Still the Golden Door

With best wishes,

David Reimers

Second Edition

Still the Golden Door

THE THIRD WORLD COMES TO AMERICA

DAVID M. REIMERS

COLUMBIA UNIVERSITY PRESS
NEW YORK

Columbia University Press
New York   Oxford
Copyright © 1985, 1992 Columbia University Press
All rights reserved

Library of Congress Cataloging-in-Publication Data

Reimers, David M.
  Still the golden door : the third world comes to
America / David M. Reimers.—2d ed.
      p.   cm.
  Includes bibliographical references (p.   ) and index.
    ISBN 0-231-07680-0 (alk. paper).—ISBN 0-231-07681-9
(pbk. : alk. paper)
      1. United States—Emigration and immigration—
History—20th century.   2. Developing countries—
Emigration and immigration—History—20th
century.   I. Title.
JV6455.R45   1992
325.73—dc20   91-32758
                                                      CIP
  ∞

Casebound editions of Columbia University Press
Books are Smyth-sewn and printed on
permanent and durable acid-free paper.

Printed in the United States of America

c 10 9 8 7 6 5 4 3 2 1

To four immigrants

MY GRANDPARENTS

Contents

Preface

SINCE THE PUBLICATION of the first edition of *Still the Gold-en Door*, some of the same issues I discussed remain unre-solved. One such area is refugees. How post-cold war refugee flows develop is still unclear. With the collapse of Communism in Eastern Europe and growth of liberalism in the Soviet Union there has been a change in the source of potential immigrants. Soviets can now emigrate, but other Eastern Europeans will have to use the regular immigration laws because they no longer qualify as refugees. Actually their immigration to the United States could increase under new legislation passed in 1990. The situation in Central America has also changed, but that area lacks stability and great pressures for emigration still exist. There are approximately 15 million refugees in the world, and it appears as if refugee issues will have to be dealt with for a long time.

In the last six years Congress has passed two major immigration laws, the Simpson-Rodino Immigration Reform and Control Act of 1986 (IRCA) and on the last day of the 101st Congress, the Immigration Act of 1990. IRCA managed to bring together various groups and produce a compromise that many thought was impossible. Because it was a compromise, it has not been fully effective in stemming undocumented immigration to the United States. INS is still underfunded to enforce the law. The United States has yet to resolve what to do about undocumented immigration. Moreover, as I argue in this book, IRCA, like the immigration reforms of 1965 and the Refugee Act of 1980, had some unforeseen consequences that made it not nearly so restrictive as some early opponents suggested. The second major measure, the Immigration Act of 1990, is a remarkable piece of legislation and sets the nation on a course to receive a record number of immigrants in the 1990s—probably over ten million. That law comes close to a national origins orientation because several parts clearly aimed at increasing Western European (and especially Irish) and Hong Kong immigration. At the same time, Congress rejected voices who wanted to decrease immigration, especially from third world nations. Indeed, the new policy makes possible increases in third world immigration, mostly through expansion of the family unification preferences for immediate family members of resident aliens. Who will come as the new immigrants with skills needed in the United States is not yet known.

In this edition I have updated individual chapters, especially to consider the issues noted above. I have ended with a short chapter on the Immigration Act of 1990, which could easily be as important as the reforms of 1965. Whatever its outcome, immigration and immigration issues will be with the United States in the years ahead.

Acknowledgments

FINANCIAL ASSISTANCE from two foundations was especially helpful in completing this project. The American Philosophical Society provided a grant-in-aid and the Rockefeller Foundation paid my salary and provided research funds for the second semester of 1982–1983. I am especially indebted to Mary Kritz of the Rockefeller Foundation for its generous support. New York University also granted me several sabbatical leaves which were essential. My chair, Carl Prince, was helpful throughout in making sure that sabbaticals came on time.

Two friends, Fred Binder and Len Dinnerstein, read the entire manuscript and gave me much help and encouragement. Len was helpful throughout the project in discussing problems and reading individual sections in addition to the entire text. At a critical time Tom Kessner read many of the chapters in a somewhat different form and was of great assistance in working through problems and concepts. Barry Chiswick also read part of the text and invited me to present some of my ideas at a conference at the University of Illinois, Chicago Circle, in 1980. The Social History Seminar at New York University also offered criticism and I am indebted to Danny Walkowitz and Molly Nolan for the invitation to speak. Different parts of the book were also presented to the Columbia University Seminar in American Civilization and the Seminar on Cultural Pluralism. Nancy Perlman was a careful research assistant during the early stages of the research. Goldie Newman typed an earlier draft of the manuscript and Kat Morgan helped put the material on a word processor. During the fall of 1983 Bill Nelson invited me to present the entire manuscript to the Legal History Seminar at New York University and I am grateful to Bill and the seminar for their criticisms and comments. Several readers from Columbia University Press made helpful suggestions.

Larry Fuchs read a complete later draft and gave me the benefit of his considerable knowledge of immigration. Of course, I am responsible for any errors and interpretations.

Material used in the second edition was presented at several conferences. I am grateful to M. Mark Stolarik of the Balch Institute for inviting me to a conference in Philadelphia in the fall of 1989 and to Barry Chiswick for participation at two conferences held in Washington in 1990 on recent immigration and immigration policy to the United States and Canada. Some issues relating to New York City were given as the Commonwealth Lecture at the University of London in February 1989.

The staffs of many libraries were very cooperative. At New York University, George Thompson, Tom Crawford, and Peter Allison located materials and kept me informed of new collections purchased by the library. The staff of Princeton University's library was also helpful as were those of the New York Public, the National Archives, and Columbia University. I also wish to thank the following organizations for use of their materials: the Center for Migration Studies, the American Council of Voluntary Agencies for Foreign Service, the American Jewish Committee, and the National Council of the Lutheran Church. I also profited a great deal from Chris Mitchell's invitation to participate in the Center for Latin American and Caribbean Studies seminars. Chapter 3 appeared in a somewhat different form in the fall 1983 issue of the *Journal of American Ethnic History.*

Finally, my wife, Cordelia, was of great help. Although she did not read a word of the manuscript nor type or edit it, she was supportive throughout the many years of work. Because of her own knowledge of immigration in another field, we discussed many of the ideas in the book. But her support went considerably beyond the discussion of ideas.

Still the Golden Door

Third World Immigration
Before World War II

A FEW IMMIGRANTS from third world nations entered the United States during the early decades of the new republic but large numbers were not recorded until the Chinese arrived in the mid-nineteenth century. The Japanese followed them beginning in the 1880s and other Asians after 1900. Migration from third world countries in the Western Hemisphere dated from the 1790s, but large numbers appeared much later.

These immigrants were not especially numerous compared to the Europeans, who comprised the bulk of American immigrants. The English were the main group in the seventeenth century. Small numbers of Dutch, Swedes, and Welsh, among others, arrived along with the early English settlers. In the next century, the Scotch Irish and the Germans dominated the statistics. With the beginning of mass immigration in the 1840s the Irish and again the Germans predominated. People from the British Isles, Canada, and the Scandinavian nations joined them throughout the nineteenth century, but in the last decade immigrants from the southern and eastern European nations became the leaders. Millions of Italians, Slavs, Jews, and Greeks poured into America from the 1890s to the 1920s, the peak years of American immigration. About twenty-five million people were recorded as entering the United States from 1880 to 1924, and the largest numbers hailed from Italy and eastern Europe.[1]

Old stock Americans had mixed feelings about the immigrants. Because Americans prided themselves on being the land of religious and political liberty and, above all, because the growing economy needed the immigrants' labor, they welcomed the newcomers. Yet they shunned social contact, and conflicts existed, especially between Protestants and immigrant Catholics. Moreover, Americans became concerned about the increasing numbers of immigrants and their shifting patterns of origin. After much discussion about restriction, in the 1920s the nation finally passed schemes to limit the flow from Europe.[2] As will be discussed below, third world immigrants became the objects of even greater hostility.

Like so many Europeans, third world peoples came largely for economic reasons. Some even intended to make money and return home and not become permanent settlers. The Chinese arrived on the West Coast in the mid-nineteenth century to work in the gold mines and later on the railroads.[3] When Japanese laborers appeared in Hawaii and California they first worked in agriculture.[4] Filipinos also came to Hawaii as agricultural laborers, a little later than the Japanese. They too found their way to the West Coast as did a few thousand East Indians and Koreans.[5]

The table indicates third world immigration to the United States from 1820, when the federal government began to record immigration arrivals, until the general restrictions of the 1920s. The figures are not precise. The government did not collect accurate statistics for some groups, such as Mexicans before 1908. Moreover, many immigrants returned, sometimes to come back to America again. In the case of the Chinese, for example, more left than entered after 1890; and the Chinese population in the United States went from 107,489 in 1890 to less than 90,000 ten years later.[6]

Some Mexicans became Americans when their land was annexed by the United States following the Mexican War. After 1850 others migrated north in search of work and crossed a loosely supervised border. Immigration officials did not even bother to record their numbers accurately until about 1908, and even after that date figures were not reliable. After the Mexican Revolution of 1910 Mexican immigration increased, in part as a response to the wretched social and economic conditions in Mexico and in part because of the need for their labor in agriculture and on the railroads of the western states. During World War I some Mexicans entered as special contract laborers, though that system ended in 1923. Larger numbers arrived during the 1920s when European immigration fell.[7]

Immigration, 1820–1930

Country	Number
China	377,245
Japan	275,643
India	9,377
Other Asia	35,895
Mexico	755,936
West Indies (including Cuba)	428,895
Central America	43,019
South America	113,499

SOURCE: INS annual reports.

Other third world people emigrated to the United States in the nineteenth and twentieth centuries. From the Caribbean, black English-speaking West Indians usually settled in the Northeast, especially New York City, while Cubans could also be found in that city and Florida as well.[8] As the table shows, immigration officials did not record especially large numbers from Central and South America but thousands did come.

Prior to World War II Mexicans constituted by far the largest number of these immigrants. Imprecise government figures recorded about three quarters of a million Mexicans before 1940. As indicated in the table, China and then Japan were next, but their combined total was less than Mexico's. The total from Korea, India, and the Philippines probably did not exceed 150,000. About four hundred thousand were recorded from a number of areas in the West Indies, usually Cuba or English-speaking colonies. Many more people entered without proper documents from immigration authorities, but exactly how many is not known. Some experts believe the number of undocumented Mexicans may have been as high as one-half million during the 1920s alone.[9]

Many third world migrants had intended to work temporarily and return home with their savings, and many did so. Mexicans commonly crossed the generally unsupervised border between their land and the United States, worked, and returned home. As noted, many Chinese laborers also went home, especially after 1890.

If European immigrants caused uneasiness among Americans, the newcomers from the third world prompted even greater suspicion. Hostility toward the Chinese took several forms. In the West,

Chinese miners found themselves faced with a Foreign Miners Tax, originally passed to tax Mexicans and other Latin Americans. While the tax was not always paid, Californians raised it in the 1850s and collected it from Chinese miners. In 1870 an anti-Chinese convention urged an end to Chinese immigration, and the state of California and local communities passed ordinances harassing Chinese businesses and aliens. By the 1880s nativist feeling against Chinese immigrants was so intense that it led to mob violence. Denver, Colorado, and Tacoma, Washington, among other cities, experienced bloody outbursts. One of the worst episodes occurred in Rock Springs, Wyoming, in 1885. In that mining community a white mob drove Chinese workers out of town and burned their homes and killed twenty-eight Chinese immigrants.[10]

Not content with violence and legal harassment, white nativists urged a ban on Chinese immigration. In 1879 they convinced Congress to pass such a law, but President Rutherford B. Hayes vetoed it on the ground that it violated the Burlingame Treaty between the United States and China. After the two nations renegotiated the treaty in 1880, Congress passed, and the President signed, the Chinese Exclusion Act of 1882. With the passage of this act the Chinese became the first and only nationality to be barred by name. The Chinese Exclusion Act suspended most immigration from China for ten years, but Congress renewed the ban when it expired.[11]

Opposition to Chinese immigrants was rooted in economics and racism. White miners, railroad workers, and other laborers accused the Chinese of working for meager wages which, they insisted, lowered the American standard of living and caused unemployment among whites. The Foreign Miners Tax and local laws hindering Chinese businesses aimed at ending what white workers called unfair Chinese competition. Yet it was not economics alone that accounted for the growing hostility toward the Chinese. Nativists claimed Chinese immigrants were of inferior morals and character and were unassimilable because of their race.[12] The late nineteenth century, with its ugly racism toward blacks and American Indians, offered fertile ground for racist attitudes toward Chinese immigrants.

The economic and racist attitudes about the Chinese could easily be directed at other Asians when they came to the United States. The Japanese were not especially numerous compared to other immigrants at the turn of the century, but many white Californians nonetheless became alarmed at their presence. The press and politicians warned of an "invasion" from Japan and called for action against these immigrants. In 1905 restrictionists organized the Asiatic Exclusion League. Although the league was not large, anti-Japanese feeling was high, especially in San Francisco.[13]

The San Francisco school board created an international incident in 1905 when it segregated Japanese students. President Theodore Roosevelt, sensitive to the rising power of Japan in the Far East, attempted to mediate the crisis and persuaded San Francisco to rescind the order in return for an executive agreement, the Gentlemen's Agreement of 1908, to restrict Japanese immigration The Japanese government agreed not to issue visas to laborers bound for the United States. California, as did some other states, still harassed the Japanese by passing restrictive laws, including preventing them from owning land.[14]

Korean immigration was considerably smaller than Chinese and Japanese. Around the turn of the century a few students had come to study in the United States along with some political refugees. Several thousand Koreans had been recruited to work on Hawaiian plantations as laborers, and a few of these Hawaiian Koreans eventually emigrated to the West Coast. Nativists were opposed to Koreans as much as to Japanese and they prevailed upon the executive branch to restrict Korean immigration by administrative action. Japan, which controlled Korea, also objected to Korean immigrants competing with Japanese migrants for jobs and agreed to halt the emigration.[15]

Their small numbers did not exempt Asians from hostility and exclusion. The few thousand Asian Indians, mostly Sikhs from the Punjab, working on the West Coast found themselves the subject of discrimination and violence. They were driven out of Bellingham, Washington, and other places by ugly mobs. Bellingham's newspaper editor declared that these immigrants were not good citizens and that "centuries" would be required "to assimilate" them.[16]

In 1917 Congress responded again to the hostility to Asians and passed another general immigration act with further limitations on immigration. For Asians, this law created an Asiatic Barred Zone, a region defined by Congress in the Far East from which immigration was banned. This particular provision cut off new immigration from India.[17]

Finally in 1924 as part of the general restrictions of that year, Congress enacted the Oriental Exclusion Act that virtually banned all immigration from Asia. The legislators used a simple scheme to exclude Asians. In 1922 the United States Supreme Court rendered a decision that Japanese aliens were not eligible for citizenship. The court cited naturalization statutes dating back to 1790 holding that only free white persons and aliens of African nativity and not Asians possessed eligibility for naturalization. Congress simply used the "aliens ineligible for citizenship" formula to exclude them. In the past, states had used this phrase for various laws to limit the rights of Japanese immigrants; now Congress used it to ban their immigration. The act excluded those "ineligible for citizenship."[18]

Congress exempted one Asian group, Filipinos, from the Oriental Exclusion Act. Filipinos, though not American citizens, had been given free immigration as American nationals because of the special status of the Philippine Islands, and that policy continued after passage of the Oriental Exclusion Act. But in the late 1920s and during the depression years of the 1930s, opposition to them appeared. Patriotic societies and the trade unions wanted them banned while the War Department and Hawaiian sugar planters, who used their labor, opposed the restrictionists. Most arguments sounded familiar and touched on economic and racial themes. Union leaders said Filipinos worked cheaply and undercut the American standard of living, while others insisted they were a "mongrel stream" that could not be assimilated into American society.[19]

During the Great Depression restrictionists not only urged a halt to further immigration but also wanted to ship unemployed Filipinos home. Advocates of repatriation argued that their policy would relieve local communities of a relief burden and would be humanitarian because the unemployed would be returning to familiar places. In the end the restrictionists won most of their goals. Filipinos were not banned, but as part of the Philippine independence bill, the Tydings–McDuffie Act, passed in 1934, they received an annual quota of only 50. When independence was scheduled to begin in 1946, they would be barred entirely under the Oriental Exclusion Act. As a final gesture Congress agreed to pay the passage of indigent Filipinos who voluntarily returned home.[20]

In passing the immigration restriction acts of the 1920s and 1930s Congress exempted the Western Hemisphere from the quotas, largely because of the legislators' sensitivity to a traditional Pan American liberal immigration policy in the Western Hemisphere. Secretary of State Paul Kellogg, for example, told a congressional committee that quotas would adversely affect American relations with Canada and Mexico.[21] Besides, those opposed to a Mexican quota noted that Mexicans would still be subject to restrictions such as the head tax and the ban on a large category of alleged undesirable immigrants. Proponents of Pan Americanism received support from economic interests in the Southwest who looked upon Mexicans as a source of cheap labor. During World War I, when the decrease of European immigration temporarily created a labor shortage, the federal government relaxed immigration restrictions against Mexico, and Southwestern agricultural growers wanted the flow of cheap labor from south of the border to continue. These interests believed that Mexicans made excellent workers because they labored for low wages and were considered docile, uninterested in labor unions. Thus, although Congress debated Western Hemisphere quotas, the legislators finally decided against them.[22]

The 1930s were another decade, however. Faced with long lines of unemployed native-born workers and unwilling to grant relief to Mexican immigrants and their children, various local governments repatriated these people. One scholar has estimated that local governments, with the aid of the federal government, repatriated about 400,000 Mexicans. This figure included a number of children who were American citizens because they had been born in the United States.[23]

While banning Asians and shipping Mexicans back home, the federal government also tightly enforced the immigration laws and quotas against others. A few West Indians still emigrated to the United States in the 1920s and 1930s. They entered under the quota of their mother country, usually Great Britain, but the numbers of such people were small in the Great Depression while the national origins system was in effect. If they would have been large, the government no doubt would have moved against them as it did against Mexicans.

Thus by the time of World War II, the United States had severely restricted most racial and ethnic minorities from third world nations and colonies. Only a few Asians were eligible for admission, for example, after the restriction laws were passed. The Chinese Exclusion Acts banned laborers but did allow groups like merchants and students to enter. These persons first had to pass through Angel Island in San Francisco Bay where officials carefully screened them as they did those who claimed to be the children of Chinese Americans.

The children of Chinese American citizens were eligible to enter. The San Francisco earthquake and fire of 1906 destroyed the city's immigration records and many Chinese claimed citizenship and became "paper citizens." They also insisted that they had children—"paper sons" or "paper children"—back in China who were eligible to enter the United States. Some of these "paper sons" were not really the sons of Chinese Americans but were other Chinese who had purchased the "slot," or claim of relationship. Immigration authorities did allow some to enter, but they were suspicious of such claims and especially tough in examining them.[24]

In the 1950s the immigration authorities began a program to allow those who had entered as "paper sons" or who claimed "paper citizenship" illegally to "confess" their fraud and then legalize their status. Several thousand did so. The Commissioner of Immigration noted some ingenious cases, including one Chinese "who had established his alleged citizenship through court proceedings in 1902 [and who] caused the illegal entry into the United States of 17 purported members of his family based on their relationship to him." Ninety-nine percent of all "confessors" were permitted to remain in the United States.[25]

Such ingenious ways to circumvent the immigration laws and the exceptions permitted were minor, however, for Americans had made it clear that third world peoples were not welcome. Nor did the opposition of their entry end their problems. Asian immigrants suffered from a wide range of legal, social, and economic discrimination that limited their rights and opportunities for advancement in American society. Black West Indians faced the same Jim Crow practices and other forms of racial discrimination plaguing native-born black Americans. Mexicans in the Southwest faced especially severe discrimination. In Texas conditions were so bad that when the United States and Mexico worked out a wartime agreement to permit Mexicans to work temporarily in the United States, the Mexican government would not let them labor in Texas.[26]

Several incidents during the war point to the intense dislike of third world minorities. Several months after Japan's attack on Pearl Harbor, the Roosevelt administration interned 110,000 Japanese Americans, many of whom were American-born citizens of the United States, in virtual concentration camps complete with barbed-wire fences. No acts of sabotage had been traced to these persons but various racists wanted them removed from the West Coast and placed in camps, and President Roosevelt, in the worse single example of violation of civil rights during the war, issued an executive order interning Japanese Americans. When challenged in the courts, the government's policy was upheld. These Japanese Americans not only lost their liberty but they lost most of their property as well in the hasty evacuation, and the federal government insufficiently compensated them after the war.[27]

A second particularly hideous incident occurred against Mexican Americans in Los Angeles. Several Mexican teenagers found themselves accused of a murder in that city in 1942. On flimsy evidence the jury convicted these unfortunate youths, who spent two years in the San Quentin prison before the courts finally overturned the verdict for lack of sufficient evidence. In 1943 Mexican Americans were subject to another incident of bigotry in Los Angeles when American sailors went on a spree and beat up many Mexican American youths in the so-called Zoot Suit riots.[28]

As bad as ethnic and racial relations were by the early 1940s, a movement began to alter American immigration policies. It gradually succeeded and the door opened slightly once again to third world immigration. In chapter 1 I shall discuss how and why American policies changed after 1940 and the growth of third world immigration to the United States up until the early 1960s, when Congress passed a 1965 immigration act that fundamentally altered the restrictions of the 1920s.

1

The Door Opens a Little, 1943–1965

THE FIRST MODIFICATION of third world immigration policy occurred largely because of America's entrance into World War II as an ally of China against Japan. In 1943 Congress repealed the Chinese Exclusion Acts. A modest alteration, the repeal nonetheless indicated future trends in shaping immigration policy. In the first place, much of the argument about repeal of Chinese exclusion centered around foreign affairs. Previously, foreign policy considerations had little influence on keeping a liberal immigration policy, especially in regard to Europe and Asia. They had of course been of some importance in the case of Mexico and the suggestion of a Western Hemisphere quota. They had also appeared in the debates about the Oriental Exclusion Act of 1924. Missionaries and other opponents of exclusion claimed, to no avail, that this exclusion insulted Japanese sensibilities and represented an unwise foreign policy.[1] The Japanese government protested to the United States over the proposed act and warned of "grave consequences." Congress rejected this protest and the Senate voted lopsidedly for exclusion: 71 to 4.[2]

Second, racial and ethnic bigotry, which had led to the exclusion of the Chinese, began to wane after 1940. Labor shortages developed as the nation mobilized for the war and minorities found better jobs. In the case of blacks, some industries that had refused to hire them now employed them. Franklin Roosevelt, under pressure in the form of a threatened march on Washington to be led by labor leader A. Philip Randolph of the Brotherhood of Sleeping Car Porters, established a Federal Fair Employment Practices Commission. The commission lacked authority, but it did help blacks obtain new jobs as mobilization created labor shortages.[3] Chinese Americans had a similar experience. Shipyards, aircraft plants, and other defense industries employed them for the first time, and educated engineers and scientists also found new opportunities. In the navy, prior to the war, Chinese Americans were limited to becoming messmen and stewards, but now they qualified as apprentice seamen.[4] One should not overestimate the degree of questioning by Americans about race relations in the 1940s, but the climate of opinion was beginning to change then, albeit slowly. And, of course, it changed mainly for those like the Chinese who were on the American side.

A third issue of importance surrounding repeal of Chinese exclusion was the role of lobbying. In the past, unions and patriotic and veterans organizations had worked for immigration restriction, and they had been opposed by various ethnic groups, so that lobbying for immigration legislation was not new in the 1940s. This time the people who wanted to liberalize immigration policy by repealing the Chinese Exclusion Acts took the offensive and orchestrated a careful campaign to steer the measure through Congress. Such lobbying for liberalization would become more important in the future development of immigration practice. By the 1960s ethnic and religious groups and those voluntary agencies (VOLAGS) responsible for refugee settlement became the major nongovernmental groups influencing American immigration policy.

Finally, although the correlation between immigration liberalization and the economy is not precise, relative prosperity between the 1940s and early 1970s aided those advocating change. Discussion about changing immigration policy to help refugees got nowhere during the Great Depression.[5] As the nation went to war the booming economy eased fears of unemployment. The repeal of Chinese exclusion occurred at the beginning of the boom. Some people still feared a postwar depression. Representative Ed Gossett of Texas proposed in 1946 that quotas be cut in half with a minimum of 100, because he feared serious unemployment after the war.[6]

Yet the predicted depression failed to materialize. Indeed, one reform group, the National Committee on Immigration Policy, suggested in 1950 that America would experience population stagnation and needed increased immigration for economic growth.[7] While this prediction, like Gossett's, proved incorrect, the surge in postwar economic growth made it possible to argue that the nation could receive additional immigration. After all, the China quota after the repeal of the exclusion acts was only 105, and most of the changes suggested for other Asians amounted to only a few hundred or thousand immigrants annually. Moreover, reformers were careful to provide special economic safeguards to placate labor unions and others when they suggested special legislation to admit refugees.[8] It is true that the consequences of immigration policy changes were often larger than predicted, but reformers usually insisted that their changes would have little economic impact.

The impetus for repeal of Chinese exclusion originated with a group of scholars interested in China and the Far East, who were joined by church leaders and writers. They knew of the opposition to repeal but the coming of World War II gave them hope that a campaign could be successful. After some discussion among interested parties, they called a meeting in the spring of 1942 that eventually led to the formation of the Citizens Committee to Repeal Chinese Exclusion. The committee was a small group with a modest budget of less than $5,000. Its key members included Pearl Buck, author of a best-selling novel about China (*The Good Earth*, 1931), and newly elected congressman from Minnesota, Walter Judd, who had been a medical missionary in the Far East. Judd became the chief tactician for repeal in Congress.[9]

From its early discussions the committee decided to emphasize the modest nature of its reform, limited to ending the ban on Chinese immigration, rather than all Asian immigration, and making Chinese immigrants eligible for naturalization. The committee also decided to stress that Americans, and not simply Chinese, wanted the exclusion acts repealed.[10]

Though its budget was small and the committee limited in size, it nonetheless ran a successful campaign to convince the public, and more importantly, Congress, of the need to remove Chinese discrimination. The committee contacted congressmen by mail and in person while using radio programs and pieces of literature to inform the public. Advocates of repeal also worked on the traditional sources of opposition to the Chinese, the unions, the West Coast, and patriotic groups, to convince them of the righteousness of their cause.

Various spokesmen for repeal make a careful case, stressing that China was our wartime ally, that this change would not open the floodgates for massive Chinese immigration with dire social and economic consequences, and that ending exclusion represented a Christian and democratic philosophy.[11] The reformers centered on repeal only for the Chinese because the United States was at war with Japan, and the American government had already removed 110,000 Japanese immigrants and their children from the West Coast and placed them in concentration camps. Any general alteration of Oriental exclusion and a law making all Asians eligible for naturalization would have included Japan and made Japanese immigrants in the camps eligible for citizenship, both of which were unpopular during World War II. Even the specter of non-Japanese Asian immigrants besides the Chinese caused uneasiness. Or as the House minority report warned in 1943, if we agree to Chinese immigration "on what valid ground can we refuse to accord similar treatment to the others?"[12]

Those favoring repeal knew of this type of opposition, hence their cautious arguments. The Reverend John G. Magee, minister of St. John's Episcopal Church in Washington, D.C., for example, said the bill would be a weapon against Japan and would aid our friendship with China. He added that he personally favored elimination of the exclusion for all Asians, but "as to the political wisdom of such a move, I do not know."[13]

Traditional opponents of Chinese immigration reiterated their arguments in congressional hearings, but little opposition developed in Congress. Some opponents also insisted that it was unwise to change immigration policy during a war. Yet, even in the South and West, long the centers of resistance to Chinese immigration, the ranks broke and repeal carried in late 1943. The law repealed the prior Chinese Exclusion Acts, made Chinese immigrants eligible for naturalization, and granted China an annual immigration quota of 105.[14] Those who worried that this law might be a prelude to further relaxation of immigration restrictions against Asians were correct. The China bill had been mainly a wartime measure, as a gesture of friendship to an ally. But America's new position in the postwar world had implications for immigration, and foreign affairs considerations could be applied to other areas of Asia, not just China. Immigration was not a matter of foreign affairs alone, for the odious racist concepts incorporated in Asian exclusion had been thoroughly discredited during the war. As the horrors of Nazism became visible for all to see and as Western colonialism began to crumble after the war, a number of Americans pointed to flaws in American racial practices and urged that American society be purged of racist laws, including Oriental exclusion.

In 1944 several congressmen introduced bills to grant quotas of 100 to several other Asian nations. Easiest to sell were those for India and the Philippines. Representative Emanuel Celler of New York introduced the India bill and raised the foreign policy implications. He insisted the bill must be passed because oppressed people throughout the world looked to the "United States for justice and equality." And he said, "Our breaking down of immigration and naturalization barriers may do much to dull the edge of this Jap propaganda against us and our Allies."[15] Celler's reference to "Jap" reveals the cautious nature of reform near the end of the war; for few expressed willingness to repeal the ban on all Asians because such a course would have included the hated Japanese. Samuel Dickstein of New York, chairman of the House Committee on Immigration and Naturalization and generally a liberal on immigration, remarked in 1945, "As far as I am concerned, I would not want to see a quota for Japan for the next thousand years." Dickstein wanted no postwar German (except Jewish) immigration either.[16]

After some debate and prompting from the administration, Congress passed the India bill in 1946. The Senate added, and the House accepted, an amendment that also allowed the Filipinos 100 slots each year. The Philippines received a quota two days before its independence. Again the same argument was heard, that granting Asian people an immigration quota and the right of naturalization represented sound foreign policy for it would demonstrate to the colored peoples of the world the openness of American democracy. Moreover, the numbers involved were not great,

only 100 quota immigrants annually from each nation. A supporter of the proposal, Congresswoman Clare Booth Luce of Connecticut, expressed the prevailing view:

I hope I make it clear that I would be the first to protest against people
from any nation, of any color, coming here in such numbers as to lower
our living standards and weaken our culture. This is a principle on which
we are all agreed. And it does so happen that the peoples of the Orient
can underlive us. They can live cheaper than our people will, or than the
people from Germany or France or Italy will live. . . . We are utterly
justified in controlling and keeping low Oriental immigration in terms of
numbers, because of the fact that they in too great numbers may under-
mine our way of life, our living standards, our form of religion. . . . The
proper reason for keeping Orientals out in great numbers is because of
those economic facts, but it is certainly improper to keep them out altogether, because they are Orientals.[17]

Of course, both the Philippines and India had been on the American side during the war and this made Congress and the public
more sympathetic to their case.

Indeed, because of the American-Philippines alliance during
the war, Congress enacted legislation to permit those who had
served in the American armed forces to become United States
citizens. Historian Ronald Takaki reported that in a single cere-
mony held at Camp Beale, California, on February 20, 1943, 1,200
Filipino soldiers became American citizens.[18]

Once China, India, and the Philippines had received quotas
and their peoples the right of naturalization, the next step was to
enact such provisions for all Asians. Congressman Walter Judd,
the chief congressional spokesman for repeal of Chinese exclusion, became the leading advocate of Asian quotas and naturalization to replace exclusion. The major beneficiaries of the Judd proposal for Asian naturalization were Japanese immigrants, most of
whom had been living in America for years, ineligible for citizenship. Judd suggested modification of the naturalization laws
to permit all races to be eligible. About 80,000 Japanese immigrants
would have been covered by this provision. In 1948 when Judd
began to push his bill, some of the wartime hostility toward Japanese Americans had waned. Second-generation Japanese Ameri-

cans had made an outstanding war record, and no espionage incidents had been recorded by the immigrant generation.

A second issue involved in Judd's bill was actual immigration. Few, if any, indicated eagerness for large-scale Oriental immigration. One could limit immigration from Asia by the use of small quotas. After all, China, the world's most populous nation, had been given a quota of only 105. But another issue loomed. If Asians became eligible for immigration and citizenship, what would prevent those persons of Asian heritage living in the Western Hemispheric nonquota nations from emigrating to the United States? They had been banned in the past because the Oriental Exclusion Act barred those ineligible for citizenship and only whites, American Indians, and blacks had eligibility. Many Asians and their children lived in the Western Hemisphere, and Americans, or at least congressmen, though perhaps ready to accept token numbers for Asian nations, remained unwilling to receive many Asian immigrants from the Western Hemisphere. As Judd put it, the problem has been "how to give a quota to people of Asian ancestry who are born in the Far East, and still not have an influx of people of Asian ancestry from nonquota countries such as Cuba. . . . These are colonies of Japanese people born in Brazil and Peru; Chinese born in Venezuela and various other places in this Hemisphere."19

To solve this "problem" Judd proposed the Asia-Pacific Triangle concept. Under this plan, as it finally evolved, a large triangle was drawn covering most of South and East Asia. Most countries within the triangle would be given minimum allotments of 100. That would limit Asian immigration from those countries. As for those persons of Asian ancestry born in the Western Hemisphere, the measure stipulated that people from the triangle whose ancestry was one-half Asian could not come in as nonquota immigrants. Rather, even if they emigrated from nonquota countries, their slot would be charged to the Asian nation of their ancestry, not the country of birth. This number would then be subtracted from that triangle nation's annual (and small) quota.

The charging of slots to the Asian nation rather than the nation of birth had been incorporated in the China bill, and Judd proposed, by creating the Asia-Pacific Triangle, to extend it to the rest of the Orient. Judd and his supporters talked of the "simple justice" of this bill, even though it contained this clearly racial discriminatory provision. On the other hand, the carefully drawn limits on Asian immigration made the proposal acceptable and it won widespread support. The administration backed it as did some representatives from California, the state which had long opposed Japanese immigration.[20] Even congressmen like Ed Gossett, a member of the House immigration subcommittee, who generally opposed liberalization of immigration in the 1940s and 1950s, supported both the Chinese exclusion repeal and the Judd bill.[21] Traditional anti-immigrant groups, the veteran's and patriotic organizations, showed little interest.

While restrictionist groups did little, the Japanese American Citizens League (JACL) worked actively to line up congressional support for this liberalization of immigration policy. Under the leadership of Mike and Etus Masaoka, JACL won over many congressmen to their cause. As journalist and historian Bill Hosokawa wrote, "In time Masaoka became a familiar sight in the halls of the Senate and House office buildings. Lawmakers who never had occasion to talk to him knew him by name."[22] The fact that Masaoka himself had been wounded in the war aided his cause. Representative Frank Chelf of Kentucky, a member of the House committee concerned with immigration, expressed the view of many when he told Masaoka, "I might say to you quite frankly, Mike, that I was one of those 'doubting Thomases,' and I was an unbeliever, and I was prejudiced, until I heard the people of your caliber speak to me, and I am for you."[23]

Instead of enacting immediate immigration reform, however, Congress at first passed a meager compensation bill, the Japanese American Evacuation Claims Act. Under this act over 23,000 claims were filed by Japanese Americans for property lost during the wartime evacuation from the West Coast. The last claim was settled in 1965 for only a fraction of the real value lost by those interned. Yet, in passing the act, Congress recognized that an injustice had been done. In a similar vein, in 1948 California voters rejected for the first time an attempt to strengthen the state's discriminatory alien land act. Several years later the courts declared such laws unconstitutional.[24]

These signs of acceptance of Japanese Americans reflected a mood of greater toleration and encouraged reformers who wished to change the immigration laws. In 1949 the House Judiciary Committee reported the Judd bill and supported it with familiar arguments. The committee pointed to the contribution of Japanese Americans during the war, the administration's support, the foreign policy implications, and concluded by explaining the bill conformed to the national origins act which "seeks to preserve the ethnic and racial composition of the United States."[25]

One final provision of the Judd bill deserves consideration: a colonial limit of 100, which the State Department suggested.[26] All quota nations had been entitled to a minimum allotment of 100; now, in the interest of uniformity, colonies were also to receive 100 places, whether in Asia or elsewhere. For instance, under the National Origins Act of 1924 the government had permitted blacks living under European control in the Western Hemisphere to enter under the quotas of the mother country. Not many Caribbean blacks arrived after 1924, but Jamaican immigration averaged about 1,000 annually in the 1940s. This provision of the Judd bill would have cut British West Indian immigration about 90 percent, to 100 annually, while independent Western Hemisphere countries had nonquota status.

Adam Clayton Powell, a black Democratic congressman from Harlem, who spoke for the large West Indian constituency in New York, along with several other New York representatives and liberals, objected to this part of the bill. Powell asked the House to strike the colonial provision, but this motion lost, and the House passed the Judd proposal on March 1, 1949.[27]

The House agreed to the bill easily, but the Senate took no action. The next year a measure permitting persons of any race to be naturalized passed both houses. In the Senate, however, the senators tacked on security measures that prompted a presidential veto.[28] President Harry Truman agreed that race naturalization reform was needed, but he would not accept the security parts of the bill. The security sections eventually found their way into the

Internal Security Act of 1950, which passed over a presidential veto, but Congress temporarily shelved naturalization issues.[29]

When the senators set aside the House proposal, they did not intend to kill it. Rather, in 1947 the Senate began a general examination of immigration issues. Three years later a subcommittee headed by Senator Pat McCarran of Nevada was still at work investigating immigration when the Judd proposal came up again. The Senate Judiciary Committee tabled the bill and decided to consider it as part of a general immigration measure. Thus, Congressman Judd's Asia-Pacific Triangle scheme failed to pass in either 1949 or 1950, but these setbacks were only temporary and it eventually became part of the McCarran-Walter Immigration Act of 1952.

The McCarran-Walter Act basically reinforced the tough immigration restrictions of the 1920s. That law reaffirmed the national origins quotas and added security provisions designed to make it almost impossible for suspected subversives to enter the United States. Liberals generally saw the 1952 immigration act as containing unduly harsh security provisions and as racist because of its inclusion of national origins quotas that gave the vast bulk of immigrant slots to the peoples of northern and western Europe. President Truman agreed with the liberal position and vetoed the bill, but Congress overrode his veto by a vote of 278 to 113 in the House and 57 to 26 in the Senate.[30]

While the McCarran-Walter Act represented a victory for the anti-communism of McCarthyism and a restatement of the bigotry of the restrictionist 1920s, it did incorporate some liberal features. With the inclusion of the Asia-Pacific Triangle all races were now eligible for both citizenship and immigration. Some observers believed that by including the popular Judd bill in the final version, McCarran assured more support for his controversial measure. This tactic was a shrewd one, for Judd became an ardent supporter of the McCarran-Walter Act and lobbied for its enactment. New York Senator Herbert Lehman later recalled to Hubert Humphrey:

I well remember how Representative Walter Judd from your own state [Minnesota] came up on the Floor of the Senate to lobby frantically with the few Republicans who were inclined to go along with us in supporting the President's veto. He buttonholed everyone of them and used all his persuasive powers while we, on the other side of the aisle, sat with bated breath to see whether he would be successful in swinging the Republicans back onto the Republican line of support for the McCarran bill. . . . Whether Judd can thus consider himself responsible for this tragic outcome, I do not know, but he certainly did his best.[31]

Whether Judd convinced anyone is hard to say. Liberals admitted that ending the ban on Oriental naturalization and immigration had merit but also noted that the ancestry provision of the Asia-Pacific Triangle was discriminatory.[32] Senator McCarran, reflecting the majority view, reiterated Judd's reason for the ancestry provision:

I would like to point out . . . there are approximately 600,000 Orientals who are natives of nonquota countries of the Western Hemisphere who would immediately become eligible for a nonquota immigrant status under our immigration laws [without the ancestry provision of the Triangle]. Coupled with the Orientals born in quota countries outside the Asia-Pacific Triangle, it is reliably estimated that approximately 2,000,000 aliens of Oriental ancestry would become eligible to enter.[33]

Critics of the McCarran-Walter Act also noted that the limit of 100 on colonies would curtail immigration from the West Indies, and they wanted the limit eliminated but they could not persuade Congress otherwise nor could they muster enough votes to sustain President Truman's veto of the McCarran-Walter Act.[34]

In addition to modifying the law for Chinese, Indians, and Filipinos and finally passing the Asia-Pacific Triangle as part of the 1952 law, Congress liberalized immigration in another area right after the war. In a series of changes beginning in late 1945 the legislators made it possible for spouses and minor children of U.S. citizens serving in the military forces to enter and be naturalized more easily. The issue appeared relatively simple: many American servicemen stationed overseas married foreigners and now wanted to bring their wives and children back to the United States with them, but some of these spouses could not get into the country because they could not comply with various provisions of the immigration laws. In December 1945, Congress passed without controversy the so-called War Brides Act that created loopholes for many of these spouses.[35] It should also be noted that those servicemen marrying Japanese or Korean women prior to 1952 still could not bring their wives to the United States because they belonged to races ineligible for immigration or naturalization. But in 1947 Congress agreed that "this discrimination should be eliminated" and changed the law. Other minor modifications were enacted relating to fiancees and extending deadlines, and eventually over 117,000 persons entered under the War Brides Act as amended, among them several thousand Asians.[36]

Although the War Brides Act had expired by 1952, the elimination of racial barriers to citizenship and immigration permitted additional Asians married to American servicemen to immigrate. In the 1920s Congress had passed a law to allow wives and minor children of American citizens to enter as nonquota immigrants and the McCarran-Walter Act continued this policy. Many spouses and children did immigrate above the small quotas placed on the triangle nations. The change after the war, of course, was coupled with the stationing of American troops in Asian nations. The importance of the change in immigration law can be seen in table 1.1, which ends in 1975 with the Communist takeover in Vietnam.

Following the enactment of the McCarran-Walter Immigration Act, liberals made half-hearted attempts to scrap the national origins system and discriminations of the Asia-Pacific Triangle. But the political climate of the 1950s was not conducive to major immigration reform, which had to wait until 1965.[37] Modest modifications in post-McCarran policy, however, did permit a growing number of third world peoples to immigrate to the United States.

In 1948, after a bitter and prolonged fight in Congress, the legislators passed the Displaced Persons (DP) Act to admit Europeans displaced and uprooted by World War II to enter outside of the annual quotas. Congress amended the 1948 act two years later, eventually admitting about 400,000 persons under the displaced persons legislation.[38] These laws aimed at helping Europeans; the legislators gave practically no thought to third world people. A few representatives and senators who opposed the DP measures suggested that friends of the displaced persons were inconsistent in their concern about European DPs and refugees while so many other uprooted peoples existed in Palestine, India, China, and elsewhere. On rare occasions DP opponents also suggested that if European refugees were admitted then a precedent might be es-

TABLE 1.1.

Asian Women Immigrants Admitted to the United States as Wives of American Servicemen

Year	Japan	Korea	Philippines	Vietnam	Thailand
1975	1,376	2,155	4,288	918	1,727
1974	1,773	2,461	5,101	806	2,141
1973	2,077	2,134	4,744	1,437	2,195
1972	1,626	2,148	4,702	1,599	1,759
1971	2,023	3,033	4,815	1,196	1,481
1970	2,104	2,646	4,056	855	983
1969	1,842	1,954	2,375	550	576
1968	1,845	1,356	2,256	331	304
1967	1,821	1,389	1,846	218	
1966	1,991	1,225	1,611	100	
1965	2,350	1,281	1,518		
1964	2,653	1,340	1,371		
1963	2,745	1,350	1,445		
1962	2,677	692	1,373		
1961	3,176	405	1,343		
1960	3,887	649	1,481		
1959	4,412	488	1,268		
1958	4,841	410	1,063		
1957	5,003	288	1,069		
1956	3,661	292	934		
1955	2,843	184	958		
1954	2,042	116	788		
1953	2,012	96	675		
1952	4,220	101	667		
1951	125	11			
1950	9	1			
1949	445				
1948	298				
1947	14				
	66,681	28,205	51,747	8,040	11,166

SOURCE: U.S. Dept. of Education, Office of Research, Development, and Improvement, *Conference on Educational and Occupational Needs of Asia-Pacific Women*, p. 365.

NOTE: The total from these Asian nations was 165,839

tablished to admit non-Europeans. Senator James Eastland of Mississippi, long a foe of immigration, told his colleagues that if the United States admitted European DPs, "How can we deny special consideration to persons who have been displaced throughout the world? No one can deny the compelling humanitarian reasons which will be advanced to obtain special consideration for millions of unfortunate displaced victims of the war in China, or approximately 10 million Pakistanian displaced persons in the partition with India or approximately 1 million Palestinian persons displaced in the Palestine war."[39]

Eastland's scare tactics failed to deter Congress from passing the Displaced Persons Act, but an issue had been raised. If special legislation could be enacted to get around national origins quotas and tight restrictions for Europeans then why not for Asians? When President Dwight Eisenhower suggested to Congress in early 1953 that another special refugee program was needed to help our European allies cope with overpopulation and their refugee problems, several congressmen called for a broader world view. Walter Judd insisted that Asians must be included in the legislation and several Arab-American organizations and church groups argued that provision should be made for Palestinians.[40] Congress responded favorably and the final 1953 refugee act included several thousand Asians, from both the Far and Near East.[41] Another change in 1957 in the Refugee Escapee Act permitted additional Chinese refugees to enter.[42]

In response to the United Nations' declaration of 1960 as World Refugee Year, Congress passed the Fair Share Law to admit a few thousand more European refugees. Senator Hiram Fong of Hawaii persuaded his colleagues in the Senate to include 4,500 Chinese refugees in the bill. He told the senators that although he knew the primary function of the Fair Share Law was to liquidate the program of refugee camps in Europe, can "we convince the man in the Far East and the man in the Middle East that this is the fact? Back of this argument is the thought that he is not wanted; that he is not as good as the refugee from Europe. This is not only a reflection on the refugee, but it will be regarded by all those of the same ethnic group that they are not wanted; that they are not as good as the people of Europe."[43] Although the Senate accepted Fong's amendment, the House rejected it and the final bill did not include the Chinese.

While Congress did not see fit to include Chinese Hong Kong refugees another means was found to admit them in the early 1960s. Following the abortive Hungarian Revolution of 1956, President Eisenhower invoked the parole power of the 1952 immigration act to admit thousands of Hungarian "Freedom Fighters." The provision used by the President through his attorney general was originally intended for individuals and not classes of immigrants like Hungarian refugees, but Eisenhower established an important precedent by using it for the Hungarians. President John F. Kennedy used the parole power again to admit Cubans and to admit about 14,000 Hong Kong Chinese.[44]

Because Congress reaffirmed the national origins quotas when passing the McCarran-Walter Act and gave a limit of 2,000 to the Asia-Pacific Triangle and aimed most refugee legislation at Europeans, the vast bulk of Eastern Hemisphere immigrants from 1945 until the major revisions of 1965 were Europeans.

Special refugee laws between 1945 and 1960 permitted about 700,000 persons to enter, of whom most were European, chiefly Italians, Greeks, Germans, and Poles. The bulk of those entering under the War Brides Act were also European, mainly Germans and English. Although Great Britain and Ireland were not affected by refugee laws, many Irish and British emigrated to American shores after the war. Among the European nations Great Britain was second behind Germany, the largest sending nation, and Italy was third.[45]

The special legislation enacted by Congress, nonquota status granted to spouses and children of U.S. citizens, and the presidential parole power also allowed Asian immigration to exceed the small quotas established by Congress. Japan had the largest quota in the Far East, but it was only 185. Yet, Japan sent 62,715 immigrants to America from 1950 to 1964 or an average of 4,479 annually. China's allotment was 105, but averaged over 3,500 in that same period. In fact, while most Asian nations still had quotas of 100, in 1965 the immigration authorities recorded over 20,000 entrants, both from the Far and Near East. These were mainly people from the Asia-Pacific Triangle nations. This figure was only 5 percent of the total American immigration for that year, but it represented a steady increase after World War II.[46]

The presence of American troops in Asia during and after World War II, especially in Japan, China, and Korea, was a key factor in explaining South and East Asian immigration from 1945 to 1965. A few Japanese entered under the War Brides Act, but most Japanese marrying American servicemen entered under the provision of the McCarran-Walter Act granting them nonquota status. Thus, the American occupation of Japan and the consequential marriages of Japanese to American GIs became the main network for postwar Japanese immigration to America. Most of these newcomers settled in nonghetto communities with their American husbands (and occasionally wives) and were largely unnoticed by the public at large. Declining postwar prejudice no doubt eased their adjustment to the United States, but little is known about these postwar Japanese immigrants.

About 6,000 Chinese entered under the War Brides Act and many others married American servicemen and citizens (either Chinese or non-Chinese) after the act expired and emigrated as nonquota immigrants under the regular immigration laws. Other Chinese entered under the annual quotas established in 1943 and especially the refugee legislation passed by Congress and Kennedy's 1961 parole. When the Communists took over mainland China in 1949, about 5,000 Chinese officials, professionals, and students were "stranded" in the United States. Many were then allowed to stay as immigrants because the 1953 Refugee Relief Act provided several thousand places for them.[47]

Not a few of these immigrants were highly educated professionals, several of whom have won international attention for their scientific achievements. Two such men at Columbia University were Chen Ning Yang and Tsung-dao Lee, who won the Nobel Prize for physics in 1957. Lee was born in China in 1926, and after receiving his early education there he came to the United States after World War II for advanced study. Upon completion of his studies he remained in the United States. Yang was born in 1922 in China and came to the United States just after World War II and, like Lee, he became an immigrant when his studies were finished.[48]

Most professionals who entered the United States after the war were European or Canadian. Yet, many were like Yang and Lee, from the third world. In 1949 as part of the "brain drain" to the United States, immigration authorities recorded 383 natural scientists along with 886 engineers and 1,148 physicians and surgeons.

By 1960 these figures had reached 1,043, 3,354, and 5,574 respectively and they continued to climb. About half in 1960 were born in Europe with England and Germany being the leading nations, but a growing number of Asians were among them.[49]

Elite Chinese scientists were apt to find posts in American universities or major research centers, but many other Chinese immigrants settled in the Chinatowns of American cities. Because so many were nonquota spouses, usually women, the women outnumbered the men among Chinese immigrants after World War II. This was characteristic also for Japanese immigration and immigration in general after 1945, reversing an historical pattern.

The nation's Chinatowns on the eve of World War II were largely bachelor societies. In 1940 the sex ratio between Chinese males and females was almost three to one. Many of the males had wives, but they lived in China.[50] The repeal of the Chinese Exclusion Act, and the granting of the right of naturalization made it possible for Chinese to bring in their spouses. From 1948 to 1952 about 90 percent of Chinese immigrants were women joining their husbands, many after years of separation. The influx of war brides and other Chinese spouses and their children changed the sex ratio. By 1960 there were 135,549 males to 101,743 females of Chinese origin living in the United States.[51] While traditional organizations still dominated the life of Chinatown, the influx of women and children strengthened the family. One scholar noted that his informants claimed that the period right after the war as the first time they recalled seeing young Chinese women and children living in New York's Chinatown.[52]

As Chinatown changed, its population declined in spite of the renewed immigration. A growing number of American-born and Chinese-born Chinese Americans found housing and employment outside Chinatown. In 1960 only about 4,000 of New York's Chinese lived in the city's Chinatown and 28,000 lived outside it. Some families still stayed in Chinatown along with those who had businesses there and elderly bachelors who had no place to go.[53] The continued existence of the nation's Chinatowns was important because they became the center of much of the new immigration after 1965.

Like Japanese and Chinese immigration, that of the Philippines in the early 1960s ran considerably above the limited quota established in 1946. As noted above, Filipinos who served in the armed forces during World War II were permitted to become American citizens. About 7,000 Filipino veterans did so. At the end of the war, however, the Attorney General evoked the authority of immigration officials to travel to the Philippines to enable other veterans to naturalize. In 1946, several months before the legislation was due to expire, immigration authorities were permitted to naturalize another 4,000 veterans in the Philippines. Some of these new American citizens then migrated to the United States with their nonquota immigrant families.[54] The Navy had permitted Filipinos to enlist in selected positions such as messboys and a number chose this escape from Philippine poverty. In 1947 the United States agreed to continue the Navy's recruitment of Filipinos, even though the Philippines was now independent, and thousands enlisted over the next few years.[55] In the late 1960s and early 1970s the enlistment program was stepped up but more wanted to enlist than places were available. In 1970, according to one historian, the 14,000 Filipinos in the United States Navy was a larger number than the entire Filipino navy.[56] Some of these men eventually became immigrants and citizens, frequently living and working near American naval bases after their term of service. Other Filipinos who had left their families behind when they emigrated became citizens after 1946 and brought their families to America.

Like the Chinese who lived in ghettoes, many Filipinos lived in "Little Manilas" prior to World War II, usually in West Coast cities like Seattle, San Francisco, and Stockton, California, or in Hawaii. They generally worked in agriculture or in other low-paying service jobs or in canneries.[57] These communities were largely male societies with few women present. From 1940 to 1960 the influx of Filipinos doubled the size of the early Filipino population. Because so many of the newcomers were women and children, the character of Filipino-American society changed. The bachelor structure of the old society began to give way to a family-oriented culture as the sex ratios narrowed. Filipinos still encountered discrimination in finding housing and jobs but, as in the case of other Asians, the social and economic climate was better than it had been during the tension years prior to the 1934 passage of the restrictive Tydings-McDuffie Independence Act.[58]

The Philippines did not furnish refugees as did China, but it did send some educated professionals, the vanguard of the large number that entered after the passage of the 1965 immigration act. These professionals, like other third world professionals in the 1960s, began to look to the United States for opportunities they found lacking at home.

In sum, Filipino immigration after World War II was largely connected to its former status as an American colony and the subsequent political and military ties between the United States and the Philippines. A similar close tie between the United States and Korea explains the growth of Korean immigration to America.

As noted, only a few thousand Koreans arrived in the United States before immigration was halted in the early twentieth century. Many Korean Hawaiian plantation workers returned home, but a few thousand of them remained in Hawaii and about one thousand migrated to the mainland. After the Gentlemen's Agreement (1908), "picture brides" could immigrate but laborers were barred. A few students and political refugees still entered, including Syngman Rhee, the future leader of South Korea. A second generation grew up in the 1930s and 1940s but their numbers were not large.[59] Several thousand Korean students entered the United States after 1945 but, like Japan, Korea was not given a quota and naturalization rights until the passage of the McCarran-Walter Act in 1952. Few Koreans lived in the United States to take advantage of that law.

What changed Korean immigration in the 1950s was the Korean War beginning in 1950. The dislocations of the war and growing ties with the United States encouraged Koreans to study in or emigrate to the United States. With a quota of only 100, however, few could enter as immigrants unless they came as nonquota ones; hence, most Koreans until the passage of the 1965 immigration law entered as nonquota spouses and children of American citizens. Altogether over 17,000 Koreans entered as immigrants from 1950 until the passage of the 1965 law. Most were war brides. During the period 1962–1970 a total of 14,554 Korean women came to the United States as wives of American citizens, mostly American soldiers.[60] Because of the growing connection between the United States and Korea economically and politically as well as militarily after 1950, Korean students and visitors increased in number in the United States and some students changed their status to immigrant after completing their studies here.[61] A few others immigrated directly to the United States under the quota. American citizens also adopted several thousand Korean orphans under special provisions of the immigration laws.[62] Because Koreans were usually nonquota family members of American citizens, they did not form distinct Korean communities in the United States. Moreover, unlike the Chinese, there were no large preexisting Korean communities to receive them.

Another Asian group, although only partly Asian, which deserves mention was the Dutch-Indonesian refugees. These people were originally Dutch who had settled in Indonesia, but many had intermarried with Indonesians and their children were of mixed blood. When Indonesia became independent after World War II, thousands fled to Holland, and several years later the new government of Indonesia expelled thousands more. In 1958 Congress passed a law permitting 22,000 Dutch-Indonesians to settle in the United States. In the case of these people, they were "doubly uprooted," first from Indonesia and then from the Netherlands. Because the Dutch government assisted them, their migration from the Netherlands to the United States was orderly. Unlike most other Asian immigrants of this period, males predominated among the Dutch-Indonesians, and they usually migrated as families. Various church groups aided these people as they did thousands of other post-World War II European refugees. Most settled in the Far West and especially California. Because of their high levels of education, middle-class status, and prior knowledge of English, the Dutch-Indonesians adjusted rather rapidly to American society, usually in neighborhoods with other Americans and not fellow refugees. No doubt their European as well as Indonesian heritage and relatively high status helped them in the new land.[63]

While Japan, China, the Philippines, Korea, and Indonesia furnished the largest number of immigrants from South and East Asia from 1943 to 1965, immigrants came from India, Thailand,

Pakistan, and other Far Eastern nations as well as the Middle East. Some Middle Eastern countries had minimum quotas of 100 since the passage of the National Origins Act and consequently experienced little migration to the United States before World War II. In the 1940s and 1950s these nations still had small quotas and lacked military or political ties with the United States such as those of China, Korea, or the Philippines to stimulate much migration.

Outside of China, the Philippines, Japan, and Korea in the Far East, India sent the most immigrants after the war, but its numbers were small. Around the turn of the century East Indian students came to study in the United States along with a few thousand agricultural workers, some after going to Canada first. As noted, the 1917 Asiatic Barred Zone aimed at halting the influx of these workers, and a few of those Indians here returned home. In 1940 the federal government reported only 2,405 East Indians in the United States, mainly in the West Coast states, although some scholars insisted that this was an undercount.[64]

The granting of naturalization and immigration rights in 1946 opened the door for renewed immigration. Unlike the earlier migration of Indians, those coming after 1946 as quota immigrants were professionals rather than unskilled agricultural laborers. In addition, larger numbers of nonquota family members also immigrated. Overall, the number of Indians arriving between 1945 and 1965 was only a few thousand, but they were the beginning of a larger immigration after 1965 of highly educated professionals.[65]

Collectively, although growing in numbers, Asian totals were still relatively small in 1965. Yet this Asian immigration was important in several respects. As noted, bigotry declined in the United States after 1945, reversing the trend of intense hostility toward Asian minorities so evident in American immigration policy from 1882 to 1924. Chinese Americans were worried during the Korean War when the United States found itself in an undeclared war with China, but there were no large-scale demands to intern Chinese Americans as had occurred against Japanese Americans only a few years before. The Asian newcomers did not cause a renewed nativism, and they, and earlier generations of Asian Americans, found increasing acceptance in American society.

Most third world immigration to the United States immediately after the war came from the nonquota nations of the Western Hemisphere, not Asia. Right after World War II, Canada was the leading Western Hemisphere sending country. However, Mexico was close behind, and by the mid-1950s Mexico overtook Canada, and in several years was the leading single source for American immigration in the world.[66] To some extent post-1945 Mexican immigration to the United States simply renewed the post-1910 migration, which was interrupted by the mass deportations of the Great Depression. During World War II labor shortages again opened the possibilities of employment for Mexican workers, and the governments of the two countries negotiated the bracero agreement for temporary Mexican immigrant workers (this program will be discussed in the next chapter).

The lure of America did not end with peace, and the generally good economic times of the 1950s and 1960s continued to attract Mexican workers, desperate to escape poverty and the lack of opportunity at home. Knowledge of the United States was certainly abundant because so many worked as braceros in the United States and returned home with stories and money in their pockets. Many other Mexicans, unable to sign up as braceros, came in without documents and labored for short periods as illegal laborers, and they too returned with news of jobs in the north. Visas as laborers were relatively easy to obtain in the mid-1950s, especially because the federal government's "Operation Wetback" program (1954) removed so many of the undocumented immigrants, and in spite of the existence of the bracero program the demand for low-paid Mexican labor, notably in agriculture, was still strong.

Unlike most other immigrants, a majority of those from Mexico were male. Mexicans were not highly skilled. In 1956, for example, of the 65,047 Mexicans recorded as immigrants by INS, 56 percent reported an occupation, and of these 17,245 were laborers and another 2,599 were farm workers. Over five thousand, mainly women, were private household workers. Only 754, or about 2 percent, came as professionals whereas about 20 percent of the Canadians with occupations were listed as professionals.[67] Hence, the Mexican immigrant was usually a single, young unskilled person seeking better wages in the United States.

Mexicans usually settled where other Mexicans or Mexican Americans lived, in the Southwest and in a few urban centers of the Midwest like Chicago. Many Mexican immigrants regarded the border as artificial and went back and forth freely, and as a group they were slow to naturalize.[68] By special arrangement the United States government recognized the artificial nature of the border and permitted some Mexican-American citizens and resident aliens to live in Mexico and commute to work in the United States. During the years of the bracero program the number of these "commuters," as they were called, grew. United States employers assisted the most desirable braceros in getting immigrant visas and immigrant status. By 1965 there were 44,000 such aliens and about 18,000 citizens living in Mexico and crossing—usually daily—to the United States for employment. Like other Mexican immigrants, these "commuters" usually worked in low-paid jobs along the border whether in agriculture or in the cities.[69] Some even entered for seasonal farm work.[70]

From elsewhere in the Western Hemisphere immigration to the United States was not substantial, amounting to about 20 percent of the hemisphere's total. It averaged 12,000 or so from the Caribbean and about the same from Central and South America. Cuba sent the largest number throughout this period and accounted for the bulk of the Caribbean immigration.[71] Of course, after the Castro revolution the number of Cubans greatly increased as the refugees poured into the United States (Cuban refugees will be discussed in chapter 6.) Prior to the enactment of the McCarran Act a steady but small stream of people entered from the British West Indies, but that law limited the number and many West Indians then went to England instead. British West Indians were also able to come as nonquota migrants, as spouses and children of American citizens, and a few did.

Chronic poverty in the Caribbean and Latin America acted as a powerful push for emigration. In addition to the quotas on colonial countries, there still existed physical, health, and economic restrictions on immigration; hence, it was not necessarily the very poor who came to America after the war. A number of physicians, scientists, and skilled workers chose to work in the United States, a few after studying here. By 1960–1965 about 600 scientists, engineers, and physicians annually were migrating from Latin America to the United States. About half of these were physicians and they amounted to about 5 percent of the Latin American medical graduates of that period, mostly from Argentina, Colombia, the Dominican Republic, Haiti, Mexico, and Peru.[72]

A few persons, generally in favor of a liberal immigration policy, uneasily noticed the shifting nature of the brain drain in the 1960s as more entered from Latin America and Asia. Senator Walter Mondale of Minnesota noted in 1967 that sixteen Nigerian doctors practiced in the United States in 1963 and that Nigeria had only one physician per 50,000 inhabitants. In addition, he expressed alarm at the growing number of highly educated Asians and Latin Americans who were leaving their countries. The senator concluded, "I do not believe we can rule out all forms of immigration restriction in looking for solutions."[73] Although proposals were made to discourage the third world brain drain to America, Congress took no action.

Not all Caribbean immigration was economically inspired. In the case of Haiti, the Duvalier regime began in 1957 when Duvalier was elected president. Under Duvalier's control, and that of his son, "Baby Doc," after him, a dictatorship reigned and some political opponents disappeared, were imprisoned, or killed. Others fled to the United States for safety. One such refugee was François Benoit, leader of the Haitian Resistance, a coalition of resistance groups in New York. Benoit had been accused as an Haitian army lieutenant in 1963 of plotting a revolt. Though he escaped, the Duvalier regime allegedly killed his infant son, parents, and others in his family.[74]

In the early 1960s political exiles were followed by the middle- and upper-middle-class Haitian professionals. About half of the immigrants of those years, who usually settled in New York City, were either professionals or white-collar workers. These people had little future in Haiti because of the police state there. Although many Haitian immigrants were professionals, they faced racial discrimination, language problems, and other difficulties in practicing their professions or securing an adequate income. To make ends meet, as well as to send money back home, many of the women worked for pay even though they had not done so in Haiti.[75]

Official immigration figures for Haitians were deceptive. In the 1950s INS recorded an average of less than one thousand annually and about 1,500 yearly in the early 1960s. New York City officials and Haitians themselves said that more than that entered. Many had come in, they said, on nonimmigrant visas and had simply overstayed after the visas expired. This illegal influx was the fore-runner of a large and controversial group-in the 1970s. Then many came in a similar manner as well as landing by boat along the Florida coast.

The largest sending nation in South America, Colombia, was also troubled by political upheaval. In Colombia economic changes in both agriculture and industry forced many out of their traditional jobs and prompted emigration. But also a fact was the rural unrest and political turmoil, "La Violenìa," as it was called, which triggered emigration in the 1950s and 1960s. Some Colombians migrated to neighboring Venezuela, but several thousand annually departed for the United States. Colombians generally settled in the borough of Queens in New York City. There they developed a community which became the focal point of large post-1965 Colombian immigration.[76]

In sum, apart from Mexicans and Cuban refugees (to be discussed later), third world immigration was not especially large from 1945 to 1965. Yet it steadily increased, and in the case of Hispanics and non-Hispanics from the Caribbean, it caused alarm in Congress by the mid-1960s. When fashioning a new act in 1965, Congress included provisions, over the opposition of the administration, to curtail this Western Hemisphere flow. Congress was not similarly alarmed about Asian immigration and was willing to see it increase after 1965. But Western Hemisphere immigration by 1965 passed 135,000, excluding Canada, while Asian immigration was only 20,000, its peak, in that year.

The growth in immigration from third world nations occurred because reformers and their organizations had fertile conditions for change; increased ethnic and racial toleration and a generally healthy economy. Moreover, America's role in world affairs made presidents, Democrats and Republicans alike, and key political leaders sensitive to relationship of migration to foreign policy. Hence, laws and practices were altered to admit refugees from World War II and Communism and to eradicate provisions offensive to America's overseas allies or to win the favor of neutral powers. These conditions continued to operate for more substantial changes after 1960.

In one other area the small but growing third world immigration of the immediate postwar years was important. Those third world people entering the United States generally had favorable experiences—or at least found conditions here better than at home. They formed the basis of future immigrant communities in the United States and they sent news and money home to enable others to follow after 1965 when the laws changed.

The fact that the system of immigration constructed in the 1920s, and renewed by the 1952 McCarran-Walter Act, was being eroded by executive action and special congressional laws gave reformers additional ammunition for change. By the 1960s two-thirds of the new immigrants were nonquota, half of whom were outside the Western Hemisphere. This erosion and the general public acceptance of these newcomers reinforced the impetus for reform. Religious, ethnic, and refugee organizations, backed by their liberal allies in Congress, saw their opportunity with the election of President John F. Kennedy, who favored scrapping the national origins quotas and the Asia-Pacific Triangle. But before looking at the 1965 amendments that fundamentally changed the old system and led to new patterns of immigration, we will turn to two other interrelated aspects of immediate postwar migration, the bracero program and the first wave of undocumented aliens.

2

Braceros and
Los Mojados

THIRD WORLD IMMIGRATION from the Eastern Hemisphere received little attention in the immediate postwar period compared to interest about displaced persons, European refugees, and general immigration policy as codified in the passage of the Mc-Carran-Walter Immigration Act. In the case of the Western Hemisphere, however, uneasy members of Congress watched growing Latin American immigration. Moreover, various public and economic groups also turned their attention to two other Western Hemisphere immigration issues: braceros and undocumented immigrants. The temporary worker (bracero) program with Mexico, established during World War II, lasted until 1964 and prompted considerable debate in Congress, among trade unions, church groups, and agricultural interests centered in the Southwestern states. Closely allied to the temporary worker program was the issue of *los mojados*, "the wetbacks," which came to a head during the 1950s, only to reappear as an important public issue in the 1970s. Braceros and mojados were largely Mexicans and became foreign policy issues as well as domestic ones.

Disputes over temporary contract laborers and illegal immigrants were not new. They dated well back into American history. Many migrants to the United States in the late nineteenth and early twentieth centuries had no intention of becoming permanent settlers in a new land. Rather they wanted to work a few months

---

Recently some observers have insisted that the term "illegal aliens" has negative implications and have suggested that "undocumented aliens" be used instead. However, many undocumented aliens do have documents, though they are fraudulent. I have used both terms for those persons who have entered or live in the United States without proper papers from the immigration authorities. No negative connotation is meant by the use of either term.

or years and return home with their fortunes or more modest savings.[1]

As noted, from south of the border, Mexicans migrated north after 1900, in search of work on the railroads and as agricultural laborers. The rapid expansion of agriculture in California, Texas, and the Southwest after passage of the Newlands Irrigation Act in 1902 generated a great demand for workers. The upheaval created by the Mexican Revolution of 1910 prompted many Mexicans to migrate. Some settled in the United States and became immigrants, and even American citizens, while others went back and forth between the two countries, working temporarily here and returning home to visit family and friends. Until 1917 few restrictions existed to stem this flow of Mexican laborers, and employers eagerly sought them. Restrictions made little difference anyway, because authorities lacked the manpower to supervise the United States–Mexican border. One student of Mexican immigration to the United States during the early twentieth century noted the laws "were enforced, little if at all, on the Mexican border."[2]

The Immigration Act of 1917 directly affected this movement of people. That law imposed a literacy test and an eight dollar head tax on prospective immigrants and it barred laborers under contract. Railroads and growers believed that Mexicans would not be able to comply with the head tax or literacy tests if the authorities enforced the laws. However, American employers could hire illegally entering Mexicans, who simply crossed the poorly supervised border.[3]

While illegal aliens provided one source of labor another developed because of the first officially sanctioned temporary workers. The ninth proviso of section three of the 1917 Immigration Act authorized the Secretary of Labor to admit temporary workers who otherwise might be ineligible for admission. Railroad operators and growers prevailed upon the Secretary of Labor to invoke this clause and he responded favorably. The war served as the rationale for the inauguration of this special migration program, and when it ended, organized labor demanded its cessation. Agricultural interests managed to keep it going for a few years after the war, until 1923. From 1917 to 1923 over 72,000 Mexicans entered under this authorization. The program was strictly unilateral for the United States did not consult the Mexican government.[4]

The termination of this program did not halt the flow of temporary workers, whether legal or illegal, from Mexico and the back and forth movement of peoples so characteristic of the Mexican-United States border. Continued political and social turmoil and economic deprivation provided the motive for migration north, and in spite of the establishment of the Border Patrol, Mexicans crossed easily into the United States during the 1920s. Congress set up a 450-man Border Patrol in 1924, but it had to supervise both the Canadian and Mexican borders, a virtually impossible task even when it was increased in size.[5] Some scholars believe that the illegal flow was equal to the legal one. The undocumented aliens, sometimes with the aid of smugglers, chose to avoid immigration inspection with its head taxes and literacy tests. As noted earlier, the Great Depression ended this migration, when several hundred thousand Mexicans, many with forcible assistance of local governments, returned home.[6]

When World War II broke out important characteristics of Mexican immigration to the United States had been established, patterns that would be repeated during the period 1943 to 1964 when the bracero program functioned and during 1954's Operation Wetback. These included the influx of many temporary workers, whether as contract laborers, regular immigrants, or those entering without documents. It also included the use of smugglers to assist the undocumented in crossing the border and finding jobs, a government-regulated contract temporary workers program, and forced repatriation. In many ways the Mexican migration to the United States from the 1940s to the early 1960s continued these traditional patterns of immigration.

The Bracero Program

The outbreak of World War II in Europe prompted a renewal of interest by growers in the Southwest for foreign labor. The Great Depression Okies who had sought jobs on California's large farms now found better-paying opportunities in the expanding defense industries. Shortly before America's entry into the war, California growers petitioned the Immigration and Naturalization Service to import temporary workers, or *braceros,* as they were called. The government rejected these pleas on the ground that enough domestic workers existed to supply the demand for farm labor. After Japan's attack at Pearl Harbor, and the direct American involvement in the war, growers renewed their pleas for braceros, but the government at first continued to resist them. As mobilization proceeded swiftly, however, the government agreed to consult with Mexico on the issues.[7]

Fearful of the impact of unilateral action upon the Good Neighbor Policy and perhaps mindful of the adverse effects of the forced repatriation of the Great Depression, the State Department did not wish to act alone to recruit Mexican labor as the United States had done in 1917. However, Mexico had reservations about a bracero arrangement. The Mexican government doubted whether a labor shortage really existed and believed that once Mexicans migrated to the United States they might be subject again to a massive repatriation like that which occurred in the 1930s. Mexicans also worried about the discriminatory treatment that their nationals and Mexican Americans suffered in certain states, especially Texas. On the other hand, the Mexican government did not want to deny earnings to her citizens as braceros, and Mexico knew that braceros sent money home.[8]

The agreement which emerged between the two countries represented a compromise among interested parties. In the United States the Department of Agriculture and the U.S. Employment Service assumed primary responsibility for the program. These agencies were to work with the Mexican government in recruiting labor. Mexico controlled supervision of individual contracts between braceros and the U.S. government, and the latter in turn was to supervise subcontracting to individual American employers. Employers had responsibility for the cost of transportation and living expenses. Mexico also won approval of a clause stating that Mexican aliens would not be subject to discriminatory actions, a provision that initially kept Texas from participating in the bracero agreement. In addition Mexico secured agreement that her citizens would be subject to the same protection enjoyed by American farm workers against disease and accidents. This was a meaningless clause because American farm workers lacked such governmental protection. Other clauses guaranteed braceros certain conditions about wages and employment.[9]

Growers expressed displeasure about many of the rights guaranteed braceros and the role of the Agricultural Department's Farm Security Administration (FSA) in supervising the program, which they considered too solicitous of the workers. In 1943 they managed to have jurisdiction switched from the FSA to the War Manpower Commission. As for the other conditions, growers either learned to live with them or to ignore them if possible. Organized labor appeared even less happy with the agreement, in part because unions did not like the very concept of a temporary workers program.[10] If unions reluctantly accepted the bracero program as a wartime measure, they certainly were not pleased to see it continued beyond the war, and renewed and renegotiated until Congress finally terminated it in 1964.[11]

The agreement reached in 1942 lasted until 1947. It included temporary workers from the Bahamas, Barbados, Canada, and Jamaica as well as Mexico, but more than 70 percent of the workers were Mexican. During these years over 200,000 temporary workers entered under the international agreements to labor in American agriculture.[12]

From 1948 to 1951 most Mexican workers entered under the regulations issued by the Secretary of Labor who invoked the ninth proviso section of the immigration law, and in the period 1948–1949 under no treaty at all. Growers found these arrangements more to their liking because the United States government paid the cost of transportation and loosely enforced whatever regulations came from Washington. However, the governments of the United States and Mexico wanted an improved and more regulated arrangement for the bracero program. Moreover, rising criticism about the braceros was being heard in Washington, both in Congress and from the administration.

In response to the growing uneasiness about farm workers, the President established the Commission on Migratory Labor in Agriculture. The commission criticized U.S. agencies involved in enforcing the contracts:

Official vigilance for the protection of living and working standards of alien farm laborers was largely abandoned in the postwar phase. Responsible United States Administrative agencies practically ceased to exert effective efforts to preserve the requirements of national immigration policy. The same ineffectiveness or laxity that undermined protective standards in the contracts spread also to the official scrutiny of the number of foreign laborers that employers claimed they needed.[13]

In addition to its criticism of the program's poor enforcement, the Truman commission believed the entire program represented "a constant eroding of immigration laws."[14] It noted that instead of recruiting laborers in Mexico, the government gave illegals already here status as braceros; hence, a premium was being placed on entering the United States without proper documents and then obtaining them. "A wetback is not admitted; he is already here, unlawfully. We have thus reached a point where we place a premium upon violation of the immigration laws," remarked the commission.[15]

During the war, the commissioners observed, the program's rationale was a shortage of farm workers, and proponents of braceros defended and justified their use on the ground of the war emergency. But after the war, the nation engaged in a contract program that lacked adequate safeguards for either the braceros or American workers affected by their importation.

In spite of such harsh words for the bracero program, the President's Commission on Migratory Labor did not recommend the elimination of braceros. With a belief in a continued shortage of agricultural workers, the commissioners urged that more Americans should be encouraged to work in agriculture, but that they should be granted more protection by the government and better working conditions. In the meantime some braceros might be necessary. If so, the Truman commission said the program should be carefully limited and improved to eradicate its abuses and bring it more into line with general American immigration policy.[16]

Congress responded and in 1951 enacted Public Law 78 which became the basis for the bracero program until 1964. Public Law 78 restricted its application to Mexico and agricultural workers, but a provision of the Immigration and Nationality Act passed the next year provided for a limited use of other temporary workers, under the so-called H-2 program. These were mainly West Indians and their numbers were not large. The bracero law also sought to protect American farm workers. It prohibited the introduction of foreign labor unless the Secretary of Labor certified that a shortage of domestic laborers existed. Moreover, it also contained additional clauses that proved to be the center of future controversies. First, the law said that the employment of foreigners must not "adversely affect the wages and working conditions of domestic agricultural workers similarly employed," and second, that "reasonable efforts have been made to attract domestic workers for such employment at wages and standard hours of work comparable to those offered foreign workers."[17]

Under the agreement finally concluded with Mexico the United States government agreed to provide transportation, medical care, and subsistence from Mexico to the United States and to guarantee that American employers would carry out their contracts. American growers were required to pay "the prevailing wages" in the area, a phrase that became difficult to define and the focus of much conflict.[18]

The use of Mexicans grew in the 1950s as table 2.1 indicates. By way of contrast, the number of temporary workers under the H-2 provision of the Immigration and Nationality Act never exceeded 30,000 in any of the years shown.[19] The late 1950s were the peak years for bracero use, after which their numbers declined and ceased altogether in 1965.

While braceros grew in the 1950s, so did criticism of the program. A writer for the *Saturday Evening Post* saw them as "Helping Hands from Mexico" who were treated well and did not harm American workers, but a correspondent for the *New Republic* wrote that bracero use amounted to running "Sweat Shops on the Farm."[20] Church groups like the National Catholic Welfare Conference called for an end to the use of braceros which they said hurt Americans, except the big growers who used them.[21]

Labor unions were especially opposed to braceros, who were not permitted to join unions, just as they had opposed the World War I temporary workers program. A representative of the United Packinghouse Workers, for example, told a congressional committee in 1955 that although the program contained written safeguards, "in actual practice, the program has become a flagrant device for depriving United States farm and shed workers of jobs

TABLE 2.1.

Braceros from Mexico

Year	Number Recruited
1951	129,000
1952	197,000
1953	201,380
1954	309,033
1955	398,850
1956	445,197
1957	436,049
1958	432,857
1959	437,643
1960	315,846
1961	291,420
1962	194,865
1963	186,865
1964	177,736

SOURCE: U.S. Congress, Senate, Committee on the Judiciary, *Temporary Worker Programs: Background and Issues*, p. 36.

in favor of lower paid imported workers, and for depressing the wages and living conditions of both the United States workers who are employed and the imported workers."[22] He said that the government sublet Mexican nationals to growers without certification of their need. Moreover, he claimed that the government failed to check on what jobs the workers did, and that in some cases the employer alone determined the "prevailing wage." Grower determination, he said, meant "the employers were given absolute power to set the wage rates as low as they chose."[23]

The Eisenhower administration supported the use of braceros, but was not immune from the criticism about laxity of enforcement and its affect on American workers. In October 1959, Secretary of Labor James Mitchell asked a team of consultants to study the program. The resulting report concluded that although the use of braceros had cut down on illegal immigration, their employment had not necessarily insured that domestic workers were not adversely affected. The consultants agreed with union complaints that the "prevailing wage" concept had not worked well and that domestic farm workers remained unprotected by American labor legislation. As a result, the consultants reluctantly recommended a continuation of the program but also suggested that the government take a more active hand in protecting farm workers.[24]

The Kennedy administration listened to the demands of organized labor and church and reform groups which wanted the braceros severely curtailed, if not ended. Employers, especially growers, defended the agreement with Mexico as a good one and claimed that all benefited from it. The Washington representative of the National Cotton Council told a congressional committee in 1961 that Americans "are simply unwilling to perform" the type of work needed in his industry and that cotton growers needed Mexican nationals. Moreover, he said, "It is unrealistic to suggest the termination of this program or to surround it with requirements and restrictions that will make its use prohibitive."[25]

Such support for braceros in the early 1960s was weaker than a decade before. Richard Craig, a leading authority on the bracero agreement, claimed that if it were not for the diplomatic complications, Congress and the administration would have ended the agreement with Mexico in 1961. However, Mexico wanted to keep the program as did the growers who employed the Mexicans. Congress extended Public Law 78 several times in the early 1960s, but added amendments to give the government additional control. Finally, Congress refused to extend it beyond 1964.[26] Thus, a twenty-year experiment in government-sanctioned temporary laborers came to an end.

Some supporters of braceros suggested that the small-scale H-2 program authorized under the McCarran-Walter Act could be expanded to replace braceros. Secretary of Labor Willard Wirtz said he was unwilling to use H-2 workers on a large scale to replace braceros because he believed that "Congress wanted this important program [of importing workers] if not stopped completely, certainly cut way down."[27]

In addition to the pressures in Congress and diplomatic considerations, a major factor in phasing out and eventually ending the bracero agreement was the increased mechanization of American agriculture in the 1950s and 1960s. Growers substituted machines for workers, and hence had less need for labor. The utilization of the cotton picker and other machines eased the demand for labor and made the termination of the bracero program more acceptable to growers. The president of the Yuma, Arizona, Producers Cooperative Association, for example, told a congressional committee in 1965 that his group had used up to 9,000 braceros in peak years but no longer employed them because "we went completely to mechanization several years ago."[28]

Not all producers could mechanize so readily as cotton growers, and citrus fruit and vegetable growers and packers still wanted to employ braceros. They maintained the labor shortage in agriculture would adversely affect other Americans as well: "The only possible result of the shortage of suitable supplemental labor in the fresh fruit and vegetable industry is a subsequent shortage of vital foods necessary to the health and welfare of the American people," remarked one spokesman for these producers.[29]

The Braceros

While politicians and pressure groups fought over the bracero program, the migrants continued to work temporarily in the United States. From the inception of the program during World War II until its end, immigration officials recorded the importation of over four million temporary workers of one kind or another. After the bracero program's termination in 1964, the number fell drastically, with only a few thousand yearly, mostly from the West Indies, migrating to America for short periods under the H-2 provision of the Immigration and Nationality Act of 1952. These migrants usually worked in the eastern states picking citrus fruit or apples.

The figures do not indicate how many different individuals actually entered the United States, for many came several times as braceros, usually during the peak employment periods in agriculture. Braceros generally returned to Mexico after their term ended, but some stayed on by renewing their contracts. A few others simply remained illegally—"skipped"—in the United States rather than return home and found other employment here.[30]

Mexican nationals accounted for the vast majority of temporary workers recruited to work in American agriculture. Most were young males who labored in the Southwest, from California to Texas. Usually single and from smaller communities in Mexico, they were generally peasants though some had sought jobs in Mexican industries before contracting as braceros. These poor rural folk sought better opportunities in America, but they lacked urban skills and education; hence, the bracero program seemed attractive. They were probably not the poorest of Mexican peasants but rather those who sought to improve their lot.[31]

Whether braceros depressed American wages and displaced native workers received much attention during the life of the program and still does today. That their working conditions were less than ideal is hardly debatable. Various government spokesmen and critics of the program pointed to the inadequate supervision of the program and a lack of labor legislation for farm workers which left braceros largely defenseless in dealing with their employers. While the government enforced guarantees of the contracts at times or benevolent employers observed them, they were frequently meaningless. Lack of agreement over the "prevailing wage" often meant that growers hired braceros for low wages and kept them as low as possible. Camp conditions were also appalling at times. Workers found themselves crowded into wooden shacks, without proper ventilation. A 1961 University of California investigation concluded that "the housing and sanitation of braceros in California is not uniformly so bad as some criticisms of the program suggest," but still reported many poor conditions in small and isolated bracero camps. Such a camp "is often partially hidden in a thicket or willows or some other type of cover. It may consist of the flimsiest sorts of buildings—perhaps nothing more than chicken coops."[32]

Sanitation was also lacking in many camps. One bracero noted, "No, it [the housing] did not have a bathroom but the river was close by. And there, in the river, we could go bathing. The restroom—well it was an outside toilet."[33] Inadequate medical care and poor diets also plagued these migrant workers. Of course they could complain to the federal government or Mexican officials about their conditions, but because of their ignorance of the law, lack of skill in English, and prohibition from joining trade unions, they found it difficult to mount protests. Church groups and reformers did try to protect the braceros against abuses and charges of repeated violations of agreements, but not with great success.[34]

Employers claimed that accommodations were adequate or insisted that these Mexican nationals came from such poor rural communities that they did not know how to take care of facilities and abused proper facilities when built. One employer said he built a new toilet, which the braceros refused to use. "Those nationals had crossed that ten-foot ditch [next to the toilet] and gone into the field rather than use a sanitary toilet. . . . They're just like animals. Now, mind you, I'm not saying they're all like this. But even if it's just a few in each camp, that's enough to make the camp into a pigsty overnight."[35] While that employer complained about sanitation habits of his workers, another noted that screens and showers were practically unknown in rural areas of Mexico and said that braceros did not know how to use them at first or would abuse the screens. "I don't know what it is but these birds seem to have a positive allergy to screens . . . the nationals kick out the screens, punch them out, do anything to get them out."[36]

If braceros received low wages and found poor housing and other living conditions, one might ask why they continued to work for American growers. As bad as conditions sometimes were here, they were better than in Mexico where these workers had practically no prospects for economic and social improvement. The same workers noted above, who spoke of bathing in the river and an outdoor toilet, said of his quarters: "The little shacks we had, at first glance, well, they did not look like much. They did not look like much from the outside, but once inside—well you should see. Very well equipped. They had their grills and heaters inside. . . . We were very comfortable there."[37]

Braceros came to make money and send it home and many did so. With life "very hard" in Mexico these remittances were valued, as were the goods acquired in the United States. "Well, I served my contract that year and when I came back I had a radio, a sewing machine, and a suitcase, a small one not too big, full of clothing. I also had a hair trimmer and all kinds of carpenter's tools," said one bracero.[38]

Los Mojados

That so many Mexican nationals hired on as braceros highlighted another aspect of migration from Mexico, *los mojados*, the illegal or undocumented aliens. Many poor Mexicans found that they could not satisfy immigration requirements or that they could not contract as braceros. Eager to work in the United States, they decided to enter without documents, as many others had done in the 1920s. Indeed, the number of undocumented aliens apprehended by immigration authorities during the life of the bracero program, some five million, actually exceeded the number of braceros. The number of expelled persons may be misleading, for individuals may have been repeatedly expelled, and therefore counted more than once. Of course, many who entered without papers were never apprehended so this figure is a mere hint of the volume of the illegal traffic. Even allowing for "repeaters" there is no doubt that the number of individuals seeking illegal entry into the United States rose sharply in the 1940s and 1950s. Table 2.2 indicates the growth in apprehensions by the INS.

Friends of unionization among American farm workers and migratory laborers insisted that these illegals, like the braceros, displaced American workers, depressed wages, and hindered the development of farm unions. Truman's commission on migratory farm laborers also turned its attention to what it called the "wetback invasion." The commission confirmed the fears of those who saw the "wetbacks" having negative impact upon American workers. "That the wetback traffic has severely depressed farm wages is unquestionable," concluded the commissioners.[39] In addition, they said these immigrants, because they escaped immigration inspections, possibly brought in diseases and caused health problems.[40]

To halt this traffic of humans required plugging the porous Mexican-American border. Most observers wanted a stronger INS Border Patrol, but they recognized that this alone would not stem the flow. Consequently, proponents of tough restraints on the illegal traffic urged that Congress focus on the employers by making it illegal for them to hire undocumented laborers. Administration officials did not completely agree on the merits of such a law or on how to enforce it if passed.[41]

TABLE 2.2.

Apprehended Undocumented Aliens

Year	Apprehended
1947	182,986
1948	179,385
1949	278,538
1950	385,215
1951	500,538
1952	543,438
1953	865,318
1954	1,075,168
1955	242,608
1956	72,442

SOURCE: INS annual reports.

If top officials within the executive departments could not arrive at a consensus, neither could Congress design a comprehensive program. One thing that could have been done easily was to halt practices by the government that encouraged undocumented aliens to come to the United States. As noted, braceros were supposed to be recruited in Mexico, but in the late 1940s the United States increasingly gave bracero status to illegals already in the United States. This process of drying out the "wetbacks" obviously encouraged Mexicans to slip into the United States without inspection in order to become braceros. The President's Commission on Migratory Labor noted in 1951 that this feature of the Mexican alien farm labor policy had become the dominant one:

For the 3 years, 1947–1949, the Mexican farm labor program amounts to this: 74,000 Mexican nationals under contract were brought from the interior of Mexico; 142,000 wetbacks already in the United States were legalized by being put under contract. Legalization of wetbacks occurred again in 1950. Meanwhile, the accelerated wetback traffic continued unabated.[42]

Mexico also worried about the "drying out" process of illegals, because it weakened Mexico's role in protecting braceros who were supposed to be recruited on Mexican soil.[43] Yet, even had this practice not been in operation, American agribusiness would have continued to hire illegals and simply use them side by side with braceros and Americans.

In the early 1950s Congress considered proposals to outlaw the employment of undocumented aliens. President Truman supported such an employer sanctions bill, as did the American Federation of Labor, but Congress was unwilling to pass it. The Senate committee investigating immigration and drawing up the eventual McCarran-Walter Act did look briefly at illegal immigration and noted its impact on wages and employment of Americans, and even acknowledged that illegal laborers were used as strikebreakers, but it did not recommend measures to halt the flow.[44] When it came to making recommendations, the legislators were unwilling to support employer sanctions. The House committee reporting on the McCarran-Walter Act wanted the law to state that "concealing and harboring aliens who are unlawfully in the United States" was a crime but it wanted the law to read that "harboring" would not include employment.[45]

In the Senate, Paul Douglas of Illinois proposed an amendment to make it a crime to hire undocumented aliens. The senator observed, "The bill as reported to the Senate by the committee does not deal with employment within the United States of persons illegally entering this country. In this amendment we are trying to reduce the volume of such illegal entries by imposing penalties upon those who knowingly employ illegal entrants. This should markedly reduce the numbers of such persons who cross the border."[46]

Senator James Eastland of Mississippi, a staunch supporter of the national origins quotas and limited immigration and an opponent of refugee bills like the Displaced Persons Act, was tolerant about admitting undocumented aliens. He insisted the Douglas amendment was "unfair to the farmer or the Mexican involved." He drew a heartrending portrait of illegal immigrants who had come to the United States. "I know of one such family which has lost a son in Europe in the American Army," said the Mississippi senator. Because these workers had faithfully labored for twenty to forty years "nothing could be more unfair to the farmers, and nothing could be more unfair to the Mexicans, because it would eliminate such laborers from the economic life of this country."[47] Eastland had strong support in the Senate and among agribusiness, and the Senate voted down the Douglas amendment. As signed into law by the President, the measure made it a felony instead of a misdemeanor to willfully import, transport, or harbor illegal aliens.[48] This measure made it possible for the government to deal more effectively with smugglers, but it did nothing about those who hired undocumented workers. Instead, the law specifically said that employment of undocumented workers did not constitute "harboring."

The exception, known as the Texas Proviso, indicated a clear victory for the growers. Yet, employer sanctions would appear again in Congress in the 1970s and 1980s when undocumented immigration increased. The opposition of Senator Eastland was important, however, for he chaired the Senate immigration committee in the early 1970s when the House twice passed an employer sanctions bill. Eastland ignored House action and did not even hold hearings on the issue for several years, thus killing another bid for employer sanctions. In the early 1980s the Senate and House passed different versions of such a bill, but could not agree on a compromise. Finally, in 1986 Congress enacted the Immigration Reform and Control Act (IRCA) that outlawed the employment of undocumented aliens. (This issue will be discussed in chapter 7.)

If neither Congress nor the Truman administration could check illegal immigration from Mexico, the situation changed during the Eisenhower years. Unions and liberals continued their complaints about the harmful impact of illegals and how they were treated. A correspondent for the *New Republic* titled his account of undocumented workers, "'Wetbacks'—Slaves of Today."[49] A writer for the *New York Times* called undocumented aliens "McCarran's Immigrants," and insisted that these aliens were not a harmless movement of workers who helped both growers and their families back home. Writing in the *Nation*, Gladwin Hill noted, "As a group they assay an inordinately high rate of such ailments as venereal disease and tuberculosis. In consequence, their presence is deplored by health officials all the way from Imperial County, California, to Michigan." He insisted that there was no evidence that "the traffic has helped the Mexican people appreciably." They hurt American farmers who tried to compete with those using this labor and retarded the assimilation into first-class citizenship of hundreds of thousands of Spanish-speaking Americans who often find themselves "lumped with the invaders."[50]

In addition, some public officials put pressure on the government to do something about the "wetback menace." The Eisenhower administration might ignore the press or trade unions, but it could not ignore the rapid rise in apprehensions of undocumented aliens, mainly along the Mexican border. As table 2.2 demonstrates, apprehensions were slightly over 500,000 in 1951 and 865,000 two years later. In August 1953 Attorney General Herbert Brownell visited southern California to observe the situation there. He obtained a firsthand look at illegal immigration and became aware of the growth in apprehensions. While these pressures mounted on the one hand, growers insisted that they needed cheap and plentiful (even if illegal) labor for farm production. In the end, Eisenhower decided that the price of an uncontrolled immigration policy and its results were too high, outweighing the interests of the growers.[51]

Brownell suggested that Congress pass a law along the lines of the Douglas proposal to penalize those who hired undocumented workers. Hearings in Congress produced the already conventional set piece debate about illegal immigration but Congress did not enact a bill.[52] Administrative action, however, did begin to rid the nation of the "wetback menace." In 1954 the Immigration and Naturalization Service, under the leadership of retired General Joseph M. Swing, newly appointed commissioner of INS, inaugurated Operation Wetback. His sweeping military-style operation, which began in California and moved across the Southwest, was carried out in the summer of 1954. INS agents picked up thousands of illegal aliens in raids among growers known to employ them and thousands more by the use of roadblocks in key areas. The immigration authorities also had the cooperation of local governments and many growers in catching and deporting the undocumented workers. In addition, the Border Patrol stepped up its activities to plug the Mexican border. INS task forces loaded the apprehended Mexicans on buses and shipped them to Mexico. INS agents not only raided growers but also seized illegals working in California cities and industries. Many thousands of other illegals in California left voluntarily rather than be taken and deported by INS agents.[53]

Texas growers naturally disapproved of the administration's efforts to remove undocumented aliens, who constituted an essential component of their work force. Although California growers generally cooperated with the government, Texas employers had a different view. Nor did Swing and his agents receive much local governmental assistance in Texas. Nonetheless, Operation Wetback moved into Texas and rounded up and deported thousands of illegals. Some Mexican Americans and Mexican officials criticized the tactics used by INS but INS moved ahead and successfully completed its goal.[54]

While most activity was concentrated in the Southwest or along the border, INS agents also rounded up illegals in mid-western cities like Chicago. There officials loaded the apprehended immigrants on planes and sent them to Mexico.[55]

Satisfied with its operation, the 1955 *Annual Report* of INS declared, "The so-called 'wetback' problem no longer exists. . . . The border has been secured."[56] The figures seemed to support this claim. Over one million illegal aliens had been apprehended in 1954 and only one fourth that number the next year. In 1956 INS reported only 72,000 apprehensions. Although Operation Wetback's military tactics helped explain the fall in illegal immigration after 1955, another issue was grower cooperation. The government generally succeeded, especially in California and Arizona, in persuading growers not to employ illegal aliens in the fields. An important consideration for the growers was the government's willingness to increase the number of braceros available to do the work. In 1953, the United States had contracted 201,380 braceros. By 1955 the number nearly doubled, and from 1956 to 1960 reached an average of over 400,000 annually. Thus, the government traded a stiff policy of keeping out illegals for a more liberal supply of braceros. In Texas during Operation Wetback the situation was so cynical in its application that some apprehended "wetbacks" were sent back to Mexico while others were "dried-out" to make them available as braceros.[57] Finally, as noted, farm technology lessened the demand for labor. This growth in mechanization, combined with the increase of braceros, made it easier to carry out a tough policy on undocumented aliens in the 1950s.

Substitution of braceros for undocumented workers and "drying-out" of illegals points to the essential similarity of braceros and undocumented workers from Mexico. Most studies of undocumented migrants concentrate on the 1970s, but there is no doubt that the 1940s and 1950s illegal workers resembled the braceros. They usually came from the same region and, like the braceros, were young Mexican males of peasant background with limited education and skills. They migrated to the United States in search of employment, mostly on the big farms of American agribusiness. They were not necessarily the poorest of Mexican peasants or the urban lower class, for it required desire and even funds for the journey north. As one observer noted, "It takes more than ordinary initiative to marshall a grubstake, get to the border, and run the Border Patrol's gauntlet, all for the purpose of working harder at lower wages than most United States citizens will accept."[58] When finished with the seasonal labor, they usually returned to Mexico to reenter again the next season. These migrants sought to contract as braceros, but if they could not, they were willing to cross illegally into the United States if necessary, "because life gets so hard here in Mexico that is why one takes a chance."[59]

The similarity of braceros and illegal agricultural workers in background and goals did not produce identical experiences in the United States. Although braceros frequently found their contractural rights loosely enforced, the illegal workers had virtually no rights at all. The President's Commission on Migratory Labor observed appalling conditions among them. In visiting camps occupied by undocumented workers the commissioners found that some had "virtually no housing, sanitary facilities, or other conditions of civilized living."[60] One California official told the commission, "The plight of the wetback I consider very serious there [in the Imperial Valley] because the majority of them live on ditch banks or in shed housing which is very, very poor. . . . I have seen lots cleaner and better chicken houses for chickens than I have seen for human beings in the Imperial Valley."[61]

In addition, labor contractors or smugglers preyed on the undocumented aliens. Smugglers, or "coyotes" as they were called, took their money to get them into the United States and had few scruples about their treatment of these workers. Some migrants found that the smuggler had deceived them and left them without funds or a job, only to be caught by the immigration authorities. If exploitation by "coyotes" were not enough, some never reached the United States. In 1953 several hundred "wetbacks" were reported to have drowned while attempting to cross rivers along the border. In August 1953, authorities reported that thirty bodies had been washed ashore near Edinburg, Texas, along the Rio Grande. "It's a scandal," said one man who worked with itinerant Mexican workers. He continued, "We of the border country are so accustomed to hearing of the drownings we have become hardened. . . . There's never any way to let their families know. No one ever knows who they are or where they come from."[62]

Most Mexicans entered on their own and the vast majority who made the journey achieved their goal. Beginning in the plazas of Mexican towns and cities immediately below the border they sought information about jobs in the United States and how to cross the border and find work. The main streams went through the deserts near El Paso and Calexico or across the Rio Grande between Rio Grande City and Brownsville. If jobs were filled near the border, they moved further up into the United States.[63] Yet, even if they found employment, these workers were exploited by growers as well as the "coyotes." Without proper legal papers, they could not expect decent wages and could not complain about poor housing and lack of sanitation facilities.

Because they desperately needed work and because they lacked immigration cards, growers and other employers paid them low wages. The President's Commission found a pattern of lower wages in areas known to employ illegals. Around 1950 the Deputy Labor Commissioner of California told the commission, "The Mexican wetbacks work for 40 cents an hour and a few of them work for between 25 and 30 cents an hour. In many of our complaints the employer will bring in records showing that the wetbacks didn't work the number of hours claimed, and I would say that, in the majority of cases, they finally settled for anywhere from 25 percent to 75 percent of the original claim, which gives the farmer an opportunity to make a little additional saving in his labor bill by just cutting it down." While these California wages of 40 cents per hour appeared meager, they were even more appalling in Texas and as low as "15, 20, 25 cents" per hour.[64]

Growers insisted that native Americans could not be found to work, hence the need for braceros and undocumented workers. What this meant, of course, was that native American workers would not work for the low wages that growers offered, but that the illegals would, because they could find little or no work in Mexico.[65] Wages could be kept down and workers held to the job because of the fear of deportation. The President's Commission noted that employers sometimes withheld the laborers' pay in part until their services were no longer needed: "Sometimes, he is deliberately kept indebted to the farmer's store or commissary until the end of the season, at which time he may be given enough to buy shoes or clothing and encouraged to return the following season."[66] What could the illegal do in the face of these wages and living conditions? Nothing, for he had no standing in the courts and was subject to deportation if caught.

Even paltry wages and inadequate living accommodations did not end their troubles. On occasions employers skipped the last paycheck and reported their workers to the immigration authorities to be deported. The State of California's Division of Labor Law Enforcement in 1953 reported that it was taking action to win back money owed to the illegals. It said such action was required if something were to be done about the "vicious practice of labor contractors and other people of working illegals and then refusing to pay them."[67]

Local merchants also charged excessively high prices for poor quality goods and services.[68] Not the least of the problems the undocumented encountered was common to other Mexicans and Mexican Americans as well, that of ethnic discrimination. Public accommodations were sometimes denied to them and segregation was not unknown. Texas possessed the reputation for the worst discrimination, and, it will be recalled, the Mexican government during the early years of the bracero program refused to allow its nationals to work in that state because of the discriminatory treatment of persons of Mexican ancestry.[69]

As bad as the conditions and wages were in the United States, these Mexicans, like the braceros, had little work at home, so they continued to come to America. The President's Commission put it,

"The wetback is a hungry human being," while others pointed to the statistics highlighting the differences in the standard of living between Mexico and the United States.[70] Most intended to save and return home, but some also hoped to contract as braceros and gain temporary legal status. Or a few even hoped to become Americans, perhaps by marrying an American and becoming a nonquota immigrant. A popular song of the "wetbacks" caught the flavor of this possibility:

> Our problem
> Can be easily be solved:
> All we need is a "gringuita"
> So that we can get married:
> And after we get our green card [legal document]
> We can get a divorce
> Long live all the wetbacks,
> Long live those that are ready to emigrate,
> Long live those that go there to get married
> So they can legally stay.[71]

Because INS concentrated its efforts along the Mexican border and because Operation Wetback aimed at undocumented agricultural workers, the immigration authorities counted Mexicans disproportionately among those apprehended. Indeed, the terms "wetbacks" and "illegals" were often used interchangeably in the 1950s and many people believed that the illegals were all Mexicans, swimming or wading the Rio Grande River. The President's Commission, for example, commented:

In recent years, literally hundreds of thousands of Mexican agricultural workers, known as wetbacks, have illegally entered the United States in search of employment. The wetback is a Mexican national who, figuratively, if not literally, wades or swims the Rio Grande. Whether he enters by wading or swimming, crawls through a hole in a fence, or just walks over a momentarily unguarded section of the long land border, he is a wetback. Since he enters by evading the immigration officers, he is, in any event, an illegally entered alien. The term wetback is widely accepted and used without derision; hence, for convenience, it is used here.[72]

Yet, other persons illegally lived in the United States too. Their numbers were minuscule compared to those of the Mexican illegals. They include merchant seamen who jumped ship while in American ports, and visitors or students who overstayed their visas. A few slipped in through the Canadian-American border. These persons were not apt to be agricultural workers. Nor were all of the Mexicans apprehended and deported engaged in temporary farm work. As noted, Operation Wetback did remove illegal aliens in Los Angeles and some mid-western cities.

Immigration authorities claimed that in addition to those apprehended by their agents, hundreds of thousands of other illegals working in the fields, or in hotels, restaurants, or small industries fled in fear, voluntarily. INS probably inflated its figures, but no doubt many undocumented workers did return to Mexico rather than risk apprehension.[73] How many escaped INS raids or the Border Patrol and managed to live in the United States illegally is not known. Their numbers were probably not large in the 1950s because most undocumented aliens worked in seasonal agricultural employment, much like the braceros, and were concentrated in the Southwest.

When the United States ended the bracero program in 1964, the Mexican ambassador to the United States noted the close connection between the program and the influx of illegal labor. He said, "The lack of an agreement to facilitate contracting as long as there is a shortage of farm labor, which the Mexican workers have been covering, would tend to bring about a return to that [the presence of illegals] situation."[74]

This argument was not unique to the Mexican ambassador. During the debates over extension of the bracero agreement, Senator James Ellender of Louisiana said, "I am certain, that if the proposed extension is not granted, there may be a recurrence of conditions that existed prior to 1951, when Mexican labor came by the thousands, some of them swimming across the Rio Grande, and become known as 'wetbacks'. . . . My fear is that there might be a recurrence of that situation."[75] These predictions proved correct. In addition to ending the bracero program the next year Congress changed the 1952 Immigration and Nationality Act to make it more difficult for people in the Western Hemisphere to emigrate to the United States; hence, many former braceros and others seeking work were willing to enter without documents.

Although the number of apprehensions had been relatively low from 1956 through 1965, after that they began to rise. But after the 1960s undocumented immigration was considerably more than temporary Mexican laborers working on American farms. The story of the renewal of this immigration deserves extension treatment and it will be discussed in chapter 7.

3

A Cautious Reform:
The Immigration Act of 1965

ERADICATING DISCRIMINATION against third world countries was not the focal point of those who disapproved of
American immigration policies. Rather, critics urged a number of
reforms, several of which would have benefited potential migrants
from third world nations, but the center of their critique was the
national origins system embedded in the McCarran-Walter Act.
Both Harry S. Truman and Dwight D. Eisenhower criticized policies established by the McCarran-Walter Act. In this veto message
Truman declared, "The basis of this quota system was false and
unworthy in 1924. It is even worse now. At the present time, this
quota system keeps out the very people we want to bring in. It is
incredible to me that, in this year of 1952, we should again be
enacting into law such a slur on the patriotism, the capacity, and
the decency of a large part of our citizenry."[1] The President wanted Congress to admit more refugees and he established a special
commission to investigate immigration and make recommendations. The commission, after holding hearings in late 1952, reported in January 1953. Given the composition of the commissioners appointed by Truman, it came as no surprise that the
report, entitled *Whom Shall We Welcome?* attacked the McCarran-
Walter Act and recommended sweeping changes in immigration
policy.[2] It also came as no surprise that Francis Walter claimed the
report was politically inspired and that he read it with disgust.
McCarran called it a "rehash of the line that was parroted in
Congress by the radical, left-wing clique in Congress" when the
legislators debated the McCarran-Walter Act.[3] Both Walker and
McCarran refused to hold hearings on the report. Although Congress took no action some of the commission's suggestions later
found their way into the 1965 act.

President Eisenhower, less critical of the McCarran-Walter Act, in 1953 successfully urged Congress to admit additional refugees, and he initiated the procedure of using executive parole power to admit refugees, at first for the Hungarians. Toward the end of his second term, Eisenhower made other recommendations, including some that would have emasculated the McCarran-Walter Act further. The president called upon the legislators to increase immigration and permit unused national origins quotas (notably those of Great Britain and Ireland) to be filled by countries with oversubscribed allotments.[4]

Truman, Eisenhower, and reformers who wanted the national origins system and the Asia-Pacific Triangle scrapped had to be content with changes noted in chapter 1. These modifications made it possible for many immigrants, especially refugees and displaced persons, to enter outside the national origins limits. Although the economy had low rates of unemployment in the 1950s and ethnic and race relations were improved over the immediate pre-World War II era, Congress was not in a reformist mood. Both McCarran and his successor, James Eastland, who chaired the Senate immigration subcommittee after the Nevada senator's death in 1953, favored the 1952 law. In the House, Francis Walter remained the key figure on immigration policy for a decade after the enactment of the McCarran-Walter Act.[5]

While reformers and presidents insisted that a liberal immigration policy was tied to anti-Communism abroad, defenders of the act maintained that it kept out subversives, and changing it would be detrimental to American national security. In the debates over its passage, McCarran and others resorted to McCarthy-like tactics. The Nevada lawmaker insisted the main opposition to his cherished law was Communist inspired and implied that those non-Communists opposed to the bill were either "soft on Communism" or duped.[6] While the security provisions of the measure clearly related to the Communist issue, it was not clear that national origins and the racially discriminatory provisions of the Asia-Pacific Triangle enhanced American security. But immigration laws were not always logical.

John F. Kennedy's victory in the close election of 1960 offered hope for a major revision of the McCarran-Walter Act. Even his

opponent, Richard M. Nixon, had endorsed Eisnehower's proposals for reform. More pressing domestic and foreign issues delayed the President's proposals for immigration reform. Moreover,
immediate concern about immigration centered on Cubans entering Florida and Chinese refugees fleeing to Hong Kong, and these
led to the enactment of the 1962 Migration Assistance Act to aid
refugees at home and abroad (third world refugees will be discussed fully in chapter 6). Nonetheless, Kennedy, author of the
pro-immigrant *A Nation of Immigrants,* intended to seek an overhaul of the 1952 Immigration and Nationality Act, and he asked
Abba Schwartz, administrator of the Bureau of Security and Consular Affairs, to prepare a new formula for the admission of immigrants.

Schwartz had joined the administration not only to help revise
immigration policy, but also to help ease American visa and travel
policies established during the anti-Communist mood of the
1950s. A friend of Kennedy's, Schwartz was a member of the
liberal Americans for Democratic Action and identified as an expert on refugee and immigration matters.[7]

Finally, in July 1963 Kennedy sent his immigration reforms to
Congress. First, the President called for the immediate abolition of
the Asia-Pacific Triangle, with its discriminatory racial ancestry
provisions and small Asian national quotas.[8] Second, Kennedy
wanted the Western Hemisphere to retain its nonquota status. All
independent nations within that hemisphere were to have that
status, a provision affecting Jamaica and Trinidad and Tobago and
any additional areas that might become independent in the future.
Under the McCarran-Walter Act, these two colonies had a quota of
100 and when they became independent in 1962, they kept that
limit and did not enjoy a nonquota status like the other independent countries within that hemisphere.

Abolition of the Asia-Pacific Triangle and retention of a nonquota position for the Western Hemisphere could enhance the
possibility of increased third world immigration, but the president's main interest was a phaseout of the national origins system
over a five-year period. Kennedy preferred a gradual rather than
an instant change to facilitate a smoother transition. During the
transitional period, each nation's unused quota would be placed in

a reserve pool, to be used by countries with over-subscribed quotas. At the end of the five years, national origins would be abolished and instead immigration would be alloted annually on a first-come, first-served basis and a preference system. All prospective immigrants would still have to satisfy health, security, and other such requirements. The President recommended that visas be granted on the basis of preference categories with one half for persons with special skills, training, or education advantageous to the United States, and the rest for those with close relatives here.[9] Aware of the growing congressional willingness to end national origins and the Asia-Pacific Triangle but unwillingness to increase immigration substantially, the President suggested that total immigration (outside the Western Hemisphere) be only 165,000 annually with no country permitted to have more than 10 percent of the total. Under the McCarran-Walter Act the Eastern Hemisphere had been allocated about 158,000 slots. Because Kennedy wanted to add parents of U.S. citizens to the list of those coming outside the numerical limits, and because some nations like Ireland and Great Britain had not fully used their quotas, immigration was expected to increase by as much as 50,000 to 60,000 annually. Some congressmen worried about any increase, but the debate centered on who gets in rather than how many.

Two other suggestions deserve mention. The President wanted to establish an immigration board to advise him on immigration issues and to set standards about the admission of skilled persons. The other proposal granted the President power to deal with refugees during emergencies.

Many in Congress recognized the unworkability of the McCarran-Walter Act and disapproved of the repeated enactment of special laws and the growing number of private member bills needed to bypass the law.[10] In the past, Francis Walter and his allies blocked all-out efforts to amend the basic law, but the death of Walter in 1963 seemed to open the possibility for major changes. Several members of Congress introduced companion bills or co-sponsored the Kennedy proposals. However, Congressman Michael Feighan of Ohio, the new chairman of the House (Immigration) Subcommittee No. 1 of the Committee on the Judiciary, exhibited little eagerness for quick reform. James Eastland, the key figure in the Senate in regard to immigration, opposed changing the McCarran-Walter Act. Eventually Eastland stepped aside, and Senators Everett Dirksen of Illinois and Sam Ervin of North Carolina played important roles. The assassination of Kennedy in Dallas in November 1963 and the elevation of Lyndon B. Johnson to the presidency caused further apprehension among reformers, who were uncertain of the new President's views. Johnson, unlike Kennedy, had voted to override President Truman's veto of the McCarran-Walter Act, and had evidenced no great interest in immigration reform as a senator. However, as in other areas of political life, Johnson became more liberal as President than he had been as a senator from the state of Texas.

In his State of the Union message of January 1964, the President endorsed immigration reform, including ending the national origins system and the Asia-Pacific Triangle, and told the House and Senate immigration subcommittee members that he supported the 1963 Kennedy proposals.[11] Both subcommittees held hearings but neither reported in 1964. In the House action was partly stalled because of a bitter feud between Michael Feighan and Emanuel Celler, chairman of the Judiciary Committee, over control over the Ohioan's subcommittee. Celler wanted to end the independence it had under Francis Walter, while Feighan saw immigration as his issue. When Feighan resisted Celler's attempts to control his subcommittee, the fight went to the floor of the House over an appropriation matter. Celler won his appeal to cut funds for Feighan's activities, but progress on the immigration bill became a casualty.[12]

In 1964 other issues preempted the attention of the administration. Immigration received scant attention in the 1964 election, except by the Republican vice presidential candidate William Miller, who warned that the Johnson proposals would open the "floodgates for virtually any and all who would wish to come and find work in this country." When criticized, he retreated and insisted that his position was misunderstood.[13]

Although immigration appeared only as a minor issue in the campaign, both parties did court ethnic voters, and the landslide victory of Lyndon Johnson and the Democratic party opened the door for the enactment of a new immigration law. Many conservative Republicans lost their seats, and in their place stood liberal Democrats more sympathetic to immigration reform and the Great Society programs of Johnson. The Democrats had a majority of 295 to 140 in the House and 68 to 32 in the Senate. Resistance to tampering with national origins traditionally centered in the South, but white southerners now found themselves on the defensive, as witnessed by the success of the Civil Rights movement in pushing through the Civil Rights Act of 1964 and the Voting Rights Act of 1965. These laws had one aim in common with amendment of the McCarran-Walter Act: ending racial and ethnic discrimination.

The election brought with it changes in the makeup of the committees responsible for immigration. In the House the Judiciary Committee went from 21 Democrats and 14 Republicans to 24 Democrats and 11 Republicans and its subcommittee on immigration increased from five to nine with a majority favoring reform. In the Senate the situation was tighter on the Senate Judiciary Committee and its Subcommittee on Immigration and Nationality, but there too reformers won control. Moreover, Congress revised its rules to expedite legislation and make it difficult, as was the case in the days of Francis Walter, for a chairman to hold up legislation.[14] These changes and the general liberal climate all pointed in the direction of the repeal of the Asia-Pacific Triangle and the national origins system, but the exact form the 1965 amendments would take remained uncertain.

Flushed with his victory in 1964, Johnson sent a number of Great Society programs to Congress and pushed them through. Among these proposals was the immigration reform measure, with minor changes, that he had supported the year before.[15] Following Johnson's message to Congress, Emanuel Celler in the House and Senator Philip Hart of Michigan, introduced the measure which became known as the Hart-Celler bill. The House subcommittee, under Feighan, began hearings in March while the Senate subcommittee, under the direction of Senator Edward Kennedy, held hearings beginning in February that lasted into the late summer. Administration spokesmen stressed that the new proposal would help American foreign policy and chose Secretary of State Dean Rusk to make one of the main statements on the need for reform and its relation to foreign affairs. Rusk and others argued that the present system was discriminatory and that passage of the new bill represented a wise foreign policy. In addition they insisted that reform was in America's self-interest economically. They also stressed its humanitarian aspects in that it aided the unification of families and assisted refugees.[16] These statements were not new; most of them had been presented before. Attorney General Robert Kennedy, for example, in 1964 told the representatives that the present system

is a standing affront to many Americans and to many countries. It implies what we in the United States know from our own experience is false: that regardless of individual qualifications, a man or woman born in Italy, or Greece, or Poland, or Portugal, or Czechoslovakia, or the Ukraine, is not as good as someone born in Ireland, or England, or Germany, or Sweden. Everywhere else in our national life, we have eliminated discrimination based on national origins. Yet, this system is still the foundation of our immigration law.[17]

Finally, the administration also assured Congress that the new law would not increase immigration significantly and would not have a negative impact upon employment in the United States.[18]

Those religious and ethnic organizations and groups working with refugees (VOLAGS) that had been clamoring for years to change the McCarran-Walter Act also favored the bill. In addition, many of these groups formed an ad hoc group, the National Committee for Immigration Reform, in early 1965 to rally support for the administration's proposals. Secular organizations long active in immigration matters, like the American Immigration Citizenship Conference, also backed the President. The voluntary organizations sent witnesses to testify for the bill and lobbied among congressmen. The various religious and ethnic organizations echoed the administration's arguments about discrimination and the need to abandon the Asia-Pacific Triangle and the national origins system.[19]

Organized labor helped the cause of reform. The CIO had supported reform during the early 1950s and had urged President Truman to veto the McCarran-Walter Act. The AFL had favored refugee legislation, like the Displaced Persons Act, but that union supported the McCarran Act. By the end of the 1950s, however, the merged AFL-CIO favored new immigration policies though it did suggest changes in the original Kennedy proposals to protect American workers. In particular, the AFL-CIO preferred that the Labor Department control prospective immigrant workers' entry.[20]

If the testimony of the AFL-CIO, the National Council of Churches, the American Committee for Italian Migration, the National Council of Jewish Women, the National Catholic Welfare Conference, and the Japanese Americans Citizens League, among others, favored the reforms, that of the patriotic, veterans, and conservative groups opposed or remained skeptical of change. The American Committee on Immigration Policies, formed in 1964, and the Liberty Lobby actively opposed the bill and a few others used the familiar arguments about the potential dangers of immigration to America.[21] Mrs. Robert Duncan, speaking for the Daughters of the American Revolution, for example, explained why her group preferred the 1952 law: "Abandonment of the national origins system would drastically alter the source of our immigration. Any such change would not take into consideration that those whose background and heritage most closely resemble our own are most readily assimilable."[22] In general, however, similar suggestions about changing patterns of immigration being detrimental to the United States, from either organizations or in Congress, were relatively few.

Moreover, a concerted effort to kill the bill by the traditional foes of immigration never materialized. Senator Edward Kennedy, the Senate floor leader for the immigration bill, later wrote:

During the course of the hearings I personally met with representatives from several of these organizations, including the American Coalition of Patriotic Societies, the American Legion, the Daughters of the American Revolution, and the National Association of Evangelicals. There was a candid exchange of the views between myself and those who joined the discussion. While most of these with whom I met were skeptical regarding various reform channels, and for reasons which varied among the organizations represented at the meetings, I believe it is fair to say that all recognized the unworkability of the national-origins quota system and at the close of the meetings expressed a willingness to cooperate in finding a new formula for the selection of immigrants. No significant opposition to eliminating the national-origins quota system was organized by any of their organizations.[23]

Kennedy was correct, and some groups like the American Legion and the American Coalition of Patriotic Societies not only did not actively oppose the bill, but the Legion even accepted the inevitable and worked to make it more to its liking.[24] "We were realistic," said one American Legion spokesman. "Many of our people, I have to admit, were not happy that we didn't go down fighting on national origins."[25]

The key to passage of the Johnson bill was winning over Michael Feighan in the House, chairman of the Subcommittee No. 1 of the Committee of the Judiciary and two senators on the Senate subcommittee, Everett Dirksen and Sam Ervin. Previously, Feighan had supported modifications of the McCarran-Walter Act, but he exhibited no enthusiasm for the 1963 Kennedy proposals and his position on important issues like national origins was not clear. Some liberals thought he opposed changing national origins. He possessed a reputation as a strong anti-Communist with close connections to patriotic groups. But Feighan also represented a district in Cleveland with many ethnic groups favorable to reform. Nor could he overlook the results of Johnson's landslide in 1964, especially because of his own political difficulty within his district. He barely won in a closely contested primary election in 1964. In early 1965 Feighan denied that he was pressured to accept reform and insisted he favored elimination of national origins quotas and had worked for a number of years to overturn them.[26]

Whatever his motives, he made a speech in February 1965 to the American Coalition of Patriotic Societies calling for the repeal of the national origins quota system and elimination of the Asia-Pacific Triangle and replacing them with a system based on family relationships, skills, and refugee status in that order. At the same time, he wanted to end the nonquota status for the Western Hemisphere and he asked for a worldwide ceiling on immigration. He opposed the immigration board suggested by both Kennedy and Johnson and wanted total immigration to be less than what he believed it would be under the administration's reforms.[27]

The Feighan proposals did not differ radically from those of the administration, and Feighan himself, after consultation with the administration, compromised. However, his proposals modified the administration ones in several key areas. When he introduced his own bill in June 1965 it became the measure that, with some modification, Congress eventually enacted.[28] The ranking minority member of the immigration subcommittee, Republican Arch Moore of West Virginia, also played an important role in shaping the final draft.[29]

Because both Feighan and the administration accepted the abolition of the Asia-Pacific Triangle and the national origins quotas as the major reforms, other issues separated the two parties. The administration stressed admitting persons with skills, education, and occupations and wanted to grant half of the visas to such people. Preference to those with close family ties in the United States came second. Feigham reversed these preferences and he won. The final proposal contained only two preference categories (the third and sixth) for those with professions, skills, occupations, or special talents needed in the United States. Congress reserved four categories for those with close American relatives. Refugees, with 6 percent of the total visas, had seventh and last preference. Moreover, of the seven categories finally enacted visas for family unification claimed 74 percent of the total while those with occupations, skills, professions, and talents had only 20 percent. Even within the two groups for occupations, skills, professions, and talents, another limitation existed. Family members of those obtaining such visas counted toward the 20 percent total. Thus, the visas for those actually having occupations, skills, professions, or talents would be less than 20 percent of the total.

The reversing of priorities by Feighan, and its acceptance by the administration and Congress, signaled a clear triumph for organized labor, which worried about competition from immigrant workers. Moreover, the bill gave the Department of Labor control over these economically oriented visas, which represented still another victory for labor control, for everyone expected the department to watch closely economic conditions in the United States. Indeed, the law contained new conditions for the issuing of visas. Under the old law, foreign labor was subject to exclusion when the Secretary of Labor said sufficient American workers existed in that prospective immigrant's occupation or that the employment of the alien would adversely affect the wages and working conditions of American workers. The Secretary of Labor enforced this exclusion loosely. Stanley Ruttenberg, the Assistant Secretary of Labor, told a congressional committee in 1968, "Under the old provision, the Department of Labor was able to prevent undue competition with U.S. workers and adverse effects on their wages and working conditions only on rare occasion. From 1957 to 1965, only 56 certifications of availability of American workers or adverse effect were issued, and more than half of these were limited to employment with one employer in one city."30

Under the Feighan bill, "this procedure is substantially changed. The primary responsibility is placed upon the intending immigrant to obtain the Secretary of Labor's clearance *prior* [italics author's] to the issuance of the visa." As finally passed, the Labor Department certification also applied to immigrants from the Western Hemisphere as well, unless they were immediate family members of American citizens or resident aliens (such as those entering with certification).31 The use of Labor Department certification before one could obtain a visa appeared to work as expected, for the department pursued a tight policy. In the future it became difficult for many unskilled, semiskilled, or skilled workers to get visas under the third and sixth preferences, and the department tended to be generous only for special occupations such as doctors, engineers, scientists, and nurses. On the other hand, the new law did not keep out working immigrants. Most immigrants arriving after 1965 worked, but only a minority, about 10 percent, arrived with Labor Department certification.32 Eighty percent or so of those who worked entered as part of family unification or as refugees and did not have to get certified.

The downgrading of economic categories and their tight control by the Department of Labor represented victories for organized labor, but emphasizing family unification was also a victory for political compromise in abolishing national origins quotas. Italy, Greece, and Poland, all nations with relatively low national origins quotas, had the largest backlogs of persons awaiting visas. Because of the pressure for emigration in those nations, not even the special laws of the 1950s eliminated their backlogs. Organizations representing people of those nationalities wanted to change the law to increase their immigration. The original Kennedy proposal provided for a total Eastern Hemisphere immigration of 165,000 annually with no nation having more than 10 percent of the total. The final bill put the figure at 170,000 and the nation limit at 20,000. The country quota of a maximum of 20,000 would have prevented an immediate elimination of an estimated backlog of about 250,000 for Italy, but nearly everyone favored some type of individual country limit so that no one nation would have too large a share of the annual visas. As the Senate Judiciary Committee put it, the limits were designed "to prevent unreasonable allocation of numbers by any one foreign state."[33] The maximum of 20,000 represented a sizeable increase for Italy with its quota of less than 6,000 or Greece with its 308, while at the same time limiting Italy's and Greece's share. Limiting nations to 20,000 annually did not appear controversial and was an accommodation to political realities, though it has since been criticized.[34]

Another way to view the proposed law which emphasized uniting families in place of national origins as a compromise is to realize that many favoring the change did not see it as having significant impact on immigration patterns. They argued that future potential immigrants would need to have close family ties in the United States, due to prior immigration, to gain entry. Greeks and Italians, for example, had those contacts. Symbolically, however, it seemed a significant change because it abolished national origins quotas and the Asia-Pacific Triangle that most observers agreed were discriminatory. But would it change immigration patterns? Special legislation had already made the quotas of McCarran-Walter somewhat meaningless. Two representatives for the American Legion explained the cautious nature of the reform. They said that while the quota system was struck down, "the national origins system wasn't . . . nobody is quite so apt to be of the same national origins of our present citizens as are members of their immediate families, and the great bulk of immigrants henceforth, will not merely hail from the same parent countries as our present citizens, but will be their closer relatives."[35]

The Legion's analysis, which explains why so much traditional opposition disappeared in 1965, does overlook the fact that many relatives would be bringing in immigrants from southern and eastern Europe, which various patriotic and veteran's groups like the Legion had opposed in the recent past. Obviously, another key issue in the mid-1960s was increased ethnic toleration in American society, the growing acceptance by old stock Americans of the children and grandchildren of the southern and eastern European immigrants. The same legion spokesmen acknowledged this acceptance tacitly and noted that act would not greatly change Asian immigration. "But Asiatics having far fewer immediate family members now in the United States than southern Europeans, will automatically arrive in far fewer numbers than Italians, Greeks and other southern European stock. Yet, there is no sting in the new law to offend Asian nations. Asians will qualify on the same basis as others, though far fewer of them will be able to do so."[36]

While the preferences given to family unification under the new immigration policy made the American Legion happy, they prompted criticism from the Japanese American Citizens League (JACL). In a letter to Senator Thomas Kuchel of California, JACL supported the bill as an improvement over the McCarran-Walter Act, but noted:

Inasmuch as the total Asian population of the United States is only about one half of 1 percent of the total American population, this means that there are very few of Asia-Pacific origin in this country who are entitled to provide the specific preference priorities to family members and close relatives residing abroad, even if all qualified family members and close relatives desire to emigrate immediately to the United States. Thus, it would seem that, although the immigration bill eliminated race as a matter of principle, in actual operation immigration will still be controlled by the now discredited national origins system and the general pattern of immigration which exists today will continue for many years yet to come.[37]

Both the American Legion and JACL observations found support from the administration and most congressmen who spoke about the impact of the proposed changes on immigration patterns. Not many congressmen discussed this issue in detail, and most who did believed that the major impact of the new law would be on southern and eastern Europe and that few could qualify from Asia or Africa. Emanuel Celler, longtime proponent of reform, assured his colleagues:

With the end of discrimination due to place of birth, there will be shifts in countries other than those of northern and western Europe. Immigrants from Asia and Africa will have to compete and qualify in order to get in, quantitatively and qualitatively, which, itself will hold the numbers down. There will not be, comparatively, many Asians or Africans entering this country. . . . Since the people of Africa and Asia have very few relatives here, comparatively few could immigrate from those countries because they have no family ties in the U.S.[38]

The administration, in supporting its own bill in 1964 and 1965, which contained even less emphasis on family unification than the final bill, minimized Caribbean and Asian immigration, and African immigration received still less discussion. In the case of the Caribbean, administration spokesmen knew that removing the one hundred limit on new West Indian nations would lead to increases, but they underestimated their extent. Experts told Congress that a "small increase" would lead to immigration of about 5,000 to 7,000 from these nations, but by the late 1970s Jamaica and Trinidad and Tobago together sent over 25,000 persons to the United States; in 1989 the combined total was just under 30,000.[39]

As for Asia, the administration spokesmen knew that abolishing the Asia-Pacific Triangle and national origins would benefit Asian nations. Eliminating the Asia-Pacific Triangle would make those persons of Asian descent in the nonquota Western Hemisphere eligible for admission as persons from the Western Hemisphere and not chargeable to the low quotas of Asian countries, which were oversubscribed. When asked how many might enter because of this change, Attorney General Robert Kennedy told a House subcommittee that only a few would come at first and then the pool would dry up. Or as he put it, "I would say for the Asia-Pacific Triangle it [immigration] would be approximately 5,000, Mr. Chairman, after which immigration from that source would virtually disappear; 5,000 immigrants would come in the first year, but we do not expect that there would be any great influx after that."[40]

If few Asians would be eligible to enter from outside of Asia because of abolition of the Asia-Pacific Triangle, what effect would changing the system have on immigration from Asian nations? Of course all nations would have a ceiling (finally set at 20,000, not including immediate family members of U.S. citizens), and that would limit any one Asian nation. Moreover, immigration was still limited by other exclusions such as rejecting those likely to become a public charge. Assistant Attorney General Norbet Schlei, for example, explained to Senator Sam Ervin about East Indian or other "underdeveloped areas":

I can foretell that there will be a relatively limited number of people who will qualify under our administrative restrictions, such as being able to demonstrate that they would not become a public charge here, that they would not come to do any work for which there are Americans available, or that would lower working standards or wages for Americans, that they are literate, that they have all these characteristics that our law requires.

I think that those provisions of law impose very real limits on the number of qualified applicants that we are liable to receive from underdeveloped areas.[41]

Numbers were not always precise, but Congress was informed by administrative officials that about 94,000 Asians from quota areas would enter during the first five years after enactment of the new policy, an average of about 19,000 annually, which was a bit less than the total number admitted in 1965, but above the average for the ten years before that date.[42] Asian immigration reached 20,000 in 1965 because of what Senator Edward Kennedy called special legislation, administrative relief, and private member bills; or as Dean Rusk noted, 109,654 of 119,677 immigrants from China, Japan and the Philippines entering between 1953 and 1963 were nonquota. Hence, the new proposal "merely updates our present law to conform more fully with our actual practice." Thus, as presented to Congress, the administration's proposal would have virtually no effect on Asian immigration, except to rid the immigration statutes of racism and eliminate backlogs within a few years or, as Senator Kennedy said, the new system "would not inundate America with immigrants from any one country or area, or the most populated and economically deprived nations of Africa and Asia." That the administration saw the changes as being "rather limited against the actual volume of immigration of Asian immigration into the United States between 1953 and 1963," is not surprising.[43] Immigration was predicted to increase only 50,000 to 60,000 and Asian nations had relatively small backlogs compared to Italy or Greece. This meant that the major impact of the reforms were projected to be on southern and eastern European nations, not Asian ones. And the final act emphasized family unification even more than the original Johnson-Kennedy bills, which made it even more cautious about initiating immigration changes.

A few congressmen who opposed the bill insisted that replacing national origins quotas, even with family preferences and tight labor controls, meant a drastic change. Senator Spessard Holland of Florida told the Senate:

What I object to is imposing no limitation insofar as areas of the earth are concerned, but saying that we are throwing the doors open and equally inviting people from the Orient, from the islands of the Pacific, from the subcontinent of Asia, from the Near East, from all of Africa, all of Europe, and all of the Western Hemisphere on exactly the same basis. I am inviting attention to the fact that this is a complete and radical departure from what has always heretofore been regarded as sound principles of immigration.[44]

In retrospect (for reasons that will be explained in later chapters), those who saw little change in the patterns were wrong. What they would have done if this issue were clear in 1965 is, of course, unknown. Third world nations dominated the immigration statistics by the 1970s, which certainly was not the intent of the reformers. The bill might have passed anyway, in the civil rights and generally liberal climate of 1965, but perhaps not so easily or without other changes.

More controversial than the method of replacing national origins by a preference system geared primarily to family unification was a suggested numerical cap on the Western Hemisphere, which aimed at limiting Latin American immigration. The ceiling, opposed by the Johnson administration, became the major issue in congressional floor debates and in the Senate committees concerned with immigration, and eventually won the reluctant support of the administration in order to get a consensus bill.

Michael Feighan favored a limit on the Western Hemisphere. Although accepting most of his other suggestions, the administration prevailed upon him to drop this idea. House Subcommittee No. 1 also originally favored a numerical limit on the Western Hemisphere, but reversed itself when two members changed their votes after receiving pressure from the administration. In the House Judiciary Committee, Clark MacGregor, a Republican from Minnesota, again offered an amendment to impose a cap of 115,000, exclusive of spouses, minor children, and parents of U.S. citizens, on the Western Hemisphere, but he lost 11 to 22.[45] Mac-Gregor then took his fight to the floor of the House, where it became the major issue affecting the House vote. Proponents of his amendment said that having a ceiling for the Eastern Hemisphere and none for the Western was unfair. "To allow unlimited immigration from the Western Hemisphere while imposing rigid ceilings on the number who can come in from the rest of the world, including our traditional friends and allies in Western Europe—and this in the name of ending a quota system labelled as discriminatory and racially prejudicial—is highly contradictory," declared the dissenting members of the House Judiciary Committee.[46]

Some representatives also worried about population pressures in Latin America and said that the United States had to regulate immigration from that source.[47] Opponents of a ceiling insisted the traditional ways of controlling Western Hemisphere immigration, such as using health and economic qualifications, were sufficient and adding a ceiling now would hurt the Good Neighbor Policy. To those who said adding a cap would harm American foreign affairs, MacGregor noted that his amendment omitted the 20,000 limit per nation and hence would not severely restrict immigration from America's immediate neighbors, Canada and Mexico.[48] On a preliminary vote his amendment barely carried, but after the administration and the amendment's opponents marshalled their forces it lost on a roll call vote, 189 to 218. The House bill did contain a rather meaningless provision telling the President to inform Congress and make recommendations if immigration from the Western Hemisphere for any year was 10 percent greater than the average for the preceding five years. After defeating MacGregor's amendment, the House then passed the bill, on August 25th.[49]

In the Senate, Senator Eastland allowed Edward Kennedy to chair the Subcommittee on Immigration hearings that began in February and ended in August. Eastland and John McClellan of Arkansas, both supporters of national origins, made only token appearances during the hearings. Instead, Senator Sam Ervin became the staunchest defender of national origins and often engaged in long question-and-answer sessions with various witnesses. Ervin insisted that immigration must be selective and that it was not discriminatory to have a national origins quota system which he argued

is based on the proposition that all men are created equal, and that the people of various nationalities have made contributions to the development of the United States in proportion to their numbers here. The McCarran-Walter Act is, therefore, based on conditions existing in the United States, like a mirror reflecting the United States, allowing the admission of immigrants according to a national and uniform mathematical formula. . . . It recognized the obvious and natural fact that those immigrants can best be assimilated into our society who have relatives, friends, or others of similar background already here.[50]

Eastland and McClellan favored the present law and the administration believed that if Dirksen and Ervin joined them, it might lack the votes to get the bill reported. Ervin and Dirksen could not block abolition of national origins indefinitely, but they managed to gain a major concession. On the day the administration won a victory in the House against the MacGregor amendment, it agreed not to wage an all-out fight in the Senate on a Western Hemisphere limitation that these two senators wanted. The senators in turn would vote for a bill abolishing national origins quotas.[51] The agreement also included a face-saving device: creation of a special commission on Western Hemisphere immigration to examine the issue and make recommendations. No one expected this commission to recommend killing the limitation. Abba Schwartz, who played an important role in drafting the original Kennedy proposal, believed the bargain was a "false theory of consensus," but the administration thought otherwise.[52] The subcommittee then approved a Western Hemisphere limit by a five to three vote. Senators Jacob Javits, Kennedy, and Hart opposed the limit on the Western Hemisphere, while Dirksen, McClellan, Ervin, Eastland, and Hiram Fong voted for it.[53]

Although insisting upon a ceiling for the Western Hemisphere, the Senate subcommittee accepted most of the changes made by Feighan and the House. The Judiciary Committee approved the bill by a vote of 14 to 2 with only Eastland and McClellan voting against it. Dirksen temporarily held up the bill in order to push a project of his own, but as part of the bargain with the administration both Ervin and Dirksen supported the bill, though Ervin did submit a special report explaining his views.[54]

When the measure reached the Senate floor on September 22, opposition predictably centered among southerners. The most extreme statement came from Senator James Ellender of Louisiana who favored a five year suspension of all immigration and expressed unwillingness to accept the bill with its projected increase and overhaul of the McCarran-Walter Act.[55] A few others worried about changing patterns of immigration and the economic impact of immigration while the bill's supporters said abolition of national origins quotas was overdue.[56] Ervin emphasized that a majority of the subcommittee favored a ceiling of 120,000 on the Western Hemisphere. This figure, 5,000 above the MacGregor amendment, nearly equalled the average immigration from the Western Hemisphere in recent years. To those favoring restriction, the worrisome aspect was the increase, especially from Latin America:

the [Senate Judiciary Committee majority] has become increasingly concerned with the unrestricted flow of immigration from the nonquota countries which has averaged 110,000 the past ten years. Last year the nonquota admissions from Western Hemisphere countries totaled 139,185 and the evidence is present that the increase will continue.[57]

Few expressed racist sentiments about Hispanics or black non-Hispanic West Indians, but some proponents of a ceiling said Latin Americans and people from the Caribbean were "different," and they insisted that the United States should not become the "dumping ground" for surplus populations.[58] The Senate accepted the restriction even though some liberals wanted it stricken.

The senators approved the bill 76 to 18, with opposition limited mainly to the South.[59]

Most differences between the two bills were minor and a conference easily reconciled them. The major stumbling block remained the Western Hemisphere limit, but House members realized that they had to accept such a cap to get the bill passed. Representative Emanuel Celler, of the House Conference Committee, told his colleagues, "We finally came to the conclusion, in order to get something done, that we should do this."[60] In the Senate, Jacob Javits explained, "We all understand that the bill is a package deal. . . . Without such a package we would not have had a bill in the Senate."[61] The Senate approved the Conference Report, which incorporated the limit, by a voice vote, while the House agreed, 326 to 69.[62]

As finally enacted the 1965 amendments to the Immigration and Nationality Act abolished the Asia-Pacific Triangle and phased out the national origins quotas over a three-year period.[63] The new system, effective July 1, 1968, provided 170,000 visas for persons from the Eastern Hemisphere and 120,000 for the Western. No country in the Eastern Hemisphere was to have more than 20,000 of these visas. However, "immediate" family members—defined as spouses, minor children (under 21), and parents of United States citizens—and a few others, such as ministers, were exempt from the numerical limits. These family exemptions soon began to run larger than predicted, and in the ten years after the law went into effect averaged about 90,000 annually, instead of projections of about half that number. They ran over 125,000 in 1978, approximately 138,000 in 1979, and by the mid-1980s topped 200,000 annually.[64] By then they became the source of debate and concern about growing immigration.

Persons in the Eastern Hemisphere received visas on a first-come, first-served basis, subject to the numerical limits and exemptions, within the following preference categories:

First Preference: Unmarried sons and daughters (over age 21) of U.S. citizens (maximum of 20 percent).

Second Preference: Spouse and unmarried sons and daughters of aliens lawfully admitted for permanent residence (20 percent plus any not required for the first preference).

Third Preference: Members of the professions and scientists and artists of exceptional ability (maximum of 10 percent).

Fourth Preference: Married sons and daughters (over age 21) of U.S. citizens (10 percent plus any not required for the first three preferences).

Fifth Preference: Brothers and sisters of U.S. citizens (24 percent plus any not required for the first four preferences). This was the largest preference and, because it was used so heavily, it prompted some to call the law "the brothers and sisters act."

Sixth Preference: Skilled and unskilled workers in occupations for which labor is in short supply (maximum of 10 percent).

Seventh Preference: Refugees (maximum of 6 percent). Refugees were to be admitted as "conditional entrants," for a period of two years, after which time they could adjust their status to permanent resident aliens. Congress defined refugees as it did under the 1957 Refugee-Escapee Act, as people fleeing persecution from Communism or the Middle East with one addition: "persons uprooted by catastrophic natural calamity as defined by the President."

Passage of the 1965 amendments can be partly attributed to the landslide election of Lyndon Johnson and the Democrats in 1964, for this election brought to power a number of new congressmen sympathetic to the goals of the act. The 89th Congress (1965–1966) became the first ever that reported Roman Catholics, many of whom descended from the large-scale immigration in the late nineteenth and early twentieth centuries, to be the leading group among various denominations. One hundred seven claimed to be Catholics; Methodists came next with eighty-eight.[65] As noted, committees responsible for immigration had solid majorities for changing the immigration laws, though the vote was closer in the Senate.

Behind these immediate reasons for the success in modifying the law lay general trends. Certainly the healthy economy played a role. Unlike the Great Depression, the prosperous sixties saw few fears about possible unfavorable results of immigration upon the economy. In addition, reformers stressed the many safeguards in the act for the American worker and they won union support. Then, too, the projected increase in immigration was only about 50,000 to 60,000 annually, of whom only half were potential workers; hence, the measure could be sold as having little more impact on the economy than current immigration.

If economic conditions favored change so did growing racial and ethnic toleration in postwar American society. Responding to the civil rights movement, in 1957 Congress passed the first civil rights law since Reconstruction, another in 1960, and two important bills in 1964 and 1965. Moreover, Supreme Court decisions and state and local laws also struck at white racism. Some blacks began to find areas of American life opening to them that heretofore had been closed. The connection between enacting civil rights legislation and abolishing the Asia-Pacific Triangle and national origins quotas was clear; as one congressman put it, "just as we sought to eliminate discrimination in our land through the Civil Rights act, today we seek by phasing out the national origins quota system to eliminate discrimination in immigration to this nation composed of the descendants of immigrants."[66]

If some blacks found expanding opportunities so did other minorities like Japanese Americans, Jews, and Catholics. As noted, Japanese immigrants had been granted naturalization rights in 1952 and a number of states that had discriminated against them repealed their discriminatory laws. Increasingly, Japanese Americans moved from the concentration camp experience of World War II into the mainstream of American society.[67]

Jews and Catholics also found increasing acceptance in American life. States began to outlaw religious discrimination after World War II and a variety of institutions that formerly barred or restricted Jews and Catholics modified their policies. Medical schools, for example, dropped numerical quotas against Jews as did Ivy League universities. Anti-Semitism, so strong in the 1930s and 1940s, peaked and began to decline in the late 1940s.[68] The same can be said for anti-Catholicism, and in 1960 the voters elected the first Roman Catholic President. Of course, the growing participation of ethnic minorities did not occur overnight, nor did prejudice disappear by the 1960s, or even today for that matter, but marked changes were noticeable by 1965.

Public opinion polls also indicated more religious toleration. A Gallup survey issued in 1979 put it, "One of the most dramatic trends in the 44-year history of the Gallup Poll has been the growth in tolerance towards persons of different religions and races. New evidence of this is found in a recent Gallup Poll in which questions first asked in 1952—and in 1965—were repeated. The finding showed steady and marked decline in the proportions of persons of the major faiths who have feelings of animosity toward each other."[69] How this affected immigration is less clear. The public did not necessarily want radical changes or increases in immigration, but two polls conducted during 1965 indicated support for changing the national origins system to one based on skills and family unification. The Harris and Gallup polls asked different questions, which obscured the issue, but they showed that only a minority favored basing immigration access on the country of one's birth.[70]

The changing public mood no doubt gave confidence to those ethnic and religious groups advocating change. Beginning with the enactment of the Displaced Persons Act, the role of ethnic lobbying for immigration reform by newer ethnic groups became apparent. The lessons learned from the 1940s and 1950s by these organizations paid dividends in the 1960s when they lobbied to change the 1952 immigration act.

Important as general trends and particular circumstances were, it is essential to note the cautious and even restrictive nature of the 1965 changes. Immigration was not projected to increase much, and Congress added tight controls for immigrant workers. Moreover, immigration from the Western Hemisphere, increasing in the early 1960s, now had a ceiling. Some saw these issues as additional restriction and they were correct even though the administration accepted them as the price for a consensus bill. Representative Joe Skubitz of Kansas, who favored the bill, noted the modest nature of the new measure. It provided only "a little more" than the present total, and the bill "includes more restrictive provisions to safeguard the American economy and jobs of American labor than the law now in effect," he said.[71] When the act becomes fully operative, Secretary of Labor Willard Wirtz said, "the total number of quota immigrants entering the work force— that is under the increase as well as under the present base—will be equal to about one tenth of 1 percent of the work force."[72] The conservative nature of the final bill can also be seen in the family preference system, which, as the *Wall Street Journal* noted, "had emotional appeal and, perhaps more to the point, insured that the new immigration pattern would not stray radically from the old one."[73]

While the family preference system was a cautious change and new labor controls and a Western Hemisphere ceiling represented increased restriction, Congress also rejected several of the administration's suggestions for further liberalization. These included flexibility in the admission of refugees and creation of an immigration board to advise the President on standards for the admission of immigrants who came to work. Both these provisions would have given the executive more control over immigration and represented a potential liberal interpretation of policy.

In spite of the new restrictions and rejection of some of the original proposals, liberals praised the act because it accomplished their essential goals of abolishing national origins and the Asia-Pacific Triangle. They saw it as a victory for toleration as did many of the major newspapers that supported the act.[74] Typical of this view was the immigration expert for the Catholic periodical *America*. "It is difficult to predict how the new immigration law will work in practice," he wrote, "but there can be little question that these changes were long overdue and that we have too long lived with an immigration law based on erroneous racial and cultural antipathies entirely inconsistent with our professed belief in the worth of and the dignity of the individual person."[75]

In signing the bill, President Johnson caught both its symbolic change and cautious reform:

This is not a revolutionary bill. It does not affect the lives of millions. It will not reshape the structure of our daily lives, or add importantly to our wealth and power. Yet, it is still one of the most important acts of this Congress and this Administration. For it repairs a deep and painful flaw in the fabric of American justice. . . . The days of unlimited immigration are past. But those who come will come because of what they are—not because of the land from which they sprung.[76]

In placing a 120,000 limit on the Western Hemisphere Congress paid little attention to details and concentrated instead on whether or not to have a ceiling. After passage of the 1965 amendments the Select Commission on Western Hemisphere Immigration reported as required and recommended that the cap be postponed for one year, but Congress took no action and it went into effect.[77] The Western Hemisphere now had a ceiling but no preference system nor individual country limit, which meant that the United States had two immigration policies. Because of the lack of a preference system for the Western Hemisphere and because more people wanted to emigrate to America than there were visas available, problems, especially for relatives of American citizens and resident aliens, soon developed. A House committee explained:

Because the Western Hemisphere has no preference system and no per-country limit, in effect, the United States has two different immigration laws for the two hemispheres. For example, under the provision determining Eastern Hemisphere immigration, the 22-year-old British citizen, daughter of a U.S. citizen, or the Spanish wife of a permanent resident alien would receive preferential treatment compared to other intending immigrants whose relational ties were more distant. . . . However, the 22-year-old Brazilian daughter of a U.S. citizen or the Canadian wife of a permanent resident alien would be required to line up behind the other intending immigrants from this hemisphere.[78]

The lack of a family preference system for the Western Hemisphere thus seemed to undercut the amendments of 1965 which in part aimed to unite families.

On the other hand, the lack of a 20,000 per nation limit in the Western Hemisphere worked to the advantage of Mexico. Mexican immigrants admitted under the hemisphere limit numbered nearly 32,000 in 1969 and they steadily increased after that; by 1974 they exceeded 45,000, excluding immediate family members. If Congress placed both the preference system and the 20,000 limit on the Western Hemisphere, immigration from Mexico would decrease.

Aware of the issues involving the preference categories and Mexico, House Subcommittee No. 1 of the Committee on the Judiciary held hearings, discussed Western Hemisphere immigration, and in 1973 reported a bill to give the Western Hemisphere a 20,000 per nation limit and a modified preference system. On the floor, the chairman of the Judiciary Committee, Peter Rodino of New Jersey, proposed an amendment: Canada and Mexico be granted special quotas of 35,000 each. Concerned about both foreign policy and illegal immigration, the administration also favored larger Mexican and Canadian totals.[79] Granting each American neighbor 35,000 was a facesaving device for those who wanted Mexico to have the extra slots. As Joshua Eilberg of Pennsylvania noted, "As a matter of fact, it is really an amendment to favor one country, and that is Mexico. The reason for that is that the Canadians do not come anywhere near using up the 20,000 per country limitation. . . . But, Mexico always exceeds it."[80] Since opponents of the amendment said favoritism of one country was wrong, it was hoped that by giving countries bordering the United States extra numbers and selling it as a foreign policy matter, the issue of favoritism would fade. They said the amendment had the endorsement of both the State and Justice departments, largely because of Good Neighbor Policy considerations, and should be adopted by Congress.[81]

Opponents of the amendment claimed that by "discriminating in favor of the Mexican immigration, we are also discriminating against other countries in the Western Hemisphere." If Mexico had more places, others would have less. "The whole thrust of this bill [without the Rodino amendment] is to take one big step toward uniformity, in our immigration policy the world over. It is, hopefully, to have a policy to rid ourselves of the national origins concept," argued Kenneth Keating of New York.[82] Joshua Eilberg, who replaced the defeated Feighan (1970) as chairman of the immigration subcommittee, noted that all countries in the Western Hemisphere already had an advantage because of the lack of a worldwide ceiling: "The Western Hemisphere, Mr. Chairman, exclusive of the United States, contains only 9 percent of the world's population yet it receives 41 percent of the visas that are allocated worldwide."[83] In the end the House rejected the State Department's contention and defeated the Rodino amendment; it then passed the bill by a vote of 336 to 30.[84] In the Senate, the Judiciary Committee under James Eastland took no action.

In the next Congress, a modified bill was reported again by the House's subcommittee on immigration and approved. By then the bill had strong support from most organizations interested in the issue and even the State Department dropped its opposition to the 20,000 per country limit:

Based on a review of existing data, a uniform ceiling for each country . . . would be preferable. This would permit an equitable distribution
of immigration from throughout the world. Problems with illegal immigration will exist whether immigration from Mexico is limited to 20,000 or
35,000 per year or not at all.[85]

Neither the House nor the Senate debated the bill at length and
it passed easily.[86] In signing the measure President Gerald Ford
indicated that he remained concerned about Mexican immigration, both legal and illegal, and that he would make a recommendation to increase the total for Mexicans because of the United
States' "very special and historic relationship with our neighbor to
the south."[87] President Jimmy Carter also requested an increase in
Mexico's share, and several congressmen introduced bills to affect
this change. Congressional committees did hold hearings, but reported no bills and Congress passed no legislation as the decade
came to an end. The issue appeared again in the 1980s.[88]

The House committee reporting the Western Hemisphere and
per nation limit bill of 1976 noted that a "unified worldwide immigration system in some form is the ultimate goal after the Western
Hemisphere situation has been resolved and after there has been
some opportunity to observe the operation of the preference system and per country numerical restriction in that hemisphere."[89]
Two years later Congress passed, without controversy, a law
providing for a worldwide immigration cap of 290,000 created by
combining both hemispheres, with a preference system and
20,000 per country limit. In 1980, when passing the Refugee Act of
that year, Congress modified the preference system and divorced
regular immigration from refugee flows. Then the legislators set
the new world ceiling at 270,000 and made the second preference
(spouses and unmarried sons and daughters of permanent resident aliens) the largest category. It had 70,200 places with the fifth
preferences (brothers and sisters of U.S. citizens) next, with 64,800
slots.

The completion of these reforms was one of the major immigration issues from 1965 to 1980. In the 1980s, however, economists,
business leaders, federal administration officials, and a growing
bloc in Congress began to examine immigration policy and push
for major changes. They succeeded in 1990 when Congress enact-

ed sweeping changes embodied in the Immigration Act of 1990. (The law will be discussed in the last chapter.)

Before passage of the 1990 Immigration Act Congress made minor adjustments in policies and procedures.[90] One change affecting third world immigration was a section of the Health Professions Educational Assistance Act of 1976 which declared "there is no longer an insufficient number of physicians and surgeons in the United States such that there is no further need for affording preference to alien physicians and surgeons to the United States under the Immigration and Nationality Act."[91]

Yet shortages of physicians and nurses still existed in a number of large cities, and in 1988 Congress passed legislation to permit nurses to extend their temporary visas. The lawmakers also tighten the rules for alleged marriage fraud as a way of migrating to the United States and established a lottery providing immigration places for those nations adversely affected by the 1965 Immigration Act. (These issues will be discussed in connection with the Immigration Act of 1990.)

Two other major issues were illegal or undocumented aliens and refugees, which will be discussed in later chapters. Regular immigration, refugees, and undocumented aliens were important matters demanding congressional attention after 1965. These, and several minor ones noted above and periodic reports of the inefficiency of the Immigration and Naturalization Service, including charges of fraud and corruption, prompted Congress to take a broad view of immigration as the decade came to an end. As part of the 1978 law creating a worldwide ceiling Congress established the Select Commission on Immigration and Refugee Policy to make a major study of immigration and recommend changes. The sixteen-member commission, composed of congressional representatives and senators, cabinet officials, and presidential appointees and armed with a budget of $700,000 (later increased), was slated to make its report in March 1981. Congress recognized, as did experts in the field of immigration, that reexamination was overdue. As Representative Eilberg said, "There is a paucity of hard data in this country on the impact of immigration, both legal and illegal. This is indeed disturbing when you consider that our immigration law has not been reviewed in over twenty-five years and that almost every aspect of the American community is affected by immigration. In my judgment, it is vital that every effort be made to reevaluate our immigration policy and that it be done in a comprehensive fashion."[92]

Father Theodore Hesburgh, president of Notre Dame University, chaired the commission, and Professor Lawrence Fuchs of Brandeis University directed its work. After lengthy investigations, hearings, and studies completed under Fuch's able direction, the Select Commission finally reported in March 1981. The commissioners disagreed over some issues, but in general recommended a humane program. They recommended that the basic immigration system be kept intact, with more flexibility, adjustments in preferences, and increases in immigration to assist in easing backlogs in particular countries. The most controversial parts of its recommendations centered on questions and policies arising from undocumented aliens.[93] Yet Congress in 1981 was preoccupied with major economic issues—taxes and budget cuts—not immigration. Hence the legislators deferred judgment on the Select Commission's recommendations. In the 1980s some parts of the commissioners' recommendations, which will be discussed later, were incorporated into the Immigration Reform and Control Act of 1986, which aimed to curb undocumented immigration. The Immigration Act of 1990 also included suggestions from the Select Commission report.

In the first years following passage of the new law, as intended, immigrants from southern and eastern Europe found it easier to come to America. Italians averaged over 20,000 annually for a decade and Greeks and Portuguese also recorded sizable increases. Poland alone of the major southern and eastern European nations did not benefit by the new law. Prior to 1965 Polish authorities were the only ones from Communist nations to permit much emigration and many Poles came to America. After 1965, the Polish government did not wish to see its well-educated and skilled people, who might have obtained Labor Department certification, go to America; and the unskilled could not get cleared or lacked family connections necessary for immigration. Hence, Polish immigration to the United States fell.[94] While Greece, Italy, Portugal, and others sent more people to America, countries in northern and western Europe sent fewer. Overall, the proportion of Europeans shifted to a majority from the southern and eastern nations after 1965.

Northern and western European countries that formerly had relatively large quotas were now having to use the family preference system or Labor Department certification. Many intending immigrants in those nations could no longer qualify. Ireland, for example, had one of the largest quotas under the National Origins Act and the McCarran-Walter Act. Under the new provisions of 1965, Irish who wished to emigrate to the United States discovered that they were in occupations that the Labor Department would not certify or that they lacked close kinship ties required by the family preference categories. Hence, Irish immigration, though not large from 1945 to 1965 compared to the migrations in the nineteenth century, plunged even further after 1965. Irish-American leaders and several congressmen protested and recommended changes. John Collins, national chairman of the American Irish National Immigration Committee, told a congressional committee in 1968, "Unfortunately, the new law, in attempting to cure the discrimination of the old law has now saddled Irishmen—and quite possibly other nationalities—with an inequitable and unfair U.S. immigration policy."[95] This unfairness, he said, was due to the fact that the majority of Irish immigrants has "always been in the unskilled labor area," and now these jobs were on the Labor Department's prohibited list. However, Congress did not change the law and Irish immigration fell further, to below 1,000 in 1979.[96] During the 1980s when a wave of Irish undocumented immigrants entered the United States, the issue of Irish immigration was raised again and was dealt with in the Immigration Reform and Control Act of 1986 and the Immigration Act of 1990. (These acts will be discussed in later chapters.)

Yet, it was not simply the new law that affected European migration. The stagnant American economy and improved conditions and opportunities in Europe combined to ease emigration pressures. Until 1960 western Europe received large numbers of refugees and was unable to employ these people because of the damage to their economies during the war. Hence, European nations looked to the Western Hemisphere to receive some of their excess population. However, rapid economic recovery created labor shortages, and by the late 1950s NATO nations, Switzerland, and Sweden began programs to import temporary foreign workers, mostly from the Mediterranean countries of southern Europe and North Africa.

Before the European governments sharply curtailed these policies after the economic slump of 1973–1974, they contributed a significant proportion of the unskilled labor force, especially in Switzerland and Germany. In Germany, which imported the largest number of foreign workers—mainly Italians, Greeks, and Turks—the aliens were called *Gastarbeiters,* or guest workers. Former colonists from North Africa migrated to France after the French lost control of their colonies, but the French economy at first absorbed these people. Great Britain received many former colonial peoples from India, Pakistan, and the West Indies, before economic woes and ethnic and racial conflict in the 1960s led to changes in British immigration policy.[97]

By the mid-1970s, however, except for Portugal, immigration from Europe fell. Even southern European nations like Greece and Italy sent fewer immigrants than they did right after passage of the 1965 act. Conditions appeared either unattractive in the United States or they had improved sufficiently at home to deter migration. In 1965, 113,424 European immigrants entered but in the 1977–1979 period, they averaged about 65,000.[98] By the late 1960s, however, a new trend was evident: the growth of Asian immigration.

4

The New Asian Immigrants

WHILE EUROPEAN IMMIGRATION shifted and then fell, that of Asia, the Caribbean basin, and South America rose significantly after 1965 and people from these third world areas accounted for about three-quarters of the four million immigrants of the 1970s, and the same pattern continued into the 1980s. By then Europeans amounted to only about 15 percent of the nation's latest immigrants, a dramatic change from historic patterns. In 1965 Asian immigrants totaled 20,683, about 5 percent of the total. By the late 1970s Asian immigration had increased sixfold and claimed over 40 percent of the newcomers. China, the Philippines, India, and Vietnam were among the leading nations sending people to America. In 1979 the seven leading exporters were all third world nations. The figures for 1980 revealed an even greater influx of third world people, for in that year over a quarter of million refugees arrived from Vietnam, Cuba, and Haiti.[1] By the late 1980s the top ten sending nations were from the third world. Table 4.1 indicates those ten for 1989, not counting immigrants covered by an anmesty passed in 1986. By that year almost one half million persons had legalized their status, but these same countries also dominated the amnesty immigrants.

Why and how did Congress and the immigration reformers fail in 1965 to see the potential surge of Asian immigration? For one thing, they saw short queues for American visas in East Asian nations, at least when compared to the long queues in Italy or Greece, and they concluded that Asians lacked a strong desire to emigrate to the United States. Yet, these relatively short lines did not provide adequate indicators of future Asian immigration. Because most Asian nations had quotas of only 100 and because the

TABLE 4.1.

Leading Nations for Immigration, 1989

Nation	Number
Mexico	58,443
Philippines	49,535
Vietnam	37,571
Korea	32,204
India	28,498
China, Mainland	27,394
Dominican Republic	25,553
Jamaica	21,899
Iran	17,128
El Salvador	13,451

SOURCE: INS, *Advanced Report*, 1989.

Asia-Pacific Triangle had a ceiling of 2,000 until 1961, Asians felt discouraged about applying for visas to America. After all, if even a few thousand wanted to compete for one hundred places, the wait could be years. Of course some qualified as refugees or non-quota immigrants, but Asians clearly encountered difficulty emigrating to the United States before the amendments of 1965 ended their small quotas.

While Asians had been discouraged from immigrating, persons from nations with large national origins quotas, such as Great Britain, Ireland, and Germany, had a relatively easy time and by the early 1960s these nations did not fully use their quotas. Greece, Poland, and Italy had smaller quotas and a great demand for emigration; hence, queues developed in these countries.

If the lines were short in Asia, applications for admission to the United States quickly grew when Congress passed the 1965 act, especially in the occupational preferences, and were a straw in the wind of things to come even before the new law was fully operative in July 1968. In early January 1968 a reporter for *Science* wrote, "A handful of American officials has been aware for several months that a dramatic shift in the composition of the brain drain was likely, but this realization did not reach a wider public until the State Department's Visa Office published a detailed analysis of the new law late in November."[2] The writer was referring to the many Asians applying for visas as the new law became effective.

Whereas under the old system scientists from Germany or Great Britain could almost immigrate at will now they were on a first-come, first-served basis in entering under the third preference for professionals. By July 1968 the backlog had reached 48,000 for that preference's 17,000 annual places (including family members). India, China, Korea, and the Philippines claimed the most persons on the waiting lists. Europeans had lost their advantages and now those who wanted to emigrate to America had to wait their turn.[3]

If short lines before 1965 fooled the politicians so did the new law's family preference system's potential for chain migration. The 1965 amendments emphasized family unification and because the Asian-American population was less than 1 percent of the American total in 1960, few believed that Asians possessed the necessary kinship networks for immigration. As noted, groups diverse as the Japanese American Citizens League and the American Legion predicted that the family unification system would keep immigration moving along its prior nationality paths. Politicians and reformers did not see how few persons were required for a network under the family preferences of the 1965 act. This new immigration can be seen by the following hypothetical example. Not untypically, and unforeseen by the 1965 reformers, an Asian student comes to America as a nonimmigrant to complete his education. While finishing his studies, he finds a job, gets Labor Department certification, and becomes an immigrant. Once an immigrant he uses the second preference to bring over his spouse and children. A few years later the new immigrant, and his spouse, become citizens and are eligible to sponsor their brothers and sisters under the fifth, the largest and most popular preference, or to bring in their nonquota parents. Needless to say, the brothers and sisters, once immigrants, can also use the second preference to bring in their spouses and children and expand the immigrant kin network still further when they become citizens. No wonder the 1965 law came to be called the brothers and sisters act.

This process is not farfetched and is exactly how many Asian nations with little pre-1965 immigration increased it so dramatically after 1965. Several INS officials noted that the new immigrants became citizens one day and returned the next to bring in nonquota close relatives or sponsor their brothers and sisters. The diagram in figure 4.1 illustrates the migratory pattern described

FIGURE 4.1

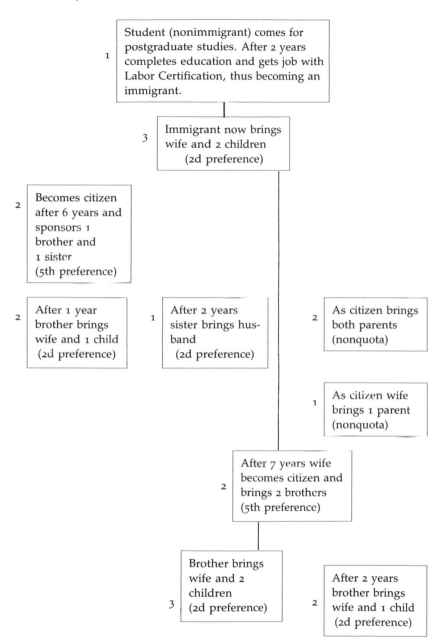

NOTE: Total is 19 after original student arrived for postgraduate education ten years earlier.

above and notes how one immigrant initially coming as a nonimmigrant can develop a chain migration.

Why the Surge from Asia

Because Congress conceived of family unification as a conservative change and because Asians lacked long lines for visas both critics and defenders of the new system generally underestimated the impact of the law on third world immigration. Yet, other signs, unclear in the early 1960s, pointed to a potential surge of Asian immigration to the United States.

In the first place, American wages and the standard of living were considerably higher than throughout Asia. Japan, of course, grew at a rapid rate after 1960 and could hardly be considered a developing third world nation; hence, Japanese immigration remained relatively low, and remained at the same level after 1965. Most other Asian nations experienced poverty, hunger, and deprivation. Yet, even the elites had incentives for emigration. Among the educated middle classes, in India, the Philippines, and Korea, people found that they possessed educations and skills not in demand in their nations, or that wages and working conditions were better in America. Moreover, unstable political and social conditions prompted uneasiness among some about the future.

Immigration is more than simply economics—low wages, low per capita income, poverty—or high birthrates or political instability. Knowledge is another important factor. In the nineteenth century railroads, steamship lines, and state bureaus of immigration promoted emigration from Europe to America by providing Europeans with information. In addition, letters from those who had already gone told families and friends in the Old World about the wonders of the new. In the past, these letters contained money to bring their countrymen to America. In the period after World War II information about America has become more plentiful than ever before and has penetrated deeply into the third world nations.

The American occupation of Japan fostered communication between those two nations. After the Korean War, Koreans became more aware of American culture. In the case of the Philippines, the American colonization, dating from 1898, brought with it knowledge of the United States, and this awareness did not end with Philippine independence in 1946. The American occupation of the Samoan Islands also accounts for awareness there of things American and helps explain the subsequent immigration of Samoans to the United States.

The outreach of American military forces was important but so was the economic and cultural penetration. Asians increasingly saw American companies and goods in their countries, and the printed word and television spread news of the good life in America. Books, newspapers, movies, and magazines told of American events and life, and in the last twenty years television has reached into even the poorest areas of the world. A United States government report in 1979 noted that in 1962 for the first time the number of television sets outside the United States surpassed the number here. By the late 1970s and early 1980s most Asian, and Latin American, nations received American-produced programs such as "I Love Lucy" and "Dallas," with their visions of bountiful consumer goods and fancy clothes and cars. Over half of all imported programs in the Philippines originated in the United States, and over 90 percent of those imported in Korea were American manufactured. These displays of the abundance of American life whetted the appetite for American goods and helped stimulate a desire to emigrate to the United States.[4]

In 1976 the South Korean newspaper *Chosun Ilbo* reported on the life of Korean immigrants in the United States. The author of the articles claimed that he wanted to tell about the difficulties of immigrant life, but the stories had the opposite effect. The news features were then published as a book, *Day and Night of Komericans: A Visit to Korea in the United States*, which became a best-seller. One scholar wrote of this book, "It has become a textbook of prospective emigrants by supplementing legal guidance on how to emigrate and secure overseas contracts."[5]

If modern communications brought the news of the good life, modern transportation made it possible. The airplane has become for Asians what the fast steamship line was to the nineteenth-century Europeans. While the media often gave the first impressions of America, actual contact, due to easy and relatively inexpensive travel, reinforced them. In 1978 exclusive of Canadians and Mexicans, over nine million people entered the United States as nonimmigrants—students, visitors, business people—most of whom arrived by air. This figure represented a fourfold increase over the early 1960s. Thousands of Asians studied in the United States after 1960. Before the enactment of the 1965 reforms, about 50,000 foreign students annually attended American universities, but by 1981 this figure had reached approximately 300,000; Asians accounted for nearly half the total.[6] The vast majority of foreign students returned after completing their education here, but some adjusted their status to resident aliens by marrying Americans or taking jobs in the United States. In 1978 over 18,000 nonimmigrant students became immigrants; of these about two-thirds were Asians.[7] A survey by the National Science Foundation (NSF) of scientists and engineers emigrating to the United States in the first five years (1966–1970) of the new immigration system, revealed that 60 percent had been in the United States on a temporary basis some time before they became immigrants, and that a majority of this group actually lived here when they became resident aliens.[8] Ten years later the NSF reported that the proportion of foreigners represented among those earning Ph.D.s in engineering, the physical sciences, and mathematics increased from the late 1960s. The Labor Department also reported that these students, once completing their education, were more likely than previously to stay and work in the United States.[9]

Nor were the trends reversed in the 1980s. When the People's Republic of China began to permit its students to study in the United States, thousands did so. By 1989, China's 40,000 students outnumbered those from any other country; Taiwan was in second place with 26,000.[10] And foreigners continued to gain a greater share of American doctorates in engineering, mathematics, chemistry, and physics. By 1989 over half of American doctorates in engineering and mathematics were being granted to foreign students.[11]

Not to be overlooked in explaining the immigration surge from Asia after 1960 is the refugee issue. Although the Vietnamese received the most attention because of their dramatic influx in 1975 and subsequent migration after that, other refugees also entered from both the Middle and Far East. President Kennedy admitted about 14,000 Chinese in the early 1960s, and other Chinese came later along with Cambodians and Laotians (The third world refugees will be discussed separately in chapter 6.) Most of the increase in Asian refugees, of course, resulted from American involvement in Asian affairs, and especially the Vietnam War. At the very time when Congress passed the new immigration act, President Johnson escalated the war in Vietnam, but few saw its future impact on immigration. But if the United States opened its doors to many anti-Communist refugees in Europe in the 1950s and to Cubans and Chinese in the early 1960s, then why wouldn't it be similarly generous to Vietnamese if disaster struck as it did after 1975? Indeed, the anti-Communist posture of the United States and the nation's constant involvement in distant and not so-distant places always has the potential for a new refugee population.

South and East Asians

Asians with professional training entered to work in a variety of fields, but none caught the public eye so much as the physicians and other medical professionals. Changes in the structure of medical service in the United States combined with the 1965 Immigration Act to increase substantially these third world medical immigrants. From the end of World War II to 1965, American medical schools graduated an almost constant number of physicians. They were inadequate to satisfy the demand and many hospitals looked abroad for their staffs. About 15,000 foreign doctors entered during the 1950s. This brain drain was predominately composed of Europeans and Canadians, with some increase in the proportion of doctors from Latin America and Asia in the early 1960s. Beginning in the 1960s the federal government encouraged with financial aid an increase in the American supply. By 1974, 121 medical schools enrolled 53,554 students compared to 35,833 in 91 schools in 1968.[12] Yet this increase was not enough; hence, hospitals still looked abroad and Asian physicians filled the need. In part, the demand was high because of population growth and America's willingness to pay for more medical care. But also important was the expansion of medical services due to federal government programs. The same year that Congress changed the immigration law, 1965, it also passed Medicare and Medicaid, which created an enlarged demand for medical services, especially in the inner city hospitals. Growing private health insurance plans also stimulated a need for more medical services.[13]

Medical Professionals

In the years 1965–1974, 75,000 foreign physicians entered the United States either to work temporarily or to practice medicine on a permanent basis. By 1974 foreign physicians made up one fifth of the total physicians in the United States and one third of the interns and residents. In some cities they were a higher proportion of interns. In New York City in the mid-1970s, Asian immigrant doctors made up more than half of the interns of the municipal hospitals, and 80 percent at voluntary hospitals like Brooklyn Hospital.[14] Of the foreign medical doctors (FMG) Filipinos were the largest nationality group. By 1980 there were over 9,000 Filipino doctors in the United States, which was a larger figure than for native black American physicians. About 40 percent of Filipino doctors practiced in America.[15] A large number also entered from Korea, Iran, and India. They also arrived from countries with little immigration to the United States. The American Medical Association reported 1,098 Thai physicians in the United States in 1970 and 1,408 in 1974. The most dramatic migration of Thai physicians occurred in 1972 when virtually the entire graduating class of the new medical school in Chiangmai, Thailand, chartered a plane and flew to America.[16]

Not a few of the Asian doctors received training that stood them well in America. Filipino doctors had been educated in schools that utilized English and American medical techniques and training, including textbooks. The Faculty of Medicine and Surgery of the University of Santo Tomas in Manila sent more of its graduates to the United States than did any other foreign medical school after 1960, and two other Filipino medical schools were close behind.[17]

Western medicine was introduced to Korea by Presbyterian missionaries in the late nineteenth century. Medical colleges established then gradually grew and the Korean War further stimulated the practice of Western medicine. After the war American funds and exchange programs also helped spread this medicine in Korea. Some pre-1965 graduates of these colleges entered the United States as nonimmigrants to work temporarily in American hospitals. When the Immigration Act of 1965 passed, it opened the door for a large movement of Korean medical professionals to the United States and Koreans were second to Filipinos in number.[18]

While doctors represented the elite of the Asian medical professionals, a large number of nurses also emigrated to the United States along with a small number of dentists, pharmacists, and other medical professionals. Inner city hospitals experienced shortages of nurses as well as doctors and they too turned to Korea, the Philippines, and other Asian nations to supply their needs. During the 1970s, for example, the Philippines' fifty nursing schools graduated about 2,000 annually, of whom about 20 percent emigrated to the United States.[19] Nurses in those countries were eager to immigrate because of the oversupply of nurses in their homelands or because of the better working conditions and higher pay in American hospitals. It was relatively easy for nurses to get licenses; hence they readily answered the recruitment policies of America.[20]

In 1976 the medical profession persuaded Congress to cut back on the supply of foreign physicians, to limit them to training and research positions. Yet urban hospitals still experienced shortages of both doctors and nurses, and the rules were modified in 1981. In 1987, the regulations were tightened again, but at that time about 15 percent of American physicians were foreign born and 22 percent foreign educated.[21]

Similar attempts were made to employ more American nurses instead of so many from the Philippines, Korea, and other nations. However, hospitals complained about shortages which they had filled by hiring alien nurses who were permitted to work in the United States for a period of up to five years. In 1988 Congress permitted these foreign nurses to work beyond their five years, and the next year the legislators passed a law that allowed them to change their status from temporary workers to resident aliens.[22]

Asian medical professionals generally settled in states where large cities, such as New York, Chicago, and Los Angeles, needed their services. Like other immigrants they often took less desirable jobs. In the case of doctors and nurses, this meant in inner city hospitals serving the poor, blacks, Hispanics, and the aged, or in rural areas where doctors were in demand, or they practiced in the lower-paid specialties of their occupation. Some had difficulty in passing state English language requirements or meeting residency or citizenship requirements.[23] Yet in spite of these difficulties, American medical practice continued to attract Asians. Advanced training, adequate hospitals, and lucrative practices were simply unavailable to many third world doctors in spite of the poor health conditions and standards in many of those countries. As one doctor in New York City put it, he came for "a higher income," but that was only part of the reason. Pointing to his laboratory the Filipino physician told a reporter, "We have good hospitals and schools at home, but nothing like this. Here you practice the best medicine in the world."[24]

The Chinese

The migration of the medical and scientific elites paved the way for others because of their ability to enter and subsequently use the family unification system. Yet most new Asian immigrants did not migrate to join professional elites. In the case of the Chinese, those who had entered in the 1950s and 1960s, though not large in numbers, became the nucleus for many future Chinese newcomers who used the family preferences for immigration. Of the Asians who benefited immediately from the changes in the law and the abolition of small quotas, the Chinese were the most apt to employ family preference categories. In the first years after the new law went into effect, Chinese immigrants mostly used the brothers and sisters fifth preference and the second preference for spouses and unmarried daughters and sons of resident aliens. In addition, a number of Chinese emigrated as quota exempt spouses or parents of American citizens. Of the countries using this latter category after the enactment of the 1965 law, China was third behind the Philippines and Italy, and by the mid-1970s had overtaken Italy.[25] The use of these nonquota categories and family unification indicated the importance of prior Chinese kinship networks in the United States. Of course, not all immigrants used family preferences; about one-fifth of the new Chinese immigrants entered under the occupational categories. This figure was less than most other large Asian nations, but higher than most European nations.[26]

Regardless of which preference or quota exemption they used, the new law certainly made it possible for the Chinese to increase substantially their immigration to the United States. The figures for the late 1960s, about 19,000 annually, were six times as large as those for the early 1960s, and Chinese immigration remained high throughout the 1970s. In the fifteen years after the passage of the 1965 act, approximately a quarter of a million Chinese emigrated to America. And in 1980, an estimated 100,000 others still waited for visas to enter the United States.[27] Moreover, in 1981 the United States government granted a separate allotment of 20,000 for both mainland China and Taiwan. While immigration from Taiwan fell in the 1980s, that of mainland China rose rapidly. Moreover, in 1986 Congress increased quotas of colonies from 600 to 5,000. This change benefited Hong Kong, and in 1990 the legislators doubled Hong Kong's quota for a three-year period and added special provisions to enable additional Hong Kong residents to come to America. When the three-year provision expired, Hong Kong would have a quota of more than 20,000.[28]

At first these immigrants differed from most other Asians in one respect: they usually did not come directly from mainland China, but rather from a second land, such as Hong Kong or Taiwan. Actually, most at first were probably refugees from China though they entered as regular immigrants. Some did utilize the preference providing for refugees, but most simply came as regular immigrants and not as refugees.[29]

Nineteenth-century Chinese immigrants had been overwhelmingly male—about 90 percent—usually between the ages of 20 and 40. As noted in chapter 1, after World War II this pattern changed with many Chinese families migrating and with more women than men arriving. The female dominance remained after the 1965 act. Nineteenth-century migrants were also rural and generally came from southern regions of China. After World War II this pattern changed with many originally from urban China.

Although the sex ratio changed after 1943, the destination of the new immigrants did not. Chinese immigrants settled in the nation's major Chinatowns, especially in San Francisco and New York City. About 60 percent of all Chinese immigrants went to New York State or California. New York City overtook San Francisco as the nation's largest Chinatown and doubled its population after 1960. Indeed, by 1990 New York City had not one but three Chinatowns. The second, mainly composed of immigrants from Taiwan, was in the Flushing section of the borough of Queens. Many other Asians also settled in that section. The third, smaller, Chinatown, grew in Brooklyn.[30]

The rapid growth of Manhattan's Chinatown strained the housing facilities of that area. Official figures indicated in 1978 that 35,000 people lived there, but some authorities estimated that both growth and undercount were high, and that between 50,000 and 60,000 resided there in 1980.[31] Newcomers who had skills, knowledge of English, and did not want to live in Chinatown moved to other boroughs, especially Queens, or the suburbs like the "stranded" group did after World War II.

Many others had no choice but to find what housing they could in Chinatown, or they preferred to live there. Some newcomers began to find housing in adjacent areas. Chinese moved east into buildings in New York's Lower East Side, at one time the homes of Jewish immigrants. Just north of Chinatown was New York's Little Italy, centered along Mulberry Street. Chinese crossed Canal Street, formerly the northern boundary, and moved into Little Italy. There they found homes and opened new businesses, some on Mulberry Street. Some newcomers from Hong Kong or Taiwan had money to buy buildings, but others were too poor and took what housing was available. In 1980, one Italian-American realtor, John Zaccaro, estimated that 40 percent of the city's Little Italy was composed of Chinese, and others put the figure higher.[32]

These newcomers bolstered the Chinese culture of Chinatown which had been losing population before 1965. Restaurants, grocery stores, movies, shops, festivals (especially the Chinese New Year), and a variety of organizations, both traditional and new, attested to the strong cultural traditions. In addition, by 1990 the city's Chinese supported nine Chinese-language newspapers.[33]

In California, San Francisco and Los Angeles experienced similar growth. San Francisco reported crowded housing and an influx of new immigrants, many of whom did not speak English. in Los Angeles the old Chinatown had been mainly a tourist attraction built in the late 1930s. Immigration after 1970 doubled the Chinese population to an estimated 16,500 in 1977 and drove up housing prices. Most of the visitors using the restaurants and other tourist facilities were reported to be Chinese.[34]

The large influx into these cities and others taxed housing and community facilities. Various community agencies reached out to the newcomers, providing social services for the aged, job placement for the young, and health services for those in need. Both New York City and San Francisco ran bilingual programs in their schools. For many of the young, once English was mastered there were opportunities in New York City's colleges and universities and similar institutions in California, including a large number at the prestigious University of California at Berkeley.

In the 1970s Chinese Americans, and Asian Americans generally, earned a reputation for high academic achievement, especially in music, mathematics, natural science, and computer science. The reputation was based on statistical evidence. In the early 1980s, Asian Americans amounted to about 1.5 percent of the nation's population and about 5 percent of California's residents, but made up 20 percent of the University of California at Berkeley's student body. They were 9 percent of Harvard's class of 1985 and a similar figure at Columbia, Yale, and Princeton. In the fall of 1990, 19.4 percent of Harvard's entering freshmen were Asian.[35] Massachusetts Institute of Technology claimed twice as many Asian as black students, even though the black population was eight times as large in the United States. Asians, at all income levels, also scored higher than other racial groups on the Math Scholastic Aptitude Tests given to high school students.[36]

Of course, these figures include native as well as foreign born, but because of the high rates of recent Asian immigration, Asian Americans were disproportionately foreign or the children of recent immigrants. A test sponsored by the United States Department of Education revealed that Asian high school students scored better than other racial groups in mathematics, and over half of the Asians taking the test were foreign born.[37] In early 1983 of the forty finalists in the Westinghouse Science Talent Search, nine were born in Asia and three others were of Asian descent. First prize that year went to Paul Ning, who had immigrated with his parents to the United States from Taiwan. The 16-year-old Ning attended New York City's elite Bronx High School of Science when he won the $12,000 prize. One of the judges said of Ning that he showed "a very sophisticated understanding of number theory not commonly found in one so young." Ning's prize-winning project did not require elaborate equipment; hence, he was able to do the work "at home." Said Ning, "with a math paper, all you need is paper and pencil. . . . I set aside days. I'd finish all my homework in half an hour and then go onto this. I often worked into the wee hours."[38]

While Asians and Chinese Americans acquired a reputation for scholarship and academic success, some youth did not fare so well. Gang wars erupted in the 1970s in the streets of the nation's Chinatowns, especially in San Francisco and New York, threatening the reputation of Chinatowns for low crime rates. Hong Kong youth, frequently lacking English and employment, formed gangs with names like the Flying Dragons and the Ghost Shadows, and resorted to crime and violence. Older Chinese residents and businessmen resented the violence, including a number of killings in San Francisco and New York, and extortion money they feared they would have to pay to stay in business. As one Chinese businessman said, "But a lot of the owners pay. They are afraid the gang will break their window or set fire to the stores."[39] Older residents called for increased police activity to check the rampaging youths in order to protect their lives and businesses as well as to continue to attract tourists.

Gang wars and youth crime spread in the 1980s, moving into New York's Queens and Brooklyn. The killing of five men in a Boston Chinatown social club raised police fears that the violence was coming to that city too.[40] Gangs composed of ethnic Chinese from Vietnam, which appeared in the late 1980s, were considered to be the most ruthless of the gangs. One such New York gang was called Born to Kill.[41] Public officials also claimed that the gangs had branched out from extortion to smuggling drugs and illegal aliens into the United States.[42]

Because many adult newcomers possessed little money, lacked skills, and did not speak English, they had limited employment prospects. Many males worked long hours in the restaurants of Chinatowns, while thousands of women labored in the hundreds of new garment shops of New York and San Francisco either in, or on the edge of, the Chinatowns. A New York City study noted in 1979 that the garment industry "provides immigrant [Chinese] women with their main source of employment," while the manager of a San Francisco shop said, "I guess almost all Chinese immigrant women who want to work come to the sewing shops."[43] Conditions and pay in nonunion factories were hardly ideal. These contemporary versions of immigrant sweatshops paid poorly, sometimes below the minimum wage, and lacked decent working conditions in spite of governmental efforts to enforce labor laws. But for many women, as well as the males who worked in the restaurants, the lack of English foreclosed other employment. Other Chinese did better. Some immigrants did own or manage many of the garment shops or Chinatown's restaurants, sometimes after initially working in garment shops or as waiters or cooks in restaurants.[44]

Not all Hong Kong or Taiwanese had poor educations or lacked English. Among the new immigrants were engineers, doctors, mathematicians, and scientists. As noted, some originally trained in China had fled after the Communist victory in 1949, or were "stranded" in the United States, but others received their education in Taiwan where the schools prepared their students for possible emigration to the United States. Not a few of these professionals completed their advanced studies in the United States and once finished, found employment in American industries and universities, and adjusted their student status to resident alien. In 1978, almost 3,000 Chinese who had entered as students changed their status to immigrant.[45] This elite found better jobs, did not necessarily settle in Chinatowns, and on the whole had an easier time adjusting to their new country.

The existence of an elite as well as many poor immigrants

prompted some commentators to describe Chinese immigration as bipolar, which was not an entirely inaccurate description.[46] Entrance of a "brain drain" group as well as many poor, non-English-speaking immigrants, was made possible by the immigration act and Chinese immigration after 1965 reflected the law.

The Filipinos

To some extent, Philippine immigration after 1965 also represented the new law's possibility for a bipolar immigration. As indicated in chapter 1, like the Chinese, the Filipinos had an older established community and had gradually increased immigration after 1946, with pockets of Filipino communities growing around American military bases.[47]

Overall, however, the Filipino-American community was considerably smaller than the Chinese-American one and Filipino emigration from 1946 to 1960 was less than Chinese. Hence for the Filipino emigration to the United States to grow as rapidly as it did after 1965, immigrants had to utilize the occupational categories as well as family kinship networks. Hence the emigration of the medical professionals and other well-educated Filipinos became important for the growth of Filipino immigration to the United States.

Once these medical professionals and other persons using occupational preferences had emigrated, they utilized the relative preferences to bring in their families. While occupational preference utilization began to decline in importance in the early 1970s, the proportion of those entering under family unification, especially the spouses of resident aliens, grew dramatically. In 1978, for example, the occupation categories had declined to about 17 percent of the quota immigrants (it had been nearly 60 percent in 1969) while family preference immigrants accounted for over 80 percent. Moreover, once they acquired American citizenship the new Americans brought in thousands of quota-exempt people, more than any other nation. In 1978, of the 17,853 nonquota Filipinos about 40 percent were parents of U.S. citizens.[48] Hence the chain of migration begun by the utilization of relative preferences and heavy use of occupational preferences opened the door to

TABLE 4.2.
Asian Immigration

Year	Nonquota immediate family members	Occupational preferences (3d and 6th)	Spouses & children of resident aliens (2d)	Brothers & sisters of U.S. citizens (5th)
1968	15,800	17,729	6,688	6,307
1972	29,585	24,758	19,364	11,985
1978	45,064	16,607	31,468	46,422
1980	58,029	15,775	42,456	43,929
1987	83,640	22,895	41,539	38,867

SOURCE: INS annual reports.

family unification and increased immigration to the United States. Table 4.2 indicates the trend for Asian immigration. In addition to the shifts from 1968 to 1987, it shows that nonquota immediate family members of U.S. citizens grew substantially. If immigrants found the preferences for family members, which had limits, were being fully utilized, they joined a growing line of those waiting for U.S. immigration visas. Indeed, by 1990 the backlog in the second and fifth preferences each ran into the hundreds of thousands, and in some countries the wait could be years.

The numbers certainly reflect this growth. Filipino immigration to the United States increased dramatically from its average of about 3,000 yearly from 1960 to 1965. In the late 1970s, outside of Mexico and the special case of Indochina, the Philippines became the largest national source for immigration to the United States. It averaged over 30,000 yearly for the 1970s, and in 1979 it topped 41,000 over half of whom were nonquota.[49] Nor did it show signs of abatement as conditions in the Philippines worsened in the decade, both politically and economically. As one Filipino businessman said in 1976, "People back home watch what goes on here. They saw how you deposed one President [Nixon] and put in another one without a drop of blood being shed. Believe me, if the immigration quota were bigger, you'd see how many more of us would leave."[50] Long lines at the American Embassy in Manila waiting for visas seemed to support his view. The Select Commission on Immigration and Refugee Policy reported in 1980 that the estimated backlog in the Philippines numbered nearly a quarter of a million.[51]

The medical professionals found jobs throughout the United States, but generally in the large cities of California, New York, New Jersey, and Illinois. Of those coming at first under the family preferences, many went to Hawaii where a fairly substantial Filipino population already lived. These persons frequently lacked good educations, came from rural background, and consequently experienced many difficulties in adjusting to the new environment. They were likely to live in a ghetto. Even those with some skills and training had difficulty finding jobs in Honolulu commensurate with their abilities and training.[52]

The Koreans

As noted in chapter 1, most Koreans who immigrated from 1950 to 1965 were nonquota wives of American servicemen. These wives continued to migrate after 1965 as the United States maintained troops in Korea, but the law opened new possibilities for immigration to the United States, especially for doctors and nurses at first, then others as family networks developed.

Lack of opportunities in Korea compared to those in America stimulated emigration, but these immigrants were mostly the urban middle classes, who were unhappy about political developments in Korea and feared another war. Some of these immigrants had been uprooted once before, from North Korea, and lacked strong ties to South Korea. Though well educated medical professionals usually came directly to the United States to work, other Koreans entered first as students, completed their education here and then adjusted their status to immigrant.[53]

The two streams of Korean immigration to the United States of the highly educated middle classes and the spouses of American citizens established the framework for additional immigration. Once these first immigrants were established, they used the family unification system to bring in others. Hence, Korean resident aliens brought in their spouses and children while those who became citizens used the popular brothers and sisters category to sponsor others.

As a result, Korean migration to the United States steadily grew. Only a few thousand entered annually from 1960 to 1965, but by 1969 it topped 6,000. In that year one half were quota exempt while about 40 percent of the remainder entered under the occupational categories. By 1977 Korean immigration exceeded 30,000, with about one third being nonquota immediate family members. These were no longer simply the wives of American servicemen, but also the families of Koreans who had emigrated previously. Although professionals still arrived, the vast bulk now entered under the family preference system. The figure of 30,000 represented the steady growth of Korean immigration. In the ten years before the 1965 act Korea sent 16,000 to America, but in the decade after the new law, the figure grew tenfold.[54] By 1980 Korea had sent about a quarter of a million immigrants to America after the enactment of the new immigration law, and excluding nations sending refugees, was one of the three largest sending nations of immigration.

In 1980 it was estimated that the backlog exceeded 74,000, while a South Korean newspaper, *Dong-a Ilbo*, found in a 1979 survey that half of the people it polled wished to emigrate.[55] As one man, who just obtained his visa, said, "I know that the first impact will be tough. But I am willing to do anything, follow the trade I know as a repairman or work in a store—anything." He said that he expected his children to become "totally American," but insisted that customs were already changing in Korea and he was prepared for Americanizing influences on his children and himself.[56]

This particular immigrant headed for New York City to join other family members, but Los Angeles claimed the largest Korean settlement, an area called Koreatown, along that city's busy Olympic Boulevard. The Korean Los Angeles community spawned organizations, newspapers, and radio and television programs that broadcast in Korean.[57] Among these organizations were Christian churches. Korea was one of the most Christian of the Asian nations and many Korean immigrants were Christians. These churches used Western practices, but combined them with Korean forms and Korean-language services.

New York City and Chicago also contained sizable Korean immigrant populations. The New York Koreans were more scattered than those in Los Angeles with less sense of community. New York's Koreans tended to be well educated, as did those in Chicago, and included a high proportion of medical professionals. In Chicago, Koreans were also scattered but the largest group was found in the Albany Park section, formerly a Jewish neighborhood. Chicago Koreans supported two newspapers and 80 to 100 Christian churches in 1981, mostly Methodist and Presbyterian. Local Korean leaders in Chicago estimated that 60 percent of the city's Koreans attended these churches. These churches administered to the spiritual needs of the new immigrants, but their ministers also helped them with problems common to recent immigrants, finding housing and employment and dealing with the bureaucracy.[58] New York's Koreans also supported many Christian churches and two daily newspapers.[59]

While the medical professionals, mainly physicians, were the elite Korean immigrants, more visible were the many small businesses. Hundreds of grocery stores, restaurants, and other establishments were run by Los Angeles' Koreans, some of whom had been professionals in Korea but who could not satisfy American state licensing requirements.[60] Chicago and New York also boasted many such Korean businesses. There were about 500 businesses in Chicago, which prompted one Korean lawyer, Jay H. Kim, to say that "owning a business is part of being Korean." The Reverend Harold Shin, director of Chicago's only social service agency for Koreans added, "A store is a goal for us. It provides independence and a good living, something many Koreans might otherwise have trouble finding."[61] No business caught the public eye or was so important to Korean immigrants as the greengrocery. One scholar dates the movement of Koreans into New York greengroceries to 1971 and estimated that seven years later 350 fruit and vegetable stores were run by Koreans in that city.[62] A journalist estimated that Koreans owned three quarters of the metropolitan area's 1200 such stores in 1982.[63]

The first Koreans into this economic activity came from Latin America, where they had been enterpreneurs having financial difficulties in those hard-pressed economies. Once established, these pioneers attracted others. The fruit and vegetable stores, formerly run by Jews and Italians, were declining economically, and

Koreans bought them with little capital. The stores competed successfully with the supermarkets because they offered better produce and stayed open long hours. to keep costs down Korean owners utilized the labor of entire families or other Koreans who had just arrived, and, without speaking English, faced limited employment prospects.[64]

The greengrocers were successful but at a price. In 1982 a journalist told of Jay Kwon of New York City and his store. Kwon arrived with three years of college and seventy-five dollars in 1972 and began work as a janitor before becoming a foreman at a wire and cable company. He then used nearly all his savings—$20,000—to purchase a store in Brooklyn. Before dawn, Kwon went to buy produce at Hunts Point, the city's central market place, a task requiring three hours. Kwon met many other Koreans there. In September 1983 many Korean greengrocers staged a protest at the United Nations against the Soviet Union's downing of a Korean airliner. They had learned of the planning for the protest at Hunts Point.[65] The rest of Kwon's day was spent, with the help of his wife and brother, cleaning, displaying, and selling produce. Kwon kept his fruit and vegetable store open 12 hours a day. He was robbed several times, but he developed good relations with the local residents and turned a modest profit for the family and its employees. Yet, typical of many immigrants, Kwon said, "I am first generation. I am not working for myself. I am working for the second generation."[66]

Building on the success of these small stores, some Koreans moved up to become wholesalers at the markets like Hunts Point and to own more than one store. Clearly their middle-class skills and aspirations stood them well in America and some were turning their greengrocer experience to less difficult businesses, such as liquor stores, fast food franchises, dry cleaners, and stationery shops.[67]

The desire to become economically established and mobile was part of the general trend of Americanization among Koreans and most other Asians, as also witnessed by the growing number seeking citizenship. In 1978 next to Cubans, who had been here longer, and the Filipinos, Koreans were third in the number of persons naturalized.[68] Of course, a desire to become Americanized does not entirely explain quick naturalization because the immigration laws encouraged citizenship in order to bring in one's brothers and sisters and nonquota relatives.

The Indians

Among Asians, East Indians trailed Filipinos, Chinese, and Koreans in numbers. Like the Koreans, few Indians had emigrated to the United States before 1950. Not many possessed the necessary family contacts in 1965 to take immediate advantage of the new law. Moreover, the United States did not have military forces stationed in India; hence, few "war brides" came from that country. Yet, India increased its immigration substantially. In the ten years after 1965, the figures topped 115,000. In 1976 immigration from India passed 17,000; in 1977 it went over 18,000 and in 1978 it was over 20,000. It topped 22,000 in 1980.[69] India was becoming one of the largest source nations for American immigration.

The first Indian immigrants entering after 1965 were predominantely males who took jobs in American urban hospitals, universities, or businesses eager to employ their skills. Next to Filipinos and Koreans, Indians made up the largest contingent of East Asian medical professionals, including nurses and physicians.[70]

Not all of the Indian professionals were physicians. They also included scientists and engineers. In 1978 the National Science Foundation reported that Asia accounted for slightly more than half of the immigrant scientists and engineers of that year. India had the largest number of any nation and accounted for one third of the Asian total. Mostly these were engineers.[71]

These immigrants found that their Westernized education in India, or sometimes in the United States, did not necessarily lead to suitable employment. Like the doctor immigrants, they found conditions in the United States to be more attractive than at home.[72] In any event, the Indian migration was truly an elite group. In 1975 immigration authorities classified the vast majority of Indian immigrants as professional/technical workers or their immediate families, a higher rate than for any other nation. Of those Indians claiming an occupation, nearly three quarters were professionals, technical, and kindred workers or managers or administrators.[73]

As the elite settled and began to bring their families and as more Indians began to use family preferences, the social base of immigrants broadened, the sex ratio of immigrants narrowed slightly, and Indian communities developed, notably in New York City. These communities included Hindu, Hare Krishna, and Gita temples and a number of social and cultural organizations. In August 1981, New York Indians decided to celebrate their ethnicity in a traditional American way. "We realized that it was time we started having a parade like other ethnic communities," said a spokesman for the Federation of India Association.[74] In New York City style, the mayor proclaimed an India Day to mark the procession which featured eighteen floats. Said New York City's then mayor, Ed Koch, "They are hard working and devoted to this city and this country. They give us their culture and their taxes—and their wonderful restaurants."[75]

Koch may have had in mind the businesses begun by one family, originally from Bangladesh, responsible for opening several restaurants on Manhattan's Sixth Street. Beginning in 1968, several brothers, some of whom originally came as students, opened an Indian restaurant along that street. Within several years, the brothers opened several more and when a brother-in-law and former waiter wanted to have his own restaurant, they assisted him. Later an uncle started another restaurant. These small eating places attracted still others so that by 1981 ten were open for business, giving that street a reputation as "Little India."[76]

In addition to restaurants, Indians also purchased many motels, at first in California and then across the country. By 1989 Indians were estimated to own 40 percent of the nation's smaller motels (those with fewer than 56 rooms), and Days Inns of America reported that one quarter of its franchises were operated by Indians. Most Indian motel owners were from the western Indian state of Gujarat, with a large number carrying the common name of Patel.[77] Motels required more capital than the greengroceries run by Koreans, but many of the Indians were from the elite classes or had many money first in Africa (Uganda) and Britain. One newly naturalized citizen, Ratan Patel of Michigan, combined engineering with business. An engineer for the Ford Motor company, he bought the Maple Lawn Motel near Detroit for his wife and brother-in-law to run, while he worked full time at Ford.[78] Asian Indians also branched out from motels. In the 1980s some began selling insurance, while others were venturing into real estate.[79]

Population Trends

The new Chinese, Filipino, Korean, and Indian communities contributed to the fast-growing Asian-American population. Traditionally, the Japanese made up the largest Asian-American groups followed by the Chinese. Table 4.3 indicates the change. These 1970 census bureau figures do not include Vietnamese or East Indians, both of whom had not been counted before. In 1980 the bureau counted about 300,000 Indochinese refugees and about one million Indochinese and their children by 1985. Practically all of the estimated 525,000 East Asian Indians in the United States in 1985 had arrived after 1970.

Apart from India, Korea, the Philippines, China (and Indochina if one counts refugees), total immigration from the Far East increased after 1965 but not so substantially as the above-mentioned nations. Thailand accounted for the next largest number, about 95,000 from 1965 to 1990. Thai immigration grew in the 1970s through the immigration of skilled and well-educated, such as the medical professionals, and family networks. A considerable proportion of Thai newcomers were nonquota spouses of American citizens who had married U.S. military personnel during the Vietnam War. Hence, a high proportion of Thai immigrants were female. While Thai physicians located in several major cities, the largest group of Thai immigrants was found in Los Angeles, a popular place for many other Asian immigrants as well.[80]

Next to Thai immigration came that of Pakistan, which also grew in the 1970s. Among the Pakistanis were the medical doctors and their families. Other Pakistanis opened stores in cities like New York. They could be seen running restaurants, food stores, and newspaper stands. Immigration from Pakistan was running about 3,000 annually in the 1970s and over 5,000 in the 1980s.[81]

The number of Samoans may have exceeded Thais but authorities did not record all of them as immigrants. Those from Western Samoa counted as immigrants, but American Samoans were American nationals; hence, they were migrants within

TABLE 4.3.
Population Gains by Asians in the U.S.

Nationality	1970	1980	1990 (estimated)
Chinese	435,062	806,127	1,260,000
Filipino	343,062	774,640	1,400,000
Japanese	591,290	700,747	804,000
Korean	100,179	354,529	814,000
Asian Indian		387,7223	684,000
Vietnamese		245,035	859,000
Laotian		47,683	
Cambodian		16,044	
Others			706,000

SOURCE: *New York Times*, July 30, 1981; Department of Commerce, Bureau of the Census, *Ancestry of the Population by State*, 1980, p. 3; Population Bulletin, *Asian Americans: Growth, Change, and Diversity*, October 1985, p. 5; and *New York Times*, Feb. 24, 1991.

American territory and not officially considered resident aliens. When the United States Navy, once the largest employer of American Samoans, closed its Samoa base in 1951, many Samoans emigrated to either Hawaii or California. Exactly how many left is not known, though some experts estimated that half of the Samoan population now lives in the United States, mostly in California. Between 20,000 and 40,000 Samoans live there, clustered around naval bases and shipping and fishing industries near Los Angeles, San Francisco, and San Diego.[82]

Middle Eastern Immigrants

A few immigrants had entered from the Middle East in the late 1940s and 1950s, including refugees from Palestine, but the small quotas available for those nations hindered their movement to the United States. Iran, Israel, Turkey, and Arab-speaking countries all recorded substantial increases in immigration after 1960. About 300,000 Arabs, including those from North Africa, came to the United States after World War II, mostly since 1970.[83] A number of the immigrants were originally Palestinians, but were recorded as being from Jordan or Syria.

The constant turmoil in the Middle East, notably the wars between Israel and her neighbors, prompted thousands to flee. The 1967 war occurred just when the new immigration system was going into effect and enabled many Arabs to emigrate to the United States. Other upheavals uprooted thousands more. The civil war in Lebanon, which dragged on for years and devastated that land, the Kuro-Iraqi War of the 1960s, and the violence in Iraq and Iran after 1978 compelled many to follow the previous waves to America. Some of these people—like the stateless Palestinians who faced limited political and economic futures—entered as refugees, but most simply came as regular immigrants. They sought both better economic opportunities and a more stable political and social order. The first newcomers established the network for others who mainly used the second and fifth family preference categories.

Many Middle Easterners were middle class and well-educated. These included the stateless Palestinians as well as other Arabs. One scholar who studied the 1980 census said that Arab immigrants as a group had higher levels of education and incomes than other immigrants and the American population as a whole.[84]

The Iranians

Many Iranians were also well-educated and middle class. Iran sent more students to American than any other country in the 1970s. These students were usually the children of affluent Iranians who sent them to America for a Westernized education. Some stayed in the United States after finishing their education. In 1977 Iranian newcomers totaled 4,261. Of that figure, 1,898 had been nonimmigrants already in the United States who adjusted their status to resident alien. That figure, 44 percent of the Iranian immigration, was more than double the adjustment rate for most other nations. Over half of those adjusting their status had been students.[85] Some officials believed that many of the students were really working or living here in violation of their visas as a way of emigrating to the United States without an immigrant visa. As one official put it, "It's a well-known dodge . . . the abuse is absolutely incredible." When the Carter administration began to investigate the status of Iranian students in 1979, it found indeed that many lived in violation of their visas.[86] Although Palestinians were known for their high educational levels, as a nation Iran accounted for the largest group of scientists and engineers from the Middle East. In 1978 the National Science Foundation reported that Iranians were about 40 percent of these people.[87] Iran also sent the largest number of physicians emigrating from the Middle East.

Iranian students and immigrants settled especially in Texas and California. Some Iranians were Jews who did not want to return to Iran after the overthrow of the shah in 1979. Indeed, for religious minorities like Jews and especially Baha'is, the new Muslim nationalist state was a hostile environment. Hence, immigration to the United States from Iran increased and it topped 8,000 in 1979, and over 10,000 in 1980. Moreover, other Iranians claimed political asylum in the United States because of the turmoil, and the United States government granted some of them permission to stay on permanently or temporarily. Indeed, Iranians were more successful than any other group in winning political asylum in the 1980s.[88] Yet the bulk of these immigrants entered under the regular laws, and their number continued to grow in the 1980s. By 1989 immigration from Iran topped 20,000, and Iran had moved into the top ten sending nations for U.S. immigrants.[89]

The Arabs

Prior to 1960 the majority of Arab immigrants were Christians, as many as 90 percent. But the new immigrants are mostly Muslims. While no one knew exactly how many Muslims were in America in 1990, most estimates placed the figures between three and four million. At the rate of post-1970 growth Islam was likely to surpass Judaism to become the third largest religious group, ahead of Judaism but behind Protestantism and Catholicism by the turn of the Century.[90] Other Arab immigrants included Maronite Christians from Lebanon and Egyptian Coptic Christians. Also included in the general migration from the Near East were Jews from Israel and elsewhere.

Arabs settled in or near prior Arab communities. The Detroit metropolitan region, especially Dearborn, attracted a steady stream of such persons after 1965. That area probably contained the largest number of recent Arab immigrants. They came from a variety of occupational backgrounds and worked in the auto industry of Detroit and other working-class employment. Several thousand of these Detroit Arabs came from Yemen with the intention of making money and returning home rather than being permanent immigrants. These peasants faced especially bleak social and economic conditions in Yemen during the 1960s, with its struggle for independence from Great Britain and economic turmoil; jobs in the auto industry looked attractive. Though they first intended to stay temporarily and send money home, the male workers began to think in terms of permanent migration and to send for their families.[91]

Not all Detroit Arabs labored in the auto industry. Christian Chaldeans, an Iraqi minority in a Muslim country, hailed at first mostly from the northern Iraqi village of Telhaif. About one thousand of them lived in Detroit when Congress passed the new immigration act. Their numbers then increased and amounted to about one seventh of Detroit's estimated 70,000 Middle Easterners in 1974. These immigrants opened grocery stores and established a reputation in that business much like the Korean greengrocers. They ran about 278 stores in Detroit in 1972. Like Korean greengrocers, the Chaldeans used their stores to assist others in emigrating to America. Chaldeans centered their community around the family and the Christian Chaldean Church, a branch of Roman Catholicism. The children mainly attended Roman Catholic schools, but a growing number entered the public schools. As the local grocery business became saturated, many Chaldeans moved to Detroit's suburbs.[92]

Another large Arab settlement was in New York City, especially the borough of Brooklyn which had attracted prior movements of Lebanese and Syrians. Los Angeles lured many Coptic Christians from Egypt who were part of the Egyptian wave to America after that nation's defeat in the Six-Day War of 1967.[93]

Because Arab immigrants came from so many different countries and had different religions and cultures, it was impossible to speak of one Arab-American community. The pre-World War II Arabs had assimilated and done well in the United States. The latest Arab immigrants were bound together, however, by the constant turmoil in the Middle East. Especially after the Arab-Israeli War of 1967, many believed that they were the victims of prejudice and adverse images in the American media. As a result new Arab-American organizations appeared. Some, like the American-Arab Anti-Discrimination Committee, were dedicated to fighting these negatives and presenting their point of view of world affairs.[94]

The Israelis

Some experts believe that like Iranians, Israelis used student and other nonimmigrant visas to enter the United States and then sometimes lived illegally once here.[95] The actual number of immigrants from Israel did increase but not spectacularly after 1965. In the decade before the 1965 act about 13,000 arrived and in the ten years after about 20,000. In the early 1960s about 1,100 Israelis emigrated to the United States annually; by the mid-1970s the figure was double that and from 1977 to 1979 it averaged over 3,000. It was 3,600 in 1989. Nonimmigrants increased more sharply. Nonimmigrants jumped from 11,000 in 1965 to over 70,000 in 1978, a higher rate of increase than recorded by most countries.[96] Return statistics for nonimmigrants are either lacking or inaccurate so that thousands of these Israelis could be still living illegally in the United States. The *Wall Street Journal* reported in early 1983 that long lines of Israelis formed at the crack of dawn outside the U.S. embassy to apply for tourist visas. One guard there was reported to have said, "All of these people won't come back, I can sense it from their conversations."[97]

In the late 1970s the Israeli government reported marked increases in emigration from Israel both of travelers, businessmen, and students as well as those choosing to emigrate permanently. More people were leaving than coming, many to escape constant military conflict, high inflation and social tensions that plagued Israel. Many of these migrants were young, which indicated that they lacked hope for their future in Israel. The exodus headed not only toward the United States but also to Canada, Australia, and Western Europe. The Israeli government grew alarmed by the exodus of these "yordim," as they were called, because of the fear of the loss of population.[98]

Regardless of their exact numbers, which were often crude guesses, if one includes the illegals, the largest number of Israeli immigrants settled in New York City, especially the Borough Park section of Brooklyn and several areas of Queens. Israeli newcomers became noted as taxi cab drivers and operators of small businesses, such as clothing boutiques, but also included some professionals. To some extent they were integrated with the larger New York Jewish community, but conflicts existed and many American Jews were embarrassed by the presence of these immigrants in their midst and the implications of emigration from Israel and the future of that land. Hence, the immigrants had their own communal life. The New York Israeli community supported a weekly newspaper, *Our Israel,* and a television and radio program.[99]

The increase of immigration of Muslims, Jews, and Christians from the Middle East, whether as refugees escaping political turmoil there, or those simply seeking economic opportunity, was part of the overall shift in patterns of immigration to the United States. Some of these trends, because of special laws, were evident before the 1965 law went into effect, but the new immigration law had a dramatic impact upon the flow of people. For the most part, Congress in 1965 did not foresee the implications of the new system and how chains of migration could be built, based on refugees, selected occupational migration, and above all on families, whether quota or nonquota. These shifts were most pronounced from the Eastern Hemisphere, but similar patterns can be seen in the Western Hemisphere in the Caribbean Basin and South America even though they lacked a preference system until 1976. How and why Western Hemisphere immigration increased and who these people were is the subject of chapter 5.

5

The Western Hemisphere: Mexico, Central and South America, and the Caribbean

IN DEMANDING a Western Hemisphere ceiling in exchange for abolishing the Asia-Pacific Triangle and national origins quotas, Congress signaled its clear desire for restricting Hispanics, black English-speaking and Creole-speaking West Indians, and other Caribbean and Latin American peoples. No one paid much attention to immigration from Canada. The Congressional face-saving Select Commission on Western Hemispheric immigration directed nearly all its attention to the Caribbean and Latin America. The commissioners examined border problems, economic conditions to the south, population growth, and the pressures for emigration to the United States.[1] Though the commissioners, it will be recalled, suggested postponing the new regulations for one year, Congress ignored this recommendation and on July 1, 1968, as scheduled, the 120,000 limit went into effect.

Labor Department certification was another compromise instituted by the legislators in 1965. Certification was more stringent in the Western Hemisphere than in the Eastern. Those entering under preference categories for refugees and family unification, composing 80 percent of the Eastern Hemisphere places, did not have to obtain Labor Department approval prior to arrival; only those coming under the occupational preferences—the third and sixth—had to convince the department they were needed.[2] But in the Western Hemisphere all prospective immigrants had to obtain certification, except immediate family members of U.S. citizens or resident aliens. It was not always easy to obtain labor certification. The congressional fight over the ceiling issue dwarfed concern over a preference system for that hemisphere. Congress finally established such a system in that region, effective in 1977, which eased the certification issue because most new immigrants could enter under family unification similar to those in the Eastern Hemisphere.

Of course, prior to the imposition of the 120,000 cap and Labor Department approval, all immigrants had to pass a literacy test, convince officials they were not likely to become a public charge, be able to satisfy health requirements, and not be on a long list— which among others, included Communists, polygamists, prostitutes, and homosexuals—considered by Congress to be undesirable. These regulations, which did limit immigration, remained in effect; Congress simply added the new restrictions on top of the old and they threatened to halt the growth of immigration from south of the border to the United States.

In anticipation of the new rules, there was a sharp increase in applications for visas at American consulates in Latin America. In Ecuador, for example, applications jumped from an average of 30 to 40 per week to between 100 and 120 in the spring of 1968. A line reportedly formed outside the American Consulate in Guayaquil to wait overnight for an interview the next day.[3]

The perception of prospective immigrants that visas to enter the United States would be more difficult to obtain was correct. The Immigration and Naturalization Service reported in 1969, the first year the new regulations were fully in effect: "In 1969, there were 129,045 special immigrants [from the Western Hemisphere] admitted, a reduction of 17 percent from the 1968 figure of 155,308."[4] By then, waiting lists were developed in Latin America, and they continued to grow, especially in Mexico. Persons who satisfied the various restrictions except the numerical ones found themselves waiting years to obtain visas.[5]

Western Hemispheric immigration was considerably less than it might have been without the numerical limit, but it nonetheless exceeded that ceiling and was much above what the restrictionists wanted in 1965. Despite the fall from 1968 to 1969, immigration rose after that date. In the 1970s about two million persons entered from the Americas. In 1978 immigration reached a decade high of 262,542 or more than double the 120,000 figure.[6] How has this been possible?

One reason Western Hemisphere immigration exceeded the

120,000 limit was the entrance of refugees. In December 1965, two months after the signing into law of the immigration amendments, the Johnson administration began an airlift to Cuba that brought about 360,000 Cubans to the United States between 1965 and 1979.[7] Most came under the Attorney General's parole power, but legislation passed in 1966 permitted them to change their status to regular immigrants. If these Cubans would have been counted as part of the ceiling that limit still would have functioned to keep numbers down. From 1968 to 1976 INS counted them, as they became resident aliens, as part of the ceiling, in spite of the apparent wish by Congress that they not be included under the 120,000 quota. After hearing criticism of this policy, Congress passed a law in 1976 declaring refugees exempt from the cap. Accordingly, in the fall of 1976 the State Department directed INS to permit Cubans to be counted above the Western Hemisphere limit. Federal court decisions in 1978 and 1979 upheld the new policy as the intent of Congress and went further. In *Silva v. Levi*, Illinois District Judge John Grady held that 144,999 places charged against the ceiling for Cubans between 1968 and 1976 be made available retroactively to others in the Western Hemisphere.[8] In accordance with this decision, INS mailed "Silva" letters to over 200,000 aliens whose status was uncertain, informing them that they might be eligible to obtain an immigrant visa.[9]

It can be argued that in passing the Cuban Adjustment Act of 1966 and additional legislation in 1976 Congress itself acknowledged that it wished refugees exempt from the limit; hence, the lawmakers weakened the ceiling only one year after passing it. Congress changed the Western Hemisphere ceiling again in 1978 when it abolished ceilings for the two hemispheres and merged them into a worldwide limit and created a uniform preference system. This change, effective the next year, opened the possibility for increased immigration from the Western Hemisphere. However, since the total for both hemispheres was the same as before, increases from the Western Hemisphere would have to be offset by corresponding losses from the Eastern. Demands for entrance were high in South and East Asia, especially in the Philippines and Korea; hence, the competition for admission to America was keen.

Another point to be made about the worldwide system in place of separate ones is that, although the Western Hemisphere limit of 120,000 was smaller than the Eastern's of 170,000, the total population of the Western Hemisphere was less. Before the creation of a unified system, the Western Hemisphere, with less than 10 percent of the world's population, had 40 percent of the numerical immigration quotas. Thus, while ending the separate ceilings potentially could have aided nations in the Western Hemisphere, it could also have taken away an advantage.

If refugees accounted for one breach in the cap, so did immediate family members of American citizens and other nonquota immigrants. In passing the 1965 amendments Congress continued a practice begun in 1928, that of not counting spouses and minor children of American citizens under numerical quotas. At the prodding of the administration the legislators added parents of U.S. citizens to the nonquota list. In advocating admission of certain immigrants—mainly immediate family members—as quota-exempt immigrants, administration officials assured Congress that the numbers would not be large, even with the addition of parents of U.S. citizens to the list, and would average about 40,000 annually.[10] Yet, in the first decade after the 1965 act passed, the figures were about double this estimate, and they continued to grow.[11] In 1978, immediate family members topped 125,000, the vast majority of whom were third world people from Asia, Mexico, or Central and South America.[12] The next year immediate family members increased again, to over 138,000. Most hailed from the same places as the year before. In 1980 third world nations in the Western Hemisphere alone sent about 75,000 immediate family members to the United States and averaged 90,000 in the 1980s.[13]

Breaches in the ceiling are only part of the story of migration from the Western Hemisphere. The above totals include only those entering legally. Because the new restrictions made it difficult to obtain visas, many entered without one, or obtained a nonimmigrant visitor's visa and simply stayed in the United States after it expired. In the past, many persons, mainly Mexicans, who intended to work temporarily in the United States came as braceros, but the bracero program ended in 1964, thus closing that avenue. Now they too were willing to become illegal aliens. While the numbers and impact of illegal immigration (which will be discussed in chapter 7) became a center of controversy, there is little debate about the geographical origins of most illegals after 1965. They were usually from the Western Hemisphere, mostly from Mexico or the Caribbean countries. Hence, illegal immigration is also part of the story of Western Hemisphere immigration.

If Congress lacked a crystal ball to see the precise future of Western Hemisphere migration, the senators and representatives wanting tighter controls knew of the growing pressures of immigration in the 1960s. The restrictionists warned about the implications for migration of poverty and high population growth in Latin America. So did the special commission on Western Hemisphere immigration.[14] If anything, these pressures grew after 1965.

Throughout Latin America and the Caribbean basin, population growth was high. As modern science conquered communicable and child-related diseases, the death rate fell while the birthrate remained high. In the nation sending the largest number of immigrants to the United States, Mexico, the population grew at over 3 percent per annum. At the height of the first massive wave of illegal aliens from Mexico, in the 1950s, Mexico's population was below thirty million. By 1970 it reached nearly fifty million and grew to over seventy million by the early 1980s. Similar rates of growth occurred throughout the countries to the south. In the twenty-five countries and ten dependencies of the Caribbean basin population doubled between the end of World War II and 1970 and continued to grow, at a somewhat lower rate in the 1970s. El Salvador, Guatemala, and the Dominican Republic all grew at a rate of about 3 percent annually.[15]

The rapid increase in population produced large numbers of people without employment or those who worked only part time or at jobs beneath their levels of skill. Latin American nations tried to solve their employment problems through economic development policies and family planning programs. Although economic growth was high and family planning did bring the rate of increase down, neither sufficed to solve the fundamental social and economic problems of unemployment and underemployment.

Poverty and deprivation remained conditions of life for millions.[16]

Economic development led to the growth of industries in the cities and less dependency on labor-intensive agriculture. Rapid urban growth characterized Mexico as well as countries in Central and South America. In Central America the proportion of the population living in cities grew from 16 percent in 1950 to 43 percent in 1980, and in Mexico it went from 51 percent in 1960 to 67 percent twenty years later, and Mexico City—like so many major third world cities—grew at a spectacular rate.[17] The cities just south of the American border, like Ciudad Juarez, Mexicali, and Tijuana, experienced sensational growth. Table 5.1 indicates the trend. People moved to these cities in response to the rapid growth of manufacturing and commerce on both sides of the border, but from these points one learned about employment prospects in the United States as well as how to cross the northern border of Mexico.

Some observers believe the familiarity of new urban workers with the manufacturing process, including plants built by American capital and utilizing American technology, made these people more inclined to migrate. If jobs were not available at home and workers were becoming acculturated to industrialization, then why not move north to similar but better-paying employment? Hence, the exportation of American capital accounts in part for the migration of labor to the United States.[18]

High population growth, economic dislocation, and poverty alone do not explain the migration of so many from the Western Hemisphere to the United States. The communication and transportation revolutions of post-World War II were also part of the process. The Puerto Rican migration of the 1940s and 1950s became a forerunner of other movements from Caribbean nations. Puerto Ricans, as American citizens, were not technically immigrants; they had the right of unrestricted migration to the mainland. Among the factors contributing to this large migration after World War II was cheap air fare between New York and San Juan. The expanding network of air connections to the Caribbean made it possible for millions of others to enter as both immigrants and nonimmigrant visitors in the post-1960 era. The journey from South America was of course longer and more expensive, but

TABLE 5.1.

Mexican Urban Growth Along the U.S. Border

City	1940 *Population*	1974 *Population*
Ciudad Juarez	55,000	650,000
Mexicali	45,000	400,000
Tijuana	25,000	750,000

SOURCE: Walter Fogel, "Mexican Migration to the United States," in Chiswick, ed., *The Gateway*, p.205.

from Mexico one could simply walk or drive an auto across the border.

Inexpensive and quick transportation (only a few hours from the Caribbean) facilitated not only immigration but also visiting as well. The number of visitors—students, tourists, and business people—increased at a faster rate than did immigrants after 1960. In 1978 over nine million persons entered the United States on nonimmigrant visas, up over fourfold from twenty years before. The number of border crossers from Mexico amounted to over 160 million in that year.[19] These visits were thus part of a firsthand information system.

As in the case of Asia, movies, magazines, books, radio, and television brought news of the United States to the Western Hemisphere. In 1978 Latin America had over 27 million TV sets. Of course those with money mostly owned these sets, but millions of others also watched television. Most Latin American countries' imported programs originated in the United States, and a significant proportion of the total programming came from America. Twenty-five percent of the total programming in the Dominican Republic and Colombia was imported from America; 33 percent of that of Mexico, Peru, and Latin America generally. American-produced programs accounted half of the programs shown in Guatemala and Nicaragua.[20]

The images of American society and American goods appearing on the TV screens were reinforced by movies and radio, though not as dramatically. More tangible reinforcement came in the form of American goods selling in the stores or being advertised on the streets. The total impact created a vision of the United States as the land of abundance with a nearly endless quantity of consumer goods.[21]

Traditional immigrant systems of information, the sending of letters and money home, also continued. The small but established communities of people from Colombia or the Caribbean Islands—Haiti, Jamaica, Trinidad and Tobago, and the Dominican Republic in the northeast—formed a link back home. The larger Mexican communities in the Southwest and cities like Chicago served the same function. The letters, as well as visits back home, told of life here and money helped support families in the home country. But money could also be used to sponsor visits or to emigrate to the United States. The Western Hemisphere lacked a family preference system until 1977, but kinship networks were nonetheless important in the immigration process. After 1960, immigrants from the Western Hemisphere generally settled where prior groups of their countrymen had, and the earlier communities helped them find jobs and housing. Often time the newcomers were simply joining their families in America. Scholars have traced the migration of virtually whole villages in the Caribbean and Mexico to large cities in the United States, where the village structure was nearly duplicated.[22] In short, immigration was not a random or crude economic process. As important as the push and pull of economics were, information, transportation, and kinship networks were also crucial in developing immigration patterns to the United States. Table 5.2 indicates trends in Western Hemisphere immigration.

As can be seen from the figures, the trend was toward increased immigration but it was not uniform. In the case of Canada, immigration dropped from the levels of the early 1960s. However, Mexican immigration increased, and Mexico became the largest sending nation in the world, excepting a few years when refugees came in large and sudden numbers.

From the West Indies Cuban refugees accounted for much of the increase after 1960. The Dominican Republic also sent substantial numbers of immigrants before 1965 and continued to do so after. As the table indicates, immigration from the Dominican Republic hit a decade high of 19,458 in 1978. By 1983 it was over 23,000, and in 1989 it topped 26,000. About two thousand of those coming in that year did so under the amnesty of the Immigration Reform and Control Act of 1986 (IRCA). Jamaica and Trinidad and Tobago

TABLE 5.2.

Western Hemisphere Immigration, 1965–1979

Country and Region	1965	1970	1975	1978	1979
North America and the Caribbean	126,729	129,114	146,668	220,778	125,573
Canada	38,327	13,864	7,308	16,863	13,772
Mexico	37,969	44,669	62,205	92,367	52,096
Cuba	19,760	16,334	25,955	29,754	15,585
Dominican Republic	9,504	10,807	14,066	19,458	17,519
Haiti	3,609	6,932	5,145	6,470	6,433
Jamaica	1,837	15,033	11,076	14,256	19,714
Trinidad and Tobago	756	7,350	5,982	5,973	5,225
Central America	12,423	9,443	9,696	20,153	17,547
El Salvador	1,768	1,698	1,416	5,826	4,479
Guatemala	1,613	2,130	1,859	3.996	2,583
South America	30,962	21,973	22,984	41,764	35,344
Argentina	6,124	3,443	2,217	3,732	2,856
Brazil	2,869	1,919	1,070	1,923	1,450
Colombia	10,885	6,724	6,434	11,032	10,637
Ecuador	4,392	4,410	4,727	5,732	4,383

SOURCE: INS, *Statistical Yearbook, 1980,* pp. 4 and 36.

recorded spectacular increases, largely due to the changes in the 1965 law and tighter restrictions in Great Britain about the same time. Prior to 1965, these two countries had a small quota imposed in 1952; but as part of the 1965 reforms, Congress placed them on the same footing as other independent Western Hemisphere nations. These two countries together passed 30,000 in 1989, partly bolstered by IRCA. Haitian immigration also increased in the 1980s; and in addition a rush of Haitian applications under IRCA made that nation's total 34,806 in 1988.[23]

In Central and South America, between 1968 and 1977, Labor Department certification made it difficult to obtain visas. The introduction of a preference system in 1977 similar to that of the Eastern Hemisphere eased the process and immigration rose from those two areas. Among Central American countries El Salvador sent more immigrants as civil war racked that country. Similar strife in Guatemala and Nicaragua sent thousands to the United States. In 1989 57,878 entered from El Salvador; 19,049 from Guatemala; and 8,830 from Nicaragua. In South America, Colombia accounted for one third of all immigration.[24]

Yet, overall, immigration from Central and South America was not especially large without the IRCA immigrants. Mexico alone, with its long-time migration ties and close proximity to the United States, annually sent more immigrants than all South and Central American nations combined.

Mexico

While the rules changed in 1965 the general character of Mexican immigration did not. It had begun to grow in the 1950s and early 1960s and it continued to do so. In 1966, 45,160 Mexicans entered and about the same number for the next three years. During the decades of the 1970s over 600,000 and another 700,000 from 1980 to 1988. From 1965 to 1977 Mexico, with its enormous pressures for emigration, benefited by the lack of a ceiling of 20,000 (exclusive of immediate family members of U.S. citizens).[25] In every year regular immigration from Mexico exceeded that limit and, overall, Mexico accounted for about one third of Western Hemisphere immigration. Beginning in 1977 Congress imposed a limit of 20,000 per country on Western Hemisphere nations, which remained when the legislators created a worldwide system in 1978. However, for several years Western Hemisphere countries had approximately 150,000 extra "Silva" visas, with Mexico getting the lion's share. Mexico also received the lion's share of IRCA's amnesty. Nearly 350,000 former undocumented Mexican aliens adjusted their status in 1989, giving Mexico about 400,000 immigrants for that year and over one million for the 1980s.[26]

Of course, after 1977 as before, many other Mexicans entered as nonquota immediate family members of American citizens and could exceed the 20,000 national limit as well as the hemisphere and worldwide ones. These exceptions, which amounted to nearly 30,000 in 1980, for example, permitted Mexican immigration to remain high, and to exceed the 20,000 limit even after it went effect.

One long-range way to beat the restrictions was more readily available to Mexicans than other immigrants. Pregnant Mexican women crossed the border and gave birth on the American side, with the child thus becoming an American citizen. That child, upon reaching the age of 21, could sponsor his immigrant parents as well as his spouse and children (if married) and his brothers and sisters. Though this might be too long a wait for the parents, for the child the advantages of being able to choose American citizenship later were evident, and the practice, according to one scholar of the Brownsville, Texas, area was "common."[27] While some of these future citizens were born in hospitals, midwives accounted for a significant proportion of new deliveries in that region. Though women did cross the border illegally to have their babies, others entered with a three-day visitor permit, which was legal. As one border guard said, "If she has a document for entry and there is no reason to deny that entry, she can come in. The local crossing card is good for 72 hours. We don't stop pregnant women at the border."[28]

Yet, immigration from Mexico would have been higher and a backlog steadily grew in the 1970s. By the early 1980s it had reached approximately 300,000, the largest of any nation. Rather than wait for years, or because they could not satisfy immigration requirements, many Mexicans simply entered illegally. As a result of this undocumented immigration, the large backlog, and foreign policy considerations, some political leaders suggested that Mexico have a larger quota than 20,000 (this issue will be discussed again later).

The backlog grew because of the immigration restrictions and Mexico's shift from labor-intensive agriculture to industrialization did not generate enough employment for its rapidly growing population. Some observers believe that in the past the economic component of Mexican immigration was as much an attractive American labor market as poverty or poor economic conditions in Mexico, but they suggest that post-1965 migration was more the result of a push from Mexico. Even though the American economy experienced difficulties in the 1970s and early 1980s, including major recessions, these problems were nothing compared to those in Mexico. The oil boom of the late 1970s promised much but did not prove to be the panacea to Mexico's problems. Indeed, it stimulated inflation and did not dent the unemployment and underemployment problem. In the early 1980s experts estimated the combined unemployment and underemployment at nearly 50 percent, where it had been for several years. Inadequate economic development, rapidly rising prices, a mounting foreign debt, and then a fall in oil prices produced another financial crisis in 1982 and further devaluation of the peso. This in turn made American dollars worth more. Although the rate of population growth had slowed as Mexico entered the 1980s, a young and still growing population looked to the north in search of work.[29]

Mexican immigrants were not poverty-stricken peasants living in rural isolation. Nor were they the educated elite—the so-called brain drain—of Mexican society. Predominately young, they frequently had experiences in urban or industrial occupations and had levels of education equal to or above the Mexican norms. They looked to the United States for a better life or better jobs. From 1965 to 1977, nonimmigrant visitors from the Western Hemisphere were not permitted to adjust their status to resident aliens while in the United States. Hence, prior to that time, Mexican immigrants came directly from Mexico, but many had been here before as visitors or as illegal aliens and knew of American life. Still others had friends or older family members who had migrated to America before as immigrants or braceros. Hence, these immigrants had knowledge of, and ties to, the United States.[30]

Prior to the implementation of a preference system, unless they were immediate family members of American citizens or residents, the prospective immigrant had to gain Labor Department approval. If one came as a spouse, child, or dependent of an immigrant with certification, one did not have to have certification even if one intended to work in the United States. Because so many Mexican immigrants entered as families of American citizens or accompanied those admitted by the labor Department, only a minority actually held certification. Here the importance of previous contacts with the United States was crucial, for they enabled the prospective immigrant to line up employment required for certification.

Mexican workers obtained certification in a variety of occupations. They included professionals, managers and clerks, but most came to labor in less prestigious jobs. Mexicans filled places in the service industries, as factory workers, or as laborers. While the demand for farm labor declined with increased mechanization, some also entered as agricultural workers. Most such immigrants were male, but a number of women initiated the immigration process. Of course many family members of those with certification or immediate family members of U.S. citizens also found employment once here, usually in similar jobs.[31]

Mexican immigrants congregated in several states. In 1978 INS reported that of its alien address cards of native Mexicans nearly one half lived in California. Southern California, especially the Los Angeles and San Diego areas of the Imperial Valley, were the centers of Mexican migration to that state. Mexican immigrants also settled in Texas, New Mexico, and Arizona, especially along the border dividing the United States and Mexico. Growing cities like Tucson, Arizona, and Brownsville and El Paso, Texas, claimed substantial Mexican populations, but the largest Mexican and Mexican American city in the United States remained Los Angeles, with its sizeable East Los Angeles barrio. Important Mexican communities also existed in Denver, Kansas City, Chicago, and Detroit.[32]

Among new large immigrant groups Mexicans were least apt to develop permanent ties to the United States. While Asians had especially high rates of obtaining citizenship, Mexicans had low rates.[33] Moreover, many Mexican immigrants returned home, perhaps to migrate again and return again, in a circulatory pattern. After 1957 immigration officials ceased to keep return rate figures for immigrant groups because the rates were low and figures considered unreliable. Hence, precise data about return rates is unknown. However, several scholars, using various sets of data, estimated that more than one million foreign-born persons left the United States during the 1960s, but they did not break their data down by ethnic groups. Two other scholars studied the 1971 cohort of immigrants and concluded that by 1979 the Mexican return emigration from the United States was as high as 56 percent. The Canadian return rate was also high, as was that for people from the Caribbean (except for Cuban refugees who had no place to go), and Central and South America. Asians were least apt to return home.[34]

As noted in chapter 1, the United States permitted some Mexican resident aliens to live in Mexico and work in the United States, either on a daily basis or for several months at a time. Challenged in the courts, the United States Supreme Court in 1974 (*Saxbe* v. *Bustos*) upheld this practice.[35] The majority of those who worked for extended periods in the United States were older married men who left their families to work in agriculture. Other "commuters" lived along the border and crossed daily for regular employment in the United States, in agriculture, service, commerce, or construction jobs. These 64,000 persons living in Mexico and working in the United States either found the cost of living less in Mexico or they simply preferred to live in a Mexican culture rather than an American one.[36] Though this group was unusual, it nonetheless fit the general character of Mexican immigration with loose ties to the United States. Thousands of others lived in Mexico; and with temporary visiting permits crossed into the United States almost daily, ostensibly to visit or shop for a few hours per day, but worked instead, usually in private household employment.[37] Several thousand other Mexicans who were American citizens either by birth or naturalization also lived in Mexico but worked in the United States.[38]

Moreover, during the 1980s the commuters increased rapidly. As Mexico's oil boom collapsed in 1982 and the peso was subsequently devalued several times, green card holders and U.S. citizens found that their American wages went much farther on the Mexican side of the border. As one commuter in the Tijuana area put it, "You can't buy a house on the California side for less than $90,000. Here though, you can get a comfortable place in a pretty nice neighborhood for $20,000 or $30,000." He concluded, "There is no real difference in living on this side. I can watch the Chargers and Padres on television just as easily from over here, so I'm not really losing any of the convenience or benefits I had."[39]

While many Mexican immigrants returned and thousands of others obtained green cards or citizenship and lived in Mexico while employed in the United States, others settled in barrios of the Southwest among other immigrants or second or third generation Mexican Americans. In those communities, families and a host of organizations and institutions formed the basis of immigrant culture. Such institutions as the Roman Catholic Church began to expand their activities among the newcomers in the 1970s and trained Spanish-speaking priests for work in Chicano parishes. The need for such priests was clear because of the importance of the native language to the new-comers. In large communities like East Los Angeles and smaller Texas towns, Spanish predominated on the streets, in the stores, on the radio, and in the display windows of the shops.[40] By 1970 Spanish had replaced Italian as America's second language. A significant proportion of the new immigrants spoke only Spanish or mainly Spanish. According to a 1976 federal government survey, of the nation's Hispanic groups, Mexican Americans were most apt to use only Spanish (35 percent) in their homes. Another 35 percent reported Spanish as their usual household language.[41] Knowledge of English was a prerequisite for citizenship and scholars studying Mexican immigrants in the Sacramento, California, area found "the most important reason that Mexican Americans do not apply for citizenship is that they do not believe that their educational skills are sufficient for them to [pass the test needed] to achieve citizenship." They also observed that many of the interviewees even lacked literacy in Spanish.[42] The development of bilingual educational programs was aimed in part at these immigrants, but more directly at their children attending the public schools. Because of this language retention, some politicians feared, as will be discussed later, that unassimilated cultural groups persisted in the United States.[43]

Because the new Mexican immigrants slowly acquired citizenship and voting rights, they generally found themselves excluded from the political process and the rising Hispanic movement in the 1970s. Most Mexican Americans, about three quarters, were American-born in the early 1980s, in spite of the large migration of the post-1960 era. In the 1970s, a variety of Chicano organizations, such as the GI Forum, the Mexican American Legal Defense and Educational Fund, and La Raza, began to speak more forcibly on Mexican American and Hispanic affairs and took positions on issues—jobs, housing, education, legal status of aliens, and discrimination—affecting immigrants, both legal and undocumented. By the late 1970s, these Chicano organizations were important enough to influence the shaping of immigration policy. Until the new immigrants became more acculturated and acquired citizenship, however, they remained a powerless minority among the large American-born Mexican American community.

Mexican immigrants' most immediate problem was employment. Though Mexican immigrants did not originate in the lowest strata of Mexico in terms of education and work experience, they were, nonetheless, considerably less educated than most Americans. In 1976 the federal government reported that Mexican immigrants age 22 to 30 had only 8.4 years of schooling compared to 13.2 for white non-Hispanics. Among those age 31 to 50 the completed years of school was 6.7 compared to 12.5 for white non-Hispanics. Mexican immigrants had the lowest educational attainments for Hispanic groups.[44]

The lack of education, coupled with language barriers and discrimination, limited the employment prospects of these new migrants. Their jobs in urban America were mainly concentrated in the lower-paid positions in the service industries such as dishwashers in restaurants or as operators in the garment industry. A large group in California was also self-employed in small service industries, such as gardening, or among the women, as houseworkers.[45] In 1976 the Bureau of the Census found that Mexican immigrants earned $6,910 less than non-Hispanic white males. Four years later the Bureau reported that the median income of Mexican-origin families was $15,200 compared to the $19,700 national median, or a gap of $4,500.[46] Only a minority of Mexican-origin families were immigrants; and traditionally they, with their lower levels of education, made less than did second- or third-generation Mexican Americans; hence the gap for immigrants was greater than $4,500.

In the past, Mexicans had improved their earnings the longer they worked in the United States, but they had not done as well as other immigrants.[47] What would be the fate of the large numbers coming in the 1970s and 1980s was not yet clear, for their presence in the United States was too recent to tell. Certainly lack of English and low levels of education severely handicapped them. Their economic progress was also tied to general patterns of assimilation, for as immigrants acquired English and moved up economically, and Mexicans were no exception, they moved out of barrios into mixed neighborhood and became part of the general American culture.

According to the Bureau of the Census, in 1980 Mexicans and Mexican Americans made up about 60 percent of the nation's estimated 14.6 million Hispanics. Then came Puerto Ricans and Cubans, with the remaining 20 percent from Central or South America or listed as "other Spanish."[48] The Bureau did not indicate the origin of these 20 percent; nor did INS have precise data. However, the largest group hailed from the Dominican Republic and will be discussed later.

Central and South America

In addition to increases from Mexico and the Dominican Republic, and the influx of Cuban refugees, Central and South American immigration also grew. Table 5.3 indicates the totals for the main sources of this immigration. INS data does not note the ethnicity, only the country of origin; hence, many Argentines, for example, may have traced their families back to Europe. Nor, as noted earlier, does INS keep data on return rates for these immigrants. The scholars who studied the 1971 immigrant cohort suggested that immigrants from Central and South America had a high rate of return.[49] Precise information about how many Central and South Americans lived in the United States was also complicated because, like many Mexicans and Dominicans, some entered illegally.

While economic conditions and poverty troubled Central and South America, these immigrants were not necessarily the poor. A high percentage of those coming to work from South America were middle-class or elite, well-educated professionals.[50] The proportion of professionals among Central Americans was also high, though not so pronounced as in the case of South Americans.[51] These persons were not unemployed or underemployed in their native lands. Rather they came to the United States because they perceived that better opportunities existed there. In the 1960s and 1970s a few Chileans, Argentines, and others also fled the tur-

TABLE 5.3.
Hispanic Immigration

Country	Total 1966–1987
Central America	
Costa Rica	29,030
El Salvador	106,390
Guatemala	66,060
Honduras	52,601
Panama	50,742
South America	
Argentina	57,423
Brazil (Portugese-speaking)	37,572
Chile	36,574
Colombia	187,560
Ecuador	101,452
Guyana	117,767
Peru	38,088

SOURCE: INS annual reports.

bulent political life and police states that characterized many Latin American countries, though not many entered as refugees under the immigration laws or as parolees by the Attorney General. As noted, after 1979, the bloody civil war in El Salvador sent thousands fleeing, but most probably entered the United States illegally and only a handful won political asylum. In 1977, El Salvador, the largest sending nation of Central America, recorded 4,426 immigrants and in 1980, 6,101. With IRCA it was 57,878 in 1989.[52]

These Hispanic immigrants were frequently downwardly mobile when they arrived and found their first jobs; many professionals and some skilled workers could not find employment in their chosen occupations. Faced with language barriers, prejudice, union rules, unfamiliarity with American culture, and citizenship and residence requirements for the practice of a profession or obtaining a skilled job, the newcomers took what employment was available. One reporter told of an immigrant from Guayaquil, Ecuador, who was forced out of a high-status governmental position and had to leave in 1969. Within a week of his arrival in New York City he found two jobs, one as a janitor in Manhattan and the other sweeping floors in a Queens toy factory. When his wife arrived she took a low-paying job, as did so many Latin Americans, in a garment factory. She had an advanced degree in psychology in Ecuador but could not find suitable employment here. They gradually found better jobs and housing, but not without a struggle and tension.[53] Of the Hispanic groups, South and Central Americans did better financially than Mexicans or Puerto Ricans but earned less than Cubans.[54]

Central and South Americans generally settled in large cities, especially in California, Florida and New York. In New York City they lived near other Hispanics in Queens where Colombians, Peruvians, Argentines, Ecuadorans, Dominicans, and Puerto Ricans mingled.[55] Many Nicaraguans, Salvadorans, and Costa Ricans settled in California cities. For example, the Bureau of the Census reported San Francisco's 1980 population to be over 12 percent Hispanic. The largest groups were from Nicaragua, then El Salvador and Mexico. The immigrants centered in the city's Mission District. The Roman Catholic Church there had originally served Italians and then a broader group of Italians, Filipinos, and Irish. In 1970, a new priest of Italian origin but reared in Argentina and fluent in Spanish arrived to work among the growing Latin American population. Fifty came to his first Spanish mass and it rapidly increased to 700. In 1981, Spanish-speakers accounted for about one third of the parish.[56]

Washington, D.C., and its environs also attracted immigrants from Central and South America.[57] In New Orleans, Latin Americans, especially immigrants from Honduras, replaced older white residents who moved to the suburbs. Hondurans supposedly came at first on the banana boats, found work and settled, and then sent for their families and friends.[58]

Colombia

Colombians were the largest South and Central American group entering after passage of the 1965 amendments. In the earlier wave of Colombia immigration to the United States many middle-class people and professionals migrated, either searching for better economic opportunities or escaping the violent political and social turmoil of the 1950s and early 1960s. In the post-1965 era the proportion of professionals dropped and those with lower educational levels and skills increased. Many women migrated as domestics in the late 1960s for which visas and jobs were available, but this group declined considerably during the late 1970s. Few Colombian farmers or farm workers emigrated and in general the migration was one of the urban lower middle classes. These immigrants usually had secondary education and did not suffer from poverty or high rates of unemployment prior to emigration.[59] Most immigrants entered as family units with the women being the majority of the newcomers. Women usually came as parts of families, but once in the United States a high proportion worked, even though many had not been in the labor market in Colombia.[60]

The largest settlement of these immigrants was in the New York City area and especially the borough of Queens. Another substantial group settled in Chicago. How many resided in the United States or New York City was unknown because of the lack of data about return migration and the size of the undocumented migrants which some scholars believed to be a sizable proportion of the Colombian community. Slightly over 100,000 immigrated between 1965 and 1980.[61] Some authorities estimate that the actual Colombian population was larger, in the area of 32,000 to 42,000 in Queens; about 50,000 to 65,000 in the boroughs of New York City and 125,000 to 160,000 nationally in 1980. The census of 1980 reported 156,176 persons of Colombian origin.[62]

Although part of the larger Hispanic community in the United States and New York City, Colombians, like most other Hispanic groups, maintained their own identity and culture. Especially crucial was the family with the husband being the center of authority. Yet, because of the difficulty of economic survival, many women entered the paid work force, usually as operators in the garment shops or in lower-paid service employment. These women had a higher proportion in the work force than did American women generally.[63] One Colombian woman told a reporter, "In Colombia the woman does not work. She dedicates herself to caring for the children and the home, whereas in New York the woman should work; it is impossible to live with only one salary."[64] As wage earners, the women took on more responsibility and authority than they had at home, with males losing some of their traditional status and power.[65]

In New York many Colombian parents were dissatisfied with the public schools that they considered lax in discipline; hence, they sent their children to the parochial schools. Colombians also attended the Catholic Church which in turn began to recruit Colombian priests and use Spanish. But many resented the Irish domination of the Church and remained somewhat aloof from it.[66] These immigrants also organized a variety of clubs and organizations, but organizational life was not meaningful to most of these immigrants. Of course, for those who lacked proper immigration papers, appearing too often in public was dangerous. Moreover, work and family life consumed most of the immigrants' time. Not only were two incomes required for support of the family, but also to send money back home to those left behind.

Some ethnic cohesion evolved around politics. Colombian law allowed overseas nationals to vote in elections, and politics became an issue in New York City. In 1970 an estimated 3,700 immigrants cast ballots in the Colombian national election, and as the 1974 poll grew near, both major political parties set up campaign headquarters in Queens.[67]

Voting in home elections, sending money back to Colombia, and undocumented status all point to the transient nature of the Colombian community and to the desire by many to return home. Many did so, but for some women the American life was more attractive. As one put it, "I'd like very much to return, but how? I'd return if I could lead an independent life, away from my parents, but that takes money. . . . I won't go back to a repressive family."[68] Still others had hopes for their children in the United States or believed that better opportunities existed there than in Colombia.

The Caribbean

Dominican Republic

From the Caribbean another important Hispanic group increased its immigration to the United States: Dominicans. In 1978 INS reported 108,291 Dominican immigrants living in the United

States, and two years later recorded 122,502.[69] But many experts said this was a gross underestimate because they believed that thousands of undocumented Dominicans were not included in the official figures. Some put the number as high as 300,000 or even higher, which would have meant two thirds of the Dominican population lacked legal documents or failed to report to INS. The 1980 census revealed 170,698 persons of Dominican origin.[70]

Dominican immigration averaged about 12,500 from 1965 through the early 1980s, but then it increased and averaged over 22,000 for the rest of the 1980s. Like most other Caribbean migrants, the return flow was high, possibly as high as 40 percent, which means that the 108,291 recorded by INS in 1978 or 122,502 noted in 1980 might be reasonably accurate for legal migrants.[71] However, as the United States tightened restrictions after 1965, many came as tourists, sometimes first to Puerto Rico, and then stayed on illegally. Although the number of immigrants increased from 1965 to 1990, the number of nonimmigrants increased even faster. It was 66,000 in 1966 and 155,900 ten years later, with a total of over one million for the decade. Only Mexico recorded more visitors to the United States from the Western Hemisphere in that period.[72] If a substantial number stayed on as claimed, then the Dominican population could include several hundred thousand illegals in the 1980s. Certainly the demand for visas was high as the pressure to leave was great amidst American restrictions imposed after 1965. In 1970, one lawyer commented, "After the sugar industry, hustling visas has become the biggest business there is in the Dominican Republic."[73]

The demand for both immigrant and nonimmigrant visas to the United States remained high because of poor economic conditions in the Dominican Republic and the lure of the United States. High unemployment, poverty, and a limited future all made many Dominicans eager to leave. Included among them were poor peasants, but a Dominican government study found that most immigrants originated in the better educated, urban, and higher strata of that society.[74] Most were under age forty and were fairly evenly divided by sex, though slightly more women than men emigrated.[75]

Many Dominican migrants took jobs beneath their skill levels in order to get certification if they did not enter as immediate family members. Once here, the bulk of the new immigrants found jobs in the restaurant, hotel, and clothing industries and a few opened their own garment shops.[76] Among the women, many entered as live-in maids, an occupation considered in short supply. In the United States, they worked as domestics, but most found employment in the garment industry at sewing machines. A high percentage of women worked whether or not they were single or part of a family with young children present.[77]

Most Dominicans settled in New York City, especially the boroughs of Manhattan on the Upper West Side and Queens, and in nearby cities and towns of Long Island and New Jersey.[78] They were drawn to these areas by economic opportunities and other Dominicans who had migrated previously. Kinship networks formed the basis of the migration process. One member of a household went first and his or her extended family would follow. Those who came first found jobs and housing for their kin and friends and even helped obtain needed papers for immigration. Ties with home were close with the immigrants frequently sending money home and returning for visits.[79]

Dominicans in New York were only one of several Hispanic groups, Puerto Ricans being the most numerous. The major Hispanic organizations at times tried to reach all the groups, and newspapers in the city like *El Diario* and *El Tempo* catered to their Dominican clientele with news of the Dominican Republic as well as announcements of Dominican affairs in the city.[80] Various voluntary associations also served the Dominican community, including the Catholic Church. With the arrival of Puerto Ricans, the church began to hold Spanish-language masses and programs for its Hispanic members.[81] Many, believing the public schools inadequate both academically and socially, sent their children to Catholic schools. As one parent put it, "In the public schools, they [the children] learned to be disrespectful of parents and older people. . . . The school in the church doesn't allow them to disobey and do all the things like fighting and using drugs like the public school does."[82]

The emphasis on respect for parents was part of the traditional importance of the extended family, which was so crucial in the migration process. Yet, the family underwent change in the

United States. Although some women had paid work before immigration, because of the need for income the vast majority of them, married and unmarried, worked and provided a vital part of the family income even in families with more than one breadwinner.[83] This change in providing family income led to a shift in traditional sex roles with growing independence of these women and in some cases a reluctance to return to the traditional ways associated with a move back home. As one man said, "In the Dominican Republic my household was authoritarian, here I have taken my lead from the Americans. My house is now run as a democracy."[84] One student of Dominican life in New York found that women and men disagreed over the wife's expenditures of her salary. The wife preferred to spend on consumer goods rather than save for a return home. She found men repeating the refrain, "Five dollars wasted today means five more years of postponement of the return to the Dominican Republic." By returning home, she concluded, the men, largely confined to menial low-paying jobs, could reassert their status.[85]

West Indies

Hispanic immigrants from Mexico, the Caribbean Islands, and Central and South America were not the only newcomers from the Western Hemisphere to the United States after 1965. English-speaking migrants from former British colonies in the Caribbean increased their numbers as did French- and Creole-speaking immigrants from Haiti. From the time the McCarran-Walter Act (1952) imposed severe restrictions on immigrants from the British West Indies until the reforms of 1965, persons from Jamaica, Barbados, and Trinidad and Tobago immigrated to Great Britain rather than the United States. In 1962 Parliament passed the Commonwealth Immigrants Act which curtained immigration from these former British colonies, and in 1983 tightened requirements further. Dependents of persons already resident in England were still allowed to enter, but adults wanting to work in Great Britain found it difficult to obtain the necessary approval. However, the abolition of quotas imposed on these new nations opened the door for substantial increased immigration to the United States.

From 1965 through 1987, over 300,000 Jamaicans emigrated to the United States and thousands more from Barbados and Trinidad and Tobago. In the 1970s Trinidad and Tobago averaged over 6,000 entrants annually, then fell in the 1980s.[86]

Emigration from the English-speaking lands of the Caribbean had a long history, the movement to the United States and Great Britain being the latest stages in that story. High population growth coupled with a migration from the land to the cities provided the immediate stimulus because the urban areas did not provide jobs. However, most of those coming were not necessarily displaced and unemployed peasants. Rather, they were frequently well-educated and skilled persons who saw greater economic opportunities in the United States than in the West Indies.[87]

Because they were exposed to the communication and transportation revolutions of the post-World War II era and because of prior West Indian emigration to the United States, these immigrants possessed ample knowledge of conditions in America. Many had visited the United States before emigration. Jamaicans had also been recruited to work in states from Florida to Vermont as temporary workers, under the H-2 program. They usually found employment in agriculture, harvesting crops such as citrus fruit in Florida or apples in Vermont.[88]

While a majority of immigrants since the 1930s have been female, most workers obtaining Labor Department certification have been male. In the case of Jamaicans, however, women usually initiated the migration process. In 1967 and 1968 over 70 percent of all Jamaican immigrants were women. In those years it was easy for women—Jamaican, Dominican, and others—to get certification as domestics, and about one half of all workers from Jamaica were listed as household workers. Once here they could bring their families. One reluctant male told a researcher, "I didn't want to come, but she kept insisting and so I came." Some Jamaican women never sent for their spouses while others were not married when they emigrated.[89]

Once established, these certified workers were not required to stay at their certified job indefinitely, and the federal government did not supervise immigrants carefully once in the United States. Hence, many left this unskilled occupation and took other, higher-paying, employment. This was not uncommon, for many immigrants entered in an occupation beneath or different than their skills in order to immigrate but switched shortly after arrival.[90]

As family members began to replace certified workers as the main groups from the West Indies the number of household workers declined. However, many women also came as professionals. Between 1962 and 1972 about one half of Jamaican professionals were nurses.[91] Jamaican women, along with Koreans, Filipinos, and others, found it easy to enter as nurses because of the nursing shortage in the United States.

The West Indian community centered in New York City, especially the borough of Brooklyn. In 1980 INS reported over 80,000 Jamaicans in the United States, of whom over half lived in New York State.[92] As in the case of other Caribbean immigrants, the exact size of the illegal population was unknown nor was it known how many of the post-1965 immigrants returned. The Jamaican community was certainly larger than 80,000 but how much could only be estimated. In addition to the substantial New York community, other communities existed in cities like Detroit, Chicago, and Los Angeles and states like Connecticut and Florida.[93]

The relatively high socioeconomic status of these immigrants and their economic motive for emigration reflected the value they placed on education and social mobility. Scholars like economist Thomas Sowell have praised West Indians for their success, both politically and economically.[94] Two popular sayings about West Indians caught the flavor of economic success and political life: "As soon as a West Indian gets ten cents above a beggar, he opens a business" and "A radical is an overeducated West Indian without a job."[95] Their knowledge of English and the education and skills they brought with them helped but they also encountered a problem that many other immigrants experienced to a much lesser degree: racial discrimination. Though class was related to race in the Caribbean, many West Indians arrived unprepared for the discrimination they found in the United States.[96]

Prior immigrants had established organizations like the Jamaican Progressive League to help West Indians. Political clubs and Protestant churches, especially the Protestant Episcopal Church, were also important associations for these newcomers, but racial prejudice was sometimes a problem within the churches.[97] In addition to joining the Jamaican Progressive League and churches, these immigrants organized various hometown associations and cricket clubs.[98] In 1948 West Indian Day was celebrated for the first time by a parade and thus began a large and growing celebration in New York each year, with emphasis on West Indian music, costumes, and food.

Haiti

West Indians were not the only black immigrants from the Caribbean. Haiti sent about 5,000 immigrants annually to the United States between 1965 and 1979 and over 9,000 annually from 1980 to 1987.[99] Economic conditions in Haiti were especially harsh and conducive to emigration. In 1980 the per capita income of Haiti, the poorest country in the Western Hemisphere, was less than $300. The World Bank estimated that 85 percent of Haiti's population lived below what it labeled the "absolute poverty level." High infant mortality rates, illiteracy, and malnutrition also afflicted Haiti. In addition, one of the Hemisphere's most oppressive rulers, Claude (Baby Doc) Duvalier, who became dictator when his father died, ruled Haiti with an iron hand until he was overthrown in 1986. Given the oppressive economic and political conditions, it is no wonder that many Haitians wanted to leave, but few could afford to do so. As one refugee worker who helped settle Haitians in Florida put it, "When you see how most Haitians live, you can understand why so many risk their lives in a leaky boat to go to Florida. Even though they've never seen anything but Haiti, they just know it has to be better here."[100]

Like other people from the Caribbean, Haitians had a history of migration in search of a better life. Some went to the neighboring Dominican Republic or the Bahamas, until the Bahamian government took action in 1978 to keep Haitians out and to expel those already there. A few Haitians settled as far north as Canada while others headed for South America.[101] The largest number migrated to the United States. Because so many entered illegally, no one knew how many Haitians lived in the United States, though estimates in the early 1980s ranged as high as 300,000 to 450,000. The 1980 census found only 90,000 who claimed Haitian origin.[102]

As noted in chapter 1, the pre-1965 exodus was of the elite, political exiles and the urban middle and upper classes. Gradually the less well off migrated too, although the very poor had difficulty coming legally. Haitians often entered as tourists, then overstayed their visas and lived and worked illegally, or made the perilous journey by boat from Haiti to the Florida coast.[103] These new immigrants generally settled where other Haitians had gone, to New York City or other urban areas such as Newark, Boston, Chicago or Miami. The largest Haitian center still remained New York, especially the borough of Brooklyn.[104]

Because Haitians immigrated from an all-black society and were not thoroughly familiar with American mores, many were unprepared for the racial discrimination they encountered in the United States. Mostly Creole speakers, they lacked a command of English. Their color and lack of English made the finding of adequate employment difficult. Friends and relatives already here helped many find jobs, usually semiskilled jobs in the garment factories or in service industries, such as hospital workers. Some women entered with Labor Department certification as domestics. Sometimes the more skilled and highly educated secured employment in their fields, but those without documents and education were forced to take the lowest paying jobs available.[105]

Like other immigrants, Haitians organized their own associations as well as using American ones. The Catholic Church played an important role among the newcomers and some Haitians preferred the parochial schools for their children. However, voodoo was also practiced in the Haitian community. While masses in Creole pleased some of these immigrants, others identified language with status and preferred French.[106] Haitians, through informal groups, their families and meetings in parks, stores, and bars, kept alive Haitian music, customs, and folklore. A few Haitians became involved in politics focusing on conditions in Haiti, but most kept contact by sending remittances to Haiti.[107]

Haitian leaders worked with black Americans, such as the black congressional caucus, on common racial problems like the refugee status of Haitians. But Haitians, like English-speaking West Indians, did not necessarily identify with native-born black Americans. The immigrants brought with them their own traditions and culture and wanted to keep them alive. Some American blacks also alleged that West Indians believed themselves to be superior to American blacks and were clannish. Of course, for Haitians, their different language set them apart.

Unless they heard French or Creole or the West Indian accent, most white Americans were probably unaware that Haitians or West Indians were immigrants rather than native-born blacks. What disturbed whites about immigration were the issues of refugee policy and illegal or undocumented aliens. Demand for restrictions by politicians to curb immigration usually centered on refugees and the undocumented immigrants; not ethnic groups per se. (These issues will be discussed in chapters 6 and 7.)

As the 1970s came to a close, however, public and political concern arose over the flow of nonrefugee legal immigrants. Mostly this did not deal with Haitians or the West Indians—or Asians for that matter. Rather, it centered on the Hispanics who entered in growing numbers after 1965 and the issue of assimilation.

During the 1970s the media and politicians began to note, and in some cases express alarm, about the growing numbers of Mexicans, Dominicans, Colombians, Cubans, and other Hispanics. In 1974 the *New York Times* incorrectly informed its readers: "The poor and huddled now come from South America."[108] The same year, *U.S. News and World Report* said, "The Newest Americans; A Second 'Spanish Invasion.'"[109] The next year, *Newsweek* remarked, "In a burst of ethnic espirit, Latin music has leapt over the boundaries of El Barrio and into the land of the Anglos."[110]

Much of the commentary echoed these themes about the Hispanic influence on American culture and the growing Hispanic community. Hence, one could read or see on TV about Hispanic political organizations and their new power. Some claimed that Hispanics would outnumber blacks as the nation's largest ethnic minority by the turn of the century. Others hinted that Hispanic political power was growing and would become a major force in American life and politics, as witnessed by the Hispanic organizational opposition to the Simpson-Mazzoli bill in Congress in 1982, 1983, and 1984.[111] The U.S. government also responded, not only by including them in affirmative action programs, but also by making a special effort to study Hispanics and to count them accurately in the 1980 census.

Not all political discussion was alarmist. The *Wall Street Journal*, for example, in 1982 noted the Hispanic increase among the general population but said they "were still far from achieving equivalent social or political standing."[112] Others noted, too, how the new immigrants, including Hispanics, revitalized dying sections of American cities.

The most disturbing issue was bilingualism, which was related to the broader issue of assimilation. The *Christian Science Monitor* wrote in 1980, "But the challenge lies not only in numbers. It involves also the digesting into the U.S. mainstream of a vast segment of the population much of which sees itself as both linguistically and culturally different. This raises in turn the question: Can it be done without disruptive collision or confrontation."[113] In his best-selling *America in Search of Itself* (1982), author Theodore White went further in discussing the assimilation issue and placed the blame on the 1965 Immigration Act which he considered an ill-conceived law for bringing about a change in traditional patterns of immigration. Now these newcomers make special demands according to White: "Some Hispanics have, however, made a demand never voiced by immigrants before: That the United States, in effect, officially recognize itself as a bicultural, bilingual nation."[114]

Before the *Nichols v. Lau* (1974) decision, in which the U.S. Supreme Court ruled that schools must teach children in a language they understand, many schools had bilingual programs. The ruling seemed to strengthen bilingual education, but exactly how remained controversial. So too were federal government requirements about bilingualism contained in the Voting Rights Act. Many public agencies—dealing with welfare, police, and health issues—hired persons fluent in Spanish or another needed language as well as English. Private and commercial groups also began to offer their services in Spanish as well as English during the 1970s, and in major American cities signs in Spanish in stores and on public transportation became common.[115] Minority representatives insisted that these services were necessary, while their critics worried that excessive use of bilingualism would perpetuate an unassimilated subculture in the United States, especially as more immigrants entered during the decade. Senator S. I. Hayakawa of California even wanted the United States Constitution amended to say that English was the national language.[116]

Senator Hayakawa's U.S. English movement was unable to amend the United States Constitution to make English the official language, but by 1990 it succeeded in having seventeen states enact some form of official English policy. The major victory occurred in 1986 when California voters amended their constitution to make English the official language of the state. What this amendment actually did is another matter.[117] While California's provision seemed to have teeth, it apparently had little effect. Los Angeles schools later expanded their bilingual programs and announced that they lacked bilingual teachers.[118] Indeed, most states reported shortages of classes for immigrants and their children, Hispanic as well as others, who indicated a strong desire to learn English. And in Arizona a federal judge ruled that that state's constitutional amendment making English the official language of all government functions and actions violated the federally protected free speech rights.[119]

Throughout the 1970s practically no one in Congress suggested a cap on legal immigration. But in July 1980 as the numbers swelled, largely because of refugees, Senator Warren Huddleston of Kentucky proposed that immigration be limited to 650,000 in that year. He said that if the nation wanted to take in large numbers of refugees, chiefly from Cuba and Vietnam, then other types of immigrants should be cut to keep the numbers down.[120] One supporter of Huddleston's amendment, Senator Robert Dole of Kansas, declared, "This amendment is one critical step toward a sound immigration policy. Setting an overall goal for immigration recognizes that our capacity to resettle people is limited. By having such a goal, the Government must confront squarely the question of whom we shall admit."[121] The Senate rejected Huddleston's proposal and ultimately the United States admitted over 800,000 persons in 1980.

Attempts to limit the legal flow did not die, however. When the Select Commission on Immigration and Refugee Policy completed its work, one of its members, Senator Alan Simpson of Wyoming, assumed Senate leadership in formulating proposals about immigration. The commission had suggested a numerical limit of 350,000 in place of the 270,000 then existing limit (excluding refugees) and preferred to allow immediate family members of United States citizens to continue to enter above the regular worldwide and individual country limits.[122] Because the additional 80,000 immigrants would no doubt sponsor some immediate family members, the total of these family immigrants would be larger than in the past. Moreover, the commission also wanted an additional 100,000 visas for the next five years to clear up the backlogs then pending. Thus, the commission recommended increases in American immigration for at least five years, no limit on the nonquota immediate family members, and flexibility on refugees.[123]

Senator Simpson thought otherwise. Although the focus of his Immigration Reform Control Act of 1986 centered on illegal aliens, in early drafts the bill restricted legal immigration as well. Simpson was worried about the growing numbers of newcomers and about federal policies "that encourage the separation of groups of people because of language and cultural differences." In a letter to the Washington Post, the Senator wrote of the new aliens that a "substantial proportion of these new persons and their descendants do not assimilate satisfactorily into our society." He argued that they "may well create in America some of the same social, political, and economic problems that exist in the countries from which they have chosen to depart. Furthermore, if language and cultural separation rise above a certain level, the unity and political stability of our nation will—in time—be seriously eroded."[124]

While wanting to restrict legal as well as illegal immigration, senators had to fashion a bill to accommodate several points of view. Hence, the Senate bill, which passed in 1982, and again in 1983, included both an amnesty for many undocumented aliens already in the United States and penalties against employers who hired undocumented immigrants.[125] As for legal migration, the Senate bill included nonquota immediate family members of U.S. citizens under the numerical limit which was set at 425,000 (except refugees), up from 270,000 under the old law. The senators set no limit on the number of these immediate family members, but their numbers were to be subtracted from the various preferences if the total reached 425,000. While 425,000 was an increase over the previous ceiling, quota-exempt family members of U.S. citizens had grown in recent years. The old ceiling plus immediate family members averaged close to 450,000 in recent years. By placing them under the ceiling the Senate was attempting to ensure that future immigration would not grow and exceed 425,000 (except refugees).

In addition, the Senate modified the fifth preference for brothers and sisters of U.S. citizens. When the 1965 amendments were being enacted, legislators knew that many Italians and other Europeans would use it, but they were not aware of how many Asians—and people from the Western Hemisphere after 1976— would be able to utilize this category. As was explained in chapter 4, the brothers and sisters fifth preference became a vital part of the snowball effect built into the 1965 immigration act. Eliminating or cutting this preference category would curtail the snowball effect of the law and open more places for "independent" immigrants, those with special skills or talents needed in the United States. As Senator Simpson said, "There seems to be some support for the concept of increasing the percentage of immigrants selected for skills and traits likely to benefit the United States. In any case, I do feel that family preference categories should be based on the U.S. concept and definition of a nuclear family and not on the definition of such a family as expressed in other nations."[126]

Restrictions on legal immigration passed the Senate twice but the House Judiciary Committee under Representative Peter Rodino killed them. The Immigration Reform and Control Act of 1986 finally dealt with the undocumented immigration issue, but the act neither capped immigration nor eliminated the fifth preference. These issues were raised again, however, and were debated anew before the passage of the Immigration Act of 1990. In the end, Congress increased immigration in 1990 and did not eliminate the fifth preference. (The 1990 act and IRCA will be discussed in later chapters.)

One final part of the Senate bill deserves attention: an increase in the allotment for Mexico. It will be recalled that when Congress created a preference system for the Western Hemisphere in 1976 and placed a 20,000 limit on each nation, the administration and some members of Congress wanted Mexico to have a higher figure. The Senate bill contained additional places for Mexico. It gave countries contiguous to the United States 40,000 each and said if one country (meaning Canada) did not use its places, then the other (Mexico) could. Because Canadian immigration averaged only around 10,000 in recent years potentially Mexico could have 70,000 immigrants slots. The purpose of this provision was twofold. First, it aimed at improving relations between the United States and Mexico over the troublesome immigration issue. Second, the senators hoped that by giving Mexico extra places, some of the pressure for illegal immigration from that source would be eased. Congress had been unwilling to give Mexico extra visas when it created a worldwide system in the 1970s, but by the mid-1980s the legislators seemed more willing to grant Mexico additional slots. However, IRCA did not do so, nor did the Immigration Act of 1990, although national limits were increased slightly.

6

The Unwanted:
Third World Refugees

THE DRAMATIC SHIFT in policy permitting large numbers of third world refugees to enter occurred after 1960. A few third world peoples had entered under the special laws enacted between 1948 and 1960, but these measures for the most part opened the door for nonquota European migrants. After 1960, however, it was the third world peoples, especially Cubans and Vietnamese, who came to America as refugees. While the ethnic composition of the refugee flow changed dramatically, in other ways refugee policy continued pre-1960 patterns. In the first place, foreign policy considerations, especially anti-Communism, loomed large in determining refugee policy. As will be discussed below, the Refugee Act of 1980 seemed to mark a departure from this anti-Communist posture, but admissions did not deviate much from pre-1980 flows in the first few years after passage of the act. Second, the role of the executive branch, emergent before 1960, became more important after that date. In December 1945, President Harry Truman directed that displaced persons be given preference under immigration quotas. A few years later President Eisenhower urged and prodded Congress to pass the Refugee Relief Act of 1953. When Hungarians poured into Austria after the abortive Hungarian Revolution of 1956, the President utilized the parole power to admit thousands above the small Hungarian quota. President John F. Kennedy again invoked the parole power after Fidel Castro won control over Cuba to admit Cubans and to admit Hong Kong Chinese in 1962. These initial uses of the parole power expanded after 1960, and the President's attorney generals paroled over a million refugees, the bulk of them being Cubans and Indochinese.

Another immediate postwar development, the active role of the voluntary agencies (VOLAGS), also continued. The American Jewish Committee, with the help of other religious and ethnic groups, had worked hard to secure enactment of the Displaced Persons Act of 1948. Protestant and Catholic groups were especially supportive of the Refugee Relief Act of 1953, which was sometimes called the "church bill." These groups, along with various secular ethnic organizations, lobbied in the 1960s and 1970s for the admission of other refugees. Some of these groups led the fight to secure asylum for Haitians and later Salvadorans. In addition, they formed a partnership with the federal government in settling refugees. This relationship had begun under the Displaced Persons Act, and by the 1960s the VOLAGS were an integral part of refugee resettlement.

The other half of the process involved the federal government. Most regular immigrants received no special aid from the federal government once they obtained their visas and prepared to enter the United States. When the Hungarians arrived, the Eisenhower administration temporarily housed them at Camp Kilmer, New Jersey, before they obtained clearance and settled into various communities. In 1975 the government housed 130,000 Vietnamese for months in special camps, which had been military bases, and repeated that practice when the Mariel Cubans arrived in 1980. Congress also voted funds to the VOLAGS for resettlement, and once the refugees were placed, aided them with money for health care, education, and general assistance. By the late 1970s these federal programs were costing several hundred million dollars annually. Because they were limited in duration and costly, the programs became a political issue, especially in local communities where refugees congregated.[1]

The steady growth of federal and VOLAG involvement in refugee policy was largely unseen in 1960. By then the severe refugee problems in Europe appeared over. In that year Congress passed the Fair Share Law, which sanctioned a limited parole program to receive a few thousand Europeans so that the remaining refugee camps operating under the United Nations High Commissioner for Refugees could be closed. But most observers did not see the future significance of the problem. As noted, European nations began to import labor in the late 1950s. Furthermore, the exodus from East Germany fell after the Communists built the Berlin Wall in 1961. From the end of the war to 1961 about 3.5 million East Germans fled to the west, but in the twenty years after the Berlin Wall was constructed, only about 185,000 crossed to the west.[2]

The Cubans

Because the United States immigration policy was so European-oriented and Europeans were now importing workers, it thus appeared that refugee issues would not be so important in the future. Beginning with Cuba in 1959, the destabilization and eventual collapse of particular pro-American third world regimes abruptly changed American policy, often without much warning or planning. The 1960 census revealed only 124,416 Cubans in the United States, of whom 75,156 were Cuban nationals and the rest Cuban Americans born in the United States. Some Cubans emigrated because they did not wish to live under the American-supported Batista government which solidified its control in 1952. Others fled in 1958 when that government was near collapse. These pre-1959 immigrants entered as regular immigrants and not as refugees. When Fidel Castro assumed power on January 1, 1959, the exodus increased and triggered the first of three waves of Cubans coming to the United States.[3]

Beginning slowly but steadily at first, it reached flood proportions just prior to the Cuban missile crisis of October 1962. By then 3,000 persons weekly were arriving from Cuba. Although precise figures are lacking, approximately 200,000 entered during the first wave. Castro canceled air flights to the United States during the missile crisis, and from then until 1965 about 9,000 entered directly from Cuba, mostly by boat and sometimes at great risks. They were the first of the "boat people."[4]

Unlike most European refugees and displaced persons who were processed in another country before coming to the United States, Cubans arrived directly, often with only a few dollars in their pockets. The federal government decided against a Camp Kilmer-style center and Cubans were left to manage for themselves, with aid from local governments, the existing Cuban-American community, and the VOLAGS. Miami civic leaders set up a committee to coordinate activities, and the state established the Cuban Refugee Emergency Employment Center to help the newcomers find jobs.[5] It quickly became apparent, as the numbers of refugees grew, that facilities and funds were inadequate; hence, local organizations and leaders requested financial aid. President Eisenhower sent Tracy S. Vorhees, who had worked with the Hungarians, to investigate. Vorhees preferred a limited federal commitment, restricted to covering transportation costs and temporary assistance to the Cuban Refugee Emergency Center to help refer Cubans to private agencies. In December 1960, Eisenhower allocated one million dollars from the International Cooperation Administration to assist in the settlement of Cubans, especially in meeting emergency needs such as housing, food, and clothing.[6]

As the numbers grew during the Kennedy administration, it became obvious that greater federal aid was required. Accordingly, the President began a nine-point program to assist the refugees with medical care, education, employment, and general cash assistance.[7] Prior to the arrival of the Mariel Cubans in 1980 federal appropriations for the Cuban Refugee Program eventually reached 1.4 billion dollars, with peak spending occurring during the 1970s.[8] To bring order to the program, Congress passed the Migration and Refugee Assistance Act of 1962. This act not only provided funds and programs for the Cubans, but also authorized aid for refugees outside of the United States.[9]

Because most Cubans were Catholic, the Catholic Refugee Committee became the most active VOLAG involved with Cubans. Yet the Protestant Church World Service also helped, as did the secular International Rescue Committee and the Hebrew Immigrant Aid Service (HIAS). HIAS had a long tradition of helping immigrants and had special interest in helping those Cubans who were Jewish; most Cuban Jews eventually left Cuba. Working with the federal government, these VOLAGS found sponsors for the refugees, mainly in the Miami area.[10]

Most refugees arriving in the early 1960s were Cubans but President Kennedy also paroled about 15,000 Chinese in 1962. Although Hong Kong's population swelled dramatically in the late 1950s, these parolees had fled China earlier, after the Communist takeover in 1949. However, they could not gain entrance into the

United States because of China's small quota of 105. Accordingly, Kennedy, through his attorney general, invoked the parole power to admit them.[11]

Paroled Chinese were not large in numbers and the Cuban exodus appeared over after the missile crisis of 1962. Consequently, when Congress received President Kennedy's July 1963 proposals to amend the 1952 McCarran-Walter Immigration Act, refugee items were not a priority issue. As noted in chapter 3, Congress mainly debated national origins, the Asia-Pacific Triangle, the Western Hemisphere ceiling, labor certification, and the family preference system. Yet a number of congressional liberals had been advocating that regular procedures be included in the immigration law for the admission of refugees. They usually used cold war arguments: that America had an obligation to help refugees throughout the world and in particular to accept some of those fleeing Communism. For example, President Truman's commission, in its report *Whom Shall We Welcome?* (1953), advocated "that effective measures should be taken and adequate appropriations be made to provide reasonable reception, care and migration opportunities for escapees from Communism." In place of national origins quotas, the commission wanted a system of immigration divided into five categories, one of which "should be based on the right of asylum, available for refugees, escapees, expellees, and other persons suffering from political, religious and economic persecution."[12]

When Congress debated the Refugee-Escapee Act of 1957 that admitted a few more refugees from Europe, Asia, and the Middle East, Congressman Michael Feighan, who played a key role in the enactment of the 1965 immigration act, noted the bill lacked procedures for the United States to act quickly in emergencies. "We should be prepared," he said, "in the event of another freedom revolution to take quicker and a more affirmative action than our response in the Hungarian revolt."[13] Still other members of Congress worried about the use of the parole power and the ad hoc nature of refugee programs. The Migration and Refugee Assistance Act brought some organization to the refugee problem, but it did not provide for regular procedures of admission.

Both Kennedy and Johnson wanted flexibility in the admission of refugees, but Congress granted only limited executive power. As eventually passed, Eastern Hemisphere refugees received a maximum of 6 percent of the 170,000 ceiling, or 10,200 places. The President had the authority to admit that many if he deemed it necessary. Yet, these immigrants had a different status than did regular resident aliens. They were admitted as "conditional entrants" for a period of two years, after which they could adjust their status to regular resident aliens. Theoretically, the government could review their status and behavior during the conditional period.[14] As the Western Hemisphere had a ceiling but no preference system until 1977, the legislators made no provision for refugees in that hemisphere.

In establishing a preference category for the admission of refugees from the Eastern Hemisphere, Congress clearly intended to limit the parole power. The Senate committee reporting the bill stated:

In as much as definite provision has now been made for refugees, it is the express intent of the committee that the parole provision of the Immigration and Nationality Act, which remains unchanged by this bill, be administered in accordance with the original intention of the drafters to authorize the Attorney General to act only in emergency, individual, and isolated situations, such as the case of an alien who requires immediate medical attention, and not the immigration of classes or groups outside the limit of the law.[15]

In addition to attempting to curtail the power of the executive, the legislators also made it clear that the basis of American refugee policy was anti-Communism. Refugees in 1965 were defined as they were in the Refugee-Escapee Act of 1957 as those fleeing Communism. That act also included refugees from the Near East, a reference to those escaping persecution under Nassar's regime in Egypt. A third group found their way into the 1965 act, those individuals uprooted by "catastrophic natural calamity as defined by the President who are unable to return to their usual place of abode."[16] The legislators had in mind those who came under special legislation enacted in 1958 when volcanic eruptions and earthquakes made many in the Azores Islands homeless. This provision was meaningless, for Presidents after 1965 never admitted such persons.

Subsequent events subverted the intention of Congress to provide regular procedures for refugees and to curtail the parole power. In the same year that the legislators reformed the McCarran-Walter Act, President Lyndon Johnson escalated the war in Vietnam. This action eventually resulted in the admission of several hundred thousand Vietnamese by the use of the parole power.[17]

If few could see the outcome of military activities in the Far East at that time, the Cuban situation lay closer to home. As noted, following the missile crisis and the halting of air flights between the United States and Cuba, only a few thousand Cubans managed to enter directly from that country. In 1965 Castro indicated his willingness to permit the departure of those Cubans who wanted to leave. On the very day that Johnson signed the 1965 act at the base of the Statue of Liberty, the President ignored the wishes of Congress and announced an open door for Cubans.[18] Because the Western Hemisphere had no preference category for refugees, the President used the parole power to admit them. Beginning in December 1965, air flights resumed, and until 1972, when the flow fell again, 368,000 additional refugees arrived. After 1972, a few thousand more entered, some directly from Cuba and others after going to another country first.[19] The third wave of Cubans—the Mariel group—arrived in 1980.

Although Cubans were usually admitted as parolees, as were Indochinese after 1975, the seventh preference did permit 10,200 (17,400 after 1977) refugees to immigrate annually until the enactment of the 1980 immigration act for refugees. These included Chinese, Near Easterners, and Eastern Europeans as well as some Indochinese. Hence, the seventh preference provided a procedure for admissions, but it was simply inadequate for the entrance of the large numbers of refugees the administration deemed necessary. From 1965 to 1980 those paroled numbered about four times the seventh preference conditional entrants.[20]

While Congress had intended to limit the parole power, the legislators were not unwilling to aid persons who migrated under this authority. As the number of Cubans grew again in 1966, the lawmakers held hearings on the situation and voted for increased aid programs requested by the administration. Appropriations did not come without controversy, however. Miami and Dade County Florida officials especially wanted full federal financial support for refugees, but many in Congress worried about both the amount and duration of federal support for Cubans. Finally, in 1977 Congress voted a six-year phaseout of the Cuban assistance programs. Of course, the issue of Cuban relief became uncertain and controversial again in 1980 when the Carter administration admitted nearly 130,000 Mariel Cubans.[21]

In 1965 the House refused a request by the administration to permit those paroled Cubans to adjust their status to resident aliens. Being permanent resident aliens would have enabled these persons to apply for citizenship, make it possible for some to bring in relatives, and eliminate problems of employment and legal issues associated with parole. The House Judiciary Committee later noted that diplomatic complications weighed heavily in its considerations. The committee said it did not want adjustment of status to be taken as "an indication that the Castro regime would be recognized as a permanent feature of Western Hemisphere political life."[22] Yet, Congress could not ignore the refugees. Without special legislation, the only way for most Cubans to become permanent resident aliens was to leave the United States for another country and apply for admission as immigrants to America from there, a costly procedure for which most Cubans lacked sufficient funds. This could also mean going through the regular immigration preference system (for the Eastern Hemisphere countries), including the cumbersome Labor Department certification process in some cases.[23]

While Congress, as well as many Cubans, might have wished for an overthrow of Fidel Castro, the unsettled status of a growing number of refugees had to be faced, especially in view of the failure of the 1961 Bay of Pigs invasion. Consequently, in 1966 the legislators passed the Cuban Adjustment Act that allowed these immigrants to become permanent resident aliens. The Cuban Adjustment Act of 1966 simply followed a precedent established when Eisenhower paroled Hungarians and Congress then permitted them to become resident aliens two years later. Congress followed a similar practice in the future for paroled Indochinese and others. In spite of congressional uneasiness about the executive parole power and control of refugee policy, in effect the law-makers' financial support for refugees and permission for adjust-ment of status was legislative support of, and sanction for, a pol-icy in which the executive branch determined the flow of refugees. Of course, permitting parolees to adjust their status could also be sold as saving federal funds in the long run; for as resident aliens and later citizens, these parolees would be eligible for better em-ployment, hence the need for welfare would drop.[24] Eventually, as will be discussed below, Congress attempted, with mixed suc-cess, to terminate this ad hoc policy when it passed the 1980 Refugee Act.

Among the first anti-Castro Cubans to leave were political offi-cials of the Batista government. They were joined by many who had been anti-Batista and even friendly toward Castro before the latter moved to the left and sought radical social and economic changes. Indeed, even before 1959, some anti-Batista Cubans had sought refuge in Miami; but they did not necessarily wish to re-turn after Castro's revolution. Some political exiles feared, because of their political connections, that their lives were in danger, or at the very least, they faced imprisonment and harassment. In the United States the more ardent and venturesome of the political exiles became involved in anti-Castro activities and organizations, and several thousand participated in the abortive CIA-sponsored Bay of Pigs invasion of April 1961. Following that fiasco, the im-prisonment of 1,300 of the invaders, and the missile crisis of 1962, many political exiles lost their hope for an overthrow of the Castro regime and the return of a non-Communist government in Cuba. Gradually, Cubans began to view their stay in America not as temporary but as permanent.[25]

The first wave of 1959–1962 was considerably more than an exodus of officeholders, non-Communist intellectuals, and key politicians. The radical changes instituted by Castro threatened the wealthy, well-educated professionals and the middle class generally. Those arriving between 1959 and 1962 were dispropor-tionately well educated, white, and of upper-echelon occupations and income. These included many landowners, bankers, doctors, lawyers, and other professionals and businessmen. Scholars found in studying samples of those here in 1962 that about one-third had obtained twelve years of education whereas only 4 percent of the Cuban population had reached that level. One-eighth of the refugees had four years or more of college, while only 1 percent of the general Cuban population could claim a college education. The refugees were also more likely than those who stayed behind to come from Havana or the nation's other urban centers. In short, the urban elites and middle class fled Cuba between 1959 and 1962.[26]

As the Castro revolution wrought fundamental changes in Cuban life, Cubans other than the rich were eager to leave. Consequently, when the exodus began anew with the airlift of December 1965, many fled to America. These included middle-class people but also a broader spectrum of Cuban society than was represented among the first refugees. The United States considered them political refugees escaping Communism, but many sought economic opportunities in America and did not necessarily face the same political fears of the first group.[27]

By the mid-1970s the two large waves of refugees subsided, but Cubans continued to trickle into the United States directly from Cuba or after spending several years in another country such as Spain. Like their predecessors, these newcomers were not from the lower classes, but represented persons of higher levels of education, income, and occupation and they were disproportionately white. They also included a number of skilled workers but many were from the lower levels of the middle class in the service and business sectors of the Cuban economy. As Cuba socialized the small entrepreneurial sector of the economy, they were adversely affected.[28]

Allowing for the shift downward in the socioeconomic status of Cubans from 1959 to 1979, without exaggeration one can say that these refugees represented the pre-1959 elites, professionals, middle class, and lower middle class of Cuban society. The motive for leaving for some was clearly political, including the fear of execution, but the vast bulk of these peoples stood to lose economically as Cuba became a Communist state. Because they had no future in a Marxist Cuba run by Castro, they chose immigration to the United States. As one journalist said of the 1959–1973 immigrants:

To a great extent these people represented the professional and business class of Cuba; the able, the educated, the successful. The struggle in most Latin American countries is to build a stable middle class; that of Cuba has been gutted. This exodus is the biggest brain drain the Western Hemisphere has known.[29]

The first Cubans settled in Florida, especially the Miami or Dade County region, thus beginning a pattern that later migrations followed. Other Cuban communities developed in New York City and New Jersey, notably West New York and Union City. Some Cubans originally settled outside of Miami but then migrated to that city's Little Havana, which claimed about half of the Cuban refugees.

A few refugees managed to bring money with them, or get it out before they left, but the vast bulk of the Cubans arrived with little or no money, and some with only the clothes they wore or could carry. When the Cubans arrived in Miami, the area's main industry was tourism and the city had a relatively high unemployment rate. Central Miami itself, like so many American cities, was experiencing urban decay. Union City, New Jersey, another center for these refugees, had similar problems. That aging community across from New York City had many vacant stores in the central district. As one realtor recalled, "When they started to come in the 1960s this place was dying."[30] Moreover, few expected such a large influx, and Miami's government and private groups lacked the facilities to handle so many people.

Not only did Cubans arrive with little money and find economically depressed conditions, but they faced problems common to other immigrants. Many could not speak or write English. For professionals, American licensing requirements for training and American citizenship were barriers. In addition to these professional obstacles, lawyers discovered that the American system of law differed radically from what they had known. As a result, many educated professionals had to take whatever jobs they could find, usually below their levels of education, experience, and skills. If no jobs were available the refugees accepted welfare until they could get on their own feet.[31] First reports about the refugees told of crowded conditions in Miami, employment problems, and tensions between the newcomers and the city's older residents. Then public attention focused on anti-Castro activities, the ill-fated Bay of Pigs invasion, and deteriorating relations between the United States and Cuba, including the war scare generated by the Cuban missile crisis of 1962.[32]

As Castro solidified his power and as the refugees settled in, the media discovered other news to report. Journalists, newspapers, magazines, and television informed the public of the rapid socioeconomic progress of the refugees and how they had revitalized Miami and smaller communities like Union City. As early as 1966 *Fortune* ran a story on "Those Amazing Cuban Emigres," and said, "A lot of talented refugees from Castro's Cuba are rapidly becoming an important American asset."[33] Five years later *Business Week* similarly told of "How the immigrants made it in Miami," and concluded, "The Cubans who fled Castro have become the city's affluent new middle class."[34] Speaking of Union City in 1980, the *Washington Post* analyzed the success more modestly in a story called "Slow Steady Climb Up the Ladder."[35]

These journalistic portraits of the Cuban economic success story recounted numerous tales of individual mobility as well as group progress and community revitalization. The *National Geographic Magazine* in 1973, for example, insisted, "By any indicator their impact has been, to say the least, profound." After backing this statement with statistics of Cuban entrepreneurship, it related individual accounts, including that of Carlos Arboleya, president of the Fidelity National Bank, South Miami. When Arboleya, chief auditor of Cuba's largest bank at the time Castro nationalized the banks in 1960, arrived with his wife and two-year-old son, he had only $40. "Overqualified," he could not get a job in the city's banks; instead he began life anew as an inventory clerk in a shoe factory for $45 per week, even though he "didn't know a thing about shoes when I started," he recalled. Within a year and a half he became vice president and controller of the company and then took a cut in salary to return to banking. By 1968 he was president of the Fidelity Bank and a U.S. citizen.[36]

Arboleya's story was typical of what impressed commentators most, for they noted the rapid rise of Cubans in Miami's construction, trade, and finance industries. The banking and trade expansion, accompanied by a building boom in Dade County, was closely connected to the Cuban arrival. In the 1970s about one third of Miami's commercial bank employees were Cuban, a number of whom were presidents and vice presidents. These included 16 of 62 bank presidents, 250 vice presidents, and more than 500 other bank officers.[37] Symbolic of Miami's status as a center of Latin American trade was the Annual Trade Fair of the Americas, begun in 1978. Largely organized by Cuban Evelio Ley, who arrived in Miami in 1961 with only $20 and practically no knowledge of English, the fair drew thousands of businessmen from all over Latin America and the United States.[38]

Governmental reports and scholarly studies partly confirm the media image of rags to riches. In 1979 Cuban median family incomes were highest of the Hispanic groups and higher than black Americans, though most Cubans had been here a shorter time than blacks and Puerto Ricans and many Mexicans.[39] Some of the difference can be explained by the fact that Cubans were older than other Hispanics (older people tend to have higher incomes than do younger Americans). Among Hispanics, Cubans also had higher levels of education. Cuban incomes, education, and occupational status still lagged behind white non-Hispanics, but considering the initial jobs open to them, their progress in a few years was remarkable. Some observers even claimed, "In the ten years since Cubans began fleeing to the U.S. from Castro, they have made faster progress in their adopted country than has any other group of immigrants in this century."[40]

Yet, the picture was not uniformly one of Horatio Algerism. While a middle class of entrepreneurs had emerged along with some professionals, not all Cubans had made it. Many were downwardly mobile at first and had not been able to move upward. Compared to white non-Hispanics, Cubans were disproportionately poor in the 1970s. Above the poor but still near the bottom of the Cuban population many remained laborers, or held low-paying semiskilled factory and service jobs. Included among those who failed to rise were professionals who were unable to overcome language, training, and legal barriers to practice their professions here, they remained underemployed. Still others had trouble mastering English, and although they found jobs in Little

Havana, their wages remained low and prospects for advancement dim.[41]

Government aid in providing emergency funds and later medical care, general assistance, special education, and vocational training, no doubt explains much of Cuban economic success. Although immediate job prospects were unfavorable in Florida when Cubans arrived, the 1960s and early 1970s were general years of economic growth, which helped Cuban refugees. The fact that Cubans were perceived as anti-Communist lessened prejudice directed at other Hispanics. Yet, it cannot be overlooked that although most Cubans arrived short of funds, they brought business skills, education, and a wish for additional schooling for their children, and a desire to get ahead—what social scientists label human capital or middle-class cultural attitudes and aspirations. These characteristics stood them well in an American society that prized economic success. This elite and middle-class population generally was quick to learn English and to get off welfare and willing to work hard and to take advantage of what opportunities existed, in spite of many initial hardships.

The immediate stimulus for the 1980 refugees lay in Cuba's decision in 1979 to allow Cuban Americans to visit their homeland; about one hundred thousand did so in 1979 and early 1980. These Cuban Americans told their relatives, old friends, and other Cubans about their success in the United States and brought physical documentation in the form of fine clothes, radios, and watches.[42] In early 1980 a dispute between Peru and Cuba erupted over the right of asylum in Peru's Cuban embassy. That embassy had been reluctantly giving asylum to those Cubans who entered after eluding the guards. When Castro withdrew his guards and allowed others to enter, unexpectedly ten thousand jammed the embassy, overwhelming the Peruvians' ability to care for them. The United States agreed to take in 3,500 of these people after screening them when they arrived in Costa Rica. But on April 18 Castro insisted that those wanting to leave must be taken directly to the country, mainly the United States, where they intended to settle. Three days later the first boats from the United States arrived at the Cuban port of Mariel and began to ferry the latest refugees to Florida.[43]

A confused Carter administration pursued a flip-flop policy. On the one hand, the administration wished to embarass the Castro regime by giving sanction to its dissidents and those who were close relatives of Cuban Americans. On the other hand, it wanted procedures to be orderly so that American immigration policy did not appear out of control and that Cubans would not seem to be another group of illegal immigrants.

While thousands of Cuban Americans raised money, bought, rented, or hired boats, and went to Mariel to bring out their relatives and friends, the administration failed to negotiate an orderly procedure for clearing and accepting refugees. Carter wavered between welcoming the Mariel refugees and stopping "the freedom flotilla" of small boats between Cuba and Key West, Florida. After imposing a few fines on the first boats, President Carter declared on May 5 that the United States would provide "an open heart and open arms" for the "tens of thousands" of Cubans pouring into Florida.44 The navy provided escorts and the government opened new refugee centers. Amid reports that Castro was emptying his jails and sending criminals along with cripples and the mentally ill, the administration shifted policy again and finally brought the exodus to a halt, but not before about 130,000 had arrived.45

The Marielitos were not as welcome as the early groups had been. A survey conducted by the Gallup organization for *Newsweek* revealed that 59 percent believed the latest Cuban immigration was bad for the United States, and only 19 percent thought it would be good. A Harris poll and the *New York Times*—CBS poll turned up similar results.46 The *Miami Herald* discovered that non-Hispanic whites and blacks in Dade County, by margins of nearly four to one, said the new wave would have a negative impact on their county; both of these groups believed that the earlier refugees had a positive impact. Only Latin or Hispanic persons in the area believed that the new refugees would have a healthy effect.47 Journalists also reported opposition to the Cubans, especially economic. One New Jersey automobile worker was blunt: "Those Cubans—we should put them back on their boats and sink them. We don't have enough work for our own people." An Illinois unemployed steelworker expressed similar sentiments while waiting in line for employment: "I bet that if we were Cubans we wouldn't have to wait this long. . . . They are just coming over here and being welcomed with open arms and pretty soon they will have all our jobs. The government is spending a lot of time and money to ship them all over the country while we, the backbone of this country, don't get any more consideration than this."[48]

The changed economic situation from the prosperous 1960s prompted such hostility about increased immigration. The 1970s had witnessed periodic high rates of unemployment and chronic inflation. The boom in Miami itself had slackened by 1980 and jobless rates were high among the city's blacks, who were potentially in competition for jobs with the new immigrants. Job competition was not the only economic concern; others worried about the status of the refugees and potential cost of supporting them. Local officials wanted the federal government to bear the cost of expenditures for refugees, but Congress had voted only three years before to phase out the Cuban program, and now a new group of penniless persons had arrived, with little notice and practically no planning.[49]

Added to the economic fears were rumors that Castro was dumping Cuba's undesirable citizens—its criminals, paupers, and mentally ill—on the United States. Stories circulated that Cuban officials forced boats landing in Mariel to carry back anyone the Cuban government wanted as the price for bringing back families and friends. The *Charleston* (S.C.) *News and Courier* put it, "Immigration officials say there is evidence that Fidel Castro is unloading his jails, pushing his criminal stream into the United States. The scope of that problem can only be guessed at."[50]

Reports of Castro's sending his criminals were greatly exaggerated, but the Mariel Cubans were somewhat different than the illustrious immigrants coming in the 1960s. The newest group was more apt to be male, of lower levels of skill and education than the earlier refugees. They tended to be young and working class.[51]

After establishing emergency centers in Florida, clearing and placing, with the help of the VOLAGS, as many as possible in local communities, the federal government housed the remainder, who numbered about sixty thousand, in four centers used only a few years before for the Vietnamese refugees. In the summer and fall of 1980, a riot erupted at Fort Chafee in Arkansas which added bad publicity to the mounting stories that many undesirables had come during the Mariel exodus.[52]

As placement proceeded, it became obvious that several thousand of the refugees were hard to place. By the end of the year over 6,000 refugees still lived at Fort Chafee, waiting clearance, sponsorship, and release to an American community.[53] Among those still interned were another 1,774 kept in federal prisons. These persons had been, or were suspected of being, criminals in Cuba and hence inadmissible under American immigration laws. Critics charged that the immigration authorities were too harsh and were holding persons in violation of due process and without substantial evidence.[54]

Gradually INS found homes for more of the Fort Chafee group and released some of those in American prisons, but a year after the Mariel exodus, the United States still incarcerated several thousand Cubans on the ground that they could not be placed or that they were inadmissible. Nor would Castro take them back.[55] Thus a small number of the Marielitos with criminal records found that the "freedom flotilla" of 1980 led to imprisonment in the United States. Over one thousand still languished in American prisons, mainly at the Atlanta facility, three years after their arrival. President Ronald Reagan closed the Fort Chafee center and moved its remaining few hundred persons to the federal prison in Atlanta. The President repeated Carter's request to have Castro take the remaining exiles back and said that unless Cuba received these aliens, the United States would cut down on future immigration from Cuba. Finally, in December 1984 an agreement was reached to return them to Cuba. About 200 Cubans were repatriated before the Cuban government announced in 1985 that it was suspending the agreement. Castro objected to the United States' new Radio Martí, a Spanish-language station which broadcast news, sports and entertainment to Cuba. Cubans said the programs were anti-Cuban, and until they stopped, no more prisoners were to be accepted.[56]

Immigration authorities did release some of the prisoners to sponsors who found them homes and jobs. By 1988 only 125 of the original Marielitos had been interned constantly since their arrival in 1980. Yet several thousand other Marielitos had been arrested and convicted for crimes committed in the United States and consequently found themselves incarcerated in jails throughout the United States; many were interned in the Atlanta Federal Penitentiary and a federal detention center in Oakdale, Louisiana.[57] When the United States and Cuba reached a new agreement in 1987 to deport many of these prisoners in return for the willingness of the United States to accept political prisoners in Cuba, inmates at Atlanta and Oakdale rioted. Seizing hostages and setting fire to several buildings in both facilities, they sought to dramatize their plight, claiming that they had been promised asylum in 1980 and were betrayed.[58]

The crisis ended when the government promised to halt deportations temporarily and to review individual cases. Reviews did lead to the release of some Cubans, but beginning in 1988 the United States began to deport those considered inadmissable under American laws. The first such individuals had been convicted in the United States of attempted rape, kidnapping, voluntary manslaughter, and armed robbery.[59]

Whether they were released from prison or had never been interned, all Marielitos faced a problem of status. President Carter failed to invoke the new 1980 Refugee Act when he admitted them. Instead, like presidents before him, he paroled the Mariel refugees and created a new status for them, the "Cuban-Haitian entrants (without status)" for a six-month period. Not officially refugees, they were not entitled to full-scale refugee benefits or eventual adjustment of their status. In October 1980 Congress voted funds to aid these latest refugees and in effect placed them on a par financially with others. Their temporary status was later extended, as was financial assistance, and finally the Reagan administration announced that it would permit the Marielitos to become resident aliens under the Cuban Adjustment Act of 1966.[60]

How these immigrants would fare was unknown. The New York Times claimed in May 1983 that most Cubans of the Mariel boatlift were adjusting well to the United States and quoted Denise Blackburn, director of the program staff of the Justice Department's

Program for Cubans and Haitians: "When you consider that we were a country of first asylum and received nearly 125,000 people between April and August 1980, we have remarkably few cases of people who are problems." The *Times* did not provide hard evidence, and others took a different view. The Union City, New Jersey, director of revenue and finance said of Marielitos, "These so-called Mariel refugees were brought here by President Jimmy Carter on behalf of the United States government and now they are saddling us with the welfare costs for them."[61] Others singled out the criminals who had been part of the Mariel exodus. Yet opposed to individual criminals were cases of success like Esteban Torres, who spoke no English upon arrival, but in 1990 was a straight A student at the Massachusetts Institute of Technology.[62] A study conducted in the mid-1980s of Marielitos in Miami revealed a mixed pattern, with most finding jobs after initial difficulties. It was clear that it would take more than a decade to judge the progress of these refugees.[63]

The Indochinese

The 800,000 or so Cubans represented the largest single nationality of post-World War II third world refugees from 1960 to 1984 but close behind were the 700,000 Indochinese arriving between 1975 and 1984. After 1985 the Indochinese passed the Cubans in numbers. A few Indochinese, such as war brides, had emigrated to the United States before the collapse of the American-backed South Vietnamese regime in 1975, but not many. As the nation deepened its involvement in the war, and as the violence increased, so did the number of refugees along with a growing concern about their welfare. Millions of innocent, wretched, and uprooted people were caught between the Vietcong and the North Vietnamese on the one hand, and the Americans and their allies in Saigon on the other. The population in Saigon and other cities swelled as the violence in the countryside left many homeless. To aid these Vietnamese, the American government assisted them with medical care, food, and other supplies and helped house them in what facilities were available. The United States government gave no thought to admitting these refugees to America. In 1973 Francis Kellogg, special assistant to the Secretary of State for Refugee and Migration Affairs, told a congressional committee that although the war was creating refugees he did not "anticipate them coming to the United States . . . it would be our opinion that they could be resettled in their own country."64

Aid to the Vietnamese was part of the general program of refugee assistance that the United States developed after World War II. In the case of the non-Indochinese, the United States worked through a variety of international organizations such as the International Refugee Organization, the Intergovernmental Committee for European Migration, the Office of the United Nations High Commissioner for Refugees, and the United Nations Relief and Works Agency for Palestine in the Near East.65 Because of the Americanization of the war, the United States assisted the Vietnamese more directly; the aid amounted to about seven hundred million dollars during the American presence in Vietnam.66 A dramatic collapse of the Saigon government in the spring of 1975 drastically changed American refugee aid in Indochina and altered immigration policy toward that country.

Weaknesses of the American-supported government had been apparent throughout the war, but the sudden collapse of the Saigon regime took nearly every American official by surprise. In March 1975, two years after the American withdrawal from South Vietnam, Secretary of Defense James Schlesinger said that there would be no significant military operations against the American-supported government in that year. Yet, within a few days, a major Communist offensive began. At first, the government of South Vietnam tried to carry out an orderly retreat and regroup its fleeing forces to defend critical areas and cities. Toward the end, American officials became increasingly aware of the weakness of the Vietnam regime in the south, but they did not anticipate the speed at which it fell.67

As the end drew near, the American ambassador to South Vietnam, Graham Martin, urged General Nguyen Van Thieu, head of the South Vietnamese government, to gain American aid and sympathy by permitting the airlift of Vietnamese orphans to the United States. Since the end of World War II, Americans had been willing to bring orphan immigrants to the United States, a move they interpreted as humanitarian. Thieu accepted Martin's proposal as a politically wise move. The Harris Poll indicated strong support for this maneuver; by a 56 percent to 32 percent majority Americans supported the airlift of Vietnamese orphan children to the United States to be adopted by American parents. Moreover, a lopsided 77 to 18 percent majorty believed that "Americans showed their real kindness and generosity by their willingness to adopt Vietnamese orphans."[68]

Operation Babylift encountered difficulties. First came the crash of a World Airways plane that took the lives of 150 children and 50 adults. Some members of Congress also criticized the American government's efforts and poor planning. Representative Joshua Eilberg, chair of the House Subcommittee on Immigration, Citizenship, and International Law, expressed annoyance at the administration's lack of consultation with Congress about the use of the attorney general's parole power to admit orphans. He told one administration official that although Congress shared the executive branch's concern about Vietnamese refugee children, "your words come as rather lip service to me at this point, because I feel that we are as near as the telephone, just as I feel I can reach you on the telephone. . . . I am concerned about your future activities. Are you going to be able to consult with us? You don't have to do this. There is no law requiring you to do this, but we are concerned. We are part of this; we would like to help you if we can."[69]

The confusion about Operation Babylift eventually appeared relatively minor compared to that surrounding the evacuation of 130,000 refugees that followed. In early April President Gerald Ford indicated that the United States had a plan to remove Vietnamese civilians, but he did not make it public, and Philip Habib of the State Department told the Senate Subcommittee on Refugees and Escapees several days later that the first priority was to remove American citizens and their dependents, numbering slightly under 4,000. As for the Vietnamese, the immediate plan called for the evacuation of 17,600 who had worked for the American government.[70] However, just before Saigon fell, the United States agreed to take all who worked for the American government at one time, along with their dependents, and those whose lives were considered in danger. The hasty decision-making process, the lack of planning, and the rapid fall of Saigon made for a pathetic situation of people desperately seeking to escape at the last moment. Some clung to helicopters as they took off, while others fled the capital and escaped by sea.[71]

Unlike the attitude toward the early Cubans or Vietnamese orphans, public opinion opposed resettling the Indochinese in the United States. The Gallup Poll found that 52 percent of those asked opposed the idea while only 36 percent favored it. The Harris Survey reported similar results. Several members of Congress disapproved accepting any rich generals who may have persecuted others or were war profiteers. Among the reasons uncovered by the polls for opposing additional newcomers was the belief that they would take jobs from Americans.[72] A few members of Congress expressed similar feelings. Representative John Conyers of Detroit, for example, said that the citizens of his city were not anti-Vietnamese, but that these refugees would aggravate unemployment in Detroit, while another Michigan congressional member suggested that any special financial aid rended the Indochinese should also be made available to Americans.[73] Most arguments against further immigration centered on economic themes and reflected the unfavorable economy of the mid-1970s, though racism might also have been a factor.[74]

Public opinion polls indicated uneasiness and even opposition to receiving Indochinese, but the refugees were not without friends. VOLAGS working with refugees favored receiving Vietnamese who wanted to come to America, although they were critical of the manner in which government policy was being carried out.[75] Major newspapers and prominent leaders also urged a humanitarian approach and liberal refugee policy. AFL-CIO President George Meany said that legislators opposed to the refugees were guilty of "meanness of spirit," and concluded, "If this great country can't absorb another 30,000 to 40,000 and find them jobs, we're denying our own heritage. The group is a drop in the bucket."[76]

While Congress watched the debacle in South Vietnam, the Ford Administration decided to use emergency funds to aid the refugees and announced that it would use the parole power to admit 130,000 of them. The Senate Judiciary Committee approved this action, though its approval was not required. When South

Vietnam fell to the Communists and when the administration decided to use the parole power the issue before Congress was largely moot and centered on how much money to appropriate for resettlement. Ford had originally wanted additional funds for military activities in Vietnam but the House rejected this request.[77] By 1975 many congressional members disapproved of any further military efforts and were suspicious of executive initiative. In spite of the reservations of some members of Congress about admitting refugees and spending money on them, Congress responded overwhelmingly in favor. The legislators did cut the administration's request for funds, but the vote in the House on its version was 381 to 31 while the senators approved their bill 77 to 2. The Senate and House disagreed over details and the amount, but by the time they agreed by voice vote and approved a $455 million aid bill, 130,000 refugees were already in the United States. The funds were to be used in resettlement, vocational training, medical care, language instruction, and other social services. In an attempt to assert some control over the process and obtain information about the resettlement program, Congress required that the administration's new Interagency Task Force on Indochina Refugees report on the resettlement of the refugees.[78]

As in the case of the Hungarians—but not the pre-1980 Cubans—who had been processed through Camp Kilmer, an army base in New Jersey, the government moved the Vietnamese through four military posts: Camp Pendleton, California; Fort Chafee, Arkansas; Eglin Air Force Base, Florida; and Fort Indian Town Gap, Pennsylvania. Working with VOLAGS, the government processed the refugees and resettled them into American society. The camp's program aimed to prepare them for their American experience while the VOLAGS found them homes and jobs. For the most part the VOLAGS were the same ones that had been working with Europeans and Cubans for years. The government also tried to disperse the refugees, although the largest group eventually settled in California. By mid-December 1975 the last camp was closed and the refugees settled.[79]

The Indochina Migration and Refugee Assistance Act of 1975 granted aid for only two years, and there still remained the problem of the refugees' status as parolees. In 1977 Congress passed legislation similar to the Cuban Adjustment Act that permitted the refugees to become resident aliens and extended aid for various social services. The program also covered several thousand who came after April and May 1975. By the fall of 1978 the federal government had spent over one billion dollars to assist the 170,000 Indochinese then in the United States.[80]

Those who came between the fall of 1975 and 1978 did not create the sensation presented by the spectacle of the mass and chaotic evacuation in the spring of 1975. Still, problems arose and the administration evoked the parole power, after consultation with some members of Congress, and requested additional funding for the Indochinese. Eleven thousand Laotians and additional Vietnamese arrived in 1976, and a steady trickle left Indochina throughout 1976 and 1977. Some of these persons had families already in the United States or had worked with the American government in South Vietnam. The Carter administration paroled an additional 15,000 in August 1977. These refugees had escaped by sea or were interned Laotians in Thailand.

Representative Joshua Eilberg said the Ford administration had promised not to ask for the admission of additional persons without specific legislation. Eilberg reminded Carter's attorney general, Griffen Bell, that in 1965 Congress had intended the parole power to be used for individuals and not large groups.[81] Bell assured the legislators he would consult with them, but that there were compelling humanitarian reasons to admit additional refugees. He expressed his reservations about the parole power and said he preferred regular refugee procedures. The attorney general admitted the 1952 Immigration Act's parole power "does not apply to groups. . . . It would appear that it was not intended for large groups."[82] Whatever Bell's reservations, within a few months he decided to consult once again with Congress and parole another 7,000 Indochinese who were escaping by boat.[83]

Events in Vietnam in 1978 precipitated a new crisis that made haggling over 7,000 or 15,000 new parolees a minor issue. The Communists proceeded to restructure their society and eliminate the business class, including the country's ethnic Chinese, who began to flee. The spreading war in Cambodia and the Communist takeover of Laos and the eruption of hostilities between Vietnam and China created still additional turmoil and more refugees. In August 1978 the number of Vietnamese seeking asylum elsewhere in Asia averaged about 6,000 per month, but by the spring of 1979 it reached 65,000 monthly. In desperation many bribed their way out and fled across the border to Thailand while others, the "boat people," escaped by sea on whatever boats they could find to Malaysia, Indonesia, Singapore, or Hong Kong. Amid horror stories of drownings, in December 1978 the UN High Commissioner for Refugees urged governments and shippers to rescue the refugees. Caring for the growing number of refugees was obviously beyond the capacity of neighboring nations in Southeast Asia. Some even turned these unfortunate people away, back to sea or forcing them to return to Cambodia.[84]

In response to the growing crisis, the Carter administration increased the number it planned to admit. In November 1978 Attorney General Bell announced that the United States would accept an additional 15,000 boat people by the next spring.[85] This addition soon proved to be inadequate to solve the growing problem. In 1978 private agencies aiding the refugees formed a Citizens Commission on Indochina Refugees and urged that the United States take more. By the spring of 1979 the administration was paroling 7,000 per month, but in June it announced that it would admit 14,000 monthly or a total of 168,000 in the next year.[86] Although the administration had the support of the VOLAGS and many national leaders and newspapers, public opinion was less enthusiastic. As in the case of the Mariel Cubans, both the Gallup Poll and the *New York Times*–CBS poll revealed majorities against relaxation of the immigration laws to admit additional boat people. However, most polled said they would personally welcome refugees if any settled nearby.[87] In September 1980 the administration concluded the crisis was still grave enough to admit another 14,000 Indochinese monthly for the next year. By that time the number of Indochinese in the United States exceeded 400,000 and the new admissions would push the total past the half million mark by early 1981.

The Reagan administration also wanted to stabilize refugee flows and policies. Consequently, refugees were encouraged to emigrate through the Orderly Departure Program (ODP). Under

ODP a system was developed to process refugees directly from Vietnam rather than the camps, and about 50,000 refugees entered the United States from 1980 and 1987 under ODP.[88] American policy makers also began to view later refugees as desiring to migrate to the United States for economic rather than political reasons.[89]

Yet the situation in Vietnam remained tragic, and thousands still fled by boat in the late 1980s. Not a few faced pirates at sea, and when they reached shore, not all were accepted in Southeast Asian refugee camps. In response the United States, which paid the bulk of refugee costs, prodded its Asian allies not to force the refugees to return. The Philippines foreign minister replied that if they would not return, then the "United States should accept all the Vietnamese refugees."[90] The State Department did agree to take thousands of refugees, but the camps were by no means emptied. In 1989 about 52,000 East Asian refugees were admitted and the Bush administration set a similar figure for 1990.[91] Some of those accepted by the United States were Amerasians, the children of American soldier fathers and Vietnamese women, who were unwanted in Vietnam.[92] As the 1980s came to a close, the United States had taken in approximately 900,000 Indochinese refugees with plans to accept more.

As in the past, Congress debated policy and voted additional funds to aid these latest refugees. For the most part, once the administration decided to use the parole power after consultation with a few congressional leaders, Congress voted funds to relieve local communities of the burden of caring for refugees which they believed to be a national matter. As Senator Alan Cranston of California, where many of them settled, said, "I do not think it is a wise or fair policy to ask only a few taxpayers to share the cost of our refugee admissions policy."[93]

Those Indochinese arriving during 1975 were on the whole an elite group. Disproportionately well educated and urban, they possessed higher incomes and held better jobs than did most Vietnamese. A considerable number were white-collar workers and even professionals. Many knew English, were Roman Catholic, and had close contacts with Americans in Vietnam. Not a few had originally lived in the north and had come south after the 1954

Geneva accords temporarily divided Vietnam.[94] Because of their contacts, sometimes as employees of the United States government or American companies, they felt particularly fearful of a Communist takeover.

Among those entering after 1975 were many ethnic Chinese who had been in business in South Vietnam. Also included were family members of those who had already left and thousands of other "high risk" persons who had fought in the South Vietnamese army or why had been associated in other ways with the governments of South Vietnam or the United States. Many had simply been unable to escape during the hectic days of April 1975. As Communism changed Vietnamese society they fled or were expelled. They were joined by thousands of uprooted peasants.[95]

Conditions in Laos and Cambodia created hundreds of thousands of other refugees. Laos became a Communist state in December 1975 and anti-Communist leaders fled. Among those seeking asylum was General Van Pao, who had led a clandestine army of Hmong hill tribesmen financed by the CIA. Their identification with the CIA made them vulnerable and they sought refuge in Thailand.[96] As Communist control tightened, others followed, including small farmers.

Conditions were worse in Cambodia, where opposing factions slaughtered one another. The Lon Nol Government, which assumed power in 1970, killed many ethnic Vietnamese and sent thousands of others fleeing to Vietnam or Thailand and other Southeast Asian nations. The continued hostilities after 1970, the bloodbath begun by Pol Pot's Khmer Rouge regime and Vietnamese invasion of Cambodia (1978) sent thousands more fleeing for safety. Although many of these persons were middle class and political elites, the vast majority, like the Laotians, represented a broader cross section of the population.[97]

The changing situation in Indochina was reflected in the new refugee population coming to the United States. After 1978 many of the refugees were commercial ethnic Chinese along with Cambodian peasants and Laotian Hmong tribesmen. Although some had been white-collar workers, these persons did not have such high levels of education and occupations as had the first group. Few of the 1975 Vietnamese were farmers, but many of the Laotians were. Nor could many refugees after 1975 speak English, and many Hmong were illiterate in their own language.[98]

Working through the VOLAGS and several special state agencies, the federal government tried to disperse the 1975 refugees throughout the United States. However, a large group congregated in California, especially the southern half of that state. Others lived for a few months or years in other states, then moved to California. Hence, California claimed about one third of this population. The next largest contingent settled in Texas, mainly in Houston and along the Gulf Coast. The rest located mostly in Virginia, Louisiana, New York, Pennsylvania, Minnesota, Oregon, Washington, and Illinois.[99] Refugees after 1975, though not coming through the camps, settled in these same areas, among or near other Indochinese. While concentration of the refugees quickly became a pattern, the dispersal program was not entirely unsuccessful. Indochinese refugees could be found throughout the United States, including small communities in New Hampshire, Iowa, and Montana.[100]

Because of their higher status, 1975 Vietnamese appeared to have had an easier time adjusting to the United States than those coming later. At first many of them had to apply for welfare or receive special English instruction. Within a few years, as they found jobs and were less apt to obtain government assistance, their employment rates matched American norms.[101] Yet, life was not always easy for them. Many professional and white-collar workers took blue-collar or low-paying jobs. These people encountered barriers of language, training, licensing, and residency requirements, similar to those of the elite Cubans. Government reports and scholars demonstrated that the initial refugees adjusted rapidly but had to work hard to make ends meet and were frequently downwardly mobile compared to their prior position in Vietnam.[102]

The success of Dung Quoch Nguyen illustrates the struggle. His family originally resided in the north and moved south after the Communists assumed control there in 1954. After graduating from law school, Nguyen became a law professor as well as a high official in the South Vietnamese government. His wife worked for an American bank, and when Saigon fell in 1975, the bank arranged to get them out. Processed through Camp Pendleton, he settled in New York and baby-sat for six months while his wife worked at the American office of her former employer, Chase Manhattan Bank. Like many of the elite, he knew some English, but Vietnamese law was quite different from American. Determined to be a lawyer, he took a clerkship as an alternative to law school, which was legal but unusual in New York. With hard work and the help of his law firm's tutoring, he passed the New York bar in 1978 on his second try, and received a license to practice law in New York the following year, the only Vietnamese immigrant up to that time to do so.[103]

Most of the 1975 exiles could not claim such success, and among the later refugees with fewer skills, greater health problems, less English, and fewer connections to the United States, the path appeared more difficult. As one worried local California official explained, "Among the initial influx of refugees in 1974 and 1975 were a high percentage of skilled and educated workers who were quickly assimilated into local communities. More recent immigration patterns, however, reveal that refugees presently entering the United States are from predominately agricultural and rural areas and have little or no education or employment skills."[104] Since they came directly to American communities without the camp experience, with its orientation about American society and English language instruction, they had additional problems.[105] Of course, the job market was especially poor during 1981–1983, which did not help. It was difficult to find adequate employment, and if they did, they aroused resentment among native Americans.

The later refugees, less familiar with American ways, also faced a greater cultural shock. Differences over family structure and roles, work, leisure, religion, social and cultural customs, and lifestyle were often sharp, promoting misunderstanding by Americans and hardship for the refugees. One example of the cultural difference occurred in the summer of 1980 when mountain tribesmen from Indochina were accused of stalking and killing squirrels, ducks, and stray dogs in San Francisco's Golden Gate Park, and then eating them. The director of the relocation program in that area noted that the refugees were simply reliving the way of life they had left behind. "Those reports do not surprise me. It's a way of life, a difference in cultures. . . . There are a lot of mountain-type people coming in. They are very basic people. It's just a way of life to hunt and trap, and they've brought it with them."106 In Philadelphia a similar situation existed. A resettlement worker there called a meeting with that city's Hmong refugees to persuade them not hunt pigeons with their crossbows.107

Other communities reported stories of cultural conflicts and resulting stress among the refugees. Authorities noted that among the refugees both in the camps and the United States, the suicide rate was higher than among the American population generally. The most tragic cases were those of sudden unexpected death syndrome (SUDS), which was linked to death of eighty refugees in the United States from 1975 to 1989. SUDS individuals died, mysteriously, in the middle of the night. SUDS was undoubtedly caused by extreme psychological stress, feelings of alienation and loneliness which are common to many refugees.108

Cultural differences and conflicts between Americans and Indochinese occasionally led to overt hostility and even violence. In New Orleans, several black leaders expressed anger at what they said were special programs and favors available to the newcomers but not the city's blacks.109 In 1979 in Denver, Colorado, clashes over jobs and housing between Mexican Americans and the refugees led to a near riot.110

Perhaps no incidents revealed the clash more than those occurring between Vietnamese and Texans in the fishing industry.111 In 1975 Vietnamese settled along the Gulf Coast to work in seafood companies and to fish. Those who were experienced quickly learned to work on their own. They became relatively successful, they used smaller boats and did not always follow American procedures and laws. Americans, for racial and economic reasons, resented the newcomers and the way they ran their businesses. High fuel prices and limited resources, coupled with low prices for shrimp and crabs made the competition especially aggravating to the Americans. "There's too many gooks and too few blue crabs," said one American. "The government gives them loans and houses but doesn't care about us. Who's gonna protect our rights? The Vietnamese are gonna take over, it just isn't right." In 1978 and 1979 violence erupted between the two groups. In the summer of 1979 in Seadrift, Texas, Vietnamese refugees killed an American trapper. The refugees were acquitted of murder charges. Two years later the Klan appeared at Seadrift but was barred after several cross burnings.[112] Although the Vietnamese appeared determined to stay and relations improved in some communities, their adjustment had not been easy.

Conflict will no doubt continue, even if in less violent ways. However, as the number of refugee admissions from Southeast Asia dropped after the early 1980s, further conflicts might be less. But the issue of assimilation of the later refugees and cost of welfare programs remained a concern, especially among communities where they settled. The turmoil along the Gulf Coast involved ethnic tensions and economic competition, but elsewhere some American officials worried that the post-1975 boat people might become a permanent welfare burden. Said Representative Romano Mazzoli in 1981, "This situation is unacceptable. All parties involved in the resettlement effort—Federal, State, and local governments, resettlement agencies, and mutual assistance associations must join together to place refugees on the road to self-sufficiency. . . . The high dependency rates of [Indochinese] refugees seriously concern members of Congress no less than the government officials in those states which contain large concentrations of refugees."[113] Whether welfare dependency would become a serious social problem depended on how well these latest refugees and their children adjusted, found jobs, and moved into the mainstream of American life.

Studies of welfare dependency revealed mixed results, but there is no doubt that many Indochinese were having a difficult time learning English and adjusting to America society. Some scholars blamed American programs for the alleged "welfare dependence," and they insisted that the refugees wanted to work. Others pointed to the horrendous experience of escaping from Southeast Asian nations and miserable conditions that many faced in refugee centers and the camps.[114]

Refugees from Right-Wing Oppression

If the American public expressed ambivalence and some hostility toward Cubans and Indochinese, the administration and Congress nonetheless received them and voted funds for their support. Such was not necessarily the case for those who could not claim flight from Communism. Outside of Cubans and Indochinese, Chinese, Soviet Jews and other Eastern Europeans, and Middle Easterners accounted for nearly all post-1960 refugees. Most were exiles from Communism. Those seeking refugee status or political asylum from right-wing dictatorships that the United States supported, or in some cases helped install, found an unsympathetic State Department and Immigration and Naturalization Service.

Chile

In 1973 rightists assassinated Chile's leftist President Salvador Allende and overthrew his government. Because the United States had backed the revolution it was reluctant to admit Chileans deposed by the coup. Of course, the Western Hemisphere lacked a refugee preference prior to 1977 but they could have been paroled like the Cubans. Citing strict security restrictions on immigration, State Department officials commented that Chilean leftists might not find the United States a "congenial" place to live.

Two years after the coup Secretary of State William Rogers told a Senate Committee that of the 12,224 persons who fled Chile, the United States took only 26. The State Department noted difficulties in getting security clearances as a major reason for the meager response to the exiles, but by way of contrast, 80,000 Vietnamese had obtained their security clearances within three months.[115] John Schauer, vice chair of the Committee on Migration and Refugee Affairs of the American Council of Agencies for Foreign Service, a group representing the major VOLAGS, noted that America's profession of being nonpolitical in receiving refugees was marred by a whole "series of comedies of error and tragedy that comes upon people who are caught in this maze of bureaucracy which exists in Washington."[116] Between 1974 and 1977 the Justice Department admitted several hundred more Chileans, and on the eve of President Carter's 1978 visit to Brazil, announced plans to accept 500 Chileans and Argentines, including some directly from prison, over a two-year period. A few more were authorized to enter later.[117]

These Latin Americans confronted another disadvantage once admitted. Congress had only allowed the Cubans and Indochinese to adjust their status, unless they came as seventh preference, conditional entrants, which was impossible for persons in the Western Hemisphere before 1977. The 1978 amendments to the Immigration and Nationality Act corrected this situation and permitted all paroled newcomers, including those in the Western Hemisphere, to adjust their status to resident aliens, providing they entered before September 1981. Chileans, as did some others, faced one final distinction between themselves and Indochinese and Cubans; the aid programs for refugees varied and they were not eligible. The 1980 Refugee Act which changed the definition of refugee from its essential anti-Communist stance finally corrected this inequity.[118]

Haiti

No group fleeing right-wing oppression and economic deprivation illustrated the anti-Communist bias and foreign policy foundations of American refugee policy more than the Haitians. Some Haitians had entered by air and overstayed their visitor visas, usually in New York City, while others arrived in rickety boats on the beaches of Florida, beginning in 1972. No one knew for certain how many had arrived and lived in Florida, but estimates ran as high as 20,000 to 30,000 in 1980 when another boat people, the Mariel Cubans, dramatized their plight.

Most of those arriving in Florida were penniless and without proper documents; hence, the federal government considered them illegal aliens who should be expelled. Periodic horror stories of sinking boats and unscrupulous smugglers dramatized their fate as did their treatment at the hands of the INS. In August 1979, for example, smugglers off West Palm Beach forced several Haitians overboard at gunpoint when police spotted their boat. Five children and their mother were drowned in this particular incident, but it was not the first, nor the last, such disaster.[119]

Unlike Cubans or the Indochinese, Haitians encountered a hostile government that refused to admit them as political refugees. However, another possiblity existed for them to become resident aliens. Because they were already on American soil when apprehended, they could claim asylum as distinct from refugee status that applies to those outside the United States. Although immigration laws contained no precise provision for those already on American soil to claim asylum, in 1968 the United States Senate had acceded to the United Nations Protocol on Refugees. This protocol, to which the United States was now bound, provided a way for those already here to claim asylum.

To win asylum, Haitians had to prove they had a "well-founded fear" that they would be subject to persecution on account of race, religion, nationality, or political opinion if they were returned home. A State Department official explained in 1974, "Asylum is only available to persons who have taken a stand in direct contradiction to their government," and this meant only those who were outspoken in their opposition.[120] This was difficult to prove and had to be done on a case-by-case basis, unlike parole given by the attorney general for large numbers of people. In 1968, for example, members of the Haitian Coast Guard who landed in Florida received asylum because they had participated in a revolt against the right-wing dictator Dr. François Duvalier.[121] But what poor Haitian who had landed in Florida could claim similar opposition? Few convinced the government to give them asylum. One obvious reason why neither the State Department nor the immigration officials were willing to admit that these people were eligible for political asylum was the fact that the United States supported the repressive Haitian government of Duvalier and then of his son who succeeded his father as dictator upon his death in 1971. The Haitian government in turn supported American objectives in organizations such as the Organization of American States. Even after ratification of the UN Protocol, the United States looked unfavorably on exiles from right-wing dictatorships like Haiti's, and during the 1970s most asylum cases involved fugitives from Communism, such as artists defecting from the Soviet Union.[122]

While asylum, like refugee status, was generally reserved for those supposedly fleeing Communism, claiming asylum did have one advantage. Because the Haitians were already here, they were entitled to a hearing and deportation proceedings. However, a House Committee in 1976 discovered that these proceedings were irregular and that few Haitians were properly prepared to present their cases. Too poor to post bail, Haitians found themselves in jail awaiting deportation.[123]

Although they lacked a well-organized community like the Cuban Americans to help them, the Haitians were not without friends. Civil rights and church groups helped them and took up their cause in the courts. The National Council of Churches, the Haitian Refugee Center of Florida, and the National Emergency Civil Liberties Union fought with class action suits. They claimed because the United States had acceded in 1968 to the United Nations-sponsored Protocol Relating to the Status of Refugees, the Haitians were entitled to asylum and due process pending their appeals. While the court battle went on, in November 1977 INS Commissioner Leonel Castillo agreed with the National Council of Churches to release, without bond, all detained Haitians seeking asylum and to grant them a hearing before an immigration judge. The INS soon changed its mind, however, and issued new regulations aimed at deporting the Haitians. The National Council of Churches challenged the new regulations in court and in July 1979 won a temporary suspension of the deportation proceedings.[124]

At issue were questions of proper procedures and the State Department's claim that these Caribbean people were economic and not political refugees. A State Department team visiting Haiti in June 1979 reported that although some cases might be considered political, their study indicated most of the migrants came for economic reasons and those deported were not subject to persecution. Concluded the State Department, "Interviews indicated that most Haitian migrants come to the U.S. drawn by the prospect of economic opportunity and not fleeing political persecution. . . . Economic motives, however admirable, do not translate into a right under the [U.N.] Protocol to asylum."[125]

Advocates of the Haitians insisted that while many were desperately poor, the regime in Haiti was guilty of brutal political repression. One journalist criticized the all-white State Department investigating team, noting it ignored an obvious dilemma, "the only people who will speak out in Haiti are those who have nothing to fear. . . . No one in Haiti is going to risk openly criticizing the government, particularly not to four white strangers." Moreover, he said, the study team stated that it used the local radio stations to advertise for people to come forth, "but they do not mention that the government owns or at least controls all the radio stations in Haiti."[126]

The congressional Black Caucus, which set up a task force on the Haitian refugees, said that continual frustration in dealing with the executive branch made it conclude that the only "practical, just and humanitarian way to resolve the plight of these . . . 'boat people' was to grant them refugee status." VOLAGS and prominent church leaders agreed, and they and the black congressional members pointed out that because Haitians were black many suspected the reason for their difficulties was racism and not politics alone.[127] Racism or not, the treatment of the Haitians also illustrated the attitude of the United States toward refugees or those seeking asylum, like Haitians and Chileans, from right-wing dictatorships supported by the United States. While Haitians had such difficulty, a Senate committee reported in 1980 that the United States considers all Vietnamese and Laotians who reach "safe haven in Asia as refugees. . . . There is no case-by-case screening to determine if the person is likely to be persecuted if returned to his country of origin, which is the definition of 'refugee' according to the 1980 U.S. Refugee Act and the United Nations usage. By contrast, American policy is more strict towards persons who flee non-Communist countries, as evidenced in the initial case-by-case screening of Haitian refugees."[128]

As a result of the class action suit, in early July 1980 the United States District Court in Florida held that INS had violated the constitutional rights of the Haitians and ordered INS to process the cases properly. Judge James King declared:

Those Haitians who came to the United States seeking freedom and justice did not find it. Instead, they were confronted with an Immigration and Naturalization Service determined to deport them. The decision was made among high INS officials to expel Haitians, despite whatever claims to asylum individual Haitians might have. A program was set up to accomplish this goal. The program resulted in wholesale violation of due process, and only Haitians were effected.[129]

Shortly before the case neared a decision, the Carter administration felt pressure to treat the Haitians the same as the Cubans, especially in view of the new 1980 Refugee Act that defined refugees broadly. Congresswoman Shirley Chisholm chided the administration for its talk of wanting to treat all equally as a "blatant lie."[130] The administration refused to use the new act to include Haitians, but in granting "entrant" status to Mariel Cubans it included the Haitians. This covered only those who were in INS proceedings as of June 19, 1980, later extended to October 10, 1980, when the status was granted. When the Reagan administration announced that it would permit the Mariel Cubans to adjust their status under the 1966 Cuban Adjustment Act, Haitians were omitted, much to the chagrin of friends of the Haitians. Finally, the Immigration Reform and Control Act of 1986 gave these Haitians the right to become resident aliens.

Government Stances

The essential anti-Communist definition of *refugee* and imprecise and crude asylum procedures and the resultant difficulties of Haitians made congressional liberals eager to change the meaning of who is a refugee and bring that definition into accord with the broader UN Protocol. They also disliked the two-year "conditional entrant" status for refugees. They noted that refugees were usually quickly cleared. Liberals urged that the conditional entry category be abolished, except for emergencies, and that refugees be admitted as regular resident aliens. Other congressional members disapproved of executive control over refugee flows by the use of the parole power, while still others worried about the growing number of refugees and federal cost of supporting them. In all, refugee policy appeared confused, ad hoc, and lacking procedures that the seventh preference of the 1965 act was supposed to have given.

As early as 1969 Senator Edward Kennedy urged changes in procedures. In 1975 he produced another bill to increase the flow to 36,000 and to broaden the definition of refugee away from "its present European and cold war framework."[131] Representative Joshua Eilberg in the House was especially agitated by the constant use of the parole power and ad hoc measures.[132] He also introduced legislation for a more permanent program though his proposal was less generous than Kennedy's. These proposals did not pass.

In 1978 when Congress created the Select Commission on Immigration and Refugee Policy to examine issues about immigration and refugees and recommend changes, Congress appeared to have postponed action until the commission reported. But the situation was so serious by 1979 that the lawmakers and the administration decided to change procedures and practices before the commission's report was due in 1981.

By 1979 a consensus emerged about the need for reform. Early that year the Carter administration proposed an overhaul of the existing refugee procedures and programs. Working with the Senate Judiciary Committee, the administration presented a bill to increase the normal flow of refugees to 50,000, which was about the average since the 1960s. The 50,000 figure would have increased total U.S. immigration to 320,000 annually, not counting immediate family members of U.S. citizens. The bill also granted the President the power to admit additional refugees after consultation with Congress, if he deemed it a humanitarian issue or in the national interest. The increase in numbers was not controversial nor was the proposed new definition to conform to the United Nation's Convention and Protocol Relating to the Status of Refugees in place of the American definition emphasizing those fleeing communism or the Middle East. The United States had already accepted the UN definition in theory though it was not written into immigration law. The new definition said a refugee was "any person who is outside any country of his nationality or in the case of a person having no nationality, is outside any country in which he last habitually resided, and who is unable or unwilling to return to, and is unable or unwilling to avail himself of the protection of that country because of persecution, or a well-founded fear of persecution, on account of race, religion, nationality, membership of a particular social group, or political opinion."[133] The bill proved to be noncontroversial in the Senate. The Senate Judiciary Committee approved it by a 17 to 0 vote, and the senators passed it 85 to 0. The floor leaders were the unusual combination of Edward Kennedy and Strom Thurman, conservative Republican of South Carolina. The only major change made on the floor of the committee's bill was an addition to federal funding to assist refugees. Senators S. I. Hayakawa and Alan Cranston, both of California, the state in which about one third of Indochinese had settled, co-sponsored an amendment to provide federal funding for two more years for those refugees already admitted but still in need. The amendment also provided for assistance for a 36-month period for all new Indochinese refugees in place of the 24 months called for in the refugee bill. The senators accepted the amendment easily, but it reflected a growing uncertainty about the cost of refugee programs.[134]

In the House, however, final passage was not easily obtained. Most representatives agreed that refugee policy needed reform, but there the agreement ended. House liberals accepted most of the Senate's bill, but many representatives had reservations not only about the Senate bill but also about the role of the administration in determining refugee policy. The Senate passed its bill in early September, but three months later the House rejected it and passed its own bill, on December 20.[135]

The House was less generous toward refugees than the Senate and insisted upon a key provision that allowed either chamber to veto a presidential determination for the admission of additional refugees, except in emergencies. Many representatives wanted this power, for they opposed the attorney general's parole power to admit refugees in large groups and believed that Congress had lost control over immigration. Other, less important, differences existed between the two chambers, and no agreement could be reached in December.

Consultation between the two houses and the administration eventually led to a Conference Report in February and the enactment of the 1980 Refugee Act. The legislators compromised most differences. As enacted, the law increased the "normal flow" to 50,000 and accepted the new definition of refugee. The House wanted to keep the two-year conditional entrant status for refugees but accepted a compromise of one year, after which time they could become resident aliens. The act also created the Office of U.S. Coordinator for Refugee Affairs, appointed by the President with the Senate's consent and with the rank of ambassador at large; centralized most programs in the Department of Health, Education, and Welfare; and provided continued funding for refugees. The controversial matter remained the power to veto the President's decisions to admit additional refugees. House opponents of the conference bill wanted either House to have a veto whereas the report merely said the President must consult with Congress. The opponents said the bill gave too much power to the President and that it was time to restore to Congress "control of the number of refugees . . . because that is where the Constitution places it."[136] Because of the increase in the number of refugees and new provisions for admitting additional ones, the bill provided for an end, effective sixty days after the passage of the bill, to the use of the attorney general's parole power. Finally, the conference bill carried, but the vote was close, 207 to 192 in the House. Southern Democrats joined with Republicans in voting against the bill, but they lost.[137]

One final provision of the 1980 act deserves notice. The legislators sought to solve the asylum issue by providing for the first time in law procedures for asylum and reserving up to 5,000 places annually for those requesting political asylum in the United States. However, the procedures were left unspecified, to be drawn up by the attorney general, and the figure of 5,000 soon proved to be inadequate if the United States intended to pursue a generous asylum policy.[138]

Senators hoped, as the Senate Committee on the Judiciary explained, to solve the refugee problem because the new act "establishes for the first time a comprehensive United States refugee resettlement and assistance policy."[139] Yet, as in the case of other pieces of immigration legislation, the Refugee Act did not resolve all problems. As noted, Carter chose not to invoke the act when he permitted Cubans and Haitians to enter as a special group of "Cuban-Haitian entrants." Moreover, the "normal flow" of 50,000 was inadequate. Both the Carter and the Reagan administrations, after consulting Congress, admitted considerably more than that figure. Such admissions, including the Cubans and Haitians, topped 300,000 in 1980 and averaged nearly 150,000 from to 1981 to 1983. The admission of these additional persons meant that Congress had to confront again the question of financing them.

Administrative decisions, larger numbers of refugees than anticipated, and the cost of refugee programs demonstrated how legislators did not control affairs. The unsettled nature of American policy was nowhere demonstrated more clearly than the issues of a definition of a refugee and the matter of asylum. The definition of a refugee was closely linked to the asylum question and the latter became an important issue which Congress did not forsee in 1980.

Congress changed the definition from its rigid anti-Communism, but neither the Carter nor the Reagan administrations showed much inclination to shift previous policies. The vast majority of refugee admissions after April 1980 were from Cuba, the Soviet Union, Eastern Europe, and Indochina, persons supposedly fleeing Communism. Refugees from Communism also included Ethiopians, added in part because of pressure by the Black Caucus and its allies, and Afghans. A few others came from non-Communist regimes unfriendly to the United States. Prospects for persons being admitted as refugees from right wing dictatorships supported financially and militarily by the United States were about as remote as before. Immediately after Congress passed the 1980 act the Carter administration proposed its refugee admissions for the next year. From Haiti none were to be admitted because, as the administration told Congress, "We are not proposing to admit any Haitians as refugees because we do not expect that a significant number of those outside the United States will meet the eligibility requirement of the Refugee Act definition and demonstrate that they are subject to political persecution in their homeland."[140] By way of contrast, the administration said about Soviet refugees: "It has been the policy of the United States to offer a haven to *any* [italics mine] refugee from the Soviet Union who wishes to resettle in this country. This will remain our policy."[141]

More Problems for Haitians

As before, except for those admitted along with the Mariel Cubans, Haitians had to come to the United States first, usually illegally, and then attempt to win asylum on an individual case-by-case basis, to prove that if they were deported they faced a "well-founded fear of persecution." The Carter administration assured

Congress that it was aware of the "abysmal series of human rights abuses that Haiti has known practically throughout its 180-year history. . . . We know how far Haiti falls short of observance of internationally accepted human rights standards, and we have labored hard to use the limited footholds a country like Haiti affords." But at the same time, the State Department insisted that criteria for asylum "must be a narrow and carefully focused standard," which made it extremely difficult for individual Haitians to win asylum.[142]

The Reagan administration went even further to expel Haitians. In early 1981 INS moved to deport those coming after October 11, 1980, the cut-off date for Cuban-Haitian entrants.[143] Next, the President ordered the Coast Guard to intercept and turn around boats suspected of carrying Haitians and place those seized in the United States in detention centers, which were little better than jails, while their applications were pending. The interdiction policy continued after the overthrow of the hated Duvalier regime in 1986 because that revolution did not immediately bring peace and democracy to Haiti. Violence, political unrest, and military rule continued in that Caribbean nation until a democratic election was held in 1991. Thus many Haitians still chose to leave, but the interdiction policy effectively cut the flow of potential refugees from Haiti. From 1982 to 1989 the Coast Guard and INS reported that 21,000 Haitians were intercepted on the high seas and that the vast bulk were returned to Haiti. Only a handful were admitted to pursue their asylum claims or for emergency medical care.[144] Congressional opponents argued that Haitians got the "short end of the stick," and that this policy was illegal, but it continued nonetheless.[145]

Litigation by groups sympathetic to the Haitians finally won a partial shift in government detention policy in the early 1980s. Beginning in the summer of 1982 the courts ordered a number of Haitians paroled to community sponsors pending their appeals. A reluctant federal government then released about 3,500 from the camps in Florida, New York, and Puerto Rico.[146] However, their chances of winning asylum were very slight. And for those who entered after 1982 by slipping through the Coast Guard's interdiction, detention and rejection of their asylum claim awaited. Both the Reagan and Bush administrations considered Haitians to be illegal economic migrants, not legitimate asylees.

Central America

Deteriorating conditions in the late 1980s in Central America send tens of thousands northward in hope of a better life, even if their chances of winning political asylum were slight. Many crossed the border at Harlingen, Texas, near Brownsville. In late 1988 INS announced a new policy to relieve the growing number of asylum requests, running at nearly 2,000 per week at that time. INS decided to hear the cases of those crossing at Harlingen immediately, without allowing them to leave the area.[147] As thousands gathered in tents and other makeshift quarters, friends of the Central Americans won a temporary restraining order suspending this policy, thus permitting thousands to flee the border area. Miami, the destination of many Nicaraguans, was not pleased; officials there said the city was overburdened with refugees and had no housing or jobs for them.[148] A federal judge eventually reinstated INS detention policy, but the aliens had other crossing points, and many requested asylum at places other than Harlingen.[149]

The government objected to these Central Americans, and especially to Salvadorans, on the same ground that it opposed giving asylum to Haitians. INS insisted that these "feet people" were economic migrants and not political refugees. INS recognized the existence of civil wars and violence in Central America, but said that each person must have a "well-founded fear of persecution" to gain asylum, which was nearly impossible to prove to the authorities. One application was granted asylum for the fiscal year 1980–1981, and as of January 31, 1982, INS granted only seven and denied 165. Over 8,900 applications were pending at that time.[150]

Like Haitians, Salvadorans had friends among church and civil rights groups and in the courts. Several judges halted INS deportation proceedings in 1982 on the ground of lack of due process.[151] Even an investigation by the United Nations High Commissioner for Refugees criticized American procedures.[152]

Reacting to political pressure, in September 1983 the Reagan administration quietly informed Congress that it would admit as many as two hundred Salvadorans as refugees. Although this action constituted an admission that the government the United States supported in El Salvador persecuted at least some of its opponents, the administration made clear that it did not intend to indicate a major shift in either refugee or foreign policy. The vast majority of the 72,000 refugees to be admitted during fiscal 1984, were to be from the usual sources, Vietnam, Cambodia, Laos, the Soviet Union, and Eastern Europe.[153]

While battles went on in the courts, several communities and church groups, including New York's large Riverside Church, pledged to house the Salvadorans. Though such protection was clearly "harboring" an undocumented alien, and hence in violation of the laws, Beverly McFarland, spokeswoman for INS offices in New York, declared in 1983, "We have absolutely no intention of provoking any confrontation with any church." In Los Angeles church women picketed INS offices when officials were deporting Salvadorans.[154]

In spite of McFarland's statement, the government did move against several churches and individuals. In Texas it successfully prosecuted Jack Elder and, in a major case, it planted an agent at a Tucson, Arizona, church which had declared itself a sanctuary for Central American refugees. In 1986 the government won its case against the Reverend John Fife, minister of the Southside Presbyterian Church, and several religious leaders associated with the sanctuary movement. Defendants were given suspended sentences, and federal prosecutors indicated that no more cases would be brought to court.[155] At the same time other sanctuary leaders said they would presevere. But the cases seemed to thwart the sanctuary movement and to shift the fight to Congress.[156]

Simply being from a country where refugees were accepted as being anti-Communist was no guarantee that asylum was automatic. Following the Soviet invasion of Afghanistan, hundreds of thousands of Afghans fled to neighboring Pakistan. The United States took several thousand of these uprooted people, but was unwilling to grant asylum to those that entered illegally and then requested asylum. In 1983 immigration authorities detained forty such Afghans in a former Navy jail in Brooklyn while their applications for asylum were pending. Immigration authorities indicated that they preferred the Afghans to apply to be admitted as refugees from Pakistan rather than enter the United States without proper papers. The situation of the Afghans was similar to most of those already in the United States asking for asylum. Asylum was difficult to obtain regardless of which country the application came from.[157] A major consideration was the consequences of a liberal asylum granting policy. Government officials worried that if asylum were easy to obtain once on American soil, would that not encourage tens of thousands of others to enter illegally or as tourists and then request asylum from the American government? The backlog of those here asking to stay grew rapidly in the early 1980s, even without a liberal policy.

Political issues aside, asylum applications by Afghans, Salvadorans, and Haitians were part of a growing number unforseen in 1980. Doris Meissner, acting commissioner of INS in 1981, told a Senate committee that year: "No one involved in the drafting of the Refugee Act of 1980 anticipated that the asylum process would come to assume the major role it occupies today in the structure of immigration law." She noted that Congress and those concerned in drafting the 1980 law centered on refugees outside the United States wanting to come here and that "the asylum process was looked upon as a separate and considerably less significant subject."[158]

From the time the immigration authorities first instituted asylum regulations in 1972 until 1980, the number of requests was never large; about 3,702 applied in 1978 and 5,801 the next year. The law projected 5,000 cases per year, but after it passed applications rose sharply. Between March 1980 and July 1981 53,000 persons in the United States applied for asylum and 50,000 more requests resulted from the Mariel boat lift. INS officials projected another 50,000 requests after July 1981. By 1983 over 170,000 applications from 53 countries were on file. S. Scott Burke, head of the State Department's asylum division, summarized the trend: "Ten years ago, we received a couple of hundred a year. Now we get 30,000 to 40,000. There's a backlog of more than 170,000 cases, and it keeps growing."[159] Most were from third world nations such as Cuba, Haiti, El Salvador, Nicaragua, Ethiopia, and Iran.

In addition to winning asylum from INS or temporarily remaining in the United States while their cases were pending, potential refugees had another recourse. Under "extended voluntary departure" (EVD) granted by the Justice Department, those in the United States could remain until that status was changed. The justification for this status was that a changed political situation in their homeland, while nonimmigrants were visiting the United States, would mean that they would be persecuted if they returned home. In the late 1970s the Justice Department granted extended voluntary departure to nationals from Iran, Nicaragua, Ethiopia, and Uganda for various periods of time.[160] When Poland declared martial law in 1981, the United States granted extended voluntary departure to several thousand Poles in the United States at that time. Friends of Salvadorans and Haitians suggested a similar status be granted to these nationals. The *New York Times* stated their case in 1983, "If El Salvador is dangerous, as the State Department reports in other contexts, then forcing Salvadorans to return home may subject them to danger and death. Why does the Reagan Administration err on the side of peril? Why not, temporarily, err on the side of safety? Why let Poles stay but not Salvadorans"?[161] The Reagan administration denied the request. In 1987 President Jose Napoleon Duarte of El Salvador made a direct appeal to President Reagan not to deport Salvadorans who were illegally in the United States. President Duarte requested a temporary stay of deportation and argued that because of "a severe economic crisis" in his country it could not absorb hundreds of thousands of Salvadorans if the United States deported them. But President Reagan refused to grant the request.[162]

Extended voluntary departure was not dissimilar to parole in that the executive branch determined who received it. Moreover, it virtually created a new category of temporary refugees. Yet, it was also a limbo state and could be changed. In late 1981 and early 1982 the State Department announced its intention to revoke this status for Ethiopians and to order INS to deport them. They had originally been granted extended voluntary departure because they were fugitives from a Marxist government that took over Ethiopia in 1974. The department said that a change was warranted for two reasons. First, the department insisted that conditions had changed in Ethiopia, and second that this status encouraged Ethiopians to enter the United States as visitors and then claim extended voluntary departure to avoid deportation once their nonimmigrant permit expired. Said one INS official, "There was a period when things were pretty grim. But bodies aren't turning up in neighborhoods anymore. Random violence is no longer occurring. We don't grant asylum just because you like the standard of living here. . . . Our policy was widely known here and in Ethiopia and it was subject to widespread abuse."[163] Protests led by the Black Caucus prompted the State Department to back down.[164]

Realizing that the administration would not grant EVD to Salvadorans or Haitians, their allies turned to Congress. Proposals were made to write into law EVD or a temporary "safe haven" for Central American refugees. Both Nicaraguans and Salvadorans were included in the first proposals. Nicaraguans, although fleeing a Marxist regime that the Reagan administration was trying to overthrow, were also unable to win asylum. Only 14 percent of the 15,856 Nicaraguan requests for asylum between 1983 and 1986 were granted.[165] The administration insisted that the vast bulk of claims were not based on a "well-founded fear of persecution," but rather represented people who wanted to come to the United States for economic reasons. While this was better than Salvadorans' success rate of under 3 percent, it was nonetheless not encouraging for potential asylees.

Because of President Reagan's support of the Contras attempt to overthrown the Sandinista government in Nicaragua, the situation was embarrassing to the Reagan administration. Indeed, the chief official of INS in Florida said in April 1986, that he would no longer deport Nicaraguans. The official declared, "I would personally—not just as a Government official, but personally—have trouble sending people from a Communist country back to that country. Morally and ethically it would be wrong to send people back to Nicaragua when we are at great odds with that Government."[166] Several months later Attorney General Edwin Meese III granted them EVD.[167] With the loss of power by the Sandinistas in the election of 1990, anti-Communists and other dissidents were free to return. How many would do so was not known, especially in view of the enormous economic problems faced by Nicaragua.

In Congress, House members, led by Representative Joe Moakley (D-Mass.), continued to push for safe haven for Salvadorans. The House passed such a bill on several occasions and managed to include a safe haven clause in their version of IRCA. But the senators thought otherwise and it was deleted in Conference. Moakley and his supporters, chiefly Dennis DeConcini (D.-Ariz.) in the Senate, did not give up. While the Bush administration appeared unenthusiastic about safe haven, Congress included an 18-month stay of deportation for Salvadorans in the liberal Immigration Act of 1990.

Safe haven represented a partial victory for those wanting to help Salvadorans. There still remained the issue of asylum and what would happen after the 18-month period ended. In the late 1980s court decisions indicated a potential shift in criteria for asylum cases. In March 1987, the U.S. Supreme Court rejected the rigid criteria the government had been using about "a well-founded fear of persecution" that asylum seekers had to demonstrate.[168] A year later a federal district judge ruled that the federal government had coerced Salvadorans seeking asylum into leaving the country and ordered INS to halt the practice. Because this case effected all Salvadorans it opened the possibility of many obtaining a fairer hearing from the government.[169] In 1990 the Bush administration went one step further and established new rules for asylum cases that lawyers and VOLAGS said would make it easier to obtain asylum. Finally, in December 1990, after passage of the 1990 Immigration Act, the federal government announced that it would no longer deport either Salvadorans or Guatemalans and would grant new hearings for several hundred thousand persons who had been denied asylum or who were waiting for their cases to be heard. And the cases were to be heard by specially trained judges and officials.[170]

Whether the new changes would lead to a drastic shift in asylum policy was not known, but a growing number of persons were being granted asylum in the late 1980s. In 1989, 9,229 received asylum while 31,547 were denied, with 77,000 cases pending.[171] In recognition of the small figure of 5,000 asylum places in the Refugee Act of 1980, the Immigration Act of 1990 increased the figure to 10,000. Because nearly that number won asylum in 1989, this gesture was simply an acknowledgment of the reality, and was by no means an answer to the asylum problem. As long as conditions remained deplorable in various nations whose citizens could get to the United States, the asylum issue would remain. It was obviously easy to cut the flow of potential refugees from an island nation like Haiti, but plugging the Mexican–U.S. border was not so easy, as the next chapter demonstrates.

Grappling with asylum for Central American refugees was not the only refugee issue faced by the United States as the 1980s came to an end. The refugee question in Eastern Europe and especially the Soviet Union suddenly loomed as the Soviets opened the door for emigration and Eastern European nations threw off their Communist regimes. In 1989 the Bush administration, citing "the democratic evolution" in Poland and Hungary, announced that it would no longer accept refugee applications for those countries. Between 1981 and that announcement some 33,000 Poles and 5,400 Hungarians had qualified as refugees to the United States. If they had close family ties to the United States, nationals from those countries could still apply for admission. Moreover, the Immigration Act of 1990 provided special places for countries disadvantaged by the 1965 immigration reforms, and Eastern European nations were among those nations, thus opening the door for possible emigration from Eastern Europe.[172]

The situation in the Soviet Union was somewhat different. After their government tightened emigration restrictions in 1981, few Soviets obtained exit visas to the United States. Then in 1987 the Soviet Union once again began to allow its citizens to emigrate. As a result thousands of Soviet Armenians, Jews, and Pentecoastals came to the United States as refugees.[173] Indeed, the bottleneck shifted from the Soviet Union to the United States, and especially the American embassy in Moscow. The Bush administration announced increases in Soviet immigration, but more people wanted to come than it was willing to admit. Angry congressmen insisted that because of anti-Semitism all Russian Jews should be considered refugees, and because the United States had been willing to take those who got out in the past, the United States should continue to do so.[174]

President Bush suggested a new immigrant category, one based on national foreign policy interest. Such a category would permit the admission of additional immigrants but they would not be eligible for refugee funds.[175] Eventually the administration agreed to increase the Soviet allotment to 50,000 (of the 1990 total of 131,000) of whom 40,000 would be refugees and 10,000 parolees whose cost of settlement would be assumed by VOLAGS. In September 1990, the State Department also made arrangements to airlift 6,000 Soviet evangelical Christians to the United States. These compromises eased the crisis, at least temporarily, but the fact that Soviet Jews were going to Israel, where they were welcome, also helped resolve it.[176]

Clearly dramatic foreign events directly effected refugee flows. Congress did try to look into the future. In the Immigration Act of 1990, with an eye toward the future absorption of Hong Kong by China, the legislators agreed to take in additional Hong Kong immigrants. But it was difficult to predict what would happen elsewhere. An unsettled world with deep American involvement had led to refugee and immigrant flows in the past (Korea, Cuba, and Vietnam, for example) and there was no reason to believe that refugee issues would be easily resolved in the future. Indeed, the "special protected status" provision of the 1990 Immigration Act granting a stay of deportation for Salvadorans could be used for others. It granted the Attorney General the right to give persons temporary status in the United States if they come from countries subject to armed conflict, natural disasters, or other extraordinary conditions. In February 1991, Attorney General Dick Thornburgh granted that one-year status, which carried with it the right to work, to an estimated 51,000 Lebanese, Kuwaitis, and Liberians.[177]

7

Undocumented Aliens: People and Politics

For a few years following the Immigration and Naturalization Service's boasting about the success of Operation Wetback in ridding the nation of the "menace" of illegal aliens there appeared to be little or no problem concerning these people. The service continued both its roundup and deportation of newcomers without proper papers and its border enforcement activities. The numbers apprehended were not especially large and averaged fewer than 100,000 annually from 1956 to 1964.[1] The Senate and House paid little attention to undocumented immigrants while reforming immigration policy in 1965. As noted, Congress debated national origins, labor controls, legal immigration size, family unification, the Asia-Pacific Triangle, and refugees. For most, illegal immigration had been effectively dealt with by Operation Wetback and the activities of INS, especially along the Mexican border.

Congress did discuss undocumented immigration while abolishing the bracero program in 1964. Several persons noted that because the program permitted Mexicans to work temporarily in the United States ending it would lead to an increase of undocumented persons streaming across the border. The Mexican ambassador to the United States, among others, had suggested at the time that illegal immigration might increase, and events were to prove him correct.[2] Not all could agree with this assessment, however, for changes in American agriculture after 1950 lessened the demand for bracero-type labor. The introduction of labor-saving devices such as the cotton picker eliminated many jobs formerly held by temporary farm workers, and the high rate of technological change continued in the years after 1964, with new machines to harvest tomatoes, cling peaches, lettuce, olives, and even more delicate crops like apricots, asparagus, and grapes. By 1979 about one third of California's grape crop was being harvested by machines, not hands. Giant wheel and track machines straddled two or four rows of grape vines and with pulsating pedals shook the vines. The grapes then fell onto a padded conveyor belt and dropped into a gondola.[3]

While these machines replaced farm labor they did not eliminate it entirely, and because wages for hired hands remained low in the Southwest, agricultural opportunities remained. If Mexicans could not manage to cross the border legally, they willingly slipped by the Border Patrol. Owners and managers of agribusiness ignored the legal status of their workers. Indeed, undocumented aliens eager for work made ideal low-cost laborers in the fields of Arizona, California, and Texas. Thus, it was not surprising that after the last of the braceros went home, INS found increasing numbers of Mexicans trying to cross the border. Apprehensions, for example, increased from 86,597 in 1964 to 283,557 in 1969.[4]

The numbers continued to grow and in the late 1970s and early 1980s INS apprehended about one million persons annually, mostly along the Mexican-American border where the service concentrated its resources and personnel. Yet, the growth in apprehensions and the movement of illegals into the United States was not simply a repeat of the 1940s and 1950s when they were usually Mexicans seeking farm work. Changes in the structure of the American economy after World War II opened up large numbers of relatively low-paying service and light manufacturing jobs in American cities. Many of these industries and jobs were found in California, especially Los Angeles, and along the United States-Mexican border stretching from California to Texas. New York City also became a center and home for many illegal workers, but so did other cities like Chicago. New York's and Los Angeles' garment factories, and restaurants, laundries, hotels, and hospitals nearly everywhere willingly employed persons without proper papers.

As early as 1969 Congress began to investigate the increase in illegal immigration along the Mexican border and its impact on

Southwest agriculture. Witnesses told a Senate committee that undocumented laborers on American farms made the organization of farm workers unions difficult.[5] Senator Walter Mondale stated, "But my basic complaint is that we have a massive poverty population coming into the country virtually every day from Mexico. We thought we stopped it when we eliminated the bracero program, but now other methods for commuting across the border perpetuate the problem so it is just as bad as it was 15 years ago. We need a rational policy to stop that hemorrhaging . . . along the Texas border and along the California border. . . . You have to be an idiot not to know how to get across that border to work in the United States."[6]

If the changing American economy provided the lure for the undocumented, conditions described in Chapter 5 explain why so many Mexicans and people from the Caribbean basin countries wanted to leave. Precise data on who undocumented aliens are is lacking, yet the many studies of the past decade do show that persons entering illegally had networks and knowledge similar to those of the legal migrants. If anything, scholars believe that persons entering without documents have even less education and are poorer than their legal counterparts. Many were nearly poverty stricken and the incentive for migration was strong.

Risks, including death, described below, abound for some persons trying to enter the United States illegally. Yet, it is important to note that, with the exception perhaps of Haitians or Salvadorans entering without documents, but claiming refugee status, few legal sanctions or penalties are imposed on those who are caught. As noted in Chapter 6, Haitians and Salvadorans sometimes found themselves in jail awaiting their claims for asylum. Most who attempted to enter without inspection (EWI) and were apprehended were simply sent home even though it was a crime to be in the United States illegally. The government in many cases even provided the transportation. Smugglers of undocumented aliens did run a risk of fines and jail sentences if caught but not the aliens themselves if they departed voluntarily. Critics such as the United States Civil Rights Commission have criticized INS's handling of apprehended suspected undocumented persons and the lack of rights these persons have in deportation proceedings.[7] But the essential point remains that the undocumented will usually be sent home quickly and not detained in American courts and jails or tried and sentenced to prison for trying to enter or live in the United States without proper immigration papers.

Given this lack of punishment, it is not surprising that many attempted to enter the United States, and if caught, voluntarily returned home only to try again to cross the border, maybe even the same day. The fact that so many of those apprehended were such "repeaters" means that approximately one million caught by INS in 1978 or 1983, for example, were not necessarily one million different people.

Available employment in the United States, lack of penalty for being caught, dire conditions at home, family and friends to help—all help explain the surge in illegal immigration after the mid-1960s. Yet, it is also important to emphasize how easy it is to enter the United States.

Because immigration authorities have concentrated their attention along the nearly 2,000-mile Mexican border, the vast majority of those caught—about 90 percent—are Mexicans or others trying to cross that border. The border between the United States and Mexico has not been sealed. At any one time in the 1970s and early 1980s the INS Border Patrol had about three hundred on duty, which means that miles and miles were left virtually unguarded.[8] Rivers, rough terrain, blistering heat, and fences aided the Border Patrol in their efforts to halt the flow. Yet, the Rio Grande can be waded at certain spots and fences were frequently full of holes, making crossing easy at night. Use of aircraft, autos and, after 1972, even electronic sensor devices helped the patrol increase its mobility and efficiency. One reporter in 1973 wrote that the patrol's sensors' "readout console becomes a Christmas tree" at night at the busy crossing cite at San Ysidro, California.[9] This technology helped, but the manpower of INS along the border was simply unable to keep up with the increase in those entering without inspection (EWI) after 1965. More than one critic has pointed out that many large cities had more police than did the Border Patrol. The federal government even employed more guards for the nation's capital than it did to police the southern border of the United States. Yet even with increases in manpower

INS had difficulties. In early 1984 INS officials said that if the Border Patrol were substantially increased it could still not stem the flow.[10]

No one knew how many escaped apprehension at the border. Estimates ranged as high as one person caught for every three entering, a figure seemingly high and alarmist. But once across the border it became easier for the undocumented to escape detection. INS barrio raids, factory inspections, bus terminal apprehensions, and surprise checks on New York's Chinatown restaurants may have terrorized many undocumented aliens and angered Hispanic and Chinese leaders and civil libertarians, but they did not necessarily lead to the deportation of large numbers of aliens.[11]

While slipping across America's southern border might have been the most popular method of EWI, countless others used false papers which they flashed at the border crossings. Still other persons had permits to enter the United States to shop or visit, but once here, intended to stay on, at least temporarily, to work. The number of daily crossings grew steadily in the post-war era, virtually overwhelming the immigration inspectors. In 1978 over 250 million crossers were recorded entering the United States, most of them across the Mexican border. At the San Ysidro station, 20 million alone crossed yearly. There 104 inspectors, working three shifts, handled the inspections, which allowed less than one minute per inspection.[12]

The border separating the United States and Canada had fewer controls. Though the volume of persons crossing between the United States and Canada was less than the southern border, it was relatively easy to slip in undetected from Canada. Indeed, some persons first went to Canada as visitors or even immigrants and then crossed unnoticed into the United States. In 1983 INS reported increased smuggling across the Canadian border. INS officials said that smugglers were paid from $1,500 to $2,000 to get aliens into the United States. The aliens flew from the Caribbean to Toronto where they arranged entry into the United States. INS was particularly unhappy because it had been shifting personnel from the northern border to the busy Mexican border and such shifts would hamper future INS controls along the Canadian border.[13]

Crossing from Mexico or Canada was not the only possibility for working and living in the United States without proper documents. The colossal growth in world travel brought increasing numbers of persons to the United States after 1960. As noted, excluding border crossers, INS recorded over nine million such nonimmigrants entering the United States in 1978, a nearly fivefold increase in eighteen years.[14] These included visitors, business people, diplomats, and students. By 1982 over 300,000 foreign students alone were studying in American colleges and universities.[15] Once here, many students stayed beyond the time allotted on their nonimmigrant temporary visas and took jobs and lived illegally.

That such visa abusers, or overstays as they were called, could do so easily occurred because the United States was fairly generous in admitting temporary visitors and because of a virtual breakdown in INS to account for them once they arrived. Member of Congress Elizabeth Holtzman, chair of the House Committee on Immigration, declared in 1980, "It's an agency out of control with nineteenth-century tools. Record-keeping is a disaster. There's not one part of the place that seems professional to me."[16] Another immigration expert, who served as general counsel to the agency from 1966 to 1974, said: "The INS has become a disaster area. They're overcrowded and understaffed. They don't have the ability to cope with the influx. It's sort of like putting your finger in the dike."[17]

Congressional funding for bureaucratic improvement and staffing was meager after 1960, not enough to police adequately the nation's borders or keep up with the mounds of paperwork created by the growing millions of nonimmigrant visitors. In 1979 INS conducted a test of apparent overstays of visas. Examination of the status of 3,374 persons thought to overstay consumed 8,700 staff hours and resulted in the location of only four deportable aliens. About a third, unknown to the agency before the test, had already left the country. Another third could not be located nor could their departure be verified. In short, INS did not know where they were.[18]

Two years later, INS officials disclosed that INS had been unable to keep track of some 30 million forms recently filed by foreigners when they entered or left the United States, and that it would take two years before that backlog would be eased.[19]

Even shifting to computers did not solve INS's bureaucratic nightmare. The associate commissioner for information service said in 1981 that over 600,000 visitors' requests for extensions of their temporary visits could not be put into the computer because they could not be matched with the original arrival forms.[20] Thus, countless thousands of temporary visitors could easily overstay their visas because the government did not know where they were, nor did INS have the manpower to chase them down if it did know.

Keeping track of foreign students was one of the most difficult tasks of INS. The point was made forcibly following the crisis precipitated by the Iranian seizure of the American embassy in Tehran in 1979. In retaliation, President Jimmy Carter asked the immigration authorities to report on the status of Iranian students in the United States. When the service admitted that it did not know where the students were or how many were here, INS asked the Iranians to come forward on their own and report. Before a federal court stopped the process, 56,000 reported, of whom about 6,000 were found to be in violation of their status. Some agency officials even suggested that the total number of Iranians might be nearly double that figure and admitted they did not even know how many Iranian diplomatic and consular staff members were in the United States.[21] Frustrated INS officials suggested in 1982 that the task of keeping track of foreign students be turned over to educational institutions, a proposal which drew immediate opposition from both colleges and universities as well as some politicians who saw the suggestion as shifting a federal agency responsibility to private and state institutions. INS officials, on the other hand, insisted that many students used their visas to enter the United States ostensibly to study, but really to work or find some way to remain in the United States permanently.[22]

A few critics suggested that understaffing and inefficiency were not the agency's only explanation for its failure to control illegal immigration. They charged the agency was rife with corruption. A *New York Times* investigation in 1980 reported the familiar charges of bribery, payoffs from ranchers and other employers, and the solicitation of sexual favors in exchange for admission to the United States.[23] A 1981 Jack Nicholson move, *The Border,* alluded to the same themes. Some INS employees were investigated, indicted, and even convicted, but not many. Even the agency's own complaint or corruption division seemed mired in inefficiency. INS deputy director Mario Noto declared when he took office in 1977, that the investigations unit was

run by a few individuals who felt that they were accountable only to themselves and to God. The net result of it was that I inherited hundreds of cases that had been hanging on, subject to investigation for years, on some of the most flimsy of allegations which should have been clarified very soon and which, unfortunately, cast a cloud upon the individuals concerned, bringing about havoc in private lives, impeding effective and efficient operations, and, in short, the unit, called the internal investigations unit, had been left to its own devices and it operated on the whim, the caprices of the people that were immediately responsible for its administration and supervision.[24]

Improvements after that date won praise from the Civil Rights Commission in 1981, but did not end the charges of corruption.[25]

While EWIs on their own or visa abusers made up the vast bulk of illegal aliens, other potential undocumented aliens sought out smugglers to help them. While it was only a misdemeanor to live in the United States illegally, and not a federal crime to employ the undocumented, smuggling persons across the border or manufacturing and selling fraudulent governmental documents were against the law. Yet, the desire of so many to enter made smuggling a lucrative business. Moreover, it was so easy to obtain counterfeit documents, such as Social Security cards, that smuggling and the use of counterfeit cards grew after 1965. Some schemes were novel and imaginative while others ran risks, especially for those being smuggled, and led to their deaths.

Fraudulent marriages were not new ways to obtain entry in the 1970s or 1980s, but the officials of INS believed their use was growing at an alarming rate, and in 1974 launched an offensive to halt them. Because of the preference given to spouses of American citizens or resident aliens under the immigration laws, years of waiting could be clipped from the long waiting lines for an American visa. Hence, in Mexico, the Philippines, the Caribbean, and elsewhere in Latin America, entrepreneurs sold false marriage papers to persons eager to enter the United States or arranged marriages to Americans whom the prospective immigrant did not know or had never seen. By the late 1970s such arrangements cost up to one thousand dollars, a high price, but to many worth the cost.26

As INS suspicion grew, the agency increased its investigations. Agents asked careful questions of those suspected of fraud, though the volume of cases overwhelmed officials and fraud was difficult to prove. Moreover, questioning suspects about their private lives raised civil liberties issues. One of the most enterprizing marriage brokers was caught in Florida where one woman allegedly arranged fourteen marriages. She was charged with marrying six men herself and helping her daughters each marry three men and her common-law husband marry two women.27

How extensive was such marriage fraud? In 1985 INS Commissioner Alan Nelson told a Senate committee investigating marriage fraud that based on his agency's surveys about 30 percent of the marriages to obtain a visa were a sham.28 In 1986, the same year that Congress was passing the Immigration Reform and Control Act (IRCA), the legislators also passed the Immigration Marriage Fraud Amendments to the Immigration and Nationality Act, which tightened the rules on all aliens' spouses and children who became permanent resident aliens by virtue of marriage.29

Marriages not exactly arranged in heaven, while perhaps ingenious at times, were not as numerous as seeking out a smuggler—called a coyote—and paying a few hundred dollars to take one across the border and perhaps even land a job, sometimes as far north as Chicago, New York City, or Washington, D.C. The coyotes, with their claimed superior knowledge of how to avoid a *la migra* (INS agent) and savvy in finding jobs, grew in demand, especially along the Mexican border, in the 1970s. The deteriorating Mexican economy in the early 1980s made the demand stronger as INS apprehended record numbers of those attempting to enter without inspection in the early 1980s as over one million annually were caught in those years. In 1986 a record 1.6 million persons were apprehended; after passage of IRCA the number dropped but still remained high.[30] The practice of smuggling, along with the price, rose steadily and ran to several hundred dollars per person by 1980. Smugglers would usually meet the prospective migrants in the northern Mexican cities and then take them across the border by foot at night. Tijuana was a popular staging area as was Ciudad Juarez where smugglers could be seen in the Plaza Monumental making deals. One Border Patrol official likened the coyotes to peddlers. "You can see negotiations being made all over the place," he noted.[31] In other cases, the coyotes packed people in trucks and vans, slipped across the border (or picked them up on the American side), and then took their human cargoes to jobs in northern cities.

Such smuggling activities ended in disaster on more than one occasion. In 1968, coyotes locked forty-five Mexican nationals in a two-ton truck for more than thirteen hours. Promised jobs in Chicago for $12 apiece, they ended up in San Antonio where they were abandoned by the driver. Locked in the truck, one died and another twelve had to be hospitalized for heat prostration. One recalled the trip as a "nightmare." Another declared: "We had no idea we were coming to San Antonio. All we had been promised was that we would be taken to Chicago where we could get jobs. . . . The truck left Eagle Pass (Texas) at daylight this morning and then the horror began. There was no ventilation and we were being bounced around like cattle in the back of the truck."[32]

Other such horror stories were not uncommon.[33] But perhaps the worst incident occurred in the summer of 1980 in Arizona. A group of Salvadorans had paid smugglers to take them across the Mexican border, for a price of $1,200 each, only to be abandoned and lost in the scorching heat of the Arizona desert where temperatures topped 110 degrees. Of the original group, thirteen died, and three of the women reported they had been raped. The group had been ill-prepared for their ordeal. Several of the women wore high-heeled shoes and others carried heavy suitcases filled with winter clothes and books. When the group became lost and separated, and desperate for water under the blazing sun, they reported drinking after-shave lotion, deodorant, and finally their own urine.[34]

After 1965 a growing number of aliens were apprehended in the process of being smuggled across the border and a growing number of coyotes were arrested. By 1976 stepped-up INS operations led to the apprehension of 9,600 smugglers; three years later the total was nearly double that. Yet, of those arrested in 1979, only about one third of the convicted served time in jail. "We get a lot of probated sentences," remarked one official. "That leaves a lot to be desired."[35] Too often those arrested were small-time operators, not the top men in large and profitable smuggling rings. Given the low risk of a jail sentence, especially for first offenders, these coyotes were willing to go back into business again. As a General Accounting Office report put it in 1980, "Penalties for those convicted were mostly minor. Hence, many are apt to remain in the smuggling business."[36] On occasion, the government did catch and indict big-time operators. In July 1982, the government arrested a Mexican national who ran a ring allegedly bringing in 24,000 persons annually.[37]

Hapless aliens found themselves victims not only at the mercy of the smugglers' neglect, but also confined in jail when these coyotes were caught. On occasion the federal government jailed these undocumented aliens, including some of their young children, as material witnesses. The American Civil Liberties Union, for example, claimed that thousands of such aliens were being detained in American jails for periods ranging up to several months.[38]

Once into the United States beyond the immediate border region, the chances of being caught dramatically dropped. Immigration authorities, badly understaffed, devoted most of their resources to policing the Mexican border, to prevent EWIs rather than to catching them once here. Within large cities like Los Angeles, Chicago, New York, or San Antonio, sizable communities of their fellow nationals awaited the undocumented aliens to help them find jobs and housing. It was not against the federal law to employ such persons, and the few state laws enacted to outlaw the employment of undocumented aliens were unenforced; hence, employers ran no risk in hiring them. If they were paid off the books, no identification was needed.

For those jobs requiring some identification and the withholding of taxes, fraudulent papers abounded. Fake "green cards" (permanent alien registration cards) were coveted and somewhat expensive, and could run over $1,000 by 1980. Counterfeit or even authentic green cards were known to have been sold in foreign lands, or "rented" temporarily to enable persons to enter. They could then be rented again and again. In 1984, a Costa Rican government official reported that hundreds of Taiwanese and Cubans had Costa Rican passports which were either forged or obtained under false pretenses and then used them to enter the United States. About the same time a reporter for the *Los Angeles Times* wrote that Hong Kong residents, fearful of the future takeover of the colony by China, were purchasing forged Paraguayan as well as Costa Rican passports. They then hoped to use these documents to migrate to the United States. Others, he reported, had paid up to $5,000 or more to obtain American documents.[39]

Many state and local documents, on the other hand, were relatively easy to obtain and much cheaper than the documents mentioned above. Each year in the 1970s several thousand state and local governments issued millions of birth certificates, mostly by mail. An undocumented alien or other person could purchase one or get one by following the obituaries, and after locating someone of about the same age who died, requesting a birth certificate in that person's name from the appropriate governmental agency.[40] Once in possession of a birth certificate, one could obtain other documents, such as state driver's licenses or Social Security cards.

Next to a green card the most important and common federal card was a Social Security card. Increasingly, this card has been used for national identification, though that purpose had not been envisioned by Congress when it enacted the Social Security law in 1935.[41] Prior to 1972 the Social Security Administration's field offices virtually issued cards over the counter without requiring proof of identity. After that time the administration tightened its procedures requiring identification to obtain a card, and in 1974 field offices began to ask for documentary evidence of age, identity, and citizenship or alien status, and to conduct interviews with those over age 18.[42] Because other identification was available, the abuse of Social Security cards did not cease after 1974. Government investigations into fraud turned up some astounding cases. In one instance an individual in Oregon procured 170 Social Se-

curity numbers and filed over 50 false income tax returns for re-
funds before being discovered. In another, officials charged a re-
cipient in California with using false identifications, including
Social Security cards, to assume the identity of eight separate
persons with a total of 47 children to cheat the government in Aid
to Dependent Children and food stamp programs.[43]

Immigration agents did raid business establishments and
homes suspected of employing and housing illegal aliens. Barrio
raids by *la migra* in Los Angeles and other cities led to the deportation of thousands of undocumented aliens. Several ethnic groups
and civil libertarians opposed such raids and they went to court to
halt them.

Raids on New York City's Chinese restaurants in 1970 and 1971,
in which INS agents searched for alleged illegal Chinese seamen
from Hong Kong and Taiwan who had jumped ship, led to protests by the Chinese-American community and a modification of
INS policy.[44] Two years later Chicano leaders in both Los Angeles
and Chicago assailed sweeping INS raids in their ethnic communities, charging the government with abuse of individual rights.[45]
A few years later in Washington, D.C., an INS raid on Blackie's
House of Beef, ended up in court action by the owner and a
decision by the U.S. District Court that this particular raid was
unlawful.[46]

Protests and legal action curtailed but did not end INS raids.
Yet, other factors were at work as well. As the 1980 census counting period approached, INS agents eased their activities because
they feared such raids and roundups would hinder an accurate
census count, especially among Hispanics.[47] Two years later in a
national series of raids, called "Project Jobs," INS agents rounded
up 5,410 employed aliens and persuaded 4,107 of them to leave
the country. These raids took place in cities from New York to
California but mainly involved Mexicans. Once again Hispanic
groups protested. "We're appalled at the raids," sad Joaquin Avila,
president general counsel of the Mexican American Legal Defense
and Educational Fund. "This will seriously affect the rights of
Hispanics when they seek employment."[48] The purpose of the
raids was to open jobs for other Americans, or as the chief of
special investigations of INS in New York said, "We are very satis-

fied with the results. . . . We have created 500 jobs for unemployed Americans, some of them paying $5 an hour or better."[49] Yet, the success of "Project Jobs" was not so apparent. Several companies reported that some of the arrested aliens, once released, returned to work a week later, and the *Wall Street Journal* reported after six months that few Americans were working in the vacated jobs, which paid an average wage of only $4.81 per hour, largely for unskilled work.[50]

The political nature of INS community and business raids, the legal complications and the dubious results pointed to the difficulty of controlling illegal immigration by such methods. As porous as the border between the United States and Mexico appeared to be, INS efforts at immigration control were still more effective when they were concentrated along the border. About 85 percent of deportable aliens were seized at border points within a few hours or minutes of their entry, the rest later during internal operations. Yet, one side effect of INS roundups was the political debate over the impact of undocumented immigration upon the American economy and the debate over employer sanctions, both of which will be discussed below.

Spectacular raids, sharply increasing apprehensions, and growing media coverage—sometimes sensational—all contributed to heightened political and public awareness of undocumented aliens after 1968, especially during the 1970s and early 1980s when inflation along the slumps hit the nation's economy. Media coverage picked up around 1972. In that year, *U. S. News and World Report* headlined: "Surge of Illegal Immigrants Across American Borders." "Never have so many aliens swarmed illegally into U.S.—millions, moving across the nation. For Government, they are becoming a costly headache."[51] The *New York Times*, among other papers, ran feature stories on the undocumented. In 1974 the paper reported of a "silent invasion," and said in a front-page story that one million lived in the New York Metropolitan area alone.[52] Two years later, the *New Orleans Times-Picayune* in reporting as estimate of INS, declared "Illegal Aliens: They Invade U.S. 8.2 Million Strong."[53] In 1977 when INS apprehensions topped one million, the *Tucson Citizen* headline read: "Highest Total Since 1954: Illegal Alien Catch: 1 Million."[54]

Sensational media coverage of an alleged invasion or horde of illegal aliens was accompanied by a debate among public officials, politicians, and scholars over just how many undocumented aliens lived and worked in the United States during the 1970s and their impact on American society. The numbers game produced wild and unsubstantiated guesses. During the mid-1970s the main source for INS figures was the commissioner of the agency, Leonard F. Chapman, a former career U.S. Marines officer, who took over in November 1973. Although Chapman's and INS's estimates were sometimes couched in admissions about the lack of hard and reliable data, these statements gave the impression of millions of illegals residing in the United States with harmful effects on American society and the American economy. Chapman repeated his estimates before congressional committees and claimed that there were at least six to seven million illegals in the United States and that the figure could be as high as ten to twelve million.[55] He gave his story a popular twist when he wrote an article for the *Reader's Digest* in 1976 entitled, "Illegal Aliens: Time to Call a Halt."[56]

In response to criticism of its figures, INS commissioned a study in 1975 to come up with better figures. The study was conducted by the Washington D.C. consulting firm of Lesko Associates. The Lesko study concluded that the number was between four and eleven million, and settled on an average of 8.2 million of whom 5.2 million were Mexicans.[57] Other researchers quickly pointed out that the Lesko report was tenuous at best and did not rest on hard data.[58] Congress funded another INS-sponsored study in 1976. However, when the organization carrying out the study, J. A. Reyes Associates, failed to produce a final report because it allegedly ran out of funds, a conflict developed between INS and Reyes. About one million dollars was eventually spent, but no study produced, nor would the firm make its interviews available when INS canceled the contract in 1975.[59] Under INS commissioner Leonel Castillo, who took over in 1977, INS generally stopped making estimates and admitted that reliable data were unavailable, though Castillo thought the number might be between three and six million.[60]

INS officials were not the only ones included in the undocumented aliens numbers game. Various other governmental officials and scholars produced studies and estimates. Evelyn Mann of the Population Office of the City Planning Department of New York, for example, told a House committee in 1978 that the figure was about 750,000 in New York City. When asked her sources, she said, "Frankly, we have no data on which to build a precise estimate," though she insisted the figure was not entirely arbitrary.[61]

Not surprisingly, a three-year study by the Mexican government, based on extensive interviews and concluded in 1979, placed the number of Mexican undocumented aliens in the United States lower than most American estimates. The Mexican figure was between 480,000 and 1.22 million, depending on the season. Mexican scholars noted that many of the illegals were not permanent residents in the United States, but lived and worked there only temporarily, only to return to Mexico.[62] This view was held by some academic scholars as well, such as Wayne Cornelius of the University of California at San Diego.[63]

The emotional and vexing numbers game could hardly be avoided by the Select Commission on Immigration and Refugee Policy when it was established by Congress in 1978. The commission recognized the magnitude, and perhaps impossibility, of accurately counting undocumented aliens, and instead received permission from the Bureau of the Census to have three of its top demographers review the literature on the subject. In 1980 the demographers noted the controversy, the lack of hard data, and the methodological errors in the various studies and reported that no reliable count was available. The bureau concluded:

Although the number of illegal residents in the United States remains uncertain, the authors are willing to make some inferences from the available studies with regard to the possible magnitude of the numbers. They offer the following cautious speculations. The total number of illegals resident in the United States for some recent year, such as 1978, is almost certainly below 6 million and may be substantially less, possibly only 3.5 to 5 million. The existing estimates of illegal residents based on empirical studies simply do not support the claim that there are very many millions (i.e., over 6 million) of unlawful residents in the United States.[64]

Since that time, most observers have concluded that an accurate figure was simply unavailable. Extreme estimates of ten to twelve million seem to be less popular, though the *Saginaw News* (Michigan) told its readers in August 1982, "As many as 15 million are already here." Most suggest, however, that several, perhaps three to five, million undocumented aliens lived in the United States in the early 1980s.[65]

While the size of the undocumented population was unknown and subject to politics and emotionally charged estimates, considerably more was known about who the undocumented migrants were. Field work by scholars in Mexico, the barrios, and other ethnic communities of American cities, interviews and studies of those apprehended, and widespread journalist reporting about these individuals and their families and their struggles to live in the United States brought to light a great deal of information. Governmental legal action in other cases revealed additional data.[66]

Undocumented aliens hailed from nearly all parts of the world. Hong Kong and Greek sailors jumping ship in American ports, students and visitors from Iran or Israel overstaying their visas, Dominicans slipping into New York City from Puerto Rico, and Mexicans crossing the border—with or without the help of coyotes—all were part of the post-1965 undocumented alien population. While Mexicans constituted 90 percent of the INS apprehensions, most observers believed this was due to the agency's concentration of enforcement along the border. At the same time it appeared that Mexicans made up the largest single nationality among the undocumented and probably accounted for about half or more of that population. But whether the figure was precisely 45 or 55 or 65 percent no one knew for certain. Mexicans along with others from the Central America and the Caribbean—from Haiti, the West Indies, and the Dominican Republic—probably accounted for the vast majority of the illegals. Israel may have also contributed a fairly large number with smaller groups from South America, China, and Greece. Africa contributed few immigrants, legal or illegal, and the numbers from northern and western Europe do not appear large.

Undocumented persons seem to settle in the same areas as other resident aliens, especially in New York, Texas, Florida, and California or in cities like Chicago. That they did so is no surprise because there low-paying jobs were available and there too their documented country people had established communities which spoke their language and helped them find jobs, housing, and recreation. Hence, in places like the East Los Angeles barrio, undocumented and documented aliens lived together, along with second- or even third-generation Mexican-American citizens. The mingling of documented and undocumented was such that observers found them in the same houses, members of the same families. Of course, being a person without proper immigration papers made one vulnerable for exploitation economically and legally, faced with the daily possibility of deportation, but for many in these communities distinctions between documented and undocumented were largely moot. They believed themselves to be part of one community, held together by the common bonds of nationality, friendship, and even kinship.

One of the earliest studies done on undocumented aliens was carried out by Marion Houstoun and immigration expert David North in 1976. Their study was of just under 800 apprehended aliens, mostly Mexicans. These aliens were generally young males with low levels of education and skills who came to the United States in search of work. Some had been here before and after returning to Mexico, again entered the United States to work. The vast bulk paid taxes and few used social services such as schools, hospitals, or unemployment insurance.[67] Political scientist Wayne Cornelius and Jorge A. Bustamente, interviewing aliens in Mexico in different studies, found similar results. They emphasized the temporary nature of undocumented migration from Mexico. A sizable proportion of those Cornelius interviewed had been to the United States before as braceros or knew someone who had been a bracero. He found that their villages had knowledge of working conditions in America, and like braceros, their motivation for migration was largely economic, an escape from poverty, underemployment, or unemployment.[68] Other studies of Mexicans generally confirm the portrait of a young, predominately male migration with low level of skills and education who often go back and forth between the two countries.[69]

Studies by scholars of Mexicans going back and forth were matched by the observations of INS officials along the border. Apprehensions by INS agents fell in December when many of the undocumented returned home for visits. Remarked one agent in Texas, "It happens every December. If they're working up north, say in Chicago, they start getting cold and homesick this time of year. Just like you and me, they want to be with their families for Christmas. So they pack up and head south. We just wave bye-bye to them." In the late 1970s INS border officials ceased to check carefully suspected illegals heading south, largely because of a lack of manpower, but also, "We quit bothering them going south—we consider it a plus if some go home."[70] Not all have accepted this view of migration; some scholars and politicians suggested that in the late 1970s, undocumented Mexicans had higher levels of education than before, were more apt to be urban in background, and were inclined to stay for longer periods of time in the United States, perhaps even permanently.[71]

Difficulties of generalizations being drawn from studies of Mexicans alone were revealed by scholars who studied samples of non-Mexican undocumented immigrants. Two scholars' research on Dominicans and Haitians in New York City turned up similarities with North and Houstoun but also some differences.[72] This study, done in 1976–1977, revealed higher educational levels and a slightly older population. While nine of ten in the North and Houstoun study were male, the sex ratios were more nearly equal in the New York City results. The migrants also appeared to stay in the United States for longer periods of time than did the Mexicans.[73]

Like Mexicans, however, most Dominicans and Haitians worked and paid taxes, but higher proportions used social services like food stamps, hospitals, and clinics, public schools, and unemployment insurance. Yet, the vast bulk came to work and not to use social services; consequently, their rate of such utilization was low. Other studies have discovered similar characteristics of non-Mexicans.[74]

The differences revealed by the studies suggested that undocumented immigrant flows were not all alike, in spite of the methodological problems in conducting such research. Interviews in the home country, for example, naturally biased the findings in favor of the temporary nature of migration, toward a pattern of circulatory migration. Interviewing those apprehended by INS could easily reveal a different type of migrant than those found by other methods. The very nature of an illegal status made so many of these persons unwilling to talk and thus made it difficult if not impossible to have representative samples in the various studies.

Regardless of the limitations of studies of undocumented aliens, they all seem to indicate common themes, whether about Mexicans in the Southwest or Caribbeans in New York City. The undocumented, generally without high levels of skills and education, come to the United States to work. Although they have contacts through kin, friends, or smugglers to find jobs, their lack of legal status, unfamiliarity with American customs and institutions, and frequently lack of fluency in English make them vulnerable in the labor market.

The most shocking episodes of exploitation involved Hispanics in agriculture and promoted federal government investigations, which eventually led to arrests and indictments under peonage laws. In Louisiana federal investigators charged a chicken farmer with enslaving two illegal Mexicans and chaining them around the neck with iron chains. In late 1979 the rancher pleaded guilty to one count of peonage in a plea bargaining agreement that permitted other charges to be dropped. The farmer received five year's probation and three month's imprisonment. That was the first successful federal conviction under the peonage laws involving Mexican undocumented aliens.[75]

The next year two Arizona ranchers were indicted for torturing several undocumented aliens. After several trials, one was convicted. The government successfully prosecuted several other individuals under these laws.[76] While the number of investigations grew and led to a few indictments on slavery and peonage charges, federal officials as well as reporters, social workers, and farm union organizers claimed that thousands more were being virtually enslaved by unscrupulous labor contractors and farmers and growers. They said these desperate and poor migrants were being shipped around the country to work for various farmers and growers during seasonal labor. "You're not talking about something isolated," lamented a Texas INS official. Another agreed, "There's a significant amount of that going on."[77]

While physical brutality was the most sensational and sadistic way of exploiting these migratory farm workers, others found themselves jammed into trucks and moved from one place to another, one equally as bad as the next. These included not only farms in Florida but also potato fields in Idaho. Because these poor workers were desperate for employment and ignorant of American law and could be threatened with deportation, they lived and labored in fear. While chains were extreme, federal officials reported some growers used armed patrols and threats of deportation to keep their workers in line. Living conditions were hardly ideal on many ranches, nor were the places where the migrants lived while awaiting to be delivered by smugglers and labor contractors to their places of employment. In March 1979, for example, immigration officials found one such place—called a "drop house"—in Houston, housing twenty-eight Mexicans. There they had lived behind boarded windows guarded by armed men for two weeks. Immigration officials claimed that they had found as many as fifty aliens living in one or two rooms or shacks for long periods with no mattresses or sanitary facilities.[78]

Most undocumented farm workers did not experience such horrendous treatment. Rather, they obtained jobs through families and friends. Yet, agricultural work was among the lowest paid in the United States and usually lacked fringe benefits. Not until the mid-1960s did the federal government begin to include farm workers under labor legislation and not until 1975 did California finally pass a law permitting farm workers to unionize. Growers complained that they could not get American citizens to supply their labor. Reminiscent of the 1950s, during the fight over the continuation of the bracero agreement, one citrus grower in California lamented in 1975, "It's impossible to get locals or domestics to do this work. It's hard work. We just don't get people coming around asking for farm work anymore." Another grower said, "The only people who will do this kind of work are Mexicans."[79] And, in many cases, he might have said, undocumented Mexicans. These growers, long used to a supply of cheap stoop labor, complained of INS raids which they insisted deprived them of their needed workers.[80]

Farm union leaders, on the other hand, griped about the use of illegal workers and how they hindered union drives. They claimed that the preference of growers for illegals was a way for them to keep wages down and unions out of the fields. Because most such workers in the Southwest were Mexicans and so many other farm workers were Mexican Americans, leaders like Cesar Chavez of the United Farm Workers (UFW) found themselves in an awkward position developing a policy on undocumented aliens. The UFW had been built on Chicano ethnic solidarity and how to approach the undocumented was a touchy issue. At times the UFW appeared to want the INS to keep illegals out of the fields as strike breakers and as cheap laborers. At other times, the UFW attempted to organize all farm workers regardless of their status.[81] "We won't decide who will eat and who won't," declared one UFW leader. "We're not going to say that one worker can feed his family and another can't because one is here legally and the other isn't."[82]

As important as illegal labor was for Southwest agribusiness and migratory labor in the South and Northeast, most undocumented immigrants after the 1960s did not work in agriculture. With increased automation phasing out agricultural employment and with higher wages being paid in the cities, the undocumented headed for urban areas in search of a better life.

Urban undocumented aliens worked in a wide variety of occupations. Ironically, illegals were even found employed by governmental law enforcement agencies, including the Immigration Service. In 1975 INS located two illegals working in a cleaning crew at its headquarters. Two more were found guarding the FBI building in Newark, New Jersey; two at INS offices at O'Hare Airport in Chicago; and two as painters at the Statue of Liberty.[83] INS agents in Chicago in 1980 reported that those seized in the last two years were working in nonagricultural jobs and that most earned more than the minimum wage.[84] The North and Houstoun study, as well as others, found workers in various jobs and not just agriculture. Nor were all working for the minimum wage or below.[85]

In spite of the diversity of working patterns for these aliens, they generally appear to be concentrated in low-paying and low-skilled jobs. Mexicans more than others were in agriculture but large numbers of them found employment in Los Angeles garment shops. An ILGWU organizer in Los Angeles, Phil Russo, estimated in 1978 that illegal workers "make up something like 70 percent of the garment industry here."[86] Garment shops in New York also employed many illegals, those from the Caribbean, especially Haitians and Dominicans.[87]

Undocumented aliens also found employment in the service industries, such as restaurants, hotels, motels, and hospitals. There they usually did the low-paid dirty work, as busboys or washing dishes, sweeping and mopping floors, or cleaning houses as domestics in Texas, California, and New York. These jobs required few skills, and in many cases little knowledge of English, only a willingness to learn unskilled tasks quickly and to work for low wages.[88] Some observers believed American service industries in some cities had become dependent upon undocumented workers. In 1980 Joseph Howerton, head of the Los Angeles office of INS, said, "There's not a business or industry of any type here that does not have undocumented workers. If we were to pick up every illegal alien in this area, we would close down not just 90 percent of the restaurants and the car washes, but many of the light industries."[89] These firms usually had smaller numbers of employees than did most American businesses and not infrequently violated the labor laws. Federal task forces in the late 1970s reported that a large number of such firms they inspected violated labor rules about working conditions and wages and hours.[90]

The existence of a pool of undocumented workers concentrating in agriculture, light industry, and the low-paying sectors of service industries led some observers to fear the undocumented immigrants would become an underclass of workers, doomed to an existence of exploitation or near poverty if they stayed in the United States. Government seizures of undocumented aliens found some who had been in the United States for several years, holding better-paying jobs. INS authorities in Los Angeles discovered in 1979 that those averaging 2.4 years on the job earned more than five dollars per hour as skilled workers, such as plumbers and electricians, positions not normally identified with the undocumented.[91] In Washington, D.C., in 1976 immigration authorities located an illegal working at St. Elizabeth Hospital as a psychiatrist at a salary of $37,000.[92] Yet, no reliable studies existed about the mobility patterns of the undocumented. They had been in the United States for too short a period, or because of their status, reliable data was unavailable for firm conclusions.

Fear of deportation added to the illegals' woes. *La migra* raids were a constant reminder of the vulnerability of an undocumented status and of the difficulties in obtaining better jobs and housing, even when such were available and the language barrier became less. As noted, inconsistent INS policy, inadequate staff, and court decisions hindered raids in the 1970s. INS agents complained that their problems in enforcing the law were even more difficult under Carter's commissioner from 1977 to 1979, Leonel Castillo. Some said he was too lenient on undocumented aliens and virtually "granted his own amnesty program" for them.[93]

Yet, INS barrio raids continued throughout the 1970s and into the 1980s as well as raids at businesses and farms, though INS dropped the term employer "raids" and called them employer "visits." If only sporadic, rumors of raids abounded among the undocumented, and the fear of getting caught was ever present. One anonymous Maryland informant told a reporter, "I live with the constant fear that they might find me someplace and deport me, send me away. Wherever I go, I have that constant fear. Before, I used to play soccer. I used to go the Spanish theaters and restaurants. Now I have no place to go. I watch TV."[94] Indeed, one never knew when INS agents might strike or where. On January 19, 1980, for example, agents made the largest roundup of illegal domestics ever in New York City. In the early morning they took 85 persons out of line or off buses at the midtown Port Authority Bus Terminal. These people were suspected of being illegal domestics, bound for work in New Jersey.[95] This case was perhaps untypical, for most raids occurred at places of work, not bus stations.

Of course, the prospect of a better life in the United States or of earning money to return home and starting their own businesses or buying and working their own land was a powerful inducement in spite of the problems of an undocumented status. Then too, there existed the possibility of an illegals' getting official papers and ending the fear of deportation. Though it was difficult to find a job that would carry with it Labor Department certification, the family unification emphasis of American policy made it possible for many undocumented persons to gain legal status. If illegal alien parents had a child born in the United States, they would be eligible for entrance as parents of an American citizen when the child turned 21.[96] Moreover, an illegal could marry an American citizen or resident alien and then be eligible for an immigrant visa. Because most illegals clustered in communities with their fellow nationals, meeting resident aliens or American citizens was not unusual, though no one knew how many undocumented aliens got their papers this way. Yet, it was probably not an uncommon practice and offered a potential way of ending an inferior and vulnerable status.

In sum, from what social scientists call "soft" evidence a picture of undocumented aliens emerged in the 1970s. Largely young males from either Mexico and the Caribbean without high levels of education and skills, these immigrants came to America in search of employment and a better life. Mexicans at first found jobs in agriculture but increasingly they turned to the cities where opportunities existed in light manufacturing such as garment shops and in low-paying service industries. Many, especially Mexicans, stayed in the United States temporarily. They sent money home or returned, only to reenter the United States again at a later date to earn more money. Most undocumented aliens settled where other immigrants did, in Texas, Florida, New York, or California. Because of their often desperate poverty and lack of official papers, they faced many hardships in the United States, including exploitation by employers and smugglers. Except for health services, few apparently used social services such as schools, food stamps, and unemployment insurance, either because they could not qualify or feared to contact government officials. It would not be an exaggeration to compare these immigrants to many of those coming in the late nineteenth and early twentieth centuries, such as Italians and Greeks who also were predominately young, uneducated males from villages or cities who went back and forth to America in search of work. While some observers thought that these persons might become a permanent underclass, the evidence for this belief was inconclusive.

Because evidence about undocumented aliens was sometimes lacking, inconclusive, or even contradictory, they became the focal point of much public debate about immigration after the enactment of the 1965 immigration reforms. The Select Commission on Immigration and Refugee Policy put it in 1981, "No policy issue received more attention from the Select Commission that that of illegal aliens—what to do about the presence of a large number of them in the United States and how to curtail future flows."[97] Not even the refugee issue drew such attention. Most of the immigration changes of 1965 seemed to be accepted by Congress and the general public after 1965, but not so with undocumented aliens. In addition to the uncertainty about their numbers and impact upon American life, the economic troubles of the post-1972 period no doubt contributed to public uneasiness about illegal immigration; some politicians blamed them in part for America's woes. It is also possible that persons uneasy about immigration generally, but fearful of being called intolerant or forgetful of America's tradition of being a land of immigrants, singled out the illegals rather than the regular immigrants. After all, they were here in violation of the nation's immigration laws and could be more easily attacked. In any event, an important public debate emerged as legislators sought a solution to the problem of undocumented aliens. The House on two occasions in the 1970s passed legislation to cope with this problem, but the Senate failed to act. In the early 1980s the Senate twice passed bills, but in the special session of Congress in 1982, after the Senate had acted, the House could not agree. Again the next year the Senate passed legislation and the House passed its own version in 1984, but the two bodies could not compromise. Most congressional leaders believed the bills to be dead, and although Congress discussed illegal immigration issues again in 1985, it took no action. Finally, somewhat unexpectedly and after crafting delicate compromises, the legislators passed IRCA in 1986. One sponsor said, "If this bill were a cat, this would be its ninth life. It can't pop out of the grave again. It can't have more life breathed back into its corpse."[98]

Proponents of keeping illegals out of the United States used several arguments. First, they insisted that these immigrants, by using food stamps, unemployment insurance, welfare, hospitals, and schools and other such social services were a drain and burden on the American taxpayer. As was the case with the numbers estimates, INS took the lead. In late 1975 INS estimated that the illegals created a $16 billion tax burden on Americans. This figure was arrived at by combining both the alleged cost of social services used by undocumented aliens and estimated taxes these migrants did not pay.[99] When the Labor Department and scholarly studies suggested that this estimate was a gross exaggeration and that undocumented workers paid more in taxes than they took out in various governmental services, INS backed off its more extreme estimates. But the issue of a tax burden did not die. While most studies of undocumented immigrants concluded that they paid taxes and did not make extensive use of social services involving income transfers, the undocumented population was concentrated in selected areas. Los Angeles, New York, or San Diego might feel the burden—whatever it was—more than such places as Minneapolis. The use by undocumented immigrants of social services, and especially local health services, was a controversial issue in some of these communities.[100]

Although most studies indicated the vast majority of undocumented aliens were not an economic burden, the studies did not always agree and could be interpreted in several ways.[101] If the data indicated little use of services, there still were the issues of the number of undocumented aliens and how long they stayed here. If one assumed the number was large and used higher estimates and studies of utilization, then the burden could be seen as large. If one assumed that illegals did not return home, but were inclined to remain in the United States and raise families here, then the potential future cost, in terms of schools and unemployment insurance and other such services, might grow.[102]

Related to the issue of social services were possible indirect cost to taxpayers. The cost could be higher if one believed that illegal immigrants contributed to unemployment by taking jobs from American citizens and resident aliens. These unemployed Americans in turn would use social services such as unemployment insurance and food stamps; hence, the cost of undocumented immigration could not be calculated by looking simply at what services they used. This was the argument of the Environmental Fund which estimated such costs in 1982 at between eight and eighteen billion dollars. The figures depended upon estimates of the size of the illegal population and how many American workers were thrown out of work by their presence.[103]

The issue of the illegals' impact on the labor market was also highly controversial. The key question was: did they displace American workers and depress wages? It will be recalled that this issue had been raised during the debates over Operation Wetback and the bracero program. It was heard again after 1970 and became especially emotional because of high unemployment and inflation.

While something was known about who the undocumented aliens were, where they worked and lived, what kinds of jobs they held and wages they received, precise data was lacking. Moreover, because estimating their numbers was often little more than guesswork, a key ingredient about their effect on wages and employment was missing. If the number was six, or an even higher figure of ten to twelve million, rather than a million or so, whatever market impact they had was much greater.

Growers and speakers for businesses like restaurants known to employ undocumented workers asserted the numbers made little difference. They argued that they could not find Americans to do the work at the prevailing wages; hence, they had to employ the undocumented immigrants. In a statement reminiscent of the bracero debates of years before, one avocado grower in California said of employing Americans, "We tried, but they don't want the jobs. Picking avocados is damn hard work. Americans work a day or two and drift away, it's easier to go on welfare. The illegals are really good workers."[104]

While such remarks were hardly surprising, neither were the assertions of INS officials and labor unions and their liberal allies that workers without papers caused unemployment and depressed wages. Union leaders added that they hindered the development of trade unions. In the mid-1970s, the International Ladies Garment Workers Union shifted policy and began to organize both illegal and legal immigrants in New York City and Los Angeles.[105] For the farm workers union, as noted above, the situation was agonizing because of its emphasis on ethnic solidarity. The UFW had periodically organized undocumented pickers, but in 1979 during a strike by West Coast lettuce pickers, UFW President Cesar Chavez demanded that the government remove the illegals, who were being used, he insisted, to break the strike. Declared Chavez, who still supported an amnesty for undocumented immigrants, "Regular workers will most likely not break strikes. The companies have to depend on the importation of people from Mexico. That is what has kept farm workers from organizing in the past. . . . If we ever get the government to enforce the law, our expansion could be pretty rapid."[106]

Leonard Chapman in the mid-1970s insisted that undocumented immigrants labored in several million jobs that paid enough so that Americans would have taken them if they could.[107] A few years later Ray Marshall, President Carter's Secretary of Labor, said in an interview with the *Los Angeles Times*, "It is false to say American workers cannot be found for all of the jobs filled by undocumented workers. . . . The truth is that there are millions of American workers in all of these low-paying occupations already. The job market in which they [undocumented workers] compete is highly competitive with a surplus of people vying for a shortage of jobs, no matter how undesirable the jobs may be."[108] Those who insisted that undocumented aliens took American jobs and depressed wages pointed to low wage rates along the Texas-Mexican border or in industries where such immigrants were known to concentrate. That illegals worked side by side with resident aliens and U.S. citizens in California agriculture or in garment shops demonstrated to them that Americans were willing to work in such jobs and at wages where one found illegal workers.[109]

Without this supply of relatively cheap labor, many businessmen might have moved or closed their doors, or as agribusiness had been doing for decades, automate. It is also possible that some of these industries could have survived even if they had to raise wages in order to attract American workers. It does appear that if undocumented aliens depressed wages and displaced American workers their impact was confined to selected geographical areas and particular industries and that other low-wage Americans—Hispanics, women, youths, and blacks—were hurt the most. Ultimately, data were missing for an accurate understanding about the impact of illegal immigration on the labor market.

This lack of precise knowledge did not stifle public debates, however, and Congress and a number of states wrestled with various solutions and proposals in an attempt to solve problems believed to be caused by illegal immigration.[110] As noted, the problems resolved around labor market impact and social service use, though some also worried about other issues too. A few opponents of undocumented immigration worried that persons entering without adequate medical inspection had the potential for bringing in contagious diseases.[111] Still others said many illegals were likely to be criminals or that the whole process of illegal immigration had an adverse effect on the American system of law and order.[112] A few liberals also wondered whether or not the nation was witnessing the growth of a permanent underclass of people confined to the secondary labor market with little prospect of escape in the future. Vernon Briggs, a professor at Cornell University, expressed this view in 1983, "Certainly the growth of a subclass of illegal aliens cannot be in the nation's long-term interest. Once before the nation tried to live with a subclass in its midst. Then the institution was slavery, and the nation is still trying to overcome the legacy of that episode. It is an experience that should not be repeated."[113]

Finally, in the mid-1970s environmentalists and supporters of Zero Population Growth raised their voices in protest about immigration and especially illegal immigration. They used traditional economic and social arguments, but added environmental and population ones. Wrote one environmentalist in the *National Parks and Conservation Magazine* in 1977:

No so very long ago an article about United States immigration policy would have seemed out of place in a publication on environmental concerns: too social, surely, and outside the realm of interests of a readership dedicated to the preservation of the natural habitat.

The continued degradation of the environment, a growing national awareness of the adverse effects of increased population pressures upon our natural resources and of the ensuing decline of the quality of life, the swelling stream of immigrants landing on our shores and crossing our borders, and an immigration policy incapable of coping with this invasion have changed our perspective during the past decade.[114]

Several states and local governments grappled with the issue of illegal aliens, but only with mixed success. While a few states denied benefits to illegals in their workers' compensation, general assistance, and temporary disability insurance programs, most did not.[115] In at least one state, Texas, the state supreme court ruled that illegals had the same right as others to collect workers' compensation if they were injured at work.[116]

In Los Angeles County, where many undocumented aliens were suspected of living and working, the human resources agencies responsible for administering several joint federal-state-local income transfer programs, for which illegal aliens were not eligible, asked persons requesting aid to present evidence that they had a legal status in the United States. In 1979 over 16,000 applicants for aid withdrew their applications. Of the 5,000 alien applications still processed each month several hundred of the most suspicious cases were sent to INS officials for verification, with the result that about 1,000 that year were found to be illegal aliens by INS.[117]

A more sensitive issue than general assistance or workers' compensation was medical care. Hospitals were faced with treating persons in their emergency rooms and outpatient clinics who were unable to prove their resident status. Although costs were mostly borne by local communities, denial of emergency and even regular care for those without funds seemed inhumane or even dangerous to public health. In Los Angeles County officials wrestled with the problem throughout the 1970s. At one point they asked the federal government, without success, to reimburse them for such care on the grounds that immigration was a national matter and the federal government should bear the cost of its inability to control the nation's borders.[118] In some California communities only emergency care was rendered to those who could not prove their status. At the University of California at Davis Medical Center those applying for the Medi-Cal program were asked to sign a statement saying that they realized their names would be forwarded to the immigration authorities.[119]

As emotional as medical care was, the issue of education was no less so. While school districts generally took the position that they should register and teach all children regardless of their status, in 1975 Texas moved to bar undocumented children from its public schools. When several school districts attempted to enforce the law, Hispanic and civil liberties groups, backed by Carter's Justice Department, contested its constitutionality. In 1982, in a five-to-four decision, the United States Supreme Court declared the law unconstitutional, and held that undocumented children were entitled to a public education. The close five-to-four vote and the sensitive nature of education of the young made it doubtful whether barring other social services to illegals, which had been increasingly done in federal programs in the 1970s, would be similarly struck down by the justices.[120]

These state actions, meager and somewhat ineffective as they were, dealt with the delivery of social services, while most observers believed the key issue was employment. In the 1970s, about a dozen states passed laws that outlawed the employment of undocumented aliens, but the laws, generally known as employer sanctions legislation, remained largely unenforced and had no effect on employment practices relating to undocumented aliens.

The California employer sanctions law, the nation's first such law, was a case in point. The state passed the law in 1971. It prohibited employers from knowingly employing aliens not entitled to lawful residence. Proponents of the law hailed it as a way to check the employment of illegals and pointed to fines that guilty employers would have to pay. Yet, after more than a decade no successful prosecution was ever brought under the law and it had become a dead letter.[121] In the first place, the state initially devoted meager resources to its enforcement.[122] Second, the law became involved in a legal tangle, and in 1974 the California Court of Appeals declared it unconstitutional.[123] Two years later the United States Supreme Court overturned the California decision but the state made no attempt to enforce it; or as one government official in the San Diego office of Labor Law Enforcement said, "Oh, that law isn't enforced. It's been declared unconstitutional."[124]

Because immigration was a federal matter, politicians ultimately looked to the federal government for a solution to the problem of illegal immigration. The chief ways in which the federal government dealt with the situation were border enforcement and internal operations of INS. Congress also barred undocumented aliens from receiving assistance in a number of income transfer programs.[125] These measures did not suffice to check the flow of illegal immigration, and politicians perceived that their numbers were growing. Thus, Congress turned to the important area of employment for a solution. The Carter administration inaugurated a limited program in its Labor Department. Beginning in 1978 the department's Employment Standards Administration (ESA) investigated firms suspected of hiring undocumented persons and of being in violation of labor laws. The idea was to take away the incentive to exploit illegal workers by paying them substandard wages under unlawful conditions. As one ESA official put it, "We are committed to eradication of illegal working conditions affecting persons regardless of their citizenship status. Enforcement efforts by this strike force team have curtailed some of the illegal practices to which undocumented workers are particularly vulnerable."[126] This would protect the undocumented but also make it less profitable to employ them rather than lawful residents. ESA task forces discovered a large percentage of the businesses they visited to be in violation of labor laws and were able to recover back wages for undocumented workers.[127]

The program was limited in scope, however, and Congress looked instead to employer sanctions as the way to check the employment of undocumented workers and remove their incentive for migrating to the United States. It will be recalled that during the 1950s, Congress passed the Texas Proviso that specifically declared it was not unlawful to employ illegal aliens. In 1974 the legislators amended the Farm Contractor Registration Law to prohibit crew leaders of farm laborers from knowingly hiring illegal aliens. Yet, this amendment was not vigorously enforced.

Even if it were, the vast majority of undocumented workers by that time were seeking employment in cities and were not being recruited by agricultural crew leaders.[128]

The House first considered a general employer sanctions bill in 1971. Hearings in that year led to House enactment of such a bill, the so-called Rodino Bill, in 1972. Proponents argued that it was necessary to remove the incentive to hire undocumented aliens. Opponents countered with suggestions that enforcement of the law would be difficult and might lead to discrimination against Hispanics.[129] The representatives passed the measure by voice on September 12, and in a lopsided vote refused to recommit it.[130]

When the Senate took no action, the House in the next session again considered and passed the Rodino Bill to prohibit employers from knowingly hiring illegal aliens. After airing similar arguments, the representatives voted 297 to 63 in favor.[131] In the Senate no action was taken. Mississippi Senator James Eastland, himself a cotton planter, who chaired the immigration subcommittee, held no hearings on this issue or any other immigration matter following the enactment of the 1965 amendments to the McCarran-Walter Act. The senator insisted that he could not even get a quorum together, but others suggested that he had no interest in stopping the employment of illegal aliens, in part because some Mississippi planters employed them.[132] Finally, in 1976, Eastland put forth his own bill.

Senator Eastland, as did others who represented grower interests, wanted any ban on the employment of illegals to be coupled with a renewal of a temporary worker, bracero-type program. Temporary worker proposals were not popular with liberals, labor unions, Hispanics, and many churches which had lobbied so hard in the 1960s to terminate the bracero agreement with Mexico and sought to keep the still-existing H-2 temporary worker program limited in scope. The temporary worker issue thus complicated a growing controversy. Although Eastland's committee held hearings in 1976, no report or Senate action resulted. By that time it was apparent that competing factions and views about illegal immigration made a congressional consensus, temporarily at least, impossible.

President Gerald Ford created a special executive committee to investigate the evidence and issues. The President's Domestic Council on Illegal Immigration, reporting in 1976, noted the growing seriousness of the issue, the lack of conclusive evidence about the impact of illegal immigration, and pointed to still another complication: foreign relations, especially with Mexico. Any policy carried out by the United States with respect to Mexican nationals illegally entering and working in the United States would affect American relations with Mexico.[133] Like Congress, the President's Council could find no simple solution.

President Carter sent a program to Congress in August 1977 that combined employer sanctions with an amnesty for those illegally in residence prior to 1970 and a temporary status for those who had come between 1970 and 1977. Congress held hearings on the Carter bill and other aspects of illegal immigration, but the proposals antagonized many and had no possibility of passage. Instead, Congress elected to postpone a decision when it created the Select Commission on Immigration and Refugee Policy, which was due to report in early 1981.

By the time the Select Commission reported in March 1981 a new President, Ronald Reagan, was in the White House and a variety of groups opposed various plans put forward to deal with the illegal issue.[134] Hispanic and civil liberties organizations said that employer sanctions would lead to discrimination against Hispanics because employers would be unwilling to hire them for fear of legal prosecution. Growers and other employers known to hire illegals also opposed sanctions and said that they would be forced to become private immigration authorities responsible for carrying out the law. Labor unions and black civil rights groups favored sanctions but insisted that they wanted no expansion of temporary workers which growers claimed was necessary to make up for a possible loss of illegal workers. Church groups, Hispanics, some unions like the ILGWU which had been organizing undocumented workers, and many liberals favored legalization for those who had been here a long time. But a generous amnesty was opposed by environmental and population groups like Zero Population Growth and the newly formed Federation of Americans for Immigration Reform (FAIR). A newly formed group, the Conservatives for Immigration Reform, argued that legalization rewarded

law breaking in the past. Others said it was unfair to those awaiting visas and would encourage future illegal immigration unless
the border was effectively controlled first, because many new illegal immigrants would enter hoping for another amnesty in the
future. Still others worried about the growing size of immigration
and feared an amnesty would only serve to increase it further.
Then there was the issue of enforcement. How could one prove
than an employer knowingly hired an illegal immigrant unless a
counterfeit proof identification of some type existed? Some critics
doubted whether an adequate card or system could be developed
while others worried about the civil liberties issues involved in
giving the government power to develop such a card or system.[135]
While some commentators favored tighter border enforcement,
Hispanic groups did not necessarily agree, and Asian-American
organizations believed INS spent too much time and effort on
enforcement policies and not enough serving the new immigrants. Hispanics also objected to internal raids by INS.[136]

After extensive hearings and deliberations the Select Commission, which was well aware that some compromise was needed if
any bill were to pass, recommended both legalization and an employer sanctions bill.[137] When the commission reported in March
1981, Congress was preoccupied with other matters. As unemployment worsened, in 1982, a coalition developed, led by Democratic Representative Romano Mazzoli and Senator Alan Simpson,
to enact a comprehensive immigration reform bill. The Reagan
administration showed great interest in the Select Commission
report. It set up a task force composed of representatives from
many agencies to examine the work of the commission and make
recommendations. It did favor many aspects of the reform proposals, but Reagan wanted an expansion of a temporary worker
program as well.[138] When this proved unpopular, the administration supported the Mazzoli-Simpson bill, but did not consider it a
priority item. Proponents of immigration reform could point to
growing unemployment and said their bill was not only immigration reform, but also a "jobs bill" as well. They also pointed to
public opinion polls taken in the 1970s and one in the fall of 1983,
all of which overwhelmingly supported employer sanctions and
expressed the public belief that undocumented immigrants caused
unemployment.[139]

Annoyed by leaders of Hispanic organizations continually opposing bills like the Simpson-Mazzoli bill, the Federation of Americans for Immigration Reform commissioned a survey of attitudes about immigration among representatives black and Hispanic Americans. The survey, conducted jointly by V. Lance Tarrance and Associates and Peter D. Hart Research Associates in the summer of 1983, revealed that substantial majorities of both groups favored employer sanctions and tighter border enforcement. Hispanics polled also indicated sympathy for an amnesty for undocumented aliens who had been in the United States for several years.[140] The survey, the first major one of its kind, indicated to FAIR and to many others as well that Hispanic leaders did not necessarily speak for the Hispanic population generally and that the Simpson-Mazzoli bill had widespread national support.[141]

Basically, the Simpson-Mazzoli bill measure was a delicate compromise providing for a limited amnesty, employer sanctions, and modifications in the H-2 temporary workers program to possibly admit more temporary agriculture workers. In the Senate the bill as finally passed in August 1982 included a limit of 425,000 on legal immigration, not counting refugees, and modified the brothers and sisters fifth preference.[142] The House committees responsible for the bill eliminated the cap on legal immigration and restored the brothers and sisters of U.S. citizens preference and instead concentrated on the illegal issue.[143]

The Senate passed their bill by an 81 to 18 vote, but in the House it was a different matter. When the representatives finally debated the bill in December, during a special session of Congress, not enough time was left to resolve the issues. Hispanic groups, especially, opposed the employer sanctions proviso, and they had allies who disliked other provisions. Supporters either lacked enthusiasm from representatives in areas where immigration was not an issue or they lacked time to overcome objections to particular parts of the bill. No doubt the confusion of the administration about immigration and its lack of interest also hurt.[144]

In 1983 the Senate again considered and passed the Simpson-Mazzoli measure by a lopsided margin.[145] In the House, however, several committees controlled by the Democrats altered the Senate version. Even these changes were inadequate to ward off defeat. Sensitive to Hispanic organizational pressures, Speaker Tip

O'Neill told reporters in October that the House would not consider the bill in 1983. The Speaker said that the bill would not be voted upon because the President would veto it.[146] While some administration leaders denied that the President would veto the act, others noted concerns about the cost of an amnesty to illegal aliens and the problems in formulating a worker identification policy.[147] Several weeks later, after much political and editorial outcry, O'Neill indicated a shift and said the bill would be considered by the House in the next session of Congress.[148]

Finally, in June 1984 the House of Representatives held a lengthy debate on the bill and passed it. The debates were heated at times, and the representatives voted on a series of amendments before considering the final bill. The Senate had passed the bill easily, by a four to one margin; but in the House the final vote was extremely close, 216 to 211.

Not all of the provisions of the Simpson-Mazzoli proposal were controversial. Without much dissent the House wanted both Mexico and Canada to have an extra 20,000 visas, with the provision that if neither country used these extra slots, the other could. Because Canada did not even use its 20,000 allotment, this obviously meant that Mexico would have 40,000 visas in addition to the 20,000 allotted each country. The representatives also wanted to increase funds for INS and to give 3,000 visas to colonies instead of the 600 then in effect, a provision primarily benefiting Hong Kong. The provisions creating procedures for asylum and restricting it somewhat were also not debated at length. Nor did many legislators dissent from provisions granting the Cuban/ Haitian entrants immigrant status. While the Senate bill had a cap, excluding refugees, on legal immigration, the House rejected such a limit. Finally, without great controversy, the House bill as passed included a sense of Congress statement that Salvadorans should be given extended voluntary departure status.[149] The Senate bill had not included this provision, which was not binding on the administration.[150] The Reagan administration had already indicated that it had no intention of granting such status to Salvadorans.

As in the past, the controversial issues dealt with undocumented aliens and temporary workers. Most of the arguments were familiar. Those who favored a compromise wanted an amnesty for undocumented aliens already here in exchange for employer sanctions. This compromise did not satisfy Hispanics and their supporters who wanted stricter enforcement of the labor laws, a generous amnesty, and no sanctions. Nor did it satisfy those, like William McCollum of Florida, who said an amnesty rewarded people for entering illegally and punished those who waited in line for visas. In the end, Romano Mazzoli and his allies won, and employer sanctions and an amnesty carried.[151]

Issues related to the enforcement of the compromise prompted considerable debate. The representatives worried about discriminations against Hispanics and by a 404 to 9 vote included provisions prohibiting discrimination against job applicants because of national origin or alienage.[152] This provision was not in the Senate bill and later caused trouble in conference. The House also rejected use of a national identification card and instead suggested that other documents could be used and left to the future other means of identification.[153]

Congressman Mazzoli had not favored a temporary worker program, but after fierce lobbying, representatives from states wanting laborers to pick their crops managed to win House support for an expanded temporary worker program. This angered organized labor and many others, but its supporters insisted these workers were needed to replace the undocumented ones.[154]

The close votes for individual parts of the bill and the narrow victory of five votes for the final bill indicated the deep divisions about immigration. Because the vote was so close and the House bill differed from the Senate one in several key areas, passage of the Simpson-Mazzoli bill appeared in doubt. Moreover, the Democratic candidates for President and Vice-President said that they opposed the bill.[155] Vice-President George Bush told a group of Hispanics that the administration did not favor any bill that might lead to discrimination against them. But the President indicated another reason for trouble. The administration said it did not wish the federal government to bear the full cost of legalization of undocumented aliens, who would become eligible for governmental assistance programs.[156]

In spite of the gloomy outlook for a conference bill that both houses could accept and the President would sign, House and Senate conferees attempted to find a solution. Although these members of Congress managed to compromise on the dates for legalization for those who had entered illegally and discrimination provisions, they could not agree on funding. But Congress was eager to adjourn so that its members would have time to campaign for the fall elections. Thus Simpson-Mazzoli failed again in 1984.[157]

When the newly elected Congress met in 1985, prospects for passage in the Senate appeared strong again, especially after Senator Simpson became assistant majority leader. Moreover, amnesty was made more acceptable because of promises for increased enforcement of the immigration laws. In September the Senate approved the bill 69 to 30, but the House was a different matter in 1985.[158] However, Peter Rodino, chairman of the House Judiciary Committee, assumed leadership for immigration when he introduced a bill of his own. Rodino had been opposed to a Simpson-Rodino earlier draft that had included cutting the fifth preference for brothers and sisters of U.S. citizens. But the brothers and sisters change was now dropped as were earlier suggestions for a cap on legal immigration. Neither was Rodino especially enthusiastic about temporary worker programs for growers, but compromise on that issue proved to be possible.[159]

As the Simpson-Rodino Act worked its way through Congress in 1986 the usual arguments were heard and critical compromises were required for final passage and acceptance by the White House. Of course, central to the final bill were amnesty and employer sanctions. The cutoff for an amnesty was finally fixed at January 1, 1982; those undocumented aliens who had entered the United States before that date and had remained there since were eligible. Employer sanctions made it unlawful to knowingly employ undocumented aliens. Congress rejected the controversial concept of a national identity card; instead employers could verify an alien's standing by examining a combination of documents and papers. For violators of the law, fines were assessed, but for a "pattern or practice" of hiring undocumented immigrants, criminal penalties could be imposed, including a jail sentence.

While employer sanctions and an amnesty were the heart of IRCA, crucial for its passage were provisions for temporary foreign workers to harvest perishable crops and a Special Agricultural Worker (SAW) amnesty. The Senate draft included a temporary agriculture worker program which many representatives opposed. Proponents of help for growers were reportedly losing strength in Congress by 1986, but they nonetheless were able to insist upon some provisions for agricultural workers, which Representative Charles Schumer provided. Schumer proposed that undocumented aliens who had worked for at least 20 (later increased to 90) days in agriculture between May 1985 and May 1986 be allowed to become temporary aliens and then permanent resident aliens. The final bill also permitted growers to bring foreign farm workers into the country if they convinced the government they were needed. Rodino called Schumer's proposal "a compromise very, very delicately arrived at," and said that "it is the only political reality that will bring together all the forces" working for the bill.[160] Moreover, the final bill included a another victory for growers: a section prohibiting INS officials from questioning a grower's farm workers unless they had a search warrant or the farm owner's permission.

In some ways the SAW program was the most remarkable part of IRCA. It was adopted without hearings and without a thorough examination of how it would work. Indeed, it had not been discussed much in the past. The House committee, using estimates from the Congressional Budget Office (CBO) said, "Workers covered under the special agriculture workers provision are estimated to total about 250,000."[161] Republican dissenters claimed that this provision was drafted in haste and that no one knew exactly how many workers SAW would produce, and said that "Guesses range from 200,000 to over 1,000,000." Furthermore, they noted, "There is nothing in the legislation to require SAW's continued employment in agriculture." The result was, as Representative Dan Lungren of California pointed out, that SAW as a "second legalization" program, one not carefully crafted like the main amnesty provision.[162] One Republican, James Sensenbrenner, Jr., noted another problem:

With document fraud at an all time high in the United States, fears have been raised about the possibility of fraudulent documents being used in the amnesty program. People must prove they have lived and worked in the U.S. since 1982. The Schumer workers only have to account for 60 [sic] days, with documents which would be difficult, if not impossible, to verify, and easy to draw up.[163]

Of course some representatives did not like any amnesty. But they lacked the votes to block SAW, and their attempts to kill the regular amnesty provision failed by a narrow margin in the House. On the other side were those who worried about employer sanctions leading to racial and ethnic discrimination. Addressing the concerns of Hispanics and civil libertarians, the representatives also insisted upon antidiscrimination provisions, which the Senate accepted. If the General Accounting Office (GAO) found discrimination against foreign-looking individuals or resident aliens, then Congress was to reconsider employer sanctions. Unacceptable to the administration, however, was a provision pushed in the House, to give Salvadorans and Nicaraguans EVD; it was eliminated in conference.[164]

In the end the various compromises won enough support from those not necessarily satisfied with individual sections of IRCA and it passed easily in the Senate (63–24) and by a 238 to 173 margin in the House.[165] Many members insisted that it was the best bill obtainable, and even 5 of the 11-member Hispanic caucus favored it. Hispanics and their allies wanted a later cutoff day for amnesty than January 1, 1982; it was the best they could get, and the amnesty coupled with the antidiscrimination provisions won their votes. Some feared a less generous bill would be enacted if IRCA went down to defeat.[166] Conservatives, on the other hand, favored the Simpson–Rodino Act because of employer sanctions and prospect of increased border supervision.

Estimates had varied as to the number of persons eligible for amnesty. After a slow start 1.7 million applied for the regular legalization. A majority were Mexican. SAW proved to be the surprise. CBO estimates were way short of the final number, and even INS's high guess of 600,000 turned out to be off by a half; when the deadline ended in 1988, 1.3 million persons had claimed amnesty under the SAW divisions. There were also mostly Mexicans who made up 2.2 million of the 3 million total amnesty applications.[167] INS officials had one explanation for the large number of SAWS: fraud on a massive scale. After reviewing the applications, INS in 1989 identified about 400,000 cases of possible fraud. At the same time it confessed that it lacked the funds and manpower to prosecute individual applicants. In some spots, said Jack Bass, assistant commissioner for Investigations, fraud was "rampant if not totally out of control." Charles Schumer, author of the compromise SAW program, admitted it was "too open," and that INS lacked the resources to track down fraud. Critics noted that it "was a weak program and it was poorly articulated in law."[168]

Growers had insisted upon provisions for temporary farm workers because they could no longer hire illegal aliens. Some growers did claim a shortage existed, but the federal government was not convinced. Farmers were able to find laborers, either by hiring SAW workers, Americans, regular immigrants or by continuing to use undocumented workers.[169]

Problems also emerged in the regular legalization program. VOLAGs and INS officials quickly discovered that families could be disrupted because of the cutoff date. If the husband arrived before January 1982, but the wife and children at a later date, the family members would have to apply for admission from their country under the second preference; but in countries like Mexico, that preference was backed up for years. INS indicated that it would not deport such individuals, but Congress wanted to be certain of avoiding hardship for families. After holding hearings on this issue the legislators included in the Immigration Act of 1990 a provision that provided for a stay of deportation for spouses and children of undocumented aliens who were eligible for amnesty. They then could wait (and work) in the United States while their applications for admission were pending.[170]

The concern by Hispanics and civil libertarians that the employer sanctions might lead to discrimination appeared to be well founded. Several investigations by state agencies and the GAO revealed that discrimination occurred.[171] Civil rights and Hispanic organizations called for a repeal of employer sanctions, and they had supporters in Congress. But Congress did not include this provision in the sweeping 1990 Immigration Act. The discrimination issue remained troubling, however, and indicated how shaky that IRCA was.

The main issue for many who believed that American borders were out of control was employer sanctions. For them IRCA was critical. The task of prosecuting employers who violated the law, even with increased funding and personnel for INS, was huge. Nevertheless, in August 1987, INS issued the first citation; and in 1988 a Maryland firm, the operator of Wendy's Restaurants, received the first criminal fine under IRCA.[172] Others followed.

In 1986 INS had reported a record 1.6 million undocumented aliens apprehended, and the first year after passage of IRCA, the number dropped; by 1989 it was approximately half of that amount. As employers reported shortages of workers, it appeared that the new law might deter undocumented immigration. But then apprehensions began to climb again, and in 1990 they topped one million. Several scholarly studies concluded that it was not possible to measure the precise impact of IRCA in such a short time; and they noted that in addition to IRCA, economic conditions also effected the illegal flow and that increased personnel along the border could account for changes in apprehensions.[173]

Moreover, effective enforcement of IRCA depended upon documentary evidence given by employees. INS officials and scholars said smugglers were still active and that the traffic in fake documents was as brisk as ever, only the price was higher.[174] For employers, there was little incentive to be sure that these documents were authentic, for they were not required to do so. Most employers had opposed IRCA, and some were convicted for employing undocumented aliens, but it was not easy to prove that employers knowingly hired illegals. In 1989, INS reported that of 900 aliens it arrested at workplaces, 233 admitted having counterfeit Social Security cards and 142 a fake green card. Wayne Cornelius, director of the Center for United States–Mexican Studies at the University of California at San Diego, put it in 1990, "Employer sanctions may have seemed a real barrier at first, but now they are just one more hurdle to overcome."[175]

Certainly IRCA did not end horror stories of desperate illegal aliens trying to enter the United States. In 1987 the Border Patrol found 19 undocumented aliens locked in a railroad trailer in West Texas in 120-degree heat. About the same time, the Patrol also found 18 such aliens who suffocated to death in a Texas box car. Two years later four dead undocumented aliens were discovered confined in a trailer.[176] And in early 1991 New York City police rescued undocumented Chinese aliens who had been smuggled from China. After paying thousands of dollars to get to America, they had been kidnapped and held as virtual slaves until rescued.[177]

That persons faced with poverty at home in Mexico or the Caribbean or civil war and violence in Central America would seek a better life in America was understandable, even after the passage of IRCA. If caught, they did as so many did before the 1986 Immigration Reform and Control Act became law—they simply tried again. And for thousands of others who overstayed their visas, there were jobs in American cities.

In response, INS and its allies called for more personnel for IRCA and border enforcement. They also suggested proposals with an old history: counterfeit-proof green cards, improved Social Security cards, and a national ID system. Another familiar proposal was to create a large ditch along the United States border with Mexico.[178] The Federation of Americans for Immigration Reform (FAIR) went further. It called for a beefed-up INS and the construction of a 12-foot-high fence along the area most used by border crossers.[179]

Proposals for elaborate fences and national ID cards ran into the usual opposition and had little chance for passage. Whatever impact IRCA had was clearly limited. Although long discussed, it contained too many compromises and hasty provisions (like SAW) to be fully effective. Moreover, the United States continued to be attractive to many people. Evidence exists that those crossing the border consisted of proportionately more Central Americans and Mexicans eager to stay in the United States rather than working seasonally. Some authorities also believed that the latest undocumented immigrants heading north included more women and children and even some professionals.[180] Among the visa abusers, those who entered with visitors' permits and then stayed, were a number of well-educated people, such as the Irish and Israelis. What they shared in common was a search for a better life. Barring a major economic collapse in the United States, which would dry up employment, they would still try to find a place in the American economy and society.

8

A New Immigration Policy

IN 1981 the Select Commission on Immigration and Refugees Policy recommended changes in legal immigration policy, and the next year the Senate included several modifications in legal immigration when it first began to draft legislation dealing with undocumented aliens. As noted in chapter 7, these consisted of placing a cap on total immigration and an alteration of the fifth preference for admitting brothers and sisters of American citizens. But these suggestions were quickly dropped, and Congress concentrated on undocumented immigration when it passed the Immigration Reform and Control Act of 1986.

IRCA did touch upon one legal issue emerging in the 1980s, although it too was closely linked to illegal immigration. When the Irish economy weakened after 1980, thousands of Irish did what so many had done before them; they emigrated to America. Because they usually could not qualify under the preference system or as refugees, they came as tourists and then stayed to live and work in the United States when their visas expired. These New Irish mostly congregated in the New York, Boston, and Chicago areas. Estimates ran to about 100,000 undocumented Irish immigrants in the United States by the late 1980s. The men usually found jobs in construction and the women in child care.[1] Although they were unlikely to be apprehended and deported, their illegal status made them vulnerable in the labor market and they lacked access to better paying jobs and health care.[2]

The latest Irish immigrants formed the Irish Immigration Reform Movement (IIRM) to lobby Congress to legalize their status and increase immigration from Ireland.[3] They achieved a small success when IRCA was passed. A provision of IRCA proposed by Representative Brian Donnelly of Massachusetts set aside 10,000 immigrant visas for those countries adversely effected by the 1965 immigration reforms. The "Donnelly visas" were to be determined by lottery and, not surprisingly, hundreds of thousands of applicants arrived from Ireland. When the drawing was held by INS, the Irish won over 40 percent of the places. Another visa lottery was passed by Congress in 1988.[4] These modest victories did not satisfy IIRM, which became a force in shaping the Immigration Act of 1990.

Apart from the Irish issue, which quickly broadened into a movement to help all countries (mostly European) disadvantaged by the 1965 act, the growing debate over immigration was dominated by the family preferences and labor considerations. Pushing for changes in the immigration system was a relatively quiet force in the past, the business community and its allies, economists and think-tank experts. Rick Schwartz, a advocate for the VOLAGS and various ethnic groups using the family preferences and asylum, put it in 1990, "The pro-immigration coalition is expanding. In 1980, it involved churches, Hispanic and Asian groups, and civil rights lawyers. Today it also includes major corporations, industry associations and conservative think tanks like the Heritage Foundation and the Hudson Institute."[5]

These reformers wanted immigration to be more responsive to labor needs in the United States. They argued that the family preference system did not adequately take into account the American economy and that in the 1990s the United States would need more highly skilled labor that immigrants could partly provide. A 1987 Hudson Institute report funded by the Labor Department, called *Workforce 2000*, popularized the concept of skilled labor shortages, and economists like Barry Chiswick, Julian Simon, Gary Becker, George Borjas, and those on the President's Council of Economic Advisers pointed to what they considered a flawed immigration policy. They differed in some respects. Julian Simon, for example, favored virtually unlimited immigration, while George Borjas worried about the decline in skills of immigrants coming after 1965, largely because of the family preference system, a concern shared by Chiswick. But they all favored changes in immigration.[6]

Moreover, most economic research convinced a growing number of businessmen and politicians that on balance the economic benefits of immigration far outweighed the liabilities. A Labor Department study summarized the consensus in 1989, "A second conclusion of the economic literature is that the overall economic contributions of immigration exceed its economic liabilities. Benefits are thought to spread through the economy in the form of lower products prices and higher returns to capital."[7] By the late 1980s these voices were becoming influential. For example, Congressman Bruce Morrison, the House leader in shaping the Immigration Act of 1990, became a convert to believing in the economic benefits of immigration. According to Morrison, "The debate has definitely shifted. In the past, few people focused on legal immigration as an economic issue. But a growing body of evidence shows that immigration creates jobs and stimulates demand. You need a growing economy to produce jobs for unemployed workers, and labor shortages can be a barrier to economic growth."[8]

Congressional advocates of a new immigration policy began to hold hearings and draft legislation after IRCA was passed. By 1988 the Senate was ready to act. A bill sponsored by Edward Kennedy and Alan Simpson passed the Senate easily by a vote of 88 to 4 on March 15. The bill placed a cap of 590,000 on total immigration, not counting refugees. While that figure was higher than immigration in most years, it would limit immigration if it grew in the future. Under the then current system, immigration had no cap. Preferences did have definite numbers, but immediate family members were not capped, and that category had been growing steadily, to over 215,000 by 1988.

As for the family preference system, the Senate measure increased the second preference, which had extensive backlogs, for spouses and children of permanent resident aliens and cut the other family preferences, such as the fifth preference for brothers and sisters of American citizens. It was argued that spouses and children of resident aliens represented closer relations than did the brothers and sisters and their children of American citizens. The children of brothers and sisters would only be nieces and nephews of the United States sponsor.[9]

A central aim of Kennedy-Simpson was to increase visas based on economic considerations. It did so by creating a category of

55,000 "independent" immigrants admitted on the basis of a point system. Prospective independent immigrants received points based on education, skills in demand in the United States, age, working experience, and English-language proficiency.

While the independent immigrants were being chosen for economic reasons, the Irish (as well as many others in Western Europe) would clearly have an advantage. The illegal Irish arriving in the 1980s were young. Moreover, Ireland had an excellent educational system and, of course, the Irish were English-speaking. Senator Kennedy put it, "By redressing the imbalances in immigration which have inadvertently developed in recent years, America will open its doors again to those who no longer have immediate family ties in the United States. For example, in 1986, because of the family restrictions, only 1,852 applicants from Ireland qualified for immigrant visas. . . Similar statistics could be cited for many other nations that have sent large numbers of immigrants to the United States in the past."10

Kennedy-Simpson was debated briefly before its lopsided passage. A few Senators objected to one of the economic categories reserved for those who invested $1 million in an American enterprize that created ten jobs for Americans. They said this was a "fat cat" program for those who could buy their way into the United States, and it was possible that rich drug dealers would get visas through the investment provision.11

Although it held hearings, the House was in no hurry to act in 1988, or in the next year for that matter. But in 1989, the Senate again passed the bill, with some modifications. This time the Senators established a flexible ceiling of 630,000, not counting refugees.12 Like the previous bill it increased the second preference, but unlike that bill it kept intact the fifth preference. Ethnic organizations joined Asian and Hispanic groups representing countries who used the backlogged fifth preference to convince the legislators to leave it untouched. Testifying in 1988, one Asian-American spokesman said suggestions for cutting the fifth, were motivated by a desire "to dampen and restrict the so-called influx of immigrants from Asia."13 The acceptance of the existing fifth preference was a condition for increasing visas for immigrants with economic credentials and a cap. This meant, of course, an increase in immigration, or as Senator Kennedy said, "Our compromise will add visas, it does not subtract visas."[14]

The 1989 Senate bill reserved 150,000 places for "independent visas" and their families, again with some awarded on a point system. This time no points were given for English proficiency. Senator Simpson's attempt to restore the English proficiency lost 56 to 43. Senators pointed out that the United States had never used such a test and that many of the ancestors of the present senators came to America without speaking English.[15] The measure also contained some minor provisions, established a commission to examine immigration and gave the President the authority to make slight adjustments in the immigration levels.[16]

The House in 1989 passed several measures dealing with immigration, but not the Kennedy-Simpson bill. The representatives and senators did agree on permitting Chinese students to remain temporarily in the United States, but President Bush vetoed this bill.[17] The legislators also passed a bill dealing with immigrant nurses. The House passed safe haven legislation for certain Central American refugees and a measure permitting Filipino veterans of World War II to apply for American citizenship. While the Senate did not agree with these last two acts, they eventually found their way into the Immigration Act of 1990. Although the House did not act on Kennedy-Simpson, House committees held hearings and began moving in the direction of making major immigration changes. Moreover, House Democrats ousted Romano Mazzoli from the chairmanship of the Subcommittee on Immigration, Refugees and International Law and replaced him with Bruce Morrison of Connecticut.

As noted, Morrison and a growing number of his colleagues were believers in the economic benefits of immigration and the need to admit more immigrants for economic reasons. Because most House leaders either favored family unification or did not wish to be labeled bigots for suggesting a cut in the family preferences, they did not speak out against those preferences used by so many Asians and Hispanics. Indeed, the 1990 act, like the 1989 Senate bill before it, substantially increased the second preference and did not cut the fifth. The early Morrison bill uncapped the second preference for family members of resident aliens, which would have meant a large increase in immigration.

Not all immigration experts and lawmakers were convinced of the need for substantial increases in immigration and a major overhaul of immigration policy, whether in the family preferences or for economic considerations. Dissenters in the House—mostly Republicans—pointed out that public opinion polls indicated no desire for increased immigration and that the Morrison bill "responds to every special interest group that has made a demand on the U.S. immigration system."[18] While not necessarily opposing increases in immigration, experts like Michael Teitelbaum and David North warned against making hasty immigration policy and that too often past changes had unexpected consequences.[19] Of course some environmental groups and the Federation of Americans for Immigration reform opposed any increases in immigration levels. As the bill moved forward FAIR called the situation an "Immigration Crisis In the Making," and said the Morrison bill attempts to solve "all controversies by appeasing all special interest demands."[20]

Apart from general opposition to immigration and skepticism about hasty reforms, changes in the economic visas or independent categories did not go unopposed. Various people pointed to the difficulty of predicting labor shortages. Labor Department witnesses and others worried about how the department would determine work force needs.[21] Several congressmen denied the existence of a labor shortage, or as Representative John Bryant of Texas said, "we do not have a labor shortage in America today. What we have in America today is a job shortage and a training shortage."[22] Others asked that if the United States recruited skilled labor from abroad, what would be the incentive to upgrade the education of Americans, especially minorities?[23] Finally, some legislators remained uneasy about the provision for investors receiving visas. One congressman put it, "It remains inescapable that America would, for the first time in its history, be granting a statutory preference for citizenship based on wealth."[24]

Compared to Kennedy-Simpson, the House final bill was more generous and would have admitted approximately 800,000 immigrants annually while the Senate's figure was 630,000. The Bush administration indicated that it favored the Senate version, and Senator Simpson thought the House bill was too generous. Senators who agreed with Simpson at first did not want to meet with the House Conference members because they thought the gap was too great for compromise, but in October a agreement was reached. It nearly died in the House when the Conference Committee added a program for a pilot ID program for drivers' licenses. Opponents, especially Hispanics, feared this was a forerunner of a national identification system.[25] When it was dropped, the Immigration Act of 1990 was passed, overwhelmingly in the Senate (88–9) by a substantial 264 to 118 vote in the House.[26]

The Immigration Act of 1990 provided for a flexible ceiling of 700,000 for the first three years and 675,000 thereafter, excluding refugees. After three years family unification would have 480,000 places and economic visas 140,000. The economic visas were divided into a number of categories emphasizing skilled, educated, and entrepreneurial immigrants. The act also included an amnesty for undocumented family members of immigrants legalized by IRCA. This amnesty differed in the Senate and House bills, and the compromise provided 55,000 visas annually for three years, provided these family members entered the United States by May 5, 1988.

For immigrant "diversity," a main goal of Senator Kennedy and the Irish Immigration Reform Movement, 40,000 places were reserved for those nations adversely effected by the 1965 act for each of the first three years, and 55,000 annually after that. During the three-year transition period, by a formula tied to Donnelly visas, Ireland was guaranteed 16,000 of the 40,000 slots. Final provisions stated that these visa holders had to have a promise of employment in the United States and that these visas would be scattered among countries and continents.

Ireland was not the only beneficiary of special provisions. Hong Kong's ceiling was increased to 10,000, and extra visas were set aside for Hong Kong residents working for American companies. And Hong Kong would be treated like a separate nation after 1994.

The individual country ceiling of 20,000 was increased to

around 25,000, and regulations were relaxed for temporary workers to make it easier for American businesses to recruit highly
skilled and managerial employees on a temporary basis. At the
same time some limits were placed on temporary workers, and
American workers were protected by several provisions.

For asylees the number permitted to become resident aliens
went from 5,000 to 10,000 annually, and Salvadorans received an
18-month grant of safe haven under the new "temporary protected status" clause. The House had been trying for several years
to grant Salvadorans safe haven, and now the Senate agreed to
include this provision in the final bill. Although EVD had been
used by various presidents for nearly two decades, Congress was
now legislating a new category to protect aliens who faced danger
if they had to return home when their visas expired.

The final bill eliminated individual bans on those wanting to
enter the United States, such as the bar on homosexuals and those
who had been members of organizations such as the Communist
Party.[27] The act also included a number of minor provisions touch-
ing on immigration and naturalization such as permitting Filipino
World War II veterans to become American citizens. About the
only things the restrictionists won were an authorization for more
INS personnel, improved maintenance of border barriers, and
tighter procedures for deporting alien criminals.[28]

The forces shaping American immigration policy since 1945
achieved a substantial victory with the enactment of the liberal
Immigration Act of 1990. Using the post-1945 growing racial and
ethnic toleration, various VOLAGS and racial and ethnic organizations defeated attempts to decrease family unification preferences
used by third world nations; indeed, they were increased. Moreover, the bill opened the door for additional Chinese immigration
from Hong Kong. The new IRCA amnesty benefited third world
migrants, chiefly Mexicans, while another Hispanic group, Salvadorans, won a stay of deportation. Restrictionist groups like
FAIR were vastly outnumbered, and they did not use racial arguments for restriction.

Foreign policy and humanitarian considerations also played a
role in finalizing the bill, as can be seen by the stay of deportation
for Salvadorans and the creation of the new temporary protected

status category. Moreover, the Bush administration had already announced increased refugee allotments for fiscal 1990 for a total of 131,000; and in February 1991, it granted temporary protected status to 50,000 Middle Easterners.

Economic factors, always important in determining immigration policy, emerged as relatively powerful force in the late 1980s and played a major role shaping the final act. Advocates of the need to import migrant labor, especially highly skilled workers, carried the day. The 1990 act was passed just as the United States was sliding into a recession, and whether Congress would have been as generous six months later is, of course, not known.

While economics, foreign policy, and humanitarian considerations, racial and ethnic lobbying and economics all help explain the final bill, the Immigration Act of 1990 was nonetheless a remarkable piece of legislation. It was not a high priority measure and almost got lost in the waning hours of the 101st Congress. Pressure groups wanted increases in immigration, but public opinion polls of the late 1980s indicated little popular enthusiasm for more immigrants, and at best an ambivalence.[29] One congressman from Tennessee put it, "Bringing in a lot of foreigners into the country does not get a lot of support back home."[30] Congress was clearly more liberal than the public, as Raul Yzaguirre, president of the National Council of La Raza, said, "Votes in both the House and Senate shattered the myth that Congress is unwilling to adopt fair, humane, generous immigration policies."[31]

Explaining passage of immigration acts is easier than predicting their eventual results, and the 1990 act is no exception. The parole provisions of McCarran-Walter Immigration Act of 1952, intended to be used for individual cases, have been invoked by presidents to permit the entrance of hundreds of thousands of refugees since the 1950s. The 1965 reforms had unintended consequences as did the Refugee Act of 1980 and IRCA. The Immigration Act of 1965 led to substantial increases in third world immigration. Drafters of the 1980 Refugee Act thought 5,000 places for asylum would be adequate, but soon INS was swamped with asylum requests. The same act pegged the "normal flow" of refugees 50,000, but during the 1980s the actual number of refugees entering annually was nearly twice that amount. In drafting IRCA Congress did not foresee the large number of SAW applications for amnesty nor the problem of additional legalization for immediate family members of those covered by amnesty.

Yet some outcomes of the Immigration Act of 1990 appear predictable. Most immigrants will continue to arrive under the family preferences, but a somewhat larger proportion will enter because of their economic skills. Regardless of how they emigrate to the United States, their numbers should grow in the 1990s. Under the new law almost 700,000 immigrants will be allowed to enter annually. In addition the nation had been admitting about 90,000 refugees annually during the 1980s, and if that figure held another 900,000 would arrive in the 1990s. IRCA produced three million applicants for amnesty. Approximately 500,000 had changed their temporary status to resident aliens in 1988 and 1989. If the others become resident aliens in the early 1990s that will add 2.5 million persons to the immigrant totals in the 1990s. Collectively, all these newcomers could amount to 10 million and make the 1990s the largest decade in American history for immigration, surpassing the previous high of 1900–1910.

These figures do not include undocumented immigration. IRCA has not been able to stem the flow completely, and the best guesses indicate that 100,000 to 200,000 undocumented immigrants enter the United States annually and remain here. Even if one uses a low figure, these immigrants could still add another one million to the immigrant stock of the 1990s. Of course not all immigrants stay, but while exact figures are missing, emigration appears to be less than in the first decades of the twentieth century.

But who will be part of this record flow of immigration? The new allotments for family unification will no doubt be used by the same groups that are currently using them, for the backlogs are over two million.[32] As for the new independent and diversity immigrants, it is difficult to predict. The 1990 reforms were crafted to increase Western European (and especially Irish) immigration. If social and economic conditions in Western Europe are satisfactory then many will not come regardless of the law. Eastern Europe countries which, except for the Soviet Union, are no longer eligible for refugee admissions, are another matter. There, unsettled social and economic conditions could easily prompt a new wave of immigration to America. These former Communist states appear willing to allow their citizens to emigrate, but this situation could change.

As for the independents, it will certainly be easier for the United States to attract investors, highly skilled "super stars" and other economically desirable immigrants, but they must be willing to come to America. Opportunities in Australia, Europe, Canada, and elsewhere could prove to be more attractive. In the past Africa has not been a major source of voluntary immigration to America. It is quite possible that Nigerians and South Africans could be major beneficiaries of the new law, rather than the Irish or Poles.

As for refugees and asylum, even a minor change such as increasing the places for asylum from 5,000 to 10,000 may have unintended consequences. Congress enacted the higher figure to ease the backlog of applicants and be more in accord with the reality. But generous court interpretations could make it easier to obtain asylum. Such decisions and the enlarged number could simply attract more undocumented aliens hoping for asylum and the asylum backlog could grow. Moreover, refugee flows are seldom predictable. American involvement in world affairs in Cuba, Korea, and Vietnam all helped trigger large immigrant movements to the United States. Will the Middle East, or some other area, follow these examples?

Of course, Congress could change policy in the near future. Major changes have occurred since 1945 and between 1980 and 1990 Congress passed three major immigration bills. The legislators themselves are more aware of the need for better information about immigration and the 1990 act established a commission to report about immigration and its impact upon the United States. Yet knowledge alone does not guarantee a consistent policy. As in the past immigration policy—and consequently immigrant flows—will continue to be determined by the interplay of forces that emerged after World War II. They brought to the United States the new third world immigrants who have already contributed to American society. In the near future they will no doubt continue to do so.

Notes

Introduction: Third World Immigration Before World War II

1. For a general history of immigration consult Leonard Dinnerstein and David Reimers, *Ethnic Americans: A History of Immigration and Assimilation;* Maldwyn Jones, *American Immigration;* Maxine Sellers, *To Seek America: A History of Ethnic Life in the United States;* and Thomas Archdeacon, *Becoming American.*

2. For immigration restriction see John Higham, *Strangers in the Land: Patterns of American Nativism, 1860–1925,* and Marion Bennett, *American Immigration Policies: A History,* especially ch. 5.

3. An excellent history of Asians in America is Ronald Takaki, *Strangers from a Different Shore: A History of Asian Americans.* For the Chinese, see Gunther Barth, *Bitter Strength: A History of the Chinese in the United States, 1850–1870;* and Jack Chen, *The Chinese of America.* Roger Daniels, *Asian America: Chinese and Japanese in the United States since 1850* covers both the Chinese and Japanese.

4. A general history of the Japanese is Bill Hosokawa and Robert Wilson, *East to America: The Story of the Japanese in America.*

5. For Filipino immigration see Bruno Lasker, *Filipino Immigration;* for the Koreans, Lee Houchins and Chan-Su Hochins, "The Korean Experience in America, 1903–1924," in Norris Hundley, Jr., ed., in *The Asian American: The Historical Experience;* for East Indians; Gary Hess, "The Forgotten Asian Americans: The East Indian Community in the United States," *The Asian American;* and Joan Jensen, *Passage from India: Asian Immigrants in North America.*

6. Diane Mei Lin Mark and Ginger Chih, *A Place Called Chinese America,* p. 173.

7. Two excellent general accounts of Mexican immigration are Lawrence A. Cardoso, *Mexican Emigration to the United States, 1897–1931;* and Mark Reisler, *By the Sweat of Their Brow; Mexican Labor in the United States, 1900–1940.*

8. For a general discussion of black immigrants, see Ira De A. Reid, *The Negro Immigrant.*

9. For Mexicans during the 1920s, see Cardoso, *Mexican Emigration*, ch. 5; and Reisler, *By the Sweat of Their Brow*, chs. 7–9.

10. Mark and Chih, *Chinese America*, pp. 29–36.

11. Bennett, *American Immigration Policies*, pp. 15–17; and Edward P. Hutchinson, *Legislative History of American Immigration Policy, 1790–1965*, pp. 70–71, 80–83.

12. For the Chinese exclusion movement, see Barth, *Bitter Strength*; Elmer Sandemeyer, *The Anti-Chinese Movement in California*; Stuart Miller, *The Unwelcome Immigrant: The American Image of the Chinese, 1785–1882*; and Alexander Saxton, *The Indepensable Enemy: Labor and the Anti-Chinese Movement in California*.

13. For the anti-Japanese movement, see Roger Daniels, *The Politics of Prejudice: The Anti-Japanese Movement in California and the Struggle for Japanese Exclusion*.

14. *Ibid.*

15. Houchins and Houchins, "Korean Experience"; and Bong-youn Choy, *Koreans in America*, p. 76.

16. Jensen, *Passage from India*, pp. 42–50.

17. Hess, "Asian Indians," pp. 159–64.

18. Daniels, *Politics of Prejudice*, pp. 98–105. For the confused status of East Indians under this act see Maxine Fisher, *The Asian Indians of New York City*, pp. 14–15; Gary Hess, "The Asian Indian Immigrants in the United States, 1900–1965," in S. Chandrasekhar, ed., *From India to America*, pp. 30–31; and Jensen, *Passage from India*, ch. 12.

19. See U.S. Congress, House, Committee on Immigration and Naturalization, *Exclusion of Immigration from the Philippine Islands*, Hearings, 71st Cong., 2d sess.; Robert A. Divine, *American Immigration Policy, 1924–1952*, pp. 68–71; and H. Brett Melendy, "The Filipinos in the United States," in Hundley, *Asian-Americans*, pp. 115–16, 119–25.

20. See U.S. Congress, House, Committee on Immigration and Naturalization, *To Return to the Philippine Islands Unemployed Filipinos*, Hearings, 72d Cong., 2d sess.; and Divine, *Immigration Policy*, pp. 68–76.

21. U.S. Congress, Senate, Committee on Immigration, *Restriction of Western Hemisphere Immigration*, Hearings, 70th Cong., 1st sess., pp. 161–62.

22. Divine, *Immigration Policy*, pp. 52–68.

23. See Abraham Hoffman, *Unwanted Mexican Americans in the Great Depression: Repatriation Pressures, 1929–1941*.

24. Mark and Chih, *Chinese America*, pp. 40–48.

25. *Interpreter Releases* (January 15, 1960), 37:9; and Takaki, *Strangers from a Different Shore*, p. 416.

26. Richard Craig, *The Bracero Program: Interest Groups and Foreign Policy,* pp. 42–46.

27. The best accounts of the camp experience are Roger Daniels, *Concentration Camps USA: Japanese Americans in World War II;* and Commission on Wartime Relocation, *Personal Justice Denied.*

28. Matt S. Meir and Feliciano Rivera, *The Chicanos: A History of Mexican Americans,* pp. 191–95.

1. *The Door Opens a Little, 1943–1965*

1. Robert Divine, *American Immigration Policy,* pp. 22–23.

2. *Ibid.,* p. 23, and Roger Daniels, *The Politics of Prejudice,* pp. 95–105.

3. Harvard Sitkoff, *A New Deal for Blacks,* ch. 12.

4. Diane Mei Lin Mark and Ginger Chih, *A Place Called Chinese America,* pp. 95–98.

5 See Henry L. Feingold, *The Politics of Rescue:The Roosevelt Administration and the Holocaust, 1938–1945,* and David Wyman, *Paper Walls.*

6. U.S. Congress, House, Committee on Immigration and Naturalization, *To Deny Admission to the United States of Certain Aliens and To Reduce Immigration Quotas,* Hearings, 79th Cong., 2d sess., pp. 3–4.

7. William Bernard, ed., *American Immigration Policy—A Reappraisal,* pp. 176, 191, and 164–65.

8. Under refugee legislation, sponsoring organizations had to find jobs and housing for immigrants. Changes in the law made in 1965 provided for careful Labor Department certification. This will be discussed in chapter 3.

9. Fred Riggs, *Pressures on Congress: A Study of the Repeal of Chinese Exclusion,* chs. 6–7.

10. *Ibid.,* p. 56.

11. See U.S. Congress, House, Committee on Immigration and Naturalization, *Repeal of the Chinese Exclusion Acts,* Hearings, 78th Cong., 1st sess.

12. U.S. Congress, House, *Repealing the Chinese Exclusion Laws,* H. Rept. 732, Part II, 78th Cong., 1st sess., p. 1.

13. Hearings, *Repeal of Chinese Exclusion,* p. 19.

14. Riggs, *Pressures on Congress,* chs. 15 and 16.

15. U.S. Congress, House, Committee on Immigration and Naturalization, *To Grant a Quota to Eastern Hemisphere Indians and To Make Them Racially Eligible for Naturalization,* Hearings, 79th Cong., 1st Sess., p. 5.

16. *Ibid.,* p. 16.

17. CR (Congressional Record), October 10, 1945, pp. 9529–30. See also Divine, American Immigration Policy, pp. 152–54.

18. Ronald Takaki, Strangers from a Different Shore, p. 361.

19. U.S. Congress, House, Subcommittee on Immigration and Naturalization of the Committee on the Judiciary, Providing for Equality Under Naturalization and Immigration Laws, Hearings, 80th Cong., 2d sess., p. 8. For an example of support for the Judd bill from a journal (Reader's Digest) not normally pro-immigrant, see Blake Clark, "Why Shouldn't They be Americans?" pp. 91–94.

20. Hearings, Providing for Equality, pp. 48–49, and CR, March 1, 1949, p. 1683.

21. Gossett was a vigorous and important opponent of the Displaced Persons Act and a strong supporter of the McCarran-Walter Act. For his view of the Judd bill see CR, March 1, 1949, p. 1681.

22. Bill Hosokawa, Nisei: The Quiet Americans, p. 443.

23. U.S. Congress, Subcommittees of the Committees on the Judiciary, Revision of Immigration, Naturalization, and Nationality Laws, Hearings, 82d Cong., 1st sess., p. 74.

24. Hosokawa, Nisei, pp. 334–50.

25. U.S. Congress, House, Providing the Privilege of Becoming a Naturalized Citizen of the United States to all Immigrants Having a Legal Right to Permanent Residence, To Make Immigration Quotas Available to Asian and Pacific Peoples, H. Rept. 65, 81st Cong., 1st sess., pp. 2–5.

26. CR, March 1, 1949, p. 1690.

27. Ibid., pp. 1690, 1692. The Powell amendment to delete the colonial limit lost 19 to 118.

28. Hosokawa, Nisei, p. 451.

29. Ibid.

30. For an excellent discussion of the McCarran-Walter Act see Marius A. Dimmitt, "The Enactment of the McCarran-Walter Immigration Act of 1952," Ph.D. diss., University of Kansas, 1970. See also Divine, American Immigration Policy, ch. 9; and Hutchinson, Legislative History, pp. 297–310.

31. Herbert Lehman to Hubert Humphrey, October 30, 1952. Papers of Herbert Lehman, Columbia University.

32. See U.S. Congress, House, Revising the Laws Relating to Immigration and Naturalization and Nationality, H. Rept. 1365, 82d Cong., 2d sess., pp. 27–28 for the view of Emanuel Celler, the leading opponent of the McCarran Act in the House. See also U.S. Congress, Senate, Revision of the Immigration and Nationality Laws, Committee on the Judiciary, Minority Report, 82d Cong., 2d sess.

33. CR, May 22, 1952, p. 5765.

34. President Truman in vetoing the bill established a committee to

make recommendations for immigration reform. The resulting report,*Whom Shall We Welcome?*, summarized the liberal approach to immigration, but Congress ignored it.

35. Bennett, *American Immigration Policies*, p. 72.

36. *Ibid.*, pp. 73–74, 79–80, 81, and 86–87, and U.S. Congress, House, *Immigration—Alien Spouses*, H. Rept. 428, 80th Cong., 1st sess.

37. One minor reform was enacted. The original Asia-Pacific Triangle had a total ceiling of 2,000, not counting China and Japan. In 1961 Congress repealed this limit.

38. For a thorough analysis of the DP issue see Leonard Dinnerstein, *America and the Survivors of the Holocaust.*

39. *CR*, February 28, 1950, p. 2476.

40. U.S. Congress, Senate, Subcommittee of the Committee on the Judiciary, *Expellees and Refugees*, Hearings, 83d Cong., 1st sess., pp. 83–95, 115–16, 195–96, and 305–6.

41. For the groups admitted under the 1953 Refugee Relief Act see Administrator of the Refugee Relief Act of 1953 as amended, *Final Report.*

42. Betty Lee Sung, *The Story of the Chinese in America*, pp. 91–92.

43. *CR*, July 1, 1960, p. 15400.

44. Abba Schwartz, *The Open Society*, pp. 139–40, and Bennett, *American Immigration Policies*, p. 204.

45. Data are drawn from the annual reports of INS, 1945–1965. The refugee acts were based on anti-communism. For a thorough discussion of the postwar refugee policies and their relation to the cold war, see Gil Loescher and John A. Scanlan, *Calculated Kindness: Refugees and America's Half-Open Door, 1945–Present.*

46. Data are drawn from the annual reports of INS, 1945–65.

47. Sung, *The Story of the Chinese*, pp. 85–86 and 91–92.

48. *Ibid.*, pp. 294–98.

49. Thomas J. Mills, "Scientific Personnel and the Professions," *The New Immigration: Annals*, pp. 34–37.

50. Mark and Chih, *Chinese America*, p. 173. For a discussion of New York's Chinatown see Bernard P. Wong, *Chinatown: Economic Adaptation and Ethnic Identity of the Chinese.*

51. Mark and Chih, *Chinese America*, pp. 173 and 99–100.

52. Wong, *Chinatown*, p. 8.

53. *Ibid.*, pp. 101–4.

54. *Congressional Quarterly Almanac*, 1989, p. 283.

55. H. Brett Melendy, *Asians in America*, pp. 6–7, and James Allen, "Recent Immigration from the Philippines and the Filipino Communities in the United States," pp. 199–203.

56. Melendy, *Asians in America*, p. 96.

57. *Ibid.*, ch. 6.

58. *Ibid.*, ch. 7.

59. *Ibid.*, chs. 9 and 11.

60. Illsoo Kim, *New Urban Immigrants: The Korean Community in New York City*, p. 41.

61. *Ibid.*, p. 37.

62. *Ibid.*, p. 42. Congress has periodically enacted legislation to permit Americans to adopt foreign orphans. In 1983, for example, the legislators made it possible for Americans to adopt Amerasian children in Korea and Indochina. These were the children left behind by American soldiers who had fathered them. See Jill Bauermeister, "Amerasians in America," pp. 331–33; *Congressional Quarterly* (October 2, 1982), 40:2470, and *CR* (daily digest), October 28, 1982, pp. S. 12410–13.

63. For a discussion of the Dutch-Indonesians, see American Immigration and Citizenship Conference, *Doubly Uprooted; Dutch-Indonesian Refugees in the United States.*

64. Melendy, *Asians in America*, pp. 202–6, and Fisher, *The Indians of New York City*, pp. 8–10.

65. Melendy, *Asians in America*, pp. 206–8.

66. Select Commission on Western Hemisphere Immigration, *Final Report*, pp. 39–48.

67. INS, *Annual Report*, 1956, pp. 44–46.

68. Select Commission, *Final Report*, pp. 111–30.

69. *Ibid.*, pp. 113–28.

70. *Ibid.*, pp. 116–18.

71. Data on Caribbean and South American immigration are drawn from INS annual reports.

72. Select Commission, *Final Report*, pp. 165–67.

73. Walter Mondale, "The Cost of the Brain Drain," p. 68. See also Ruth Jorrin, "Wealth Attracts Talent," pp. 425–27. ·

74. Martha Lear, "New York's Haitians," *New York Times Magazine*, October 10, 1971. Data on occupations are drawn from annual reports of INS.

75. *Ibid.*

76. Elsa M. Chaney, "Columbian Migration to the United States (Part 2)," pp. 107–11.

2. Braceros and Los Mojados

1. Michael Piore, *Birds of Passage: Migrant Labor and Industrial Societies*, pp. 154–57. For an extended discussion of this migration see Thomas

Kessner, "Repatriation in American History," Select Commission on Immigration and Refugee Policy, *Appendix A to Staff Reports*, pp. 187–387.

2. Lawrence A. Cardoso, *Mexican Emigration to the United States, 1897–1931*, p. 34.

3. Mark Reisler, *By the Sweat of Their Brow: Mexican Labor in the United States, 1900–1940*, pp. 25–27.

4. Otey Scruggs, "The First Mexican Farm Labor Program," pp. 319–26.

5. Cardoso, *Mexican Emigration*, p. 84.

6. See Abraham Hoffman, *Unwanted Mexican Americans in the Great Depression: Repatriation Pressures, 1929–1941*.

7. Richard Craig, *The Bracero Program: Interest Groups and Foreign Policy*, pp. 37–40. This is an excellent discussion of the bracero program.

8. *Ibid.*, pp. 41–42.

9. Otey Scruggs, "Evolution of the Mexican Farm Labor Agreement of 1942," pp. 140–49; and Craig, *Bracero Program*, pp. 42–46.

10. Craig, *Bracero Program*, pp. 46–68.

11. *Ibid.*, pp. 42–46. For general treatments of the bracero program, see also Ernesto Galarza, *Merchants of Labor: The Mexican Bracero Story;* and U.S. Congress, Senate, Committee on the Judiciary, *Temporary Workers Programs; Background and Issues*, A Report for the Select Commission on Immigration and Refugee Policy, Committee Print, 96th Cong., 2d sess.

12. Craig, *Bracero Program*, p. 63.

13. President's Commission on Migratory Labor in American Agriculture, *Final Report*, p. 64.

14. *Ibid.*, p. 65.

15. *Ibid.*

16. *Ibid.*, pp. 66–67. Peter Kirsetein has argued that agribusiness got its way and that organized labor was omitted from the commission. This certainly appears to be the case until 1964 when the bracero program was finally ended. Peter N. Kirstein, "Agribusiness, Labor, and the Wetbacks: Truman's Commission on Migratory Labor," pp. 650–67.

17. Public Law 78, July 12, 1951.

18. Craig, *Bracero Program*, p. 80.

19. Committee on the Judiciary, *Temporary Worker Programs*, p. 36.

20. E. Elridge, "Helping Hands from Mexico," pp. 28–29; and Jean Begeman, "Sweatshops on the Farm," pp. 16–17.

21. Ted Le Berthon, "At the Prevailing Rate," pp. 122–25; *Commonweal* (July 4, 1958), 68:341–42; and *New York Times, December 1, 1964*.

22. U.S. Congress, House, Subcommittee on Equipment, Supplies, and Manpower of the Committee on Agriculture, *Mexican Farm Labor*

Program, Hearings, 84th Cong., 1st sess., p. 128. See also *Time*, February 7, 1961, p. 18, for an account of union attempts to organize agricultural workers and fight braceros.

23. Subcommittee on Equipment, *Mexican Farm Labor*, pp. 260–62. Other statements against the program can be found in the above hearings and also U.S. Congress, House, Subcommittee on Equipment, Supplies, and Manpower of the Committee on Agriculture, *Extension of the Mexican Farm Labor Program*, Hearings, 86th Cong., 2d sess.; Ted Le Berthon, "At the Prevailing Rate," pp. 122–25; Jean Begeman, "Sweatshops on the Farm," pp. 16–17; and Galarza, *Merchants of Labor*, especially chs. 12–16.

24. Craig, *Bracero Program*, pp. 153–55. A copy of the consultants' report can be found in U.S. Congress, Senate, Committee on Agriculture and Forestry, *Extension of the Mexican Farm Labor Program*, 87th Cong., 1st sess., pp. 267–84.

25. Committee on Agriculture and Forestry, *Extension of the Mexican Farm Labor Program*, pp. 26–27.

26. Craig, *Bracero Program*, ch. 5.

27. Committee on the Judiciary, *Temporary Worker Programs*, pp. 65–67. Wirtz also said before the termination of the program that he would make every effort to place unemployed Americans in seasonal jobs usually held by braceros. *New York Times*, November 15, 1964.

28. U.S. Congress, Senate, Committee on Agriculture and Forestry, *Importation of Foreign Agricultural Workers*, Hearings, 89th Cong., 1st sess., p. 134.

29. *Ibid.*, p. 169.

30. Juan Ramon Garcia, *Operation Wetback: The Mass Deportation of Mexican Undocumented Workers in 1954*, pp. 53–57. This is an excellent account of undocumented workers and the issues in the 1940s and 1950s.

31. *Ibid.*, p. 43.

32. Henry P. Anderson, *The Bracero Program in California*, pp. 67–68.

33. Maria Herrera-Sobek, *The Bracero Experience: Elitelore versus Folklore*, p. 45.

34. See Galarza, *Merchants of Labor*, especially chs. 11 to 17.

35. Anderson, *Bracero Program*, p. 75.

36. *Ibid.*

37. Herrera-Sobek, *Bracero Experience*, p. 45.

38. *Ibid.*, p. 71.

39. President's Commission, *Final Report*, p. 80.

40. *Ibid.*, p. 88.

41. Garcia, *Operation Wetback*, pp. 142–43.

42. *Ibid.*, pp. 35–43, and President's Commission, *Final Report*, p. 53.

43. Craig, *Bracero Program*, pp. 68–71.

44. U.S. Congress, Senate, Committee on the Judiciary, *Immigration and Naturalization Systems of the United States*, S. Rept. 1515, 81st Cong., 2d sess., pp. 584–86. The Committee wanted permanent features in the law to permit the entry of temporary agricultural workers, but recommended no action in dealing with the employment of illegal aliens.

45. For the House committee's report, see U.S. Congress, House, Committee on the Judiciary, *Immigration and Nationality Act*, H. Rept., 1365, 82d Cong., 2d sess.

46. *CR (Congressional Record)*, Feb. 5, 1952, p. 812.

47. *Ibid.*

48. Craig, *Bracero Program*, pp. 93–99, and Garcia, *Operation Wetback*, pp. 127–131.

49. Jean Begeman, "Slaves of Today," p. 16.

50. Gladwin Hill, "The Wetbacks—McCarran's Immigrants," pp. 151–52.

51. Garcia, *Operation Wetback*, pp. 157–60.

52. *Ibid.*, pp. 161–67. The Senate Judiciary Committee later approved a modified employer sanctions measure, but Congress did not vote on it. *Interpreter Releases* (August 25, 1954), 31:269.

53. Garcia, *Operation Wetback*, chs. 6–7, and Julian Samora, *Los Mojados. The Wetback Story*, pp. 51–55.

54. Garcia, *Operation Wetback*, chs. 7–8.

55. *Ibid.*, pp. 224–25.

56. INS, *Annual Report*, 1955, pp. 14–15.

57. Garcia, *Operation Wetback*, pp. 219–21.

58. *New York Times*, January 31, 1954.

59. Herrera-Sobek, *Bracero Experience*, p. 74.

60. President's Commission, *Final Report*, p. 85.

61. *Ibid.*

62. Garcia, *Operation Wetback*, p. 144, and *New York Times*, August 12, 1954.

63. President's Commission, *Final Report*, pp. 76–78.

64. *Ibid.*, pp. 80–83.

65. Garcia, *Operation Wetback*, p. 144.

66. President's Commission, *Final Report*, p. 78.

67. Garcia, *Operation Wetback*, p. 148.

68. *Ibid.*, p. 146, and President's Commission, *Final Report*, pp. 78–80.

69. Craig, *Bracero Program*, pp. 50–51.

70. President's Commission, *Final Report*, p. 78.

71. Herrera-Sobek, *Bracero Experience*, pp. 100–1.

72. President's Commission, *Final Report*, p. 69.

73. Garcia, *Operation Wetback*, pp. 227–29.

74. U.S. Congress, Senate, Committee on the Judiciary, *Selected Readings on U.S. Immigration Policy and the Law,* Committee Print, 96th Cong., 2d sess., p. 162.

75. *CR*, December 3, 1963, p. 23157.

3. *A Cautious Reform: The Immigration Act of 1965*

1. Report of the President's Commission on Immigration and Naturalization, *Whom Shall We Welcome?*, p. 177.

2. *Ibid.*, pp. 263–64. The commission wanted an end to national origins, an increase in immigration, and the flexibility to admit more refugees and those with skills needed in the United States. The commission also believed that immigration could be increased without being harmful economically to the United States. The attitudes of organizations and persons critical of the McCarran-Walter Act can be found in the commission's hearings. U.S. Congress, House, Committee on the Judiciary, *Hearings Before the President's Commission on Immigration and Naturalization*, 82d Cong., 2d sess.

3. *New York Times*, January 2, 1953.

4. *Interpreter Releases* (April 1, 1960), 37:70–71.

5. An interesting view of Walter can be found in Meg Greenfield, "The Melting Pot of Francis E. Walter," pp. 24–28, and *New York Times*, February 2, 1957.

6. *CR (Congressional Record)*, May 13, 1952, pp. 5094–95. For Walter's view see Francis Walter, "The Truth About the Immigration Act," p. 126.

7. Schwartz's role in the 1965 act can be found in his book, *The Open Society*. General accounts of the 1965 act are in *Congressional Quarterly Almanac*, 1965, pp. 259–80; William S. Stern, "H.R. 2580: The Immigration and Nationality Amendments of 1965—A Case Study," Ph.D. dissertation, New York University, 1974; Charles Keely, "The Immigration Act of 1965: A Study of the Relationship of Social Science Theory to Group Interest and Legislation," Ph.D. dissertation, Fordham University, 1970; and Jethro K. Lieberman, *Are Americans Extinct?* Kennedy's bill can be found in *CR*, July 23, 1963, pp. 13132–33. His message can be found in Schwartz, *Open Society*, pp. 210–14.

8. As noted, in 1961 Congress had lifted the 2,000 ceiling on immigration from the Asia-Pacific Triangle, but most Asian nations still had small quotas, usually 100.

9. Under the 1952 law preferences to relatives and those with skills

were granted within the individual national origins quotas. The Kennedy proposals simply replaced the national origins system with a family preference and skill system.

10. Because the Immigration and Nationality Act of 1952 was so restrictive private member bills had grown steadily in the late 1950s and early 1960s to circumvent the requirements and quotas. A number of congressmen, as well as committees concerned with immigration, found these bills time consuming. See Representative Michael Feighan's comment that reform should reduce private bills to "manageable proportions consisting of only a very few cases." *CR*, June 1, 1965, p. 12089.

11. *CR*, January 8, 1964, p. 115; and U.S. Dept. of State, *Bulletin* (February 19, 1964), 50:211–12.

12. Lieberman, *Are Americans Extinct?*, pp. 127–28; and *CR*, April 10, 1964, pp. 7617–28.

13. *New York Times*, September 8, 1964, and October 10, 1964.

14. Stern, "Immigration and Nationality Act," pp. 55–56; and *Congressional Quarterly Almanac*, 1965, pp. 463–64.

15. U.S. Congress, House, H. Doc. 52, 89th Cong., 1st sess.

16. U.S. Congress, Senate, Subcommittee on Immigration and Naturalization of the Committee on the Judiciary, *Immigration*, Hearings, 89th Cong., 1st sess., pp. 8–29, 47–67, and 85–103; and U.S. Congress, House, Subcommittee No. 1 of the Committee on the Judiciary, *Immigration*, Hearings, 88th Cong., 2d sess., pp. 410–12 and 442–57. According to Abba Schwartz, Dean Rusk personally favored the retention of national origins but he supported the administration's bill in public. Schwartz, *Open Society*, pp. 119–21.

17. U.S. Congress, House, 1964 Hearings, p. 412.

18. *Ibid.*, pp. 445–57.

19. See the testimony in both the 1964 and 1965 hearings and Stern, "Immigration and Nationality act," pp. 184–88.

20. Stern, "Immigration and Nationality Act," pp. 105–10. For the views of labor unions in the McCarran-Walter Act debates, see Marius Dimmitt, "Enactment of the McCarran-Walter Act of 1952," pp. 188–89.

21. U.S. Congress, Senate, 1965 hearings, pp. 637–40.

22. U.S. Congress, House, 1964 hearings, p. 736.

23. Edward Kennedy, "The Immigration Act of 1965," in *The New Immigration: The Annals*, p. 142.

24. Deane and David Heller, "Our New Immigration Law," pp. 6–7, and Stern, "Immigration and Nationality Act," pp. 132–44. Michael Feighan also played a role in winning over the opposition of the patriotic groups.

25. *Congressional Quarterly* (October 8, 1965), 23:2042. For the shifting position of the Legion see U.S. Congress, House, 1965 hearings, pp. 266–67, and *CR*, August 25, 1965, p. 21815.

26. *Congressional Quarterly* (October 8, 1965), 23:2041, and Stern, "Immigration and Nationality Act," pp. 84–89. See also *Wall Street Journal*, October 4, 1965.

27. *CR*, February 4, 1965, pp. 2058–59; and *Congressional Quarterly* (October 8, 1965), 23:2041.

28. Stern, "Immigration and Nationality Act," pp. 100–101; Schwartz, *Open Society*, pp. 116–18 and 121–23; and Lieberman, *Are Americans Extinct?* pp. 160–61. For Feighan's bill see *CR*, June 1, 1965, pp. 12088–93.

29. Moore exaggerated when he said the final bill was practically his: "The most significant changes made by the subcommittee as it completely rewrote the administration bill came from H.R. 9139, the Moore bill." *CR*, August 25, 1965, p. 21821. However, he was especially sensitive to the concerns of organized labor and played an important role in tailoring the bill to labor's wishes. See Stern, "Immigration and Nationality Act," pp. 107–10, and *Wall Street Journal*, October 4, 1965.

30. U.S. Congress, House, Subcommittee No. 1 of the Committee on the Judiciary, *Immigration*, Hearings, 90th Cong., 2d sess., p. 111. See also Frank H. Cassell, "Immigration and the Department of Labor," in *The New Immigration: The Annals*, pp. 107–8.

31. U.S. Congress, Senate, S. Rept. 748, 89th Cong., 1st sess., pp. 6–7; and Stern, "Immigration and Nationality Act," pp. 105–8.

32. U.S. Departments of Justice, Labor, and State: Interagency Task Force on Immigration Policy, *Staff Report*, pp. 197–319; and Robert Goldfarb, "Occupational Preferences in the U.S. Immigration Law: An Economic Analysis," Barry Chiswick, ed., *The Gateway: Issues in American Immigration*, pp. 412–48.

33. S. Rept. 748. p. 5. The exact size of Italy's backlog, and that of other nations as well, was unclear. Some administration leaders believed that the actual number of Italians desiring to emigrate was considerably less than the list of nearly 250,000. For the statements of Attorney General Nicholas Katzenbach, see U.S. Congress, House, 1965 hearings, pp. 57–58.

34. Colonies such as Hong Kong were given quotas of 600. This limit has also been criticized. U.S. Civil Rights Commission, *The Tarnished Door*, pp. 132–33. The Simpson-Mazzoli bill increased the number to 3,000, but Congress did not pass it.

35. Heller and Heller, "New Immigration Law," p. 8.

36. *Ibid.*, p. 9.

37. *CR*, September 20, 1965, p. 24503; and *Wall Street Journal*, October 4, 1965.

38. *CR*, August 25, 1965, p. 21812.

39. U.S. Congress, House, 1965 hearings for the estimates, pp. 15 and 45. Figures of nonquota immigrants are taken from INS, *Statistical Yearbooks*.

40. U.S. Congress, House, 1964 hearings, p. 418. On several other occasions the administration used a similar figure. I am indebted to Stephen Wagner for clarification of this point.

41. U.S. Congress, Senate, 1965 hearings, pp. 279–80.

42. Administration estimates provided by Schwartz can be found in U.S. Congress, House, 1964 Hearings, pp. 589–91.

43. *Ibid.*, pp. 388–89, and U.S. Congress, Senate, 1965 Hearings, p. 2.

44. *CR*, September 22, 1965, p. 24779. See also U.S. Congress, House, 1965 hearings, pp. 157–58.

45. *CR*, August 25, 1965, pp. 21808–9 and 21811; and Stern, "Immigration and Nationality Act," pp. 95–96 and 100–2. and *Congressional Quarterly Almanac*, 1965, p. 471.

46. U.S. Congress. H. Rept. 745, 89th Cong., 1st sess., p. 46.

47. *CR*, August 25, 1965, pp. 21812, 21809, 21772, 21776, and August 24, 1965, pp. 21573 and 21575–77.

48. *CR*, August 25, 1965, p. 21813.

49. *Ibid.*, p. 21819, and *Washington Post*, August 16, 1965.

50. S. Rept. 748, p. 22; and U.S. Congress, Senate, 1965 hearings, pp. 63–67.

51. Schwartz, *Open Society*, pp. 123–24; *Congressional Quarterly Almanac*, 1965, p. 477; Stern, "Immigration and Nationality Act," pp. 146–49; and *New York Times*, August 28, 1965.

52. Schwartz, *Open Society*, p. 124.

53. *Washington Post*, August 27, 1965.

54. *Congressional Quarterly Almanac*, 1965, p. 477.

55. *CR*, September 22, 1965, p. 24773.

56. *Ibid.*, pp. 24739–24781.

57. S. Rept. 748, p. 10.

58. *CR*, September 22, 1965, pp. 24739 and 24773. For similar comments during the House debates see U.S. Congress, House, 1965 hearings, pp. 157–58 and *CR*, August 24, 1965, pp. 21537 and 21575–77, and August 25, 1965, pp. 21771 and 21812.

59. *CR*, September 22, 1965, pp. 24777 and 24783.

60. *CR*, September 30, 1965, p. 25657.

61. Quoted in *Congressional Quarterly* (October 8, 1965), 23:2043.

62. *CR*, Sept. 30, 1965, pp. 25616 and 25657.

63. For the provisions of the amendments see Public Law 89–236, October 3, 1965, 89th Cong., 1st sess.

64. Figures are taken from INS, *Statistical Yearbooks*.

65. *Congressional Quarterly Almanac*, 1965, p. 33.

66. *CR*, August 25, 1965, p. 21783.

67. Frank F. Chuman, *The Bamboo People: The Law and Japanese Americans*, chs. 20–21. See also Hosokawa and Wilson, *East to America*, chs. 16–18. In 1983 a federal court overturned the conviction of a Japanese American who had violated the curfew imposed by the military on the West Coast. That same year a government commission recommended that the President apologize to those interned during the war and that Congress vote funds to compensate them. See *New York Times*, November 11, 1983, and Commission on Wartime Relocation, *Personal Justice Denied; Recommendations*, p. 8. While Congress had not responded by the end of 1983, Washington, California, and Los Angeles voted to compensate those Japanese Americans who had lost their government jobs during World War II. See *New York Times*, May 5, 1983, and February 19, 1984. A federal court also overturned the conviction of a Japanese American who had been arrested in 1942 for refusing to obey wartime evacuation orders. See *New York Times*, November 11, 1983.

68. Marcia Synnott, *The Half-Opened Door: Discrimination in Admissions at Harvard, Yale, and Princeton: 1900–1970*, especially ch. 7; *New York Times*, July 29, 1981; Charles Stembler et al., *Jews in the Mind of America*; and Leonard Dinnerstein, "Anti-Semitism in America, 1945–1950," pp. 150–60.

69. "Dramatic Growth in Tolerance During the Last Quarter Century," Gallup Poll, August 1979; Paul Sheatsley, "White Attitudes Toward the Negro," pp. 217–19; and *New York Times*, January 19, 1981.

70. "Immigration," Gallup Poll, August 1965; and *Washington Post*, May 31, 1965.

71. *CR*, August 25, 1965, p. 21780.

72. U.S. Congress, House, 1964 hearings, p. 116. Wirtz's statement was made about the administration's bill. Feighan's revision had fewer positions for workers.

73. *Wall Street Journal*, October 4, 1965.

74. Stern, "Immigration and Nationality Act," pp. 296–312.

75. *America* (January 19, 1965), 114:170. Of the three major national news weeklies, *Newsweek*, *Time*, and *U.S. News and World Report*, only the last saw much potential change in immigration and even it underestimated the future shifts.

76. *New York Times*, October 4, 1965.

77. Select Commission on Western Hemisphere Immigration, *Final Report*, p. 9.

78. U.S. Congress, House, H. Rept. 94–1553, 94th Cong., 2d sess., p. 6.

79. *Interpreter Releases* (August 16, 1973), 50:246–48.

80. *CR*, September 26, 1973, p. 31548.

81. *Ibid.*, and U.S. Congress, House, Subcommittee No. 1 of the Committee on the Judiciary, *Western Hemisphere Immigration*, Hearings, 93d Cong., 1st sess., pp. 22–35.

82. *CR*, September 26, 1973, p. 31457.

83. *Ibid.*, pp. 31457 and 31460.

84. *Interpreter Releases* (October 24, 1973), 50:285–88; *CR*, September 26, 1973, pp. 31457, 31460, 31463–64, and 31477–78. Rodino's amendment lost 174 to 203.

85. U.S. Congress, House, H. Rept. 94–1553, p. 9, and U.S Congress, House, Subcommittee on Immigration, Citizenship and International Law of the Committee on the Judiciary, *Western Hemisphere Immigration*, Hearings, 94th Cong., 1st and 2d sess., pp. 50–51. Most witnesses favored the bill, but John McCarthy, director of Migration and Refugee Service of the Catholic Conference of the United States wanted Mexico and Canada to have 35,000 each, with the provision that either nation could have unused visas of the other. *Ibid.*, pp. 166–67.

86. *CR* (daily digest), September 29, 1976, p. H. 11685, and October 1, 1976, p. S. 17692.

87. *Weekly Compilation of Presidential Documents* (October 21, 1976), p. 1548.

88. U.S. Congress, House, H. Doc. 95–202, 95th Cong., 1st sess., p. 6, and U.S. Congress, Senate, Committee on the Judiciary, *Immigration and Nationality Efficiency Act of 1979*, Hearings, 96th Cong., 1st sess. The Reagan administration also favored a higher quota for Mexico. *New York Times*, May 30, 1981. By the late 1970s much of the argument for a 35,000 allotment for Mexico not only was related to foreign policy but also to the issue of undocumented immigration. These issues will be discussed in chapters 5 and 7.

89. H. Rept. 94–1553, p. 7.

90. U.S. Congress, Senate, Committee on the Judiciary, *U.S. Immigration Law and Policy*, A Report Prepared by the Congressional Research Service, 96th Cong., 1st sess., pp. 68–70. Not all changes related to third world immigration. In 1978 Congress also changed the law to make it easier to deport Nazi war criminals who had allegedly entered the United States after World War II.

91. *CR*, July 30, 1976, p. 32705. See also Lauren LeRoy and Philip R.

Lee, eds., *Deliberations and Compromise: The Health Professions Act of 1976,* especially pp. 46–76.

92. *CR* (daily digest), July 18, 1978, p. H. 6854.

93. Select Commission on Immigration and Refugee Policy, *U.S. Immigration Policy and the National Interest,* pp. 301–14.

94. All immigration data taken from the annual reports of INS. The Polish quota of 6,488 was generally filled from 1961 to 1965, but Polish immigration from 1965 to 1977 was less than that average. See *New York Times,* May 6, 1966.

95. U.S. Congress, House, Subcommittee No. 1 of the Committee on the Judiciary, *Immigration,* Hearings, 90th Cong., 2d sess., pp. 4 and 6.

96. Irish immigration was 982 in 1979. It had been averaging about 5,000 to 7,000 in the decade before the 1965 amendments went into effect. Data from annual reports of INS.

97. For general discussions of European labor and migration see Jonathan Power, *Migrant Workers in Western Europe and the United States,* and Mark M. Miller, *Foreign Workers in Western Europe: An Emerging Political Force.* Great Britain first restricted immigration from commonwealth nations in 1962 and subsequently placed additional limitations on this immigration, which virtually halted the entrance of new workers.

98. Data from annual reports of INS. In 1979 European immigration was only 60,845, the lowest of the decade.

4. The New Asian Immigrants

1. Because most of those refugees entered as parolees, they were not counted as regular immigrants; hence, the figures for 1980 totaled only 530,639 and not 808,000 persons who actually entered. When they later adjusted their status they were counted as resident aliens.

2. Philip M. Boffey, "The Brain Drain: New Law Will Stem Talent Flow from Europe," p. 282.

3. *Ibid.,* pp. 283–84.

4. Interagency Task Force on Immigration, *Staff Report,* pp. 232–33.

5. Illsoo Kim, *New Urban Immigrants: The Korean Community in New York,* pp. 59–61. Kim's book is an excellent account of the Korean immigration to New York City and the United States generally.

6. Institute of International Education, *Open Doors: 1981/1982,* pp. 2, 18–21.

7. INS, *Statistical Yearbook,* 1978, p. 11. In recent years the number of students changing their status has been close to 20,000 annually. Some officials and American consuls were alarmed by this brain drain. For a

defense of this system see the comments of Professor Jagdish N. Bhagwati of Columbia University in *New York Times*, August 4, 1984.

8. National Science Foundation, *Immigrant Scientists and Engineers*, p. vii.

9. *New York Times*, July 5, 1981.

10. *Washington Post*, May 2, 1989.

11. *New York Times*, July 20, 1988 and November 22, 1990. see also U.S. Congress, House, Committee on Science and Technology, *Demographic Trends and the Scientific and Engineering Work Force*, Background Rept., 99th Cong., 2d sess.

12. Kim, *New Urban Immigrants*, pp. 152–53. An excellent study of the changes in American medicine can be found in Paul Starr, *The Transformation of American Medicine*.

13. Starr, *Transformation of American Medicine*, pp. 360 and 363–68.

14. For a general discussion of foreign physicians see Rosemary Stevens, Louis Good, and Stephen S. Mick, *The Alien Doctors: Foreign Medical Graduates in American Hospitals*, and Alfonso Mejia, Helena Pizurki, and Erica Royston, *Foreign Medical Graduates: The Case of the United States*.

15. Stevens et al., *The Alien Doctors*, pp. 1 and 5.

16. Myron D. Fotter and Thanin Thanapisitikul, "Some Correlates of Residence Among Foreign Medical Graduates: A Case Study of Thai Medical Graduates in Buffalo," p. 779.

17. Stevens et al., *The Alien Doctors*, p. 18.

18. Kim, *New Urban Immigrants*, ch. 5.

19. U.S. Department of Education, *Conference on Asian-Pacific Women*, pp. 106–28.

20. *Ibid.*, pp. 106–28; Kim, *New Urban Immigrants*, pp. 167 and 174–76; *Time*, September 22, 1980, pp. 93–95; and *Wall Street Journal*, July 18, 1980.

21. *President's Comprehensive Report on Immigration*, 1989, pp. 152–57.

22. *Ibid.*, p. 157 and *Congressional Quarterly Almanac*, 1989, p. 283. Some nurses (especially from the Philippines) had applied to enter under the occupational preferences but, because of limits, were on a waiting list. The new law would enable them to change their status without reference to the usual country by country quota. For the issues about the nursing shortage, see U.S. Congress, House, Subcommittee on Immigration, Refugees, and International Law of the Committee on the Judiciary, *Immigration Nursing Relief Act of 1989*, Hearings, 101st Cong., 1st sess.

23. Bradley W. Parlin, *Immigrant Professionals in the United States; Discrimination in the Scientific Labor Market*; James Allen, "Recent Immigration the Philippines," p. 201; and U.S. Commission on Civil Rights: A Report of the California Advisory Committee to the U.S. Commission on Civil

Rights, *A Dream Unfulfilled: Korean and Pilipino Health Professionals in California*.

24. *New York Times*, December 30, 1978.

25. Interagency Task Force, *Staff Report*, p. 174, and INS, *Annual Report*, 1975, p. 37.

26. Interagency Task Force, *Staff Report*, p. 146.

27. Select Commission on Immigration and Refugee Policy, *U.S. Immigration Policy and the National Interest*, p. 146.

28. The first increase was part of the Immigration Reform and Control Act of 1986 and the second was part of the Immigration of 1990. These acts will be discussed in later chapters. Congress no doubt had in mind the crackdown on Chinese students in 1989 and the absorption by mainland China of Hong Kong, scheduled for 1997.

29. Interagency Task Force, *Staff Report*, p. 159; and William S. Bernard, *Chinese Newcomers in the United States*, pp. 7–8.

30. *New York Times*, November 19, 1987, and September 13, 1988.

31. *New York Times*, July 30, 1980, and Betty Lee Sung, *Chinese Population in Lower Manhattan, 1978*, pp. 1–12.

32. *New York Times*, July 13, 1980.

33. General accounts of Chinatown can be found in Bernard Wong, *Chinatown;* Tom Kessner and Betty Caroli, *Today's Immigrants; Their Stories;* Betty Lee Sung, *Chinese Population in Lower Manhattan;* and Peter Kwong, *The New Chinatown*.

34. *(Bergen) Record*, September 18, 1977.

35. *New York Times*, October 7, 1990. See also *ibid.*, September 11, 1990. Asians were about 30 percent of Berkeley's students by 1990 and 20 percent of Stanford's.

36. *New York Times*, October 24, 1982. Asian verbal scores were above those of blacks and Hispanics, but below whites. As recent immigrants, some Asian youth reported difficulty with English. *Washington Post*, July 21, 1981,and U.S. Dept. of Commerce, Bureau of the Census, *Ancestry and Language in the United States, 1979*, pp. 15–16.

37. *Washington Post*, July 21, 1981.

38. *New York Times*, March 8, 1983; and *Time*, March 28, 1983, p. 52. For the success of Asians in classical music, see *(Bergen) Record*, September 24, 1984. In 1984 one-third of the college-level students in New York's Juilliard School of Music were Asians and half of those in the precollege division were Asians. They were also well represented in other prestigious schools.

39. *New York Times*, December 6, 1979; and Berkely Rice, "New Gangs of Chinatown," pp. 60–69.

40. *New York Times*, January 15, 1991. For San Francisco see *San Francisco Chronicle*, July 9, 1987.

41. *New York Times*, July 30 and 31, 1990, and October 16, 1990.

42. See Kwong, *The New Chinatown*, pp. 107–23; and *New York Times*, January 6, 1991.

43. New York City Planning Commission, *Manhattan Bridge Area Study: Chinatown*, p. 55; *New York Times*, May 6, 1967; and Rinker Buck, "The New Sweatshops: A Penny for Your Collar," pp. 40–46. An excellent study of the garment industry in New York City is Roger Waldinger, *Through the Eye of the Needle: Immigrants and Enterprise in New York's Garment Trades*.

44. For restaurant workers see Thomas Baily and Marcia Freedman, *Immigrant and Native-Born Workers in the Restaurant Business*.

45. INS, *Statistical Yearbook*, 1978, p. 11.

46. Betty Lee Sung, "Polarity in the Makeup of Chinese Immigrants," in Roy Bryce-Laporte, ed., *Source Book on the New Immigration*, pp. 167–84.

47. Allen, "Recent Immigration from the Philippines," pp. 202–3.

48. INS, *Statistical Yearbook*, 1978, p. 9.

49. INS, *Statistical Yearbook*, 1980, p. 34.

50. *New York Times*, December 30, 1976.

51. Select Commission on Immigration and Refugee Policy, *U.S. Immigration Policy and the National Interest*, p. 146.

52. *New York Times*, March 28, 1974, and Charles J. McCarthy, "Emigration from the Philippines," pp. 14–16.

53. Kim, *New Urban Immigrants*, ch. 5.

54. Interagency Task Force, *Staff Report*, p. 124.

55. *New York Times*, November 26, 1979; and Select Commission on Immigration and Refugee Policy, *U.S. Immigration Policy and the National Interest*, p. 146.

56. *New York Times*, November 26, 1979.

57. *Los Angeles Times*, February 1, 1976; *New York Times*, October 10, 1977; and *Newsweek*, May 26, 1975, p. 10.

58. *Chicago Tribune*, April 27, 1981.

59. Kim, *New Urban Immigrants*, especially chs. 6–7 and 9; and *Daily News*, December 11, 1990.

60. U.S. Civil Rights Commission, *A Dream Unfulfilled*, passim; and Edna Bonacich, Ivan Light, and Charles Choy Wong, "Koreans in Business," pp. 54–59.

61. *Chicago Tribune*, April 27, 1981; and Won Moo Hurh, Hei Chu Kim, and Dwange Chung Kim, *Assimilation and Patterns of Immigration in the United States: A Case Study of Korean Immigrants in the Chicago Area*.

62. Kim, *New Urban Immigrants*, p. 112.

63. Marlys Harris, "Making It: How the Koreans Won the Greengrocer Wars," p. 192.

64. Kim, *New Urban Immigrants*, pp. 112–21.

65. *New York Times*, September 3, 1983.

66. Harris, "Making It," pp. 192–93.

67. *Ibid.*, pp. 196–97.

68. INS, *Annual Report* 1978, pp. 52–53. For Asian naturalization in general see Elliott Barkan, "Whom Shall We Integrate? A Comparative Analysis of the Immigration and Naturalization Trends of Asians Before and After the 1965 Immigration Act (1951–1978)," pp. 29–57.

69. Interagency Task Force, *Staff Report*, p. 142; INS, *Annual Report*, 1977, p. 68; INS, *Statistical Yearbook*, 1978, p. 2 and INS, *Statistical Yearbook*, 1980, p. 34.

70. National Science Foundation, *Scientists and Engineers*, pp. 15–16. For physicians see Rosemary Stevens, Philip J. Leonhard-Spark, and Parmatma Saran, "The Indian Immigrant in America: A Demographic Profile," in Parmatma Saran and Edwin Eames, eds., *The New Ethnics: Asian Indians in the United States*, pp. 136–62. Indians also began to run a large number of New York City's newsstands. *New York Times*, February 14, 1977.

71. National Science Foundation, *Scientists and Engineers*, pp. 15–16.

72. B. N. Ghosh, "Some Aspects of India's Brain Drain into the U.S.A.," pp. 280–89.

73. Parmatma Saran, "Cosmopolitans from India," pp. 65–66, and *New York Times*, August 7, 1977. For a general picture of Indians in New York City, see Maxine Fisher, *The Indians of New York City*. See also Manoranjan Dutta, "Asian Indian Americans—Search for an Economic Profile," and S. Chandrasekhar, "Some Statistics on Asia Indian Americans in the United States," both in S. Chandrasekhar, *From India to America*, pp. 79–84 and 90.

74. *New York Times*, August 17, 1981. See also December 18, 1983.

75. *New York Times*, August 17, 1981.

76. *New York Times*, March 4, 1981.

77. *Wall Street Journal*, August 25, 1989.

78. *Detroit Press*, May 4, 1981.

79. *Wall Street Journal*, January 27, 1987, and August 25, 1989.

80. Jacqueline Desbarats, "Thai Migration to Los Angeles," pp. 302–18 and INS, *Statistical Yearbook*.

81. Data based on INS, *Annual Reports* and *Statistical Yearbooks*.

82. Ramsay Shu and Adele Samanasian Satele, *The Samoan Community of California: Conditions and Needs*, pp. 9–12.

83. Gregory Orfalea, *Before the Flames: A Quest for the History of Arab Americans*, pp. 316–17; *New York Times*, February 10, 1991; and INS, *Annual Reports*.

84. By Jim Zogby, President of the Arab American Institute. Zogby also reported that Arab Americans were more apt to be in poverty. *New York Times*, February 10, 1991.

85. INS, *Annual Report*. 1977, p. 41.

86. *New York Times*, September 22, 1980.

87. National Science Foundation, *Scientists and Engineers*, p. 16 and Mick, "The Foreign Medical Graduate," pp. 15–17.

88. About half of the aslyees during the 1980s were from Iran. *President's Comprehensive Report*, pp. 21–24.

89. INS, *Advanced Report*, 1989. This figure includes those legalized under IRCA.

90. *(Bergen) Record*, March 6, 1989. For a general discussion of post-1948 Arab immigration, see Orfalea, *Before the Flames*, chs. 4–5.

91. Nabeel Abraham, "Detroit's Yemeni Workers," pp. 3–9. See also *Washington Post*, October 30, 1978; Nabeel Abraham," The Yemeni Immigrant Community of Detroit: Background Emigration and Community," in Sameer Y. Abraham and Nabeel Abraham, eds., *Arabs in the New World: Studies on Arab-American Communities*, pp. 106–34; and Sameer Y. Abraham, Nabeel Abraham, and Barbara Aswad, "The Southend: An Arab Muslim Working-Class Community," in Abraham and Abraham, *Arabs in the New World*, pp. 163–85.

92. For the Chaldeans see Mary C. Sengstock, *The Chaldean Americans: Changing Conceptions of Ethnic Identity; New York Times*, February 16, 1975; and *(Bergen) Record*, June 2, 1986.

93. *New York Times*, May 23, 1977; *Los Angeles Times*, February 16, 1975; and Orfalea, *Before the Flames*, pp. 177–95. For Yemeni restaurant workers in Brooklyn, see Shalom Staub, *Yemenis in New York City: the Folklore of Ethnicity.*

94. For a general discussion of Arab identity, see Orfalea, *Before the Flames* and *New York Times*, December 31, 1985, August 3, 1987, and February 10, 1991.

95. Drora Kass and Seymour Martin Lipset, "Israelis in Exile," pp. 70–77; and Moshe Shokeid, *Children of Circumstances: Israeli Emigrants in New York*, pp. 19–22.

96. Data based on INS, *Annual Reports* and *Statistical Yearbooks*.

97. *Wall Street Journal,* January 17, 1983. See also *Los Angeles Times,* March 29, 1981. For the lure of the United States, see Zvi Sobel, *Migrants from the Promised Land.*

98. Shokeid, *Children of Circumstances,* pp. 30–34; Doron P. Levin, "Israelis in the United States," pp. 15–24; *Wall Street Journal,* January 17, 1983; and Dov Elizur, "Israelis in the United States: Motives, Attitudes, and Intentions," pp. 53–67.

99. Ellen Joy Kay, "The Sephardic Israelis: A Case Study of Forest Hills and Borough Park"; Levin, "Israeli Settlers in the U.S.," *New York Times,* January 16, 1977; and Shokeid, *Children of Circumstances,* especially chs. 3–4.

5. The Western Hemisphere: Mexico, Central and South America, and the Caribbean

1. See Select Commission on Western Hemisphere Immigration, *Final Report.*

2. Family members of those entering under the third and sixth preferences were counted as part of the allotments in those preferences, but they did not have to have certification.

3. *New York Times,* June 6, 1968.

4. INS, *Annual Report,* 1969, p. 3.

5. Mexico had the largest backlog, roughly 300,000, of any nation. For some persons the wait could be over three years or even longer.

6. INS, *Statistical Yearbook,* 1980, pp. 34–35. It averaged about 250,000 from 1980 to 1987.

7. The refugee issue will be discussed fully in the next chapter.

8. The 144,999 places were to be used by 1983.

9. *Interpreter Releases* (September 27, 1976), 53:322–23; *ibid.* (August 23, 1979), 56:419; and *Chicago Tribune,* October 12, 1978.

10. U.S. Congress, Senate, Subcommittee on Immigration and Naturalization of the Committee on the Judiciary, *Immigration,* Hearings, 89th Cong., 1st sess., pp. 12–15 and 105ff.

11. Interagency Task Force on Immigration, *Staff Report,* pp. 176–88.

12. INS, *Statistical Yearbook,* 1978, p. 8.

13. INS, *Annual Reports* and *Statistical Yearbooks.*

14. See Select Commission on Western Hemisphere Immigration, *Final Report.*

15. Robert A. Pastor, "Migration in the Caribbean Basin: The Need for an Approach as Dynamic as the Phenomenon," in Mary Kritz, ed., *U.S. Immigration and Refugee Policy: Global and Domestic Issues,* pp. 101–2.

16. *Ibid.*, pp. 103–4; and Wayne Cornelius, *Mexican Migration to the United States: Causes, Consequences, and U.S. Response,* pp. 36–43.

17. Pastor, "Migration in the Caribbean Basin," pp. 102–103. Mexico City and its suburbs had about 17 million people by the early 1980s. *(Bergen) Record,* December 14, 1983.

18. This view can be found in Saskia Sassen-Koob, *Exporting Capital and Importing Labor: The Role of Caribbean Migration to New York City.*

19. INS, *Statistical Yearbook,* 1978, pp. 51–57.

20. Interagency Task Force on Immigration, *Staff Report,* p. 232.

21. *Ibid.*, pp. 232–34.

22. See Glenn Hendricks, *The Dominican Diaspora;* and Patricia Pessar, *Kinship Relations of Production in the Migration Process: The Case of the Dominican Emigration to the United States.*

23. INS, *Advanced Report,* 1988 and 1989.

24. INS, *Advanced Report,* 1989, and *Annual Reports* and *Statistical Year books.*

25. INS, *Annual Reports* and *Statistical Yearbooks.*

26. INS, *Advanced Report,* 1989.

27. Michael Miller, *Economic Growth and Change Along the U.S.-Mexico Border: The Case of Brownsville, Texas,* p. 21; and *New York Times,* November 22, 1982.

28. *New York Times,* November 22, 1982; and *(Bergen) Record,* April 8, 1983.

29. Cornelius, *Mexican Migration: Causes, Consequences; and U.S. Response,* pp. 38–41.

30. Wayne Cornelius, *Mexican Migration to the U.S.: The View from the Rural Sending Communities,* pp. 6–7.

31. Data on occupations derived from INS annual reports.

32. INS, *Statistical Yearbook,* 1978, p. 78; Wayne Cornelius, Leo R. Chaney, and Jorge G. Castro, *Mexican Immigrants in Southern California: A Survey of Current Knowledge,* pp. 11–13; and Gilbert Cardenas, "Los Desarraigados: Chicanos in the Midwestern Regions of the United States," pp. 153–86. An excellent discussion of Mexican immigration to California is Thomas Muller and Thomas J. Espenshade, *The Fourth Wave: California's Newest Immigrants.*

33. Alejandro Portes and Ruben G. Rumbaut, *Immigrant America: A Portrait,* pp. 116–23.

34. Robert Warren and Jennifer Marks Peck, "Foreign-Born Emigration from the United States: 1960–1970," pp. 71–81; and Guiliermina Jasso and Mark Rosenzweig, "Estimating the Emigration Rates of Legal Immigrants

Using Administrative and Survey Data: The 1971 Cohort of Immigrants to the United States," pp. 279–90.

35. INS, *Annual Report*, 1978, pp. 5–6.

36. Cornelius, Chaney, and Castro, *Mexican Immigrants*, pp. 15–16, and Miller, *Economic Growth*, pp. 19–21.

37. Cornelius, Chaney, and Castro, *Mexican Immigrants*, p. 16, and Miller, *Economic Growth*, pp. 21–22.

38. Miller, *Economic Growth*, p. 22.

39. *New York Times*, May 19, 1987.

40. For Hispanic supermarkets see *New York Times*, February 11, 1987 and for cable television, see *ibid.*, May 5, 1989.

41. U.S. National Commission for Employment Policy, *Hispanics and Jobs: Barriers to Progress*, p. 29.

42. Quoted in Cornelius, Chaney, and Castro, *Mexican Immigrants*, p. 59.

43. For a discussion of language and immigration see Portes and Rumbaut, *Immigrant America*, ch. 6.

44. National Commission, *Hispanics and Jobs*, p. 28.

45. Cornelius, Chaney, and Castro, *Mexican Immigrants*, pp. 25–29.

46. *Ibid.*, p. 66.

47. Barry Chiswick, "The Effect of Americanization on the Earnings of Foreign-Born Men," pp. 987–921; and Marta Tienda and Lisa J. Neident, "Segmented Labor Markets and Earnings: Inequality of Native and Immigrant Hispanics in the U.S."

48. U.S. Dept. of Commerce: Bureau of the Census, *Persons of Spanish Origin in the United States: March 1980 (Advance Report)*.

49. See Jasso and Rosenzweig, "Estimating Emigration."

50. Stephen Mick, "The Foreign Medical Graduate," pp. 14–21; National Science Foundation, *Scientists and Engineers from Abroad, 1976–1978*; INS, *Annual Reports*; and Adriana Marshall, "Emigration of Argentines to the United States," in Patricia Pessar, ed., *When Borders Don't Divide: Labor Migration and Refugee Movements in the Americas*, pp. 129–41.

51. Data from INS, *Annual Reports*.

52. INS, *Statistical Yearbook*, 1980, p. 36; and INS, *Advanced Report*, 1989. The refugee question will be discussed in chapter 6.

53. *New York Times*, June 22, 1975.

54. National Commission, *Hispanics and Jobs*, pp. 38–39 and 41. Central and South Americans also had higher levels of education than Puerto Ricans and Mexicans. See also Portes and Rumbart, *Immigrant America*, ch. 3.

55. *New York Times*, May 6, 1976, May 11 and 12, 1980.

56. *Ibid.*, August 3, 1981. For a sketch about Hispanics in Los Angeles, see Zena Pearlstone, *Ethnic L.A.*, pp. 53–66.

57. *New York Times*, February 13, 1978; *Washington Post*, April 1 and 3, 1979.

58. *New York Times*, May 2, 1975.

59. Fernando Urrea Girald, *Life Strategies and the Labor Market*, pp. 9–18; Juanita Castano and Carmen Cruz, "Colombian Migration to the United States, Part I," pp. 55–64; and Elsa Chaney, "Colombian Migration to the United States, Part II," pp. 109–10.

60. Mary Garcia Castro, "Women in Migration: Colombian Voices in the Big Apple," pp. 24–30; Gurak and Kritz, "Immigrant Women," pp. 17–20; and Elsa Chaney, "Women in Migration: Colombia Migration to the U.S.," pp. 8–12.

61. INS, *Statistical Yearbook*, 1980, pp. 4 and 36.

62. Girald, *Life Strategies*, p. 10.

63. Mary C. Castro, *"Mary" and "Eve's" Social Reproduction in the "Big Apple*," pp. 56–58.

64. *New York Times*, May 12, 1980.

65. Elsa Chaney, "Colombian Migration to the U.S., Part II," pp. 116–17.

66. *Ibid.*, pp. 118–19.

67. *New York Times*, February 13, 1974.

68. Quoted in Castro, *"Mary" and "Eve*," p. 73.

69. INS, *Statistical Yearbook*, 1978, p. 78; and INS, *Statistical Yearbook*, 1980, p. 43. INS no longer requires alien address cards each year.

70. U.S. Dept. of Commerce: Bureau of the Census, *Ancestry of the Population by States, 1980*, p. 3.

71. Phillip Kayal, "Dominicans in New York," p. 12; and Antonio Ugalde, Frank Bean, and Gilbert Cardenas, "International Migration from the Dominican Republic: Findings from a National Survey," pp. 235–36.

72. Data taken from the annual reports of INS.

73. *New York Times*, May 15, 1970; Hendricks, *The Dominican Diaspora*, pp. 57–64; and Nancie L. Gonzalez, "Peasants Progress: Dominicans in New York," pp. 163–64.

74. Ugalde, Bean, and Cardenas, "Migration from the Dominican Republic," pp. 239–45. For an emphasis on the migration of the rural poor, see Gonzalez, "Peasants Progress"; and Hendricks, *Dominican Diaspora*.

75. Data taken from the annual reports of INS.

76. Kayal, "Dominicans in New York," p. 12; and Hendricks, *Dominican Diaspora*, pp. 75–79.

77. Douglas T. Gurak and Mary Kritz, "Immigrant Women in New York City: Household Structure and Employment Patterns," pp. 18–19.

78. Ugalde, Bean, and Cardenas, "Migration from the Dominican Republic," pp. 256–57, and Kayal, "Dominicans in New York," p. 12.

79. Hendricks, *Dominican Diaspora*, ch. 4; Pessar, "Kinship Relations"; and Vivian Garrison and Carol J. Weiss, "Dominican Family Networks and United States Immigration Policy: A Case Study," pp. 264–83.

80. Hendricks, *Dominican Diaspora*, pp. 106–13.

81. *Ibid.*, pp. 117–21.

82. *Ibid.*, p. 138.

83. Gurak and Kritz, "Immigrant Women," pp. 17–20.

84. Pessar, *Kinship Relations*, p. 27.

85. *Ibid.*, p. 27.

86. Data from annual reports of INS.

87. See Dawn I. Marshall, "Toward an Understanding of Caribbean Migration," in Kritz, ed., *U.S. Immigration and Refugee Policy*, pp. 113–32.

88. INS, *Statistical Yearbook*, 1978, p. 78.

89. *Ibid.*; Nancy Foner, *Jamaican Migrants: A Comparative Analysis of the New York and London Experience*; Ransford Palmer, "A Decade of West Indian Migration to the United States, 1965–1972. An Economic Analysis," pp. 571–87; and Virginia Dominquez, *From Neighbor to Stranger: The Dilemma of Caribbean Peoples in the United States*, pp. 14–16.

90. David North and William Weissert, *Immigrants and the American Labor Market*, pp. 114–19 and 133.

91. Foner, *Jamaican Migrants*, p. 15.

92. INS, *Statistical Yearbook*, 1980, p. 43. Virginia Dominquez estimates that about 70 percent of the West Indians live in the New York City area. Dominquez, *Neighbors to Strangers*, p. 34.

93. For the Los Angeles West Indian community see Joyce B. Justus, "West Indians in Los Angeles: the Community and Identity," in Smithsonian Institution, *Caribbean Migration to the United States*, pp. 130–48.

94. Foner, *Jamaican Migrants*, pp. 130–34; Dennis Forsythe, "Black Immigrants and the American Ethos; Theories and Observations," in Smithsonian Institution, *Caribbean Migration to the United States*, pp. 68–74; and Thomas Sowell, "West Indian Immigrants," in Thomas Sowell, ed., *American Ethnic Groups*, pp. 41–48.

95. Forsythe, "Black Immigrants," p. 68.

96. Foner, *Jamaican Migrants*, pp. 24–28.

97. *Ibid.*, pp. 28–29.

98. *New York Times*, June 12, 1974, and July 11, 1983.

99. Data from annual reports of INS.

100. *Newsweek,* February 1, 1978, p. 27. Franck Larague has argued that political oppression is the main thrust behind Haitian emigration. See his "Haitian Emigration to New York," pp. 28–31.

101. James Allman, "Haitian Migration: 30 Years Assessed," pp. 7–11.

102. Allman estimated the figure at 450,000. Another high estimate can be found in Charles Foster, "Creolo in Conflict," p. 10.

103. Undocumented aliens will be discussed in chapter 7.

104. Michel S. Laguerre, "The Haitian Niche in New York City," pp. 12 and 18; Laguerre, *American Odyssey: Haitians in New York City;* and Pierre-Michel Fontaine, "Haitian Immigrants in Boston: A Commentary," in Smithsonian Institution, *Caribbean Migration to the United States,* pp. 111–29. For Haitians in Miami see *Miami Herald,* February 26, 1989.

105. *New York Times,* March 13, 1974; and Susan H. Buchanan, "Haitian Women in New York City," pp. 19 and 23.

106. Susan H. Buchanan, "Language and Identity: Haitians in New York City," pp. 298–312; Fontaine, "Haitian Immigrants," pp. 118–19; and Foster, "Creole in Conflict," pp. 10–13.

107. Laguerre, "The Haitian Niche," pp. 15–18, and Buchanan, "Haitians in the Arts," pp. 33–38.

108. *New York Times,* August 18, 1974.

109. *U.S. News and World Report,* July 8, 1974, pp. 34–36.

110. *Newsweek,* May 26, 1975, pp. 58–59.

111. The Mazzoli-Simpson bill will be discussed in chapter 7.

112. *Wall Street Journal,* June 9, 1982. For a different view see *Christian Science Monitor,* December 16, 1975.

113. *Christian Science Monitor,* April 28, 1980.

114. Theodore White, *America in Search of Itself: The Making of the President,* p. 367. See also the discussion in John Crewdson, *The Tarnished Door,* pp. 286–305.

115. John Crewdson, *The Tarnished Door,* pp. 290–306, and Abigail Thernstrom, "Language: Issues and Legislation," in Stephan Thernstrom, ed., *The Harvard Encyclo-edia of American Ethnic Groups,* pp. 619–28.

116. Crewdson, *The Tarnished Door,* pp. 327–28.

117. Rosalie P. Porter, *Forked Tongue: The Politics of Bilingual Education,* p. 211. For a general discussion of U.S. English, see Dennis Baron, *The English-Only Question: An Official Language for Americans?.*

118. *New York Times,* May 5, 1988 and December 15, 1988.

119. *Ibid.,* February 8, 1990.

120. *CR* (daily digest), June 18, 1980, p. S. 7354.

121. *Ibid.,* p. S. 7360.

122. Select Commission on Immigration and Refugee Policy, *U.S. Immigration Policy and the National Interest,* pp. 305–6.

123. The Select Commission also wanted to allow grandparents and adult unmarried sons and daughters of U.S. citizens be on the nonquota list. These changes would have increased immigration several thousand annually.

124. *Washington Post*, April 28, 1981.

125. The undocumented alien controversy will be discussed in chapter 7.

126. U.S. Congress, Senate, Subcommittee on Immigration and Refugee Policy of the Committee on the Judiciary, *The Preference System*, Hearings, 97th Cong., 1st sess., p. 19.

6. The Unwanted: Third World Refugees

1. Excellent discussions of refugee programs can be found in David North, Julia Taft, and Daniel Ford, *Refugee Resettlement in the U.S.: Time for a New Focus;* U.S. Congress, Senate, Committee on the Judiciary, *Revision of U.S. Refugee Resettlement Programs and Policies*, Committee Print, 96th Cong., 2d sess; Select Commission on Immigration and Refugee Policy, *Appendix C to Staff Reports;* and Barry Stein and Silvano Tomasi, eds., *Refugees Today: International Migration Review.*

2. *New York Times*, August 13, 1981.

3. Raul Moncraz and Antonio Jorge, "International Factor Movement and Complementarity Growth and Entrepreneurship Under Conditions of Cultural Variation," pp. 3–4.

4. North, Taft, and Ford, *Refugee Resettlement*, pp. 66–67. For a general discussion of Cuban refugee policy, see Felix Roberto Masud-Piolot, *With Open Arms.*

5. *Ibid.*, p. 69.

6. *Ibid.*, p. 69, and "Mr. Vorhees Submits Final Report on Cuban Refugee Problem," *Dept. of State Bulletin* (February 13, 1961), pp. 220–24.

7. "President Outlines Measures for Aiding Cuban Refugees," *Dept. of State Bulletin* (February 27, 1961), pp. 309–10.

8. North, Taft, and Ford, *Refugee Resettlement*, p. 80.

9. Schwartz, *Open Society*, pp. 139–41.

10. North, Taft, and Ford, *Refugee Resettlement*, pp. 84–87.

11. Schwartz, *Open Society*, pp. 138–39.

12. President's Commission on Immigration and Naturalization, *Whom Shall We Welcome?* pp. 59 and 118.

13. *CR*, August 23, 1957, p. 16302.

14. U.S. Congress, Senate, *Immigration and Nationality Act: Amendments*, S. Rept. 748, 89th Cong., 1st sess., pp. 7–8.

15. *Ibid.*, p. 17.

16. Public Law 89–236:79 Stat. 911.

17. Some Indochinese refugees were admitted under the Eastern Hemisphere's seventh preference, but the vast majority entered through the parole power.

18. *New York Times,* October 3, 1965.

19. North, Taft, and Ford, *Refugee Resettlement*, pp. 66–67.

20. Refugee admissions averaged about 50,000 annually during the 1970s.

21. North, Taft, and Ford, *Refugee Resettlement*, pp. 78–84.

22. U.S. Congress, House, Committee on the Judiciary, H. Rept. 1978, 89th Cong., 2d sess., p. 3. See especially the comments of Arch Moore, ranking minority member on the House subcommittee on immigration, in *CR*, September 19, 1966, p. 22917.

23. The problems of Cubans are discussed in U.S. Congress, Senate, Subcommittee to Investigate Problems Connected with Refugees and Escapees of the Committee on the Judiciary, *Cuba Refugee Problems*, Hearings, 89th Cong., 2d sess. Some Cubans did settle first in Spain and other nations before coming to the United States.

24. Certain professions and jobs in most states required resident alien or citizenship status as prerequisites for employment.

25. See the excellent article by Susan Jacoby in the *New York Times Magazine*, September 29, 1974. See also Jose Llanes, *Cuban Americans: Masters of Survival.*

26. Richard Fagen, Richard A. Brody, and Thomas J. O'Leary, *Cubans in Exile: Disaffection and Revolution*, pp. 16–28.

27. Lourdes Casal and Andres R. Hernandez, "Cubans in the U.S.A.: Survey of the Literature," pp. 25–51.

28. Alejandro Portes, Robert Bach, and Juan Clark, "The New Wave: A Statistical Profile of Recent Cuban Exiles to the United States," pp. 1–32.

29. Quoted in Robert L. Bach, "The New Cuban Immigrants: Their Background and Prospects," p. 44.

30. *Washington Post,* July 7, 1980. For Cubans in Union City, New Jersey, see Eleanor M. Rogg, *The Assimilation of Cuban Exiles. The Role of Community and Class.*

31. The literature on Cubans is large. For the professionals generally see Raul Moncraz, "A Model of Professional Adaptation of Refugees: The Cuban Case in the U.S., 1959–1970," and "Professional Adaptation of Cuban Physicians in the United States, 1959–1969." See also Raul Moncraz and Antonio Jorge, "A Case of Substitution and Misallocation of Human Resources. The Cubans in the United States," and "The Cuban

Influx into South Florida; Cultural Entrepreneurship and the Emergence of New Growth Patterns in an Advanced Society." For a history of Cuban Americans see Jose Llanes, *Masters of Survival.*

32. John Scanlan and Gilburt Loescher, "U.S. Foreign Policy, 1959–80; Impact on Refugee Flow from Cuba," in John Scanlan and Gilburt Loescher, eds., *The Global Refugee Problem: U.S and World Response,* especially pp. 17–27.

33. *Fortune* (October 1966), 74:144.

34. *Business Week,* May 1, 1971, p. 88.

35. *Washington Post,* July 7, 1980.

36. *National Geographic Magazine* (July 1973), 144:88–95.

37. Antonio Jorge and Raul Moncraz, "Cubans in South Florida; A Social Science Approach," and Robert Bach, "The New Cuban Immigrants," p. 44.

38. *New York Times,* September 21, 1980.

39. U.S. Bureau of the Census: Current Population Reports, *Persons of Spanish Origin in the United States: March 1979;* Moncraz and Jorge, "Cubans in South Florida" and "Cuban Immigration to the United States," in Dennis L. Cuddy, ed., *Contemporary American Immigration,* pp. 146–75.

40. "How the Immigrants Made It in Miami," *Business Week.* May 1, 1971, p. 88. For a general discussion of the Cuban refugee programs and the mobility and assimilation of Cubans, see Silvia Pedraza-Bailey, *Political and Economic Migrants in America: Cubans and Mexicans,* especially chs. 2 and 4–5.

41. Moncraz and Jorge, "Cuban Immigration to the United States," pp. 158–71.

42. Ronald Copeland, "The Cuban Boatlift of 1980: Strategies in Federal Crisis Management," in Scanlan and Loescher, eds., *Global Refugees,* pp. 141–42. Copeland's article is a comprehensive account of the Mariel exodus.

43. *New York Times,* April 9, 1980, and April 15, 1980; *Newsweek,* April 28, 1980, pp. 38–43.

44. *New York Times,* May 6, 1980.

45. *New York Times,* May 18, 1980. In late May the administration finally began to seize boats and levy fines on boat owners who defied a new ban on the flotilla.

46. *Newsweek,* May 26, 1980; ABC News-Harris Survey May 26, 1980, and *New York Times*-CBS Poll, June 1980.

47. *Miami Herald* survey, May 11, 1980, completed May 1–4, 1980.

48. *New York Times,* June 30, 1980, and October 19, 1980. See also *New*

York Times, May 10, 1980; *(Bergen) Record,* June 11, 1980; and *Daily News,* May 14, 1980.

49. Copeland, "The Cuban Boatlift of 1980," pp. 139–47.

50. *Charleston News and Courier,* May 8, 1980, in *Editorials on File,* 1980, p. 533. For an optimistic view of the Cubans see the report of the Heritage Foundation in *CR* (daily digest), August 4, 1980, p. S 10635.

51. Robert Bach, "The New Cuban Immigrants," pp. 39–46.

52. *New York Times,* August 29, 1980; June 2, 1980; June 3, 1980; and November 30, 1980.

53. *Ibid.,* December 18, 1980, and December 21, 1980; and James Conway, "Unwanted Immigrants: Cuban Prisoners in America," pp. 72–81.

54. *New York Times,* September 27, 1980, and December 7, 1980.

55. *Ibid.,* April 27, 1981; August 9, 1981; and May 26, 1983.

56. *Ibid.,* May 26, 1983, June 28, 1983, December 15, 1984, and May 21, 1985.

57. U.S. Congress, House, Subcommittee on Immigration, Refugees and International Law of the Committee on the Judiciary, *Cuban Detainess, Hearings,* 100th Cong., 2d sess., pp. 22–37, 132 and 27a–34a.

58. *New York Times,* November 21, 23, 24, and 25, 1987. The Oakdale facility was completely destroyed.

59. *Ibid.,* November 11, 1988.

60. *Ibid.,* November 20, 1984. The administration said it waited for Congress to pass special legislation, but when the legislators failed to act, it decided to use the 1966 law.

61. *Ibid.,* May 17, 1983. See also *(Bergen) Record,* May 19, 1984, and *Time,* September 12, 1983, pp. 24–25.

62. *New York Times,* March 31, 1985 and April 15, 1990.

63. *Ibid.,* September 29, 1985, and Alejandro Portes and Juan Clark, "Mariel Refugees: Six Years After," *Migration World* (1987), 15(5):14–18.

64. U.S. Congress, House, Subcommittee No 1 of the Committee on the Judiciary, *Western Hemisphere Immigration,* Hearings, 93d Cong., 1st sess., p. 105.

65. U.S. Congress, House, Subcommittee on Immigration, Citizenship, and International Law of the Committee on the Judiciary, *Admission of Refugees into the U.S.,* Hearings, 95th Cong., 1st sess., pp. 21–23.

66. *Ibid.,* p. 23.

67. Gail P. Kelly, *From Vietnam to America: A Chronicle of the Vietnamese Immigration to the United States,* ch. 2.

68. "Public Approves of Babylift," the Harris Survey, April 28, 1975.

69. U.S. Congress, House, Subcommittee on Immigration, Cit-

izenship and International Law of the Committee on the Judiciary, *Refugees from Indochina; Evacuation from South Vietnam (Orphan Airlift)*, Hearings, 94th Cong., 1st and 2d sess., p. 12.

70. U.S. Congress, Senate, Subcommittee to Investigate Problems Connected with Refugees and Escapees of the Committee on the Judiciary, *Indochina Evacuation and Refugee Problems*, Part II, Hearings, 94th Cong., 1st sess., pp. 28–35. Assistant Secretary of State Philip Habib said that if the 17,600 Vietnamese employees were removed along with their families the total could reach 167,000. But he said, "Quite obviously, we are not simply thinking in terms of bringing them all to the United States." He added that if the situation was chaotic there would probably be no mass evacuation.

71. Several senators and a Senate committee investigating evacuation said it was characterized by interagency "squabbling" and that plans for orderly decisions about whom the Americans would evacuate were a "charade." U.S. Congress, Senate, Subcommittee to Investigate Problems Connected with Refugees and Escapees of the Committee on the Judiciary, *Indochina Evacuation and Refugee Problems*, Hearings, Parts II, III, and Staff Rept. See also Kelly, *From Vietnam to America*, pp. 18–21; Frank Snepp's account in *Decent Interval*; and Alan Dawson, *55 Days: The Fall of Saigon*, pp. 326–47.

72. "Majority Opposes Resettling Viet Refugees in this Country," Gallup Poll, May 1975, and "Viet Refugees Given Cold Reception by Public," the Harris Survey, June 26, 1975. The administration said its mail was running slightly against aiding the refugees. *New York Times*, May 7, 1975. See also *New York Times*, May 27, 1975.

73. *CR*, May 14, 1975, pp. 14327, 14341, and 14348.

74. Kelly, *From Vietnam to America*, p. 18.

75. *Congressional Quarterly Almanac*, 1975, p. 316.

76. *New York Times*, May 7 and 13, 1975.

77. *CR*, May 14, 1975, pp. 14372–73 and May 16, 1975, pp. 14863–64.

78. For the resettlement programs, see Kelly, *From Vietnam to America*.

79. See Kelly, *From Vietnam to America*.

80. U.S. Comptroller General, *Response to the Indochinese Exodus—A Humanitarian Dilemma*, p. 100.

81. *New York Times*, July 4, 1977, and U.S. Congress, House, Subcommittee on Immigration, Citizenship, and International Law of the Committee on the Judiciary, *Admission of Refugees into the United States*, Hearings, Part II, 95th Cong., 1st and 2d sess., p. 13.

82. House, Hearings, *Admission of Refugees into the United States*, p. 13.

83. *New York Times*, July 4, 1977, and December 22, 1977.

84. See Barry Wain, "The Indochina Refugee Crisis," pp. 160–80; and Wain, *The Refused; the Agony of the Indochina Boat People.*

85. *New York Times,* November 15 and 28, 1978.

86. *Ibid.,* June 29, 1979.

87. "Indochinese Refugees," Gallup Poll, August 1979, and *New York Times,* July 15, 1979. See also *Congressional Quarterly* (August 14, 1982), 40:1963–68.

88. James W. Tollefson, *Alien Winds: The Reeducation of America's Indo-chinese Refugees,* pp. 10–12. The United States and Vietnam do not have diplomatic relations which has caused complications for ODP. See Valerie O'Connor Sutter, *The Indochinese Refugee Dilemma,* pp. 69–71.

89. Tollefson, *Alien Winds,* p. 11.

90. *New York Times,* February 14, 1987 and July 30, 1990. See also Sutter, *The Indochinese Refugee Dilemma,* ch. 2; and Tollefson, *Alien Winds,* ch. 2.

91. *New York Times,* October 16, 1990.

92. Tollefson, *Alien Winds,* p. 11. The United States also permitted similar children from the Korean War to enter.

93. CR (daily digest) August 3, 1979, p. S. 71103.

94. Robert Marsh, "Socio-economic Status of Indochinese Refugees in the United States; Progress and Problems," pp. 13–14.

95. Wain, *The Refused,* pp. 39–44, 61–64. Most of Wain's excellent book deals with the boat people. See also Tollefson, *Alien Winds.*

96. *Ibid.,* pp. 55–61.

97. *Ibid.,* pp. 47–55.

98. U.S. Congress, House, Subcommittee on Immigration, Refugees, and International Law of the Committee on the Judiciary, *Refugee Act of 1980—Amendments,* Hearings, 97th Cong., 1st sess., pp. 73–74; Comptroller General, *The Indochina Exodus: A Humanitarian Dilemma,* pp. 68–69; Research Project on Indochinese Refugees in the State of Illinois, *Survey of Indochinese Refugees,* 1:12; *Los Angeles Times,* November 29, 1979; and U.S. Dept. of Health and Human Services, *Refugee Resettlement Program, 1983,* pp. 24–25.

99. American Public Welfare Association, *Refugee Reports,* March 6, 1981 and U.S. Dept. of Health and Human Services, *Refugee Resettlement 1983,* p. 20.

100. See, for example, *Washington Post,* July 5, 1980; *New York Times,* May 8, 1979, and March 1, 1981. Iowa alone among the states maintained an Indochinese resettlement agency after 1975.

101. Barry Stein, "Occupational Adjustment of Refugees; The Vietnamese in the United States," pp. 25–41; Robert Bach and Jennifer Bach,

"Employment Patterns of Southeast Asian Refugees," pp. 31–38; and David W. Haines, "Southeast Asian Refugees in the United States: An Overview," pp. 9–13. Darrel Montero's book, *Vietnamese Americans: Patterns of Socioeconomic Adaptation in the United States*, deals with the first wave of Indochinese refugees, and, based on government task force reports, gives an optimistic picture. See also U.S. Dept. of Health and Human Services, *Refugee Resettlement Program*, 1983, pp. 22–26.

102. Bach and Bach, "Employment Patterns," pp. 31–38; and Stein, "Occupational Adjustment," pp. 25–41.

103. *New York Times*, June 16, 1980.

104. U.S. Congress, House, Subcommittee on Immigration, Refugees, and International Law of the Committee on the Judiciary, *Refugee Act of 1980 Amendment*, p. 5, and *New York Times*, July 7, 1981.

105. See Lutheran Council in the U.S.A.: Dept. of Immigration and Refugee Service, *The Adjustment of Indochinese Refugees in the United States 1979–1980; One Year Later*, pp. 30–32; and Marsh, "Socio-economic status of Indochinese Refugees," pp. 13–14. The *New York Times* in early 1984 reported that the ethnic Chinese, with their contacts in the United States and business skills, were doing well in New York City's Chinatown. *New York Times*, February 19, 1984.

106. *New York Times*, August 14, 1980.

107. *Washington Post*, July 5, 1980.

108. Tollefson, *Alien Winds*, p. 33.

109. *New Orleans Picayune-Tribune*, April 24, 1978, and May 12, 1978.

110. *New York Times*, August 24, 1979. For community opposition to a Laotian settlement in rural West Virginia, see *(Bergen) Record*, January 2, 1983, and November 27, 1983. For friction on California farms, see *New York Times*, August 19, 1983. For hostility in Philadelphia, see *New York Times*, September 17, 1984.

111. For an account of the fishing controversy, see *Wall Street Journal*, August 10, 1979, *New York Times*, April 6, 1980, and two articles by Paul D. Starr, "Vietnamese Fisherfolk and How they Grew," pp. 11–16, and "Troubled Waters: Vietnamese Fisherfolk on America's Gulf Coast," pp. 226–238.

112. *New York Times*, April 6, 1980.

113. U.S. Congress, House, Subcommittee on Immigration, Refugees, and International Law of the Committee on the Judiciary, *Refugee Act of 1980 Amendment*. Hearings, p. 1. See also *Congressional Quarterly* (August 14, 1982), 40:1963–68, and the comments of Representative Daniel Lungren of California during the debates over refugee aid in 1982 in *CR* (daily digest), June 22, 1982, p. H. 3755.

114. For a critical look at Americanization programs for the Indochinese refugees, see Tollefson, *Alien Winds*. For a positive view of the achievements of the "boat people," especially educationally, see Nathan Caplan, John Witmore and Marcella H. Choy, *The Boat People and Achievement in America*.

115. U.S. Congress, Senate, Subcommittee to Investigate Problems Connected with Refugees and Escapees of the Committee on the Judiciary. *Refugees and Humanitarian Problems in Chile*, Hearings, 94th Cong., 1st sess., Part III, pp. 34–37, 45, 59–60.

116. *Ibid.*, pp. 6–7. Schauer was equally critical of Congress for its lack of direction. See also *The Progressive* (November 1978), 39:8–9.

117. North, Taft, and Ford, *Refugee Resettlement*, p. 93.

118. Sylva R. Guendelman, "South American Refugees: Stresses Involved in Relocating in the San Francisco Area," pp. 20–25.

119. *Chicago Tribune*, August 14, 1979, and August 15, 1979. See also *New York Times*, September 10, 1980. General accounts of the Haitians are numerous. See Michelle Bogre, "Haitian Refugees: Haiti's Missing Persons," p. 10, and Peter Schey, "The Black Boat People Flounder on the Shoals of American Immigration Policy," pp. 7–10.

120. U.S. Congress, House, *Haitian Immigration*, Report of the Subcommittee on Immigration, Citizenship, and International Law of the Committee on the Judiciary, 94th Cong., 2d sess., p. 1.

121. *Ibid.*, p. 1. According to testimony by Durward E. Jowell, Southern Regional Commissioner of INS, before the Select Commission on Immigration and Refugee Policy a group of Haitians who arrived in 1963 were not granted asylum. Select Commission on Immigration and Refugee Policy, hearings held in Miami, 1979.

122. Excellent reviews of Haitian difficulties are Naomi Zucker, "The Haitians versus the United States: The Courts as a Last Resort," in Scanlan and Loescher, eds., *Global Refugees*, pp. 151–62; Paul Lehman, "The Haitian Struggle for Human Rights," pp. 941–43; and Alex Stepick, "Haitian Boat People: A Study in the Conflicting Forces Shaping U.S. Immigration Policy," in Richard Hofstetter, ed., *U.S. Immigration Policy: Law and Contemporary Problems*, pp. 163–92. In early 1984 the Reagan administration certified that, despite problems, Haiti was making progress in human rights and should continue to receive American aid. Such a certification was required by law. The administration also noted another condition for aid; namely that Haiti was taking steps to halt illegal immigration to the United States. *New York Times*, February 5, 1984.

123. U.S. Congress, House, Subcommittee on Immigration, Citizenship, and International Law, *Haitian Emigration*, pp. 1–9.

124. *Haitian Refugee Center v. Civiletti*, 503 F. Supp. 442 1980, pp. 510–18.

125. U.S. Congress, Senate, Committee on the Judiciary, *Caribbean Refugee Crisis*, Hearings, 96th Cong., 2d sess., pp. 202–203.

126. Michelle Bogne, "Haitian Refugees: (Haiti's) Missing Persons," p. 10.

127. *CR* (daily digest), December 20, 1979, pp. H. 12432 and H. 12438.

128. U.S. Congress, Senate, *Indochina Refugees; The Impact of First Asylum and Implications for American Policy*, A Study for the Use of the Joint Economic Committees of Congress, 96th Cong., 2d sess., p. 48. Cambodians were not so fortunate as Vietnamese and Laotians. Beginning in 1982 INS began to screen Cambodians on a case by case basis, thus making it more difficult for them to gain entrance. INS was concerned about the Khmer Rouge, the Communists, being admitted. See William Shawcross, *The Quality of Mercy: Cambodian, Holocaust and Modern Conscience*, pp. 412–14.

129. *Haitian Refugee Center v. Civiletti*, 503 F. Supp. 442 (1980), p. 532.

130. *New York Times*, June 18, 1980.

131. Most of these criticisms can be found in the testimony in U.S. Congress, Senate, Committee on the Judiciary, *The Refugee Act of 1979*, Hearings, 96th Cong., 1st sess., and U.S. Congress, House, Subcommittee on International Operations of the Committee on Foreign Affairs, *The Refugee Act of 1979*, Hearings, 96th Cong., 1st sess. See also North, Taft, and Ford, *Refugee Resettlement*.

132. U.S. Congress, House, Subcommittee on Immigration, Citizenship, and International Law of the Committee on the Judiciary, *Admission of Refugees into the United States*, Hearings, 95th Cong., 1st sess., p. 1.

133. *Ibid.*, pp. 98–134. See also Ted Kennedy's account of the act in "Refugee Act of 1980," in Barry Stein and Silvano Tomasi, eds., *Refugees Today; International Migration Review*, pp. 141–56.

134. *New York Times*, July 11, 1979, and *CR* (daily digest), September 6, 1979, p. S. 12027. In December 1983 the federal government designated 18 counties as too "impacted" to receive more refugees. A spokesman for the Dept. of Health and Human Services said the government was "trying to make sure that when refugees came into the country, they are located in an area where they can find work and be assimilated into an American community as quickly as possible." *New York Times*, December 12, 1983.

135. *CR* (daily digest), December 20, 1979, pp. H. 12369–75 and H. 12410. The vote in the House was 318 to 47.

136. *CR* (daily digest), March 4, 1980, p. H. 1519.

137. *Ibid.*, and *Congressional Quarterly* (March 8, 1980), 38:690.

138. Refugee Act of 1980, Public Law 96–212.

139. U.S. Congress, Senate, Committee on the Judiciary, *Refugee Act of 1980*, S. Rept. 96-256, 97th Cong., 2d sess., p. 1.

140. *CR* (daily digest) April 21, 1980, p. S. 3962.

141. *Ibid.*, p. S. 3959.

142. Dept. of State, *Bulletin* (August 1980), p. 77.

143. *New York Times*, January 31, 1981.

144. U.S. Congress, House, Subcommittee on Immigration, Refugees, and International Law of the Committee on the Judiciary, *Haitian Detention and Interdiction*, Hearing, 101st Cong., 1st sess., pp. 26–30 and 220–26.

145. *Ibid.*, p. 69. For a critical view of American refugee policy, including the Haitian issue, see Norman L. Zucker and Naomi Flink Zucker, *The Guarded Gate: The Reality of American Refugee Policy*.

146. *New York Times*, June 19, 1982, and July 24, 1982.

147. *Ibid.*, December 14, 1988.

148. *Ibid.*, January 11 and 14, 1989.

149. *Ibid.*, February 18, 21, and 27, 1989, and March 12, 1989. See also *Time*, February 27, 1989, pp. 14–15.

150. *Ibid.*, March 1, 1981, July 4, 1983, and July 25, 1983; *CR* (daily digest) February 11, 1982, p. S. 817; Mary Solberg, "El Salvador," pp. 8–12; and *The Voice*, December 13, 1983. The Reagan administration disagreed with the decisions but drew up a plan to parole Haitians. In August 1983 the administration gained an appellate court's agreement to rehear arguments about Haitian detention. *New York Times*, August 17, 1983. Those Haitians who were free pending their asylum application decision faced difficulties finding jobs. *New York Times*, June 18, 1983.

151. *Interpreter Releases* (May 6, 1982) 59:305–306, and (August 27, 1982), 59:551–52; *New York Times*, May 2, 1982, and June 26, 1982.

152. *CR* (daily digest), February 11, 1982, pp. S. 827–30.

153. *New York Times*, September 22, 1983.

154. *Ibid.*, April 8, 1983, September 9, 1983, and October 2, 1984; *Los Angeles Times*, September 4, 1983; *Newsweek*, July 11, 1983, p. 27 and December 5, 1983, pp. 72–73; and the *(Bergen) Record*, October 7, 1984.

155. *New York Times*, May 2, 1986.

156. *Ibid.*, May 3 and May 6, 1986. A good discussion of the sanctuary movement is Ann Crittenden, *Sanctuary: A Story of American Conscience and the Law in Collusion*.

157. *New York Times*, May 5, 1983. In July the government began to

release some Afghans on parole. *New York Times*, July 3, 1983. The U.S. Catholic Conference reported in 1983 that even Poles were having difficulties gaining asylum. *New York Times*, September 21, 1983. However, in New Jersey INS admitted that it did not usually raid work places if they knew the illegal aliens were Poles as opposed to Latin Americans. *(Bergen) Record*, March 4, 1984. See also *Christian Science Monitor*, January 26, 1983. For an excellent discussion of asylum cases in New York see Patricia W. Fagen, *Applying for Political Asylum in New York: Law, Policy and Administrative Practice*. In fiscal 1982 just over 4,000 persons were granted asylum. More than half were from Iran, followed by people from Nicaragua, Afghanistan, Ethiopia, and Poland. U.S. Dept. of Health and Human Services, *Refugee Resettlement Program, 1983*, p. 35.

158. U.S. Congress, Senate, Subcommittee on Immigration and Refugee Policy of the Committee on the Judiciary, *Asylum Adjudication*, Hearings, 97th Cong., 1st sess., pp. 7–8. See also Kennedy, "The Refugee Act of 1980," in *Refugees: International Migration Review*, pp. 141–56, and Arnold H. Leibowitz, "The Refugee Act of 1980: Problems and Congressional Concern," in Scanlan and Loescher, eds., *Global Refugees*, pp. 163–71.

159. U.S. Congress, Senate, Subcommittee on Immigration and Refugee Policy of the Committee on the Judiciary, *Asylum Adjudication*, p. 7; *(Bergen) Record*, June 29, 1982; *New York Times*, July 7, 1983, June 10, 1983, and February 19, 1984; and Peter Schuck, "The Transformation of Immigration Law," pp. 39–41. The Reagan administration's decision to permit the Mariel Cubans to become resident aliens cut the backlog substantially.

160. *CR* (daily digest), February 11, 1982, p. S. 832.

161. *New York Times*, May 31, 1983. See also the comments of J. Michael Myers of the Church World Service in the *New York Times*, August 19, 1983, and the protests by civil liberties and church groups in the *Times*, May 5, 1983. The State Department's position, stated by Assistant Secretary of State for Human Rights and Humanitarian Affairs Elliott Abrams, can be found in the *Times*, August 5, 1983.

162. *Ibid.*, April 26 and May 15, 1987.

163. *Ibid.*, January 27, 1982.

164. *Ibid.*, July 7, 1982; *Interpreter Releases* (October 29, 1982), 59:699–700; and Lynn Norment, "Are Black Refugees Getting a Dirty Deal?" pp. 132–34.

165. Zucker and Zucker, *The Guarded Gate*, p. 144.

166. *New York Times*, April 17, 1986.

167. *Washington Post*, July 9, 1987.

168. *New York Times*, March 10, 1987.

169. *Ibid.*, May 1, 1988.

170. *Ibid.*, July 1, July 19 and December 20, 1990.

171. *Ibid.*, July 1, 1990. See also President's Comprehensive Report, pp. 21–23.

172. *Washington Post*, November 23, 1989, and *New York Times*, November 22, 1989. Czechoslovakia, Romania, and Bulgaria were taken off the refugee list in 1990.

173. *Christian Science Monitor*, March 1, 1988; *New York Times*, July 13 and September 16, 1989.

174. *New York Times*, September 15, 1989. See also the reactions of congressmen in U.S. Congress, House, Subcommittee on Europe and the Middle East of the Committee on Foreign Affairs and the Subcommittee on Immigration, Refugees and International Law of the Committee on the Judiciary, *Processing of Soviet Refugees*, Jt. Hearing, 101st Cong., 1st sess. In 1989 the House passed a bill to restore the presumption that Soviets and certain Indochinese refugees should be considered refugees.

175. Subcommittee on Europe and the Middle East, *Processing of Soviet Refugees*, pp. 3–10 and 42–43.

176. *New York Times*, September 24, 1989, September 22, 1990, and October 16, 1990.

177. *Ibid.*, February 26, 1991. When it passed the Immigration Act of 1990, Congress had recommended that the Attorney General take this action.

7. *Undocumented Aliens: People and Politics*

1. INS, *Annual Report*, 1969, p. 83.

2. See the conclusion of chapter 2.

3. *New York Times*, July 27, 1979.

4. INS, *Annual Report*, 1969, p. 83.

5. See U.S. Congress, Senate, Subcommittee on Migratory Labor of the Committee on Labor and Public Welfare, *Migrant and Seasonal Farm Labor Powerlessness*, Hearings, 91st Cong., 1st and 2d sess.

6. *Ibid.*, p. 4548. See also Sheldon L. Greene, "Wetbacks, Growers, and Poverty," pp. 403–06.

7. U.S. Civil Rights Commission, *The Tarnished Door: Civil Rights Issues in Immigration*, pp. 79–95.

8. See Paul Ehrlich et al., *The Golden Door: Internal Migration, Mexico, and the United States*, pp. 292–310; and John Crewdson, *The Tarnished Door*, ch. 7.

9. *New York Times*, July 22, 1973; and *Chicago Tribune*, October 28, 1975.

By 1978 the Border Patrol had a fleet of 28 aircraft along the border with Mexico. INS, *Statistical Yearbook, 1978*, p. 21.

10. Eugene Sofer, *Illegal Immigration; Background to the Current Debates*, p. 18; and Michael S. Teitelbaum, "Right vs. Right: Immigration and Refugee Policy in the United States," p. 55. For the recent position of INS see *New York Times*, February 13, 1984.

11. See, for example, *Chicago Tribune*, October 28, 1975, and *New York Times*, July 22, 1973. Over 90 percent of deported aliens were those seized along the border, usually within a few hours of their entry.

12. *New York Times*, July 22, 1973, and July 7, 1980. See also INS, *Statistical Yearbook, 1978*, p. 17, and *New York Times*, January 17, 1980.

13. *New York Times*, May 1, 1983.

14. INS, *Statistical Yearbook, 1978*, p. 51.

15. Institute of International Education, *Open Doors: 1981/1982*, p. 2.

16. *New York Times*, January 17, 1980. Visitors wishing to enter the United States do have to gain permission at American embassies overseas. Such permission is by no means automatic. A House committee, for example, reported that the acceptance rate in Colombia was about 50 percent and that of Mexico 70 percent. By way of contrast the *New York Times* reported that in 1983 of 92,000 applications for tourist visas in the Philippines, 74,561 were accepted. American officials are concerned that persons are entering with the intention of staying after their visas expired. Yet the numbers involved prevent adequate checks and the numbers granted permission has steadily risen. In Mexico City the House committee said the interviews of prospective visitors lasted only a few minutes. See U.S. Congress, House, Subcommittee on Inter-American Affairs of the Committee on Foreign Affairs, *United States-Mexican Relations: An Update*, Hearings, 97th Cong., 1st sess., pp. 4–5; and *New York Times*, March 15, 1984.

17. *New York Times*, January 17, 1980. For the situation four years later see *ibid.*, July 23, 1984.

18. Comptroller General of the United States, *Prospects Dim for Effectively Enforcing Immigration Laws*, pp. 20–21.

19. *New York Times*, November 23, 1981.

20. *Ibid.*, November 23, 1981. See also Crewdson, *The Tarnished Door*, ch. 5.

21. *New York Times*, November 23, 1981; and U.S. Congress, Senate, Committee on the Judiciary, *Department of Justice Authorization and Oversight*, Hearings, 97th Cong., 1st sess., pp. 527–33.

22. *New York Times*, July 13, 1982.

23. *Ibid.*, January 13–17, 1980. See also *Los Angeles Times*, December

12, 1972; and the *(Bergen) Record*, February 12, 1980. Based on his immigration reporting Crewdson wrote *The Tarnished Door*. See especially ch. 6 about corruption in INS.

24. Civil Rights Commission, *The Tarnished Door*, p. 119. See also the statement of David Crossland, Commissioner of INS, in U.S. Congress, Senate, Committee on the Judiciary, *Dept. of Justice Authorization*, p. 523.

25. Civil Rights Commission, *The Tarnished Door*, pp. 119–20. See also *New York Times*, January 20, 1980.

26. *New York Times*, February 26, 1974; *Wall Street Journal*, October 29, 1975; and Crewdson, *Tarnished Door*, pp. 37–38.

27. *Wall Street Journal*, October 29, 1975.

28. U.S. Congress, Senate, Subcommittee on Immigration and Refugee Policy, *Immigration Marriage Fraud*, Hearing, 99th Cong., 1st sess., pp. 35–37.

29. The main change was to create a two-year "conditional" status for all alien spouses, sons, and daughters who become permanent resident aliens as immediate relatives of U.S. citizens or under the second preference by virtue of a marriage entered into less than two years before obtaining that status. The law was modified again in 1990. For the 1986 provisions see U.S. Congress, House, Committee on the Judiciary, *Immigration Marriage Fraud Amendments of 1986*, H. Rept. 99–106, 99th Cong., 2d sess.

30. Data from INS, *Annual Reports* and *Statistical Yearbooks*.

31. *New York Times*, July 2, 1981.

32. *Ibid.*, October 1, 1968.

33. *Ibid.*, February 4, 1981, and October 6, 1982.

34. *Ibid.*, July 7 and 8, 1980.

35. *Ibid.*, July 21, 1980.

36. Comptroller General of the United States, *Prospects Dim*, p. 15.

37. *New York Times*, June 24, 1982, and July 12, 1982.

38. *Ibid.*, August 22, 1980; and *Los Angeles Times*, May 27, 1974.

39. *Los Angeles Times*, October 14, 1983. In April 1979 an illegal alien from Trinidad was arrested in Brooklyn and charged with selling green cards for $1,000 each. The police said he made $100,000 monthly selling the cards. *New York Times*, April 5, 1979. For another recent case see *New York Times*, February 7, 1984.

40. *New York Times*, August 22, 1977, and July 10, 1984.

41. Comptroller General of the United States, *Issuing Tamper-Resistant Cards Will Not Eliminate Abuse of Social Security Numbers*, pp. 8–10.

42. *Ibid.*, pp. 4–6.

43. *Ibid.*, p. 13. The Social Security Administration reported in 1971

that an estimated four to five million persons held more than one number. *Ibid.*, p. 11. In 1983 a Senate committee stated that the economic impact of false identification on commerce and the government cost large sums of money annually. The committee, like others before it, found little cooperation between government agencies and loose standards to protect against fraud. See *New York Times*, September 9, 1983; and U.S. Congress, Senate, Permanent Subcommittee on Investigations of the Committee on Government Affairs, *Federal Identification Cards*, S. Rept. 98–84, 98th Cong., 1st sess.

44. *New York Times*, March 12 and November 1, 1971.

45. *Chicago Tribune*, April 12, 1973; *Los Angeles Times*, June 27, 1973, and December 1, 1974.

46. U.S. Civil Rights Commission, *The Tarnished Door*, pp. 79–80. For a general discussion of legal actions resulting from INS raids see *ibid.*, pp. 80–91, and Comptroller General of the United States, *Illegal Aliens: Estimating their Impact on the United States*, pp. 40–41.

47. *New York Times*, March 28 and 29, 1980. Following the census count, INS announced it would continue its crackdown on illegal aliens, but these raids have been sporadic.

48. *New York times*, April 27 and May 7, 1982. For other protests, see *ibid.*, April 30, 1982.

49. *Ibid.*, May 4, 1982, and INS, *Annual Report*, 1982, p. 5.

50. *New York Times*, May 4, 1982, and *Wall Street Journal*, December 12, 1982. INS has an apparent fondness for "projects" and "operations." In early 1984 federal raids in Florida allegedly netted 62 illegals and 11 smugglers in "Operation Everglades." *New York Times*, February 15, 1984.

51. *U.S. News and World Report*, January 17, 1972, pp. 32–33.

52. *New York Times*, December 29,1974.

53. *New Orleans Times-Picayune*, June 23, 1976.

54. *Tucson Citizen*, November 24, 1977. This style of reporting was common for the next decade. In 1983, for example, *U.S. News and World Report* ran a feature story entitled, "Invasion from Mexico: It Just Keeps Growing," March 7, 1983, pp. 37–44. About the same time *Time* called its feature "Losing Control of Our Border," *Time*, June 13, 1983, pp. 26–27.

55. U.S. Congress, Senate, Subcommittee on Immigration and Naturalization of the Committee on the Judiciary, *Immigration 1976*, Hearings, 94th Cong., 2d sess., pp. 26–28. An excellent discussion of the numbers game is Arthur E. Corwin, "The Numbers Game: Estimating Illegal Aliens in the United States, 1970–1981," in Hofstetter, ed., *U.S. Immigration Policy: Law and Contemporary Problems*, pp. 228–84.

56. Leonard Chapman, "Illegal Aliens: Time to Call a Halt," pp. 188–92.

57. A copy of the Lesko Survey can be found in U.S. Congress, Senate, Subcommittee on Immigration and Naturalization of the Committee on the Judiciary, *Immigration 1976,* pp. 133–43.

58. Ehrlich, *The Golden Door,* pp. 178–85; Bureau of the Census, *Illegal Residents,* pp. 2–3; and Charles Keely, "Counting the Uncountable: Estimates of Undocumented Aliens in the United States," pp. 473–81.

59. *Los Angeles Times,* September 13 and 23, 1978.

60. U.S. Congress, House, Select Committee on Population, *Immigration to the United States,* Hearings, 95th Cong., 2d sess., pp. 497–515.

61. *Ibid.,* pp. 175–79.

62. *New York Times,* October 13, 1980; Jorge A. Bustamente and Geronimo Martinez, "Undocumented Immigration from Mexico: Beyond Borders but Within Systems," pp. 265–84; and Warren Sanderson, "The Problems of Planning for the Unexpected: Demographic Shocks and Policy Paralysis," in Clark W. Reynolds and Carlos Tello, eds., *U.S.-Mexican Relations: Economic and Social Aspects,* pp. 293–95.

63. See, for example, Wayne A. Cornelius, *Mexican Migration to the United States; the View from the Rural Sending Communities.*

64. Bureau of the Census, *Illegal Residents,* p. 19. For reports on other studies see U.S. Dept. of Commerce: Bureau of the Census, *Preliminary Review of the Existing Studies of the Number of Illegal Resident in the United States,* and Ellen Sehgal and Joyce Vialet, "Documenting the Undocumented: Data, Like Aliens, are Elusive," p. 19. In 1983 the Bureau of the Census reported that it counted 2,047,000 undocumented aliens in the 1980 census, but said the actual figure could be higher. *New York Times,* June 19, 1983.

65. The *Saganaw News,* August 26, 1982, reported in *Editorials on File* (1982), p. 998. The *New York Times* in a series of articles in 1980 reported that the State Department believed the figure was ten million. See *New York Times,* January 16, 1980.

66. A useful summary of research on Hispanic undocumented aliens is Douglas S. Massey and Kathleen M. Schnabel, "Background and Characteristics of Undocumented Hispanic Migrants to the United States: A Review of Recent Research," pp. 7–13.

67. David North and Marion F. Houstoun, *The Characteristics and Role of Illegal Aliens in the U.S. Labor Market; An Exploratory Study.*

68. Cornelius, *Mexican Migration: the View from the Sending Communities,* pp. 6–13.

69. Bustamente and Martinez, "Undocumented Immigration," pp. 265–84; Wayne Cornelius, *Mexican Migration to the United States: Causes, Consequences, and U.S. Response,* pp. 19–30; and Douglas Massey and Josh Reichert, "Patterns of U.S. Migration from a Mexican Sending Communi-

ty: A Comparison of Legal and Illegal Migrations," pp. 624–48. The entire issue of *International Migration Review* (Winter 1978) is devoted to undocumented Mexican migration to the United States.

70. *New York Times,* December 23, 1977.

71. See the statement of Prof. Ronald A. Grennes of the Border Research Institute of Trinity University, San Antonio, Texas, reprinted in *CR* (daily digest), June 6, 1980, pp. S. 6424–25.

72. Patricia J. Elwell et al., "Haitian and Dominican Undocumented Aliens in New York City: A Preliminary Report," pp. 5–6.

73. *Ibid.,* pp. 6–7.

74. For a study of Salvadorans and Costa Ricans see Guy Poitras, "The U.S. Experience of Return Migrants from Costa Rica and El Salvador," in Select Commission on Immigration and Refugee Policy, *Appendix E,* pp. 45–196.

75. *New York Times,* October 19, 1980, and November 23, 1979.

76. *Ibid.,* February 24, 1981, and *Houston Post,* February 19, 1981. In a Texas case two men were convicted of holding 19 Mexicans in slavery, but the judge only fined them $1,000 each and gave them five years of probation, and not a jail sentence. *New York Times,* February 11, 1984. For an account emphasizing the ill-treatment of undocumented aliens, see Sasha G. Lewis, *Slave Trade Today; American Exploitation of Illegal Aliens.*

77. *New York Times,* October 19, 1980.

78. *Ibid.*

79. *Ibid.,* November 20, 1975.

80. *Ibid.*

81. *Ibid.,* May 4, 1969, and July 31, 1983; *Los Angeles Times,* April 18, 1979; and *U.S. News and World Report,* May 28, 1979, p. 60. For the statement of Cesar Chavez on illegals and the role of INS, see U.S. Congress, Senate, Committee on Labor and Human Resources, *Farmworker Collective Bargaining,* Hearings, 96th Cong., 1st sess., pp. 5–30 and 639–43.

82. Jonathan Kirsch, "California's Illegal Aliens; They Give More than They Take," p. 28.

83. *Washington Post,* March 4, 1975.

84. *New York Times,* November 10, 1980.

85. See North and Houstoun, *Illegal Aliens;* Elwell, "Haitian and Dominican Undocumented Aliens"; and Poitras, "Migrants from Costa Rica and El Salvador." For an excellent summary of the issues relating to undocumented aliens see Charles Keely, "Illegal Migration," pp. 41–47.

86. *Los Angeles Times,* November 11, 1978.

87. *New York Times,* March 18, 1979, February 16, 1981, and October 12, 1983. See also Rinker Buck, "The New Sweatshops: A Penny for Your Collar," pp. 40–46.

88. *Washington Post*, February 2, 1975; and Comptroller General, *Illegal Aliens*, pp. 10–14.

89. *New York Times*, November 10, 1980.

90. "Protective Labor Laws and Illegal Migrants," in Select Commission on Immigration and Refugee Policy, *Appendix E*, pp. 239–42.

91. *New York Times*, November 10, 1980.

92. *Washington Post*, December 16, 1976.

93. *Los Angeles Times*, November 11, 1978, and December 5, 1978.

94. *Washington Post*, December 16, 1976.

95. *New York Times*, January 30, 1980.

96. It will be recalled that brothers and sisters of American citizens were also part of the preference system.

97. Select Commission on Immigration and Refugee Policy, *Appendix E*, p. 5.

98. *Congressional Record* (daily digest), October 15, 1986, H 10586.

99. *New York Times*, December 1, 1975.

100. Select Commission on Immigration and Refugee Policy, *Appendix E*, p. 39.

101. U.S. Congress, House, Select Committee on Population, *Immigration to the United States*, Hearings, 95th Cong., 2d sess., pp. 574–76. For the literature on the use of social services, see North and Houstoun, *Illegal Aliens*; Keely, "Illegal Migration"; Wayne Cornelius et al., *Mexican Immigrants and Southern California: A Summary of the Current Knowledge*, pp. 47–56; *Washington Post*, July 15, 1982; Texas Advisory Commission on Civil Rights, *Without Papers: The Undocumented in Texas*; *Houston Post*, April 7, 1982; and Maggie Sullivan, "The Economic Impact of Undocumented Immigrants: The Orange County Report," pp. 7–9.

102. Select Commission on Immigration and Refugee Policy, *Appendix E*, p. 38. For an example of a critic of scholarly studies showing little use of social services and an insistence that later reports demonstrated greater usage, see Roger Conner, "Breaking Down the Changing Relationship Between Illegal Immigration and Welfare," *FAIR Immigration Papers, IV*.

103. The Environmental Fund News as reported in FAIR Information Exchange, September 13, 1982.

104. *Wall Street Journal*, September 19, 1977.

105. *New York Times*, February 16, 1978, June 3, 1979, and May 4, 1980; and *Los Angeles Times*, January 30, 1975.

106. *U.S. News and World Report*, May 28, 1979, p. 60; and *Los Angeles Times*, April 18, 1979. The controversy over organizing illegals in California fields went back to the 1960s. See *New York Times*, May 4, 1969.

107. Chapman, "Illegal Aliens," pp. 188–92.

108. *Los Angeles Times*, December 2, 1979.

109. For general discussions on the economic impact of undocumented immigration see Keely, "Illegal Migration"; Comptroller General of the United States, *Illegal Aliens;* Select Commission on Refugee and Immigration Policy, *Immigration and the National Interest,* pp. 38–45 and *Appendix E;* President's Domestic Council: Committee on Illegal Aliens, *Preliminary Report.* Many congressional committees held hearings on the subject. An example of testimony of these issues can be found in U.S. Congress, House, Select Committee on Population, *Immigration to the United States,* Hearings, 95th Cong., 2d sess.

110. A good summary of the pros and cons on the impact can be found in an article by reporter Barry Stein in *Los Angeles Times,* December 14, 1982.

111. *New York Times,* May 18, 1975 and December 4, 1983.

112. For statements about criminal activities of the undocumented aliens by the police see *Los Angeles Times,* January 30, 1977.

113. Vernon Briggs, "Illegal Immigration from Mexico and Its Labor Implications." p. 2.

114. Gerda Bikalis, "Immigration Policy: The New Environmental Battlefield," p. 13. The issue of the impact of immigration on population growth was first raised in 1972 by the President's Commission on the Future of the American Population. By the late 1970s groups like Zero Population Growth and the Environmental Defense Fund had taken strong positions on controlling illegal immigration.

115. David North, *Immigration and Transfer Policies in the United States: An Analysis of a Non-Relationship,* pp. 16–18.

116. *Los Angeles Times,* June 11, 1976, and David North, *Government Records: What They Tell Us About the Role of Illegal Immigrants in the Labor Market and in Income Transfer Programs,* pp. 67–69.

117. North, *Immigration and Transfer Policies,* pp. 60–61.

118. *Los Angeles Times,* August 15, 1974, February 19, 1975, July 19, 1977, and April 23, 1978.

119. *Ibid.,* January 7 and February 7, 1979. See also Leo R. Chavez, "Undocumented Immigrants and Access to Health Services: A Game of Pass the Buck," pp. 16–19.

120. *New York Times,* March 13 and April 22, 1980, and June 16, 1982. A good account of the entire controversy is Peter Schey, "Unnamed Witness Number 1: Now Attending the Texas Public Schools," pp. 22–27.

121. Kitty Calavita, *California's "Employer Sanctions": The Case of the Disappearing Law,* pp. 3–4.

122. *Ibid.,* pp. 41–42.

123. *Ibid.,* pp. 43–44.

124. *Ibid.*, p. 47. See also Carl E. Schwartz, "Employers Sanctions Laws: The State Experience as Compared with Federal Proposals," in Wayne Cornelius and Ricardo A. Montoya, eds., *America's New Immigration Law: Origins, Rationales, and Potential Consequences*, pp. 83–102.

125. North, *Immigration and Income Transfer Policies*, pp. 7–15.

126. U.S. Dept. of Labor; Employment Standards Administration, News Release, February 15, 1980.

127. North, *Government Records*, pp. 29–37, and *Houston Post*, October 23, 1979.

128. *Congressional Quarterly Almanac*, 1974, pp. 30–31. In the four-year period 1978–1981, the government reported that the Justice Department won only six convictions in cases brought under this act. See U.S. Congress, Senate, Subcommittee on Immigration and Refugees, *Knowing Employment of Illegal Immigration*, Hearings, 97th Cong., 1st sess., pp. 41–42.

129. See U.S. Congress, House, Subcommittee No. 1 of the Committee on the Judiciary, *Illegal Aliens*, Hearings, 92d Cong., 1st sess., and *CR*, September 12, 1972, pp. 30154–185.

130. *CR*, September 12, 1972, p. 30186.

131. *CR*, May 3, 1973, pp. 14179–208.

132. *New York Times*, December 26, 1974.

133. President's Domestic Council: Committee on Illegal Aliens, *Preliminary Report*, pp. 52–55 and 224–25. See also Jorge Bustamente, "Mexican Migration: The Political Dynamic of Perceptions," and Sanderson, "The Problems of Planning for the Expected: Demographic Shocks and Policy Paralysis," in Reynolds and Tello, eds., *U.S.-Mexican Relations: Economic and Social Aspects*, pp. 272–75 and 287–98; and U.S. Congress, House, Subcommittee on Inter American Affairs of the Committee on Foreign Affairs, *United States-Mexican Relations: An Update*, pp. 14–19.

134. For a general discussion of the work of the Select Commission on Immigration and Refugee Policy leading to the Simpson-Mazzoli bill see Lawrence Fuchs, "Immigration Reform in 1911 and 1981: The Role of Select Commissions," pp. 59–65 and 66–85.

135. These arguments can be found in Select Commission on Immigration and Refugee Policy, *Immigration and the National Interest*, pp. 66–69, and several hearings held by the Commission; Civil Rights Commission, *The Tarnished Door*, pp. 57–58; and testimony in U.S. Congress, Senate, Subcommittee on Immigration and Refugee Policy of the Committee on the Judiciary, *Systems to Verify. Authorization to Work in the United States*, Hearings, 97th Cong., 1st sess.; U.S. Congress, Senate, Subcommittee on Immigration and Refugee Policy of the Committee on the Judiciary, *The Knowing Employment of Illegal Immigrants*, Hearings, 97th Cong.,

1st sess.; U.S. Congress, Senate, Subcommittee on Immigration and Refugee Policy of Committee on the Judiciary, *Legalization of Illegal Immigrants*, Hearings, 97th Cong., 1st sess.; and U.S. Congress, Senate, Committee on the Judiciary, *Alien Adjustment and Employment Act of 1977*, Hearings, 95th Cong., 2d sess.

136. Select Commission on Immigration and Refugee Policy, *Immigration and the National Interest*, pp. 302–5.

137. Select Commission on Immigration and Refugee Policy, *Appendix H*, pp. 259–61. The legislative history of Simpson-Rodino can be found in Nancy Humel Montwieler, *The Immigration Reform Law of 1986*. An excellent discussion of the compromises and issues surrounding passage is Aristide R. Zolberg, "Reforming the Back Door: The Immigration Reform and Control Act of 1986 in Historical Perspective," in Virginia Yans-McLaughlin, ed., *Immigration Reconsidered: History, Sociology, and Politics*, pp. 315–39.

138. Fuchs, "The Role of Select Commissions," pp. 66–85; *Washington Post*, August 30, 1981; *New York Times*, May 11, 1981, and July 31, 1981. President Reagan did not work with Simpson and Mazzoli but submitted his own proposal. In addition to supporting the unpopular temporary worker program the administration had reservations about the need for an identity card to implement an employer sanctions law. The administration also expressed concern about the cost of an amnesty. The Reagan administration later recommended tough controls on those seeking asylum from the Western Hemisphere and emergency power to cut off illegal immigration. These were radical in scope and were opposed in Congress. The different bills passing Congress did modify procedures for asylum. See *Washington Post*, July 31, 1981, and October 22, 1981; and *New York Times*, November 4, 1981, and June 21, 1984.

139. "Majority Would Prosecute Those Who Hire Illegal Aliens," Gallup Poll, June 1977, "Public Backing Away from its Hard Stand on Hiring Illegal Aliens but Rejects Amnesty," Gallup Poll, February 1978, and "Majority Favors Law Against Hiring Illegal Aliens," Gallup Poll, November 1980; Roper Report, July 30, 1980; *Los Angeles Times*, July 30, 1980; CBS-*New York Times* Index Poll, January 1979; "Americans Strongly Back Laws Forbidding the Hiring of Illegal Aliens and Requiring All U.S. Citizens to Carry I.D. Cards," Gallup Poll, November, 1983; and *Newsweek*, June 25, 1984, p. 21. Most polls also indicated opposition to an amnesty for illegal aliens who had been in the country several years.

140. FAIR, Information Exchange, August 4, 1983. In the mid-1970s a poll by the University of San Diego Law School revealed Hispanics were more divided on the issue of illegals than the public at large. President's

Domestic Council: Committee on Illegal Aliens, *Preliminary Report*, pp. 208–209. The Gallup Poll of November 1983, also discovered Hispanics in favor of employer sanctions and amnesty. However, the sample, less than 100, was too small for reliable conclusions. Gallup Poll, Nov. 1983. A poll conducted by the *Los Angeles Times* of Hispanics in California in 1983 found Hispanics generally opposed to employer sanctions and heavily in favor of a legalization program for undocumented aliens. *Los Angeles Times*, July 25, 1983.

141. FAIR, Information Exchange, August 4, 1983.

142. *New York Times*, August 13, 14, and 18, 1982. See also Fuchs, "The Role of Select Commissions," pp. 66–85.

143. *Congressional Quarterly* (September 18, 1982), 40:2300 and (September 25, 1982), 40:2360–61.

144. *Ibid.* (December 15, 1982), 40:3097–98; *New York Times*, December 17 and 19, 1982. For the House debates see *CR* (daily digest), December 16, 1982, pp. H. 9959–60, H. 10070–93, and *CR* (daily digest), December 17, 1982, pp. H. 10251–265.

145. *New York Times*, July 31, 1983.

146. *Ibid.*, October 2, 5, and 6, 1983.

147. *Ibid.*, May 30, 1983, January 4 and 19, 1984; and U.S. Congress, House, Subcommittee on Immigration, Refugees, and International Law of the Committee on the Judiciary and Senate, Subcommittee on Immigration and Refugees of the Committee on the Judiciary, *Immigration Reform and Control Act of 1982*, Jt. Hearings, 97th Cong., 2d ses., pp. 322–41.

148. *New York Times*, November 11, 1983. For editorial opinion see FAIR, Information Exchange, October 27, 1983, and January 23, 1984. O'Neill delayed consideration until June 1984 because of division among Democrats. See *New York Times*, April 22, 1984, and May 3, 1984.

149. For the provisions of the House bill see *CR* (daily digest), June 20, 1984, H. pp. 6667–70.

150. Earlier attempts to pass such a sense of Congress resolution failed.

151. The House debates can be found in *CR* (daily digest), June 11–19, 1984. The employer sanctions provision carried 321 to 97 while an amendment by William McCollum to omit an amnesty failed 195 to 233. The Hispanic proposal of Edward Roybal to strengthen the labor laws instead of sanctions failed 120 to 304.

152. *CR* (daily digest), June 12, 1984, p. H. 5644.

153. *Ibid.*, June 20, 1984, pp. H. 6167–68.

154. *Ibid.*, June 14, 1984, pp. H. 5837–70. The vote for a temporary worker program was 228 to 172. See also *New York Times*, June 15, June

23, and July 21, 1984; and *Congressional Quarterly* (June 23, 1984), 42:1497.

155. *New York Times*, July 18, 1984.

156. *Ibid.*, July 16 and August 9, 1984.

157. *Ibid.*, September 13, 14, 15, 18, 20, 22, 25, 26, and 27, 1984; October 4, 6, 10, and 12, 1984.

158. *Ibid.*, September 20, 1985.

159. Zolberg, "Reforming the Back Door," pp. 326–30.

160. *New York Times*, September 14, 1986. See also *Congressional Quarterly*, October 5, 1985, pp. 2010–11.

161. U.S. Congress, House, *Immigration Reform and Control Act of 1986*, H. Rept. 99-682 (I), 99th Cong., 2d sess., p. 137.

162. *Ibid.*, pp. 212 and 220; and U.S. Congress, House, *Immigration Reform and Control Act*, H. Rept., 99-682 (II), 99th Cong., 2d sess., pp. 47–48.

163. H. Rept. 99-682 (I), pp. 211–12 and 220.

164. For the bill's provisions see the Conference Report in *Congressional Record* (daily digest), October 15, 1986, p. H. 10585–86.

165. *Ibid.*, pp. H. 10598–99 and *New York Times*, October 18, 1986.

166. *New York Times*, November 11, 1986.

167. INS, *Statistical Yearbook*, 1989, p. xxiv.

168. *New York Times*, November 5, 1987; July 17 and November 17, 1988, and November 12, 1989.

169. *Washington Post*, May 26, 1987; *Wall Street Journal*, September 22, 1987; and Philip L. Martin and J. Edward Taylor, *The Initial Effects of Immigration Reform on Farm Labor in California.*

170. U.S. Congress, House, Subcommittee on Immigration, Refugees, and International Law of the Committee on Judiciary, *Family Unification, Employer Sanctions, and Anti-Discrimination Under IRCA*, Hearings, 100th Cong., 2d sess. INS wanted to give a stay of deportation only to those who had arrived before passage of IRCA. See *New York Times*, February 3, 1990. The 1990 act was more generous and made the cutoff date May 5, 1988. See U.S. Congress, H. Rept. 101-955, *Conference Report to Accompany S. 358*, 101st Cong., 2d sess., p. 126. The act provided for 55,000 places annually for a three-year period. The final figures could be higher. In any case it was another unforseen consequence of IRCA. Under the INS guidelines, called "family fairness," 60,000 persons had applied during the first months of the program.

171. *New York Times*, November 5, 1988, January 12 and March 30, 1990; and *Los Angeles Times*, July 12, 1989.

172. *New York Times*, August 4, 1987; and *Washington Post*, November 3, 1988.

173. *New York Times*, December 7, 1986, June 24, 1988, March 13, June 18, and October 9, 1989. See also Frank D. Bean, Georges Vernez, and Charles B. Keely, *Opening and Closing the Doors: Evaluating Immigration Reform and Control;* Robert Bach and Doris Meissner, *Employment and Immigration Reform: Employer Sanctions Four Years Later;* and Frank Bean, Thomas Espenshade, Michael White, and Robert Dymowski, *Post IRCA Change in the Volume and Composition of Undocumented Migration to the United States.*

174. *New York Times*, August 4, 1990, March 2, 1989, and November 26, 1990.

175. *Ibid.*, November 26, 1990.

176. *Ibid.*, October 11, 1989; and *Washington Post*, July 9, 1987.

177. *New York Times*, January 2 and 8, 1991.

178. *Ibid.*, January 26 and August 24, 1989.

179. FAIR, *Ten Steps to Securing America's Borders*. See also *Christian Science Monitor*, January 26, 1989.

180. Bean, Espenshade, White, and Dymowski, *Post IRCA Changes*, p. 35, *New York Times*, February 28, 1989 and January 21, 1991.

8. A New Immigration Policy

1. *U.S. News and World Report*, March 2, 1987; *New York Times*, April 17 and 27, 1987; *Irish Voice*, March 16, 1991; and *Boston Globe*, August 4, 1987.

2. *New York Times*, November 25, 1990.

3. *Irish Echo*, May 21, 1988.

4. *New York Times*, November 27, 1988, March 1 and 17, 1989; and *Irish Echo*, December 3, 1988.

5. *New York Times*, August 15, 1990. See also *Fortune*, January 29, 1990, p. 12; *Business Week*, October 30, 1989, p. 128; Scott McConnell, "The New Battle Over Immigration," *Fortune*, May 9, 1988, pp. 90–99; and Constance Holden, "Debate Warming Up on Legal Migration Policy," *Science*, July 15, 1988.

6. These economists' views can be found in the hearings held by Congress from 1986–1990. See for examples, U.S. Congress, Subcommittee on Economic Resources, Competitiveness and Security Economics of the Jt. Economic Committee, *Economic and Demographic Consequences of Immigration*, 99th Cong., 2d sess. See also Barry Chiswick, "A Troubling Drop in Immigrant 'Quality,'" *New York Times*, December 21, 1986; George Borjas, *Friends or Strangers: The Impact of Immigrants on the U.S. Economy;* Ben Wattenburg, "The Case for More Immigrants," *U.S. News and World Report*, February 13, 1989, pp. 29–31; Gary Becker, "Opening

the Golden Door Wider to Newcomers with Knowhow," *Business Week*, June 11, 1990, p. 12; and James Cook, "The More the Merrier: Interview with Julian Simon," *Forbes*, June 11, 1990, pp. 77–81.

7. U.S. Dept. of Labor, *The Effects of Immigration on the U.S. Economy and Labor Market*, p. 180.

8. *New York Times*, August 15, 1990.

9. The fifth preference was to be limited to unmarried brothers and sisters of U.S. citizens. For Kennedy's defense of this change, see *Congressional Record*, March 15, 1988, p. S. 2214. Kennedy-Simpson did provide 30,000 extra visas for a three-year period for the fifth preference.

10. *Congressional Record* (daily digest), March 14, 1988, p. S. 2120.

11. *Congressional Quarterly*, March 19, 1988, pp. 711–13; and *Congressional Record* (daily digest), March 14, 1988, p. S. 2126.

12. Family preferences and immediate family members of U.S. citizens accounted for 480,000 places. If immediate family members rose substantially above its present level of around 215,000, it would be subtracted from family preferences when the total hit 630,000. However, family preferences could not fall below the current 216,000, thus the cap could be exceeded.

13. U.S. Congress, House, Subcommittee on Immigration, Refugees and International Law of the Committee on the Judiciary, *Reform of Legal Immigration*, Hearings, 100th Cong., 2d sess., p. 312.

14. *Congressional Record* (daily digest), July 11, 1989, p. S. 7631.

15. *New York Times*, July 14, 1989; and *Congressional Record*, July 13, 1989, p. S. 7860–66.

16. Minor adjustments included changing the per-country limit, an. increase in Hong Kong visas, permission for Chinese students to remain temporarily in the United States, and amnesty for immediate family members of IRCA legalized immigrants and more Donnelly visas.

17. President Bush did allow the students to remain in the United States until 1994. Congress wanted to cover the extension by legislation, but the President said it could be done by executive authority.

18. U.S. Congress, *Family Unity and Employment Opportunity Immigration Act of 1990*, H. Rept., 101st Cong., 2d sess., pp. 137–39.

19. U.S. Congress, House, Subcommittee on Immigration, Refugees and International Law of the Committee on the Judiciary, *Immigration Act of 1989*, Hearings (Part I), 101st Cong., 1st sess., pp. 380–83; and U.S. Congress, House, Subcommittee on Immigration, Refugees and International Law of the Committee on the Judiciary, *Legal Immigration*, Hearing, 99th Cong., 2d sess., pp. 373–77.

20. FAIR, *Immigration Report*, September 1990.

21. U.S. Congress, Senate, Subcommittees on Immigration and Refugee Affairs of the Committee on the Judiciary, *Immigration Reform*, Hearings, 101st Cong., 1st sess., pp. 292–96; and U.S. Congress, House, *Immigration Act of 1990*, Hearings (Part 3), pp. 87 and 112–19.

22. *Congressional Record* (daily digest), October 27, 1990, p. H. 12359. See also the comments of labor economist Vernon Briggs in U.S. Congress, Subcommittee on Immigration, Refugees, and International Law of the Committee on the Judiciary and the Immigration Task Force of the Committee on Education and Labor, *Immigration Act of 1990*, Jt. Hearings (Part 3), 101st Cong., 3d sess., pp. 232–47.

23. U.S. Congress, House, *Immigration Act of 1990*, Hearings (Part 3), p. 71.

24. *Congressional Record* (daily digest), October 27, 1990, p. H. 12362.

25. *Washington Post*, October 27, 1990; *Los Angeles Times*, October 25, 1990; and *Congressional Record* (daily digest), October 26, 1990, pp. H. 12980 86.

26. *Washington Post*, October 28, 1990.

27. The Secretary of State still retained some power to bar persons with unpopular beliefs.

28. For the law's main provisions, see U.S. Congress, *Conference Report to Accompany S. 358*, H. Rept. 101-955, 101th Cong., 2d sess.

29. *New York Times*, July 1, 1986; FAIR, "California State Poll on Border Security and Immigration," *Information Exchange*, May 9, 1989; "American Attitudes Toward Immigration," Roper Organization; June 1990; and *Newsweek*, September 10, 1990, p. 48.

30. *New York Times*, October 4, 1990.

31. *Washington Post*, October 28, 1990.

32. Comptroller General of the United States, *Immigration Reform: Major Changes Likely Under S. 358*, pp. 34–42.

Bibliography

Books, Periodicals, Articles, and Pamphlets

Abraham, Nabeel. "Detroit's Yemeni Workers." *MERIP Reports* (1977), 57:30–39.

Abraham, Sameer Y. and Nabeel Abraham, eds. *Arabs in the New World: Studies on Arab-American Communities.* Detroit: Wayne State University Press, 1983.

Abrams, Elliott and Franklin S. Abrams. "Immigration Policy—Who Gets In and Why." *Public Interest* (Winter 1975), 3–29.

Adams, Walter, ed. *The Brain Drain.* New York: Macmillan, 1967.

Allen, James P. "Recent Immigration from the Philippines and the Filipino Community in the United States." *The Geographical Review* (April 1977), 67:195–208.

Allman, James. "Haitian Migration: 30 Years Assessed." *Migration Today* (1982), 10(1):7–11.

American Immigration and Citizenship Conference. *Doubly Uprooted: Dutch Indonesian Refugees in the United States.* New York: AICC, 1965.

"America's Changing Face." *Newsweek* (September 10, 1990), 116:46–48.

Amundson, Robert H. "Breakthrough in Immigration." *America* (January 29, 1966), 114:168–70.

Amundson, Robert H. "Immigration Policy and Refugees." *America* (February 6, 1960), 102:556.

Amundson, Robert H. "The McCarran–Walter Act." *America* (July 20, 1957), 97:423–25.

Anderson, Henry P. *The Bracero Program in California.* Berkeley: School of Social Work, University of California, 1961.

Ansari, Abdolmaboud. *Iranian Immigrants in the United States: A Case Study of Dual Marginality.* New York: Associated Faculty Press, 1988.

Archdeacon, Thomas. *Becoming American.* New York: Free Press, 1983.

Arizpe, Lourdes. "The Rural Exodus in Mexico and Mexican Immigration to the United States." *International Migration Review* (Fall 1981), 15:629–49.

Bach, Robert L. "Employment Characteristics of Indochinese Refugees." *Migration Today* (1980), 8(3):10–14.

Bach, Robert L. "Mexican Immigration and the American State." *International Migration Review* (1978), 12(4):536–58.

Bach, Robert L. "The New Cuban Exodus: Political and Economic Motivations." *Caribbean Review* (Winter 1982), 11:22–25.

Bach, Robert L. "The New Cuban Immigrants: Their Background and Prospects." *Monthly Labor Review* (October 1980), 103:39–46.

Bach, Robert L., Juan M. Clark, and Alejandro Portes. "The New Wave: A Statistical Profile of Recent Cuban Exiles to the United States." *Cuban Studies* (January 1977), 7:1–32.

Bach, Robert L. and Doris Meissner. *America's Labor Market in the 1990s: What Role Should Immigration Play?* Washington: Carnegie Endowment for International Peace, 1990.

Bach, Robert L. and Doris Meissner. *Employment and Immigration Reform: Employer Sanctions Four Years Later.* Washington: Carnegie Endowment for International Peace, 1990.

Baily, Thomas and Marcia Freedman. *Immigrant and Native-Born Workers in the Restaurant Industry.* New York: Conservation of Human Resources, Columbia University, 1981.

Balmori, Diana. *Hispanic Immigrants in the Construction Industry: New York City, 1960–1982.* New York: Center for Latin American and Caribbean Studies, New York University, 1983.

Baras, Victor and Milton Himmelfarb, eds. *Zero Population Growth—For Whom?* Westport, Conn.: Greenwood Press, 1978.

Barkan, Elliott R. "Whom Shall We Integrate? A Comparative Analysis of the Immigration and Naturalization Trends of Asians Before and After the 1965 Immigration Act (1951–1978)." *Journal of American Ethnic History* (Fall 1983), 3:29–57.

Baron, Dennis. *The English-Only Question: An Official Language for Americans?* New Haven: Yale University Press, 1990.

Barth, Gunther. *Bitter Strength: A History of the Chinese in the United States, 1850–1870.* Cambridge: Harvard University Press, 1964.

Bauermeister, Jill. "Amerasians in America." *America* (November 17, 1982), 147:331–33.

Bean, Frank, Allan King, and Jeffrey Passel. "The Number of Illegal Migrants of Mexican Origin in the United States: Sex Ratio-Based Estimates for 1980." *Demography* (February 1980), 20:99–109.

Bean, Frank D., Thomas J. Espenshade, Michael J. White, and Robert F. Dymowski. *Post-IRCA Changes in the Volume and Composition of Undocu-

mented Migration to the United States: An Assessment Based on Apprehensions Data. Washington: Urban Institute, 1990.

Bean, Frank, Georges Vernez, and Charles B. Keely. *Opening and Closing Doors: Evaluating Immigration Reform and Control.* Santa Monica, Calif.: Rand, 1989.

Beauchamp, Marc. "Welcome to Teheran, Calif." *Forbes* (December 12, 1988), 142:60–66.

Becker, Gary. "Opening the Golden Door Wider—To Newcomers with Knowhow." *Business Week* (June 11, 1990), p. 12.

Begeman, Jean. "Wetbacks—Slaves of Today." *New Republic*, March 10, 1952, 126:16–17.

Bennett, David. *The Part of Fear: From Nativist Movements to the New Right in American History.* Chapel Hill: University of North Carolina Press, 1988.

Bennett, Marion T. *American Immigration Policies: A History.* Washington: Public Affairs Press, 1963.

Bernard, William. *Chinese Newcomers in the United States: A Sample Study of Recent Immigrants and Refugees.* New York: American Immigration and Citizenship Conference, 1974.

Bernard, William S., ed. *American Immigration Policy—A Reappraisal.* New York: Harper, 1948.

Bernard, William, ed. *The United States and the Migration Process.* New York: American Immigration and Citizenship Conference, 1975.

"Beyond the Melting Pot," *Time* (April 9, 1990), pp. 28–35.

Bikales, Gerda. "Immigration Policy: The New Environmental Battlefield." *National Parks and Conservation Magazine* (December 1977), 51:13–16.

Boffey, Philip M. "The Brain Drain: New Law Will Stem Talent Flow from Europe." *Science* (January 19, 1968), 159:282–84.

Bogen, Elizabeth. *Immigration in New York.* New York: Praeger, 1987.

Bonacich, Edna, Ivan H. Light, and Charles Choy Wong. "Koreans in Business." *Society* (September/October 1977), 14:54–59.

Borjas, George. *Friends Or Strangers: The Impact of Immigration on the U.S. Economy.* New York: Basic Books, 1990.

Boyd, Monica. "The Changing Nature of Central and Southeastern Asian Immigration to the United States: 1961–1972." *International Migration Review* (Winter 1974), 8:507–19.

"Breathing New Life into Small Business." *Forbes* (September 1979), 124:196–98.

Briggs, Vernon, Jr. *Chicanos and Rural Poverty.* Baltimore: Johns Hopkins University Press, 1973.

Briggs, Vernon, Jr. "Illegal Immigration and the American Labor Force." *American Behavioral Scientist* (January/February 1976), 19:353–63.

Briggs, Vernon, Jr. "Illegal Immigration from Mexico and Its Labor Force Implications." *Industrial Relations Report* (Spring 1983), 20:6–11.

Briggs, Vernon, Jr. *Immigration Policy and the American Labor Force.* Baltimore: Johns Hopkins University Press, 1984.

Briggs, Vernon, Jr., Walter Fogel, and Fred Schmidt. *The Chicano Worker.* Austin: University of Texas Press, 1977.

Brown, Peter G. and Henry Shue, eds. *The Border that Joins.* Totowa, N.J.: Rowman & Littlefield, 1983.

Bruce, J. Campbell. *The Golden Door: The Irony of Our Immigration Policy.* New York: Random House, 1954.

Bryce-Laporte, Roy S., ed. *Sourcebook on the New Immigration: Implications for the United States and the International Community.* New Brunswick, N.J.: Transaction Books, 1980.

Buchanan, Susan H. "Language and Identity: Haitians in New York City." *International Migration Review* (1979), 13(2):298–312.

Buchanan, Susan H. "Scattered Seeds: The Meaning of Migration for Haitians in New York City." Ph.D. dissertation, New York University, 1980.

Buck, Rinker. "The New Sweatshops: A Penny for Your Collar." *New York* (January 29, 1979), 12:40–46.

Burton, Eve. "Khmer Refugees in Western Massachusetts: Their Impact on Local Communities." *Migration Today* (1983), 11(2/3):29–34.

Bustamente, Jorge. "Structural and Ideological Conditions of the Mexican Undocumented Immigration to the United States." *American Behavioral Scientist* (January/February 1976), 19:364–76.

Bustamente, Jorge and Geronimo Martinez. "Undocumented Immigration from Mexico: Beyond Borders but Within Systems." *Journal of International Affairs* (Fall/Winter 1979), 33:265–84.

Cafferty, Pastore, Barry Chiswick, Andrew Greeley, and Teresa Sullivan. *The Dilemma of American Immigration: Beyond the Golden Door.* New Brunswick: Transaction Books, 1983.

Calavita, Kitty. *California's "Employer Sanctions" The Case of the Disappearing Law.* La Jolla, Calif.: Center for U.S.–Mexican Studies, University of California, San Diego, 1982.

Caplan, Nathan, John Whitmore, and Marcella H. Choy. *The Boat People and Achievement in America.* Ann Arbor: University of Michigan Press, 1989.

Cardenas, Gilbert. "Los Desarraigados: Chicanos in the Midwestern Region of the United States." *Aztlan* (1978), 7(2):153–86.

Cardoso, Lawrence A. *Mexican Emigration to the United States, 1897–1931.* Tucson: University of Arizona Press, 1980.

Caroli, Betty Boyd. "Recent Immigration to the United States." *Trends in History* (Summer 1982), 2:49–69.

Case, Clifford D. "Toward a New Immigration Policy." *The Reporter* (March 7, 1957), 16:26–27.

Castano, Juanita and Carmen Cruz. "Colombian Immigration to the United States, Part I." Interdisciplinary Communications Program, Smithsonian Institution. *The Dynamics of Migration: International Migration.* Occasional Monograph Series, no. 5, pp. 41–86.

Castles, Stephen and Godula Kosack. *Immigrant Workers and Class Structure in Western Europe.* London: Oxford University Press, 1973.

Castro, Mary. *"Mary" and "Eve's" Social Reproduction in the "Big Apple."* New York: Center for Latin American and Caribbean Studies, New York University, 1982.

Castro, Mary. "Women in Migration: Colombian Voices in the Big Apple." *Migration Today* (1982), 10(3/1):23–30.

Chandrasekhar, S. ed. *From India to America: A Brief History of Immigration; Problems of Discrimination; Admission, and Assimilation.* La Jolla, Calif.: Population Review, 1982.

Chavez, Leo R. "Undocumented Immigrants and Access to Health Services: A Game of Pass the Buck." *Migration Today* (1983), 11(1): 16–19.

Chen, Jack. *The Chinese of America.* New York: Harper and Row, 1980.

Chen, Ronald, ed. *Foreign Medical Graduates in Psychiatry: Issues and Problems.* New York: Human Sciences Press, 1981.

Ching, Frank. "Crime in New York's Chinatown." *Bridge* (April 1974), 3:11–14.

Chiswick, Barry. "An Analysis of Earnings Among Mexican Origin Men." Paper, Hoover Institution, Stanford University, October 1977.

Chiswick, Barry. "The Economic Progress of Immigrants: Some Apparently Universal Patterns." In William Fellner, ed., *Contemporary Economic Problems.* Washington: American Enterprize Institute, 1979.

Chiswick, Barry. "The Effect of Americanization on the Earnings of Foreign-Born Men." Paper, Hoover Institution, Stanford University, June 1977.

Chiswick, Barry, ed. *The Gateway: Immigration Issues and Policy.* Washington: American Enterprise Institute, 1982.

Chiswick, Barry. "Sons of Immigrants: Are They at an Earnings Disadvantage?" *American Economic Review* (February 1977), 67:376–80.

Choy, Bong Youn. *Koreans in America.* Chicago: Nelson-Hall, 1979.

Chuman, Frank F. *The Bamboo People: The Law and Japanese-Americans.* Del Mar, Calif.: Publishers, 1976.

Clark, Blake. "Why Shouldn't They Be Americans?" *Reader's Digest* (August 1951), 59:91–94.

Cohen, Lucy M. *Culture, Disease, and Stress Among Latino Immigrants.* Washington: Smithsonian Institution Press, 1979.

Committee on the International Migration of Talent. *The International Migration of High Level Manpower.* New York: Praeger, 1970.

"Controversy in Congress Over Proposed Amnesty for Illegal Aliens." *Congressional Digest* (October 1977), no. 56. Entire issue.

"Controversy Over Proposals to Reduce the Number of Illegal Aliens in the U.S." *Congressional Digest* (January 1975), no 54. Entire issue.

Conway, James. "Unwanted Immigrants: Cuban Prisoners in America." *Atlantic Monthly* (February 1981), 247:72–80.

Coobs, Orde. "Illegal Immigrants in New York: The Invisible Subculture.: *New York* (March 15, 1976), 9:33–41.

Cornelius, Wayne A. *Illegal Migration to the United States: Recent Research Findings, Policy Implications, and Research Priorities.* Cambridge: Center for International Studies, MIT, 1977.

Cornelius, Wayne A. *Immigration, Mexican Development Policy and the Future of U.S.-Mexican Relations.* Working Paper, Program in U.S.-Mexican Studies, San Diego University, 1980.

Cornelius, Wayne A. *Mexican Migration to the United States: Causes, Consequences, and U.S. Responses.* Cambridge: Center for International Studies, MIT, 1978.

Cornelius, Wayne A. *Mexican Migration to the United States: The View from the Rural Sending Communities.* Cambridge: Center for International Studies, MIT, 1976.

Cornelius, Wayne A. "Outgrowth from Rural Mexican Communities." Interdisciplinary Communications Program, Smithsonian Institution. *The Dynamics of Migration: International Migration*, no. 5, pp. 1–40.

Cornelius, Wayne A., Leo R. Chavez, and Jorge G. Castro, eds. *Mexican Immigrants and Southern California: A Summary of Current Knowledge.* La Jolla, Calif.: Program in United States-Mexican Relations, University of California, San Diego, 1982.

Cornelius, Wayne A. and Ricardo Anzaldua Montoya, eds. *America's New Immigration Law: Origins, Rationales, and Potential Consequences.* La Jolla, Calif.: Center for U.S.-Mexican Studies, University of California, San Diego, 1983.

Craig, Richard B. *The Bracero Program: Interest Groups and Foreign Policy.* Austin: University of Texas Press, 1971.

Crewdson, John. *The Tarnished Door: The New Immigrants and the Transformation of America*. New York: New York Times Books, 1983.

Crittenden, Ann. *Sanctuary: A Story of American Conscience and the Law in Colllusion*. New York: Weidenfeld and Nichlson, 1988.

Crouchett, Lorraine J. "California: 1965–1978, Third Wave Filipino Immigration." *Migration Today* (June 1979), 7:17–23.

Cuddy, Dennis L., ed. *Contemporary American Immigration*. Boston: Twayne, 1982.

Daniels, Roger. *Asian America: Chinese and Japanese in the United States Since 1850*. Seattle: University of Washington Press, 1988.

Daniels, Roger. *Coming to America: A History of Immigration and Ethnicity in American Life*. New York: Harper Collins, 1990.

Daniels, Roger. *Concentration Camps U.S.A*. New York: Holt, Rinehart, and Winston, 1972.

Daniels, Roger. *The Politics of Prejudice: The Anti-Japanese Movement in California and the Struggle for Japanese Exclusion*. Berkeley and Los Angeles: University of California Press, 1962.

Davidson, John. *The Long Road North*. Garden City, N.Y.: Doubleday, 1979.

Del Mar, Marcia. *A Cuban Story*. Winston Salem, N.C.: John F. Blair, 1979.

Desbarats, Jacqueline. "Thai Migration to Los Angeles." *Geographical Review* (July 1979), 69:302–18.

Dimmitt, Marius. "The Enactment of the McCarran-Walter Act of 1952." Ph.D. dissertation, University of Kansas, 1971.

Dinnerstein, Leonard. *America and the Survivors of the Holocaust*. New York: Columbia University Press, 1982.

Dinnerstein, Leonard. "Anti-Semitism in America, 1945–1950." *American Jewish History* (September 1981), 71:134–49.

Dinnerstein, Leonard, Roger Nichols, and David Reimers. *Natives and Strangers: Ethnic Groups in the Building of America*. New York: Oxford University Press, 1990.

Dinnerstein, Leonard and David Reimers. *Ethnic Americans: A History of Immigration and Assimilation*. New York: Harper and Row, 1988.

Divine, Robert A. *American Immigration Policy, 1924–1952*. New Haven: Yale University Press, 1957.

Dominquez, Virginia R. *From Neighbor to Stranger: The Dilemma of Caribbean Peoples in the United States*. New Haven: Atilles Research Program, Yale University, 1975.

Donohue, John W. "The Uneasy Immigration Debate." *America* (March 20, 1982.), 146:206–209.

Duke, Paul and Stanley Meisler. "Immigration: Quotas vs. Quality." *The Reporter* (January 14, 1965), 32:30–32.

Ehrlich, Paul R., Loy Bilderback, and Anne H. Ehrlich. *The Golden Door: International Migration, Mexico, and the United States*. New York: Ballantine Books, 1979.

Elridge, Fred. "Helping Hands from Mexico." *Saturday Evening Post* (August 10, 1957), 230:229.

Elizur, Dov. "Israelis in the United States: Motives, Attitudes and Intentions." *American Jewish Yearbook* (1980), 80:53–67.

Epenshade, Thomas J. *A Short History of U.S. Policy Towards Illegal Migration*. Washington: Urban Institute, 1990.

Fagen, Patricia Weiss. "Applying for Political Asylum in New York: Law, Policy, and Administrative Practice." Paper, Center for Latin American and Caribbean, New York University, 1983.

Fagen, Richard, Richard Brody, and Thomas O'Leary. *Cubans in Exile: Disaffection and the Revolution*. Stanford: Stanford University Press, 1968.

Fallow, James. "The New Immigrants: How They Are Affecting Us." *The Atlantic* (November 1983), 252:45–101.

Feingold, Harry L. *The Politics of Rescue: The Roosevelt Administration and the Holocaust, 1938–1945*. New Brunswick: Rutgers University Press, 1970.

Fenyvesi, Charles. "Immigration Amnesty." *New Republic* (June 14, 1980), 182:19–20.

Fermi, Laura. *The Illustrious Immigrants: The Intellectual Migration from Europe, 1930–1941*. Chicago: University of Chicago Press, 1971.

Ferris, Elizabeth G. *The Central American Refugees*. New York: Praeger, 1987.

"Fewer 'Brains' Hear U.S.A.'s Siren Song." *Business Week* (May 27, 1967), pp. 100–101.

Field, Sandra. "Cubans to Cuban Americans: Assimilation in the United States." *Migration Today* (1983), 11(4/5):34–41.

Fitzhugh, David. "The Silent Invasion." *Foreign Service Journal* (January 1976), 53:8–26.

Fisher, Maxine. *The Asian Indians of New York City*. New York: New Asia Books, 1980.

Fogel, Walter. *Mexican Illegal Workers in the United States*. Los Angeles: UCLA, 1978.

Foner, Nancy. *Jamaican Migrants: A Comparative Analysis of the New and London Experience*. New York: Center for Latin American and Caribbean Studies, New York University, 1983.

Foner, Nancy, ed. *New Immigrants in New York*. New York: Columbia University Press, 1987.

Foner, Nancy. "West Indians in New York City and London: A Comparative Analysis." *International Migration Review* (1979), 13(2):284–96.

"Foreign Talent Heads Where the Action Is." *Business Week* (September 9, 1967), pp. 196–98.

Foster, Charles. "Creolo in Conflict." *Migration Today* (1980), 8(5):9–18.

Fottler, Myron D. and Thanin Thanapisitikul. "Some Correlates of Residence Preference Among Foreign Medical Graduates: A Case Study of Thai Medical Graduates in Buffalo." *Medical Care* (September 1974), 12:778–87.

Fuchs, Lawrence H. *The American Kaleidoscope: Race, Ethnicity and the Civic Culture.* Hanover, N.H.: University Press of New England, 1990.

Fuchs, Lawrence H. "Immigration Reform in 1911 and 1981; The Role of Select Commissions." *Journal of American Ethnic History* (Fall 1983), 3:58–89.

Galarza, Ernesto. *Farm Workers and Agri-Business in California, 1947–1960.* Notre Dame, Ind.: University of Notre Dame Press, 1977.

Galarza, Ernesto. *Merchants of Labor. The Mexican Bracero Story.* Santa Barbara, Calif.: McNally & Loftin, 1964

Gallup Poll. *Public Opinion, 1935–1971.* New York: Random House, 1972.

Garcia, John A. "Political Interpretation of Mexican Immigrants: Exploration into the Naturalization Process." *International Migration Review* (Winter 1981), 15:611–24.

Garcia, Juan. *Operation Wetback: The Mass Deportation of Mexican Undocumented Workers in 1954.* Westport, Conn.: Greenwood Press, 1980.

Gardner, Robert W., Bryant Robey, and Peter C. Smith. *Asian Americans: Growth, Change, and Diversity.* Washington, D.C.: Population Reference Bureau, 1985.

Garrison, Vivian and Carol I. Weiss. "Dominican Family Networks, and United States Immigration Policy." *International Migration Review* (1979), 13(2):264–83.

Ghosh, B. N. "Some Economic Aspects of India's Brain Drain to the U.S.A." *International Migration* (1979), 17(3/4):280–89.

Giralde, Fernando Urrea. *Life Strategies and the Labor Market: Colombians in New York in the 1970s.* New York: Center for Latin American and Caribbean Studies, New York University, 1982.

"Giving Immigration Points to the Skilled and Educated." *Insight* (September 5, 1988), pp. 41–42.

"Give Me Your Rich, Your Very Rich . . . " *Business Week* (September 4, 1989), p. 31.

"Give Me Your Tired Engineers, Your Poor Biochemists, Your Huddled Computer Scientists Earning Big Fees." *U.S. News and World Report* (July 24, 1989), p. 12.

Glazer, Nathan, ed. *Clamor at the Gages: The New American Immigration.* San Francisco: Institute for Contemporary Studies, 1985.

Glazer, Sarah. "Bilingual Education: Does It Work?" *Editorial Research Reports* (March 11, 1988), pp. 126–39.

Gonzalez, Nancie. "Garifuna Settlement in New York: A New Frontier." *International Migration Review* (Summer 1979), 13:255–63.

Gonzalez, Nancie. "Peasants' Progress: Dominicans in New York." *Caribbean Studies* (October 1970), 10:154–71.

Gordon, Monica H. *The Selection of Migrant Categories from the Caribbean to the United States: The Jamaican Experience.* New York: Center for Latin American and Caribbean Studies, New York University, 1983.

Graham, Otis L., Jr. "Illegal Immigration." *Center Magazine* (July-August 1977), 10:56–65.

Grasmuck, Sherri. *The Impact of Emigration on National Development: Three Sending Communities in the Dominican Republic.* New York: Center for Latin American and Caribbean Studies, New York University, 1982.

Greene, Sheldon L. "Wetbacks, Growers, and Poverty." *Nation* (October 20, 1969), 209:403–6.

Greenfield, Meg. "The Melting Pot of Francis E. Walter." *The Reporter* (October 26, 1961), 25:24–28.

Grubel, Herbert G. and Anthony Scott, eds. *The Brain Drain: Determinants, Measurement and Welfare Effects.* Waterloo, Ont.: Wilfrid Laurier University Press, 1977.

Grubel, Herbert G. and Anthony Scott. "The Immigration of Scientists and Engineers to the United States, 1949–61." *Journal of Political Economy* (August 1966), 74:368–77.

Guendelman, Sylva R. "South American Refugees: Stresses Involved in Relocating in the San Francisco Area." *Migration Today* (1982), 9(2):19–25.

Gurak, Douglas T. and Mary M. Kritz. "Immigrant Women in New York City: Household Structure and Employment Patterns." *Migration Today* (1982), 10(3/4):15–21.

Hadley, Eleanor M. "A Critical Analysis of the Wetback Problem." *Law and Contemporary Problems* (Spring 1956), 21:336–50.

"Haitians: Special Issue." *Migration Today* (September 1979), no. 7. Entire issue.

Halsell, Grace. *The Illegals.* New York: Stein and Day, 1978.

Hambro, Dr. Edward. *The Problem of Chinese Refugees in Hong Kong.* Leyden: A. W. Sigthoff-Leyden, 1955.

Handlin, Oscar. "At Last a Fair Deal for Immigrants." *Reader's Digest* (May 1966), 88:29–34.

Harper, Elizabeth J. *Immigration Laws of the United States.* Indianapolis: Bobbs-Merrill, 1975.

Harris, Maryls. "How the Koreans Won the Greengrocer Wars." *Money* (March 1983), 12:190–98.

Harwood, Edwin. "Can Immigration Laws Be Enforced?" *Public Interest* (Summer 1983), pp. 107–23.

Haug, J. N. *Foreign Medical Graduates in the United States, 1970.* Chicago: American Medical Association, 1971.

Heimlich, William F. "Immigration Visas for Sale." *American Mercury* (February 1956), 82:26–27.

Heller, David and Deane Heller. "Our New Immigration Law," *American Legion Magazine* (February 1966), 80:6–9, 14.

Hendricks, Glenn. *The Dominican Diaspora: From the Dominican Republic to New York City—Villagers in Transition.* New York: Teachers College Press, 1974.

Herrera-Sobek, Maria. *The Bracero Experience: Elitelore versus Folklore.* Los Angeles: University of California at Los Angeles, Latin American Center Publications, 1979.

Heureux, Hervie J. L. "America's New Front Door Policy." *Reader's Digest* (August, 1954), 65:61–65.

Hewlett, Sylvia Ann. "Coping with Illegal Aliens." *Foreign Affairs* (Winter 1981/82), 60:358–78.

Higham, John. *Strangers in the Land: Patterns of American Nativism, 1860–1925.* New York: Atheneum, 1963.

Hill, Gladwin. "The Wetbacks—McCarran's Immigrants." *Nation* (August 22, 1953), 177:151–52.

Hoffman, Abraham. *Unwanted: Mexican Americans in the Great Depression, Repatriation Pressures, 1929–1939.* Tucson. University of Arizona Press, 1974.

Hofstetter, Richard R., ed. *U.S. Immigration Policy: Law and Contemporary Problems* (Spring 1982), no 45. Entire issue.

Holborn, Louise. *Refugees: A Problem of Our Time.* 2 vols. Metchen, N.J.: Scarecrow Press, 1975.

Holden, Constance. "Debate Warming Up on Legal Immigration Policy." *Science* (July 15, 1988).

Hosokawa, Bill. *Nisei: The Quiet Americans.* New York: Morrow, 1969.

Hosokawa, Bill and Robert Wilson. *East to America: The Story of the Japanese in America.* New York: Morrow, 1980.

"How the Immigrants Made it in Miami." *Business Week* (May 1, 1971), pp. 88–89.

Humphrey, Hubert H. Jr. *The Stranger at Our Gate.* New York: Public Affairs Committee, 1954.

Hundley, Norris, ed. *The Asian American: The Historical Experience.* Santa Barbara, Calif.: American Bibliography Center, CLIO Press, 1976.

Hurh, Won Moo, Hei Chu Kim, and Dwange Chung Kim. *Assimilation Patterns of Immigrants in the United States States: A Case Study of Korean Immigrants in the Chicago Area.* Washington: University Press of America, 1978.

Huss, John D. and Melanie Wirken. "Illegal Immigration; The Hidden Population Bomb." *Futurist* (April 1977), 2:114–20.

Hutchinson, Edward P. *Legislative History of American Immigration Policy, 1790–1965.* Philadelphia: University of Pennsylvania Press, 1981.

Iganzcio, Lemuel F. *Asian Americans and Pacific Islanders (Is there Such an Ethnic Group?).* San Jose, Calif.: Pilipino Development Associates, 1976.

"Illegal Immigration." *The Humanist* (November/December 1981), no. 41. Entire issue.

"Illegal Mexican Immigrants to the U.S." *International Migration Review* (Winter 1978), no 12. Entire issue.

"The Immigration Mess." *Time* (February 27, 1989), pp. 14–15.

"Immigration—Why the Lady Still Beckons." *Forbes* (October 30, 1978), 122:63–67.

Jacoby, Susan. "The New Americans (series)." New York: Alicia Patterson Foundation, 1974.

Jacoby, Susan. "The Roots of Immigration." *New York Affairs* (Winter 1976), 3:54–67.

Jasso, Guiliermina and Mark R. Rosenzweig. "Estimating the Emigration Rates of Legal Immigrants Using Administrative and Survey Data: The 1971 Cohort of Immigrants to the United States." *Demography* (August 1982), 19:279–90.

Jasso, Guiliermina and Mark R. Rosenzweig. *The New Chosen People: Immigrants in the United States.* New York: Russell Sage Foundation, 1990.

Jensen, Joan. *Passage from India: Asian Indian Immigrants in North America.* New Haven: Yale University Press, 1988.

Johnson, Kenneth A. *Illegal Aliens in the Western Hemisphere.* New York: Praeger, 1981.

Jones, Maldwyn. *American Immigration.* Chicago: University of Chicago Press, 1960.

Jones, Richard C. *Undocumented Migration from Mexico: Some Geographical Questions.* San Antonio: Human Resources Management and Development Program, University of Texas at San Antonio, 1981.

Jorge, Antonio and Raul Moncraz. *A Case of Subutilization and Misallocation of Human Capital Resources; The Cubans in the United States.* San Antonio: Human Resources Management and Development Program, University of Texas at San Antonio, 1981.

Jorge, Antonio and Raul Moncraz. *The Cuban Influx into South Florida: Culture, Entrepreneurship, and the Emergence of New Growth Patterns in an Advanced Society*. San Antonio: Human Resources Management and Development Program, University of Texas at San Antonio, 1981.

Jorge, Antonio and Raul Moncraz. "Cubans in South Florida: A Social Science Approach." *Metas* (Fall 1980), 1:37–87.

Jorrin, Ruth. "Wealth Attracts Talent." *Nation* (April 3, 1967), 204:225–27.

Kayal, Philip M. "Dominicans in New York." *Migration Today* (October 1978), 3:11–15.

Kaye, Ellen Joy. "The Sephardic Israelis: A Case Study of Forest Hills and Borough Park." Paper in American Social History Seminar, New York University, 1980.

Keely, Charles B. "The Development of U.S. Immigration Policy since 1968." *Journal of International Affairs* (Fall/Winter 1979), 33:240–64.

Keely, Charles B. *Global Refugee Policy: The Case for a Development Oriented Strategy*. New York: The Population Council, 1981.

Keely, Charles B. "Illegal Migration." *Scientific American* (March 1982), 246:41–47.

Keely, Charles B. "The Immigration Act of 1965; A Study of the Relationship of Social Science Theory to Group Interest and Legislation." Ph.D. dissertation, Fordham University, 1970.

Keely, Charles B. "Philippine Migration: International Movements and Emigration to the United States." *International Migration Review* (Summer 1973), 7:177–87.

Keely, Charles B. *U.S. Immigration: A Policy Analysis*. New York: The Population Council, 1979.

Keely, Charles B. and S. M. Tomasi. *Whom Have We Welcomed?* New York: Center for Migration Studies, 1975.

Kelly, Gail P. *From Vietnam to America: A Chronicle of the Vietnamese Immigration to the United States*. Boulder, Colo.: Westview Press, 1977.

Kessner, Thomas and Betty Boyd Caroli. *Today's Immigrants: Their Stories*. New York: Oxford University Press, 1981.

Kim, Hyung-chan, ed. *The Korean Diaspora*. Santa Barbara; ABC-CLIO, 1977.

Kim, Illsoo. "New Urban Immigrants; The Korean Community in New York." Ph.D. dissertation, City University of New York, 1981.

Kim, Illsoo. *New Urban Immigrants: The Korean Community in New York City*. Princeton: Princeton University Press, 1981.

Kirsch, Jonathan. California's Illegal Aliens: They Give More Than They Take." *New West* (May 23, 1977), pp. 26–33.

Kiser, George and Martha Kiser, eds. *Mexican Workers in the United States.* Albuquerque: University of New Mexico Press, 1979.

Koehler, Charles. "Recruiting Abroad: Does It Pay?" *American Journal of Nursing* (December 1978), 78:2086–90.

Kritz, Mary M., ed. *U.S. Immigration and Refugee Policy: Global and Domestic Issues.* Lexington, Mass.: D. C. Heath, 1983.

Kuo, Chia-ling. *Social and Political Change in New York's Chinatown: The Role of Voluntary Associations.* New York: Praeger, 1977.

Kuvlesky, William P. *Gender Differences Among Mexican American Youth: A Synthesis of Results from Texas Research, 1967–1980.* San Antonio: Human Resources Management and Development Program, University of Texas at San Antonio, 1981.

Kwong, Peter. *The New Chinatown.* New York: Hill and Wang, 1987.

Laguerre, Michel S. *American Odyssey: Haitians in New York City.* Ithaca: Cornell University Press, 1984.

Laiken, Judith. "Our Irrational Nationality Quotas." *The Reporter* (March 7, 1957), 16:28–30.

Lasker, Bruno. *Filipino Immigration.* Chicago: University of Chicago Press, 1931.

Le Berthon, Ted. "At the Prevailing Rate." *Commonweal* (November 1, 1957), 67:122–25.

Lega, Leonor I. "The 1980 Cuban Refugees: Some of Their Initial Attitudes Toward Their Future in a New Society." *Migration Today* (1983), 11(4/5):23–25.

Lehman, Paul. "The Haitian Struggle for Human Rights." *Christian Century* (October 8, 1980), 97:941–43.

LeMay, Michael C. *From Open Door to Dutch Door: An Analysis of U.S. Immigration Policy Since 1820.* New York: Praeger, 1987.

"Let's Change the Immigration Law—Now." *Fortune* (January 29, 1990), p. 12.

Levin, Doron P. "Israeli Settlers in the U.S." *National Jewish Monthly* (October 1978), pp. 17–24.

Lewis, Sasha G. *Slave Trade Today: American Exploitation of Illegal Aliens.* Boston: Beacon, 1979.

Lieberman, Jethro K. *Are Americans Extinct?* New York: Walker, 1968.

Linehan, Edward J. "Cuba's Exiles Bring New Life to Miami." *National Geographic Magazine* (July 1973), 144:68–95.

Lipset, Seymour Martin and Drora Kass. "Israelis in Exile." *Commentary* (November 1979), 68:68–72.

Liskofsky, Sidney. "American Immigration Policy: Today and Tomorrow." *Jewish Frontier* (September 1952), 19:7–16.

Liskofsky, Sidney. "The Refugee Relief Act of 1953." *Jewish Frontier* (October 1953), 20:21–26.

Llanes, Jose. *Cuban Americans: Masters of Survival.* Cambridge: ABT Books, 1982.

Loescher, Gilburt D. and John A. Scanlan. *Calculated Kindness: Refugees and America's Half-Open Door, 1945–Present.* New York: Free Press, 1986.

Loescher, Gilburt D. and John A. Scanlan, eds. "The Global Refugee Problem: U.S. and World Response." *The Annals of the American Academy of Political and Social Science* (May 1983), no. 467. Entire issue.

Lowenthal, David. "New York's New Hispanic Immigrants." *Geographical Record* (January 1976), 66:90–94.

Lutheran Council in the USA: Dept. of Immigration and Refugee Services. *One Year After Arrival: The Adjustment of Indochinese Women in the United States, 1979–1980.* New York: Lutheran Council, no date.

Lutton, Wayne and Palmer Stacy. *The Immigration Time Bomb.* Alexandria, Va.: American Immigration Control Foundation, 1985.

Mamot, Patricio R. *Foreign Medical Graduates in America.* Springfield, Ill.: Charles C. Thomas, 1974.

Mandel, Michael J. "Roll Out America's Red Carpet for the Skilled." *Business Week* (October 30, 1989), p. 128.

Mariano, Honorante. *The Filipino Immigrants in the United States.* San Francisco: R & E Associates, 1972.

Mark, Diane Mei Lin and Ginger Chih. *A Place Called Chinese America.* San Francisco: The Organization of Chinese Americans, 1982.

Marrus, Michael R. *The Unwanted: European Refugees in the Twentieth Century.* New York: Oxford University Press, 1985.

Marsh, Robert. "Socio-economic Status of Indochinese Refugees in the United States: Programs and Problems." *Social Security Bulletin* (October 1980), 43:11–20.

Martin, Philip and Edward J. Taylor. *The Initial Effects of Immigration Reform on Farm Labor in California.* Washington: The Urban Institute, 1990.

Martinez, Vilma. "Illegal Immigration and the Labor Force." *American Behavioral Scientist* (January/February 1976), 19:335–51.

Massey, Douglas. "Dimensions of the New Immigration to the United States and the Prospects for Assimilation." *Annual Review of Sociology* (1981), 7:57–85.

Massey, Douglas and Josh Reichert. "History and Trends in U.S. Bound Migration from a Mexican Town." *International Migration Review* (1980), 14(4):477–91.

Massey, Douglas S. and Josh Reichert. "Patterns of U.S.—Migration from a Mexican Sending Community: A Comparison of Legal and Illegal Migrants." *International Migration Review* (Winter 1979), 13:599–623.

Massey, Douglas S. and Kathleen Schnabel. "Background Characteristics of Undocumented Hispanic Migrants to the United States: A Review of Recent Research." *Migration Today* (1983), 11(1):9–13.

Masud-Piloto, Félix Roberto. *With Open Arms: Cuban Migration to the United States.* Totowa, N.J.: Rowman and Littlefield, 1988.

Matthews, J. B. "Immigration: 1956 Issue." *American Mercury* (October 1955), 81:51–57.

McCarthy, Charles J. "Emigration from the Philippines." *Migration News* (November/December 1972), pp. 14–19.

McCarthy, Kevin F. and Burclaga R. Valdez. *Current and Future Effects of Mexican Immigration in California.* Santa Monica, Calif.: Rand, 1986.

McConnell, Scott. "The New Battle Over Immigration." *Fortune* (May 9, 1988), 117:89–102.

Meier, Matt S. and Feliciano Rivera. *The Chicanos.* New York: Hill and Wang, 1972.

McNeill, William H. and Ruth S. Adams, eds. *Human Migration Patterns and Policies.* Bloomington: Indiana University Press, 1978.

Meijia, Alfonso, Helena Pizurki, and Erica Royston. *Foreign Medical Graduates: The Case of the United States.* Lexington, Mass.: D. C. Heath, 1980.

Melendy, H. Brett. *Asians in America: Filipinos, Koreans, and East Indians.* New York: Hippocrene Books, 1981.

Melendy, H. Brett. *The Oriental Americans.* Boston: Twayne, 1972.

Mick, Stephen S. "The Foreign Medical Graduate." *Scientific American* (February 1975), 232:14–21.

Miller, Mark J. *Foreign Workers in Western Europe: An Emerging Political Force.* New York: Praeger, 1981.

Miller, Michael V. *Economic Growth and Change Along the U.S.-Mexico Border: The Case of Brownsville, Texas.* San Antonio: Human Resources Management and Development Program, University of Texas at San Antonio, 1981.

Miller, Stuart C. *The Unwelcome Immigrant: The American Image of the Chinese, 1785–1882.* Berkeley and Los Angeles: University of California Press, 1969.

Moncraz, Raul. "A Model of Professional Adaptation of Refugees: The Cuban Case in the U.S., 1959–1970." *International Migration* (1973), 11(4):171–83.

Moncraz, Raul. "Professional Adaptation of Cuban Physicians in the United States, 1959–1969." *International Migration Review* (Spring 1970), 4:80–86.

Mondale, Walter. "The Cost of the Brain Drain." *The Atlantic* (December 1967), 220:67–69.

Montero, Darrel. *Vietnamese Americans: Patterns of Socioeconomic Adaptation in the United States.* Boulder, Colo.: Westview Press, 1979.

Montero, Darrel. "The Vietnamese Refugees to America: Patterns of Socio-economic Adaptation and Assimilation." *International Migration Review* (Winter 1979), 13:624–48.

Montwieler, Nancy Humel. *The Immigration Reform Law of 1986: Analysis, Text, Legislative History.* Washington: Bureau of National Affairs, 1986.

Morgan, Thomas B. "The Latinization of America: What Does it Mean When You Walk the Streets of Your Own Country and You Don't Understand a Word of the Language?" *Esquire* (May 1983), 5:47–56.

Morris, Milton D. *Immigration: The Beleagured Bureaucracy.* Washington: The Brookings Institution Press, 1985.

Muller, Thomas and Thomas Espenshade. *The Fourth Wave: California's Newest Immigrants.* Washington: Urban Institute, 1985.

Munoz, Alfredo. *The Filipinos in America.* Los Angeles: Mountain View, 1971.

Myers, John. *The Border Wardens.* Englewood Cliffs, N.J.: Prentice Hall, 1971.

"Needed: A New Immigration Law." *Christian Century* (December 30, 1964), 81:1611–12.

"The New Immigration." *Annals of the American Academy of Political and Social Science* (September 1966), no. 367. Entire issue.

Nishi, Setsuko Matsuanaga. "The New Wave of Asian Americans." *New York Affairs* (Spring 1979), 5:82–96.

Norment, Lynn. "Are Black Refugees Getting a Dirty Deal?" *Ebony* (October 1983), 38:132–36.

North, David. *The Border Crossers: The People Who Live in Mexico and Work in the United States.* Washington: National Technical Information Service, 1969.

North, David (with the assistance of Jennifer R. Wagner). *Government Records: What They Tell Us About the Role of Illegal Immigrants in the Labor Market and in Income Transfer Programs.* Washington: New TransCentury Foundation, 1980.

North, David (with the assistance of Jennifer R. Wagner). *Immigration and Income Transfer Policies in the United States: An Analysis of a Non-Relationship.* Washington: New TransCentury Foundation, 1980.

North, David and Marion Houstoun. "The Characteristics of Illegal Aliens." *Industrial Relations Review* (Spring 1983), 20:12–15.

North, David and Marion Houstoun. *The Characteristics and Role of Illegal*

Aliens in the U.S. Labor Market: An Exploratory Study. Washington: Linton, 1976.

North, David, Julia Taft, and David Ford. *Refugee Resettlement in the U.S.: Time for a New Focus.* Washington: New TransCentury Foundation, 1979.

Orfalea, Gregory. *Before the Flames: A Quest for the History of Arab Americans.* Austin: University of Texas Press, 1988.

O'Grady, John. "The McCarran Immigration Bill." *Commonweal* (June 20, 1952), 56:263–65.

Open Doors: 1981/1982: Report on International Educational Exchange. New York: Institute of International Education, 1983.

Palmer, Ransford W. "A Decade of West Indian Migration to the United States, 1962–1972: An Economic Analysis." *Social and Economic Studies* (December 1974), 23:571–87.

Papademetriou, Demetrios G. and Mark J. Miller, eds. *The Unavoidable Issue: U.S. Immigration Policy in the 1980s.* Philadelphia: Institute for the Study of Human Issues, 1983.

Parlin, Bradley W. *Immigrant Professionals in the United States: Discrimination in the Scientific Labor Market.* New York: Praeger, 1976.

Pearlstone, Zena. *Ethnic L.A.* Beverly Hills, Calif.: Hill Crest Press, 1990.

Pedraza-Bailey, Silvia. *Political and Economic Migrants in America: Cubans and Mexicans.* Austin: University of Texas Press, 1985.

Peerman, Dean. "Haitian Refugees: Calamity Compounded." *Christian Century* (November 18, 1981), 98:1180–82.

Pernia, Ernesto M. "The Question of the Brain Drain from the Philippines." *International Migration Review* (Spring 1976), 10:63–72.

Pessar, Patricia R. *Kinship Relations of Production in the Migration Process: The Case of Dominican Emigration to the United States.* New York: Center for Latin American and Caribbean Studies, New York University, 1982.

Pessar, Patricia R., ed. *When Borders Don't Divide: Labor Migration and Refugee Movements in the Americas.* New York: Center for Migration Studies, 1988.

Piore, Michael J. *Birds of Passage: Migrant Labor and Industrial Societies.* Cambridge: Cambridge University Press, 1979.

Polenberg, Richard. *One Nation Divisible.* New York: Living Press, 1980.

Porter, Rosalie. *Forked Tongue: The Politics of Bilingual Education.* New York: Basic Books, 1990.

Portes, Alejandro. "Illegal Immigration and the International System: Lessons from Recent Legal Mexican Immigration to the United States." *Social Problems* (April 1979), 26:425–32.

Portes, Alejandro. "Return of the Wetback." *Society* (March/April 1974), 2:40–46.

Portes, Alejandro and Robert L. Bach. *Latin Journey: Cuban and Mexican Immigrants in the United States.* Berkeley: University of California Press, 1985.

Portes, Alejandro and Rubén Rumbaut. *Immigrant America: A Portrait.* Berkeley: University of California Press, 1990.

Portes, Alejandro and Kenneth L. Wilson. "Immigrant Enclaves; An Analysis of the Labor Market Experiences of Cubans in Miami." *American Journal of Sociology* (September 1980), 86:295–320.

Power, Jonathan. *Migrants and Workers in Western Europe and the United States.* Oxford: Pergamon Press, 1979.

Powers, Thomas. "The Scandal of U.S. Immigration: The Haitian Example." *Ms.* (February 1976), 4:62–64 and 81–84.

"Proposed Sanctions Against Employers of Illegal Aliens." *Congressional Digest* (October 1981), no. 60. Entire issue.

Ramchandani, R. R. *Uganda Asians; The End of An Enterprize.* Bombay: United Asian Publications, 1976.

"Refugee Policy." *Editorial Research Report* (May 30, 1980), 20:387–403.

Reid, Ira De. *The Negro Immigrant.* New York: Columbia University Press, 1939.

Reisler, Mark. *By the Sweat of Their Brow.* Westport, Conn.: Greenwood Press, 1976.

Reubens, Edwin P. *Interpreting Migration: Current Models and a New Integration.* New York: Center for Latin American and Caribbean Studies, New York University, 1981.

Reynolds, Charles W. and Carlos Tello, eds. *U.S.-Mexican Relations: Economic and Social Aspects.* Stanford: Stanford University Press, 1983.

Rice, Berkeley. "The New Gangs of Chinatown." *Psychology Today* (May 1977), 10:60–69.

Riggs, Fred W. *Pressures on Congress: A Study of the Repeal of the Chinese Exclusion Act.* New York: King's Crown Press, 1950.

Rockett, Ian. "Immigration Legislation and the Flow of Specialized Human Capital from South America to the United States." *International Migration Review* (Spring 1976), 10:47–62.

Rogg, Eleanor M. *The Assimilation of Cuban Exiles: The Role of Community and Class.* New York: Aberdeen Press, 1974.

Rogg, Eleanor M. "The Influence of a Strong Refugee Community on the Economic Adjustment of its Members." *International Migration Review* (Winter 1971), 5:474–81.

Rothchild, Sylvia. *A Special Legacy: An Oral History of Jewish Emigres in the United States.* New York: Simon and Schuster, 1985.

Rowan, Carl T. and David M. Mazie. "Our Immigration Nightmare." *Reader's Digest* (January 1983), 122:87–92.

Samora, Julian. *Los Mojados: The Wetback Story.* Notre Dame, Ind.: University of Notre Dame Press, 1971.

Sandemeyer, Elmer C. *The Anti-Chinese Movement in California.* Urbana: University of Illinois Press, 1939.

Saran, Parmatma. *The Asian Indian Experience in the United States.* Cambridge: Schenkman, 1985.

Saran, Parmatma. "Cosmopolitans from India." *Society* (September/October 1977), 14:65–69.

Saran, Parmatma and Edwin Eames, eds. *The New Ethnics; Asian Indians in the United States.* New York: Praeger, 1980.

Sassen-Koob, Saskia. *Exporting Capital and Importing Labor: The Role of Caribbean Migration to New York City.* New York: Center for Latin American and Caribbean Studies, New York University, 1981.

Saxton, Alexander. *The Indispensable Enemy: Labor and the Anti-Chinese Movement in California.* Berkeley and Los Angeles: University of California Press, 1971.

Schey, Peter. "The Black Boat People Founder on the Shoals of U.S. Policy." *Migration Today* (1981), 9(4/5):7–10.

Schey, Peter. "Unnamed Witness Number I: Now Attending the Texas Public Schools." *Migration Today* (1982) 10(5):22–27.

Schmidt, Aurora. "Refugees and Immigrants: In Conflict with the American Poor?" *Migration Today* (1981), 9(4/5):17–21.

Schuck, Peter. "The Transformation of Immigration Law." *Columbia Law Review* (January 1984), 84:1–80.

Schwartz, Abba P. *The Open Society.* New York: Wm. Morrow, 1968.

Scruggs, Otey. "Evolution of the Mexican Farm Labor Agreement of 1942." *Agricultural History* (July 196), 34:140–49.

Scruggs, Otey. "The First Mexican Farm Labor Program." *Arizona and the West* (Winter 1960), 2:319–26.

Seller, Maxine. *To Seek America: A History of Ethnic Life in the United States.* Englewood Cliffs, N.J.: Jerome S. Ozer, 1977.

Semler, H. Michael. "The New Immigration Law and 'Guest Workers.'" *America* (September 4, 1982), 147:106–8.

Sengstock, Mary C. *The Chaldean Americans: Changing Conceptions of Ethnic Identity.* New York: Center for Migration Studies, 1982.

Sengstock, Mary C. "Traditional and Nationalist Identity in a Christian Arab Community." *Sociological Analysis* (Autumn 1974), 35:101–10.

Sheatsley, Paul. "White Attitudes Toward the Negro." *Deadalus* (Winter 1966), 95:217–29.

Shokeid, Moshe. *Children of Circumstances: Israeli Emigrants in New York.* Ithaca: Cornell University Press, 1988.

Shu, Ramsay. *The Samoan Community in Southern California: Conditions and Needs.* Chicago: Asian American Mental Health Research Center, 1977.

Simon, Daniel T. "Mexican Repatriation in East Chicago, Indiana." *Journal of Ethnic Studies* (Summer 1974), 2:11–23.

Simon, Julian. *The Economic Consequences of Immigration.* Oxford: Basil Blackwell, 1989.

Simon, Julian L. *The Ultimate Resource.* Princeton: Princeton University Press, 1981.

Simon, Rita. *New Lives: The Adjustment of Soviet Jewish Immigrants in the United States and Israel.* Lexington, Mass.: Lexington Books, 1985.

Simon, Rita. *Public Opinion and the Immigrant: Print Media Coverage, 1880–1980.* Lexington, Mass.: Lexington Books, 1985.

Sitkoff, Harvard. *The Struggle for Equality: 1954–1980.* New York: Hill and Wang, 1981.

Snepp, Frank. *Decent Interval.* New York: Random House, 1977.

Sobel, Zvi. *Migrants from the Promised Land.* New Brunswick: Transaction Books, 1986.

Sofer, Eugene F. *Illegal Immigration: Background to the Current Debate.* Policy Research Center, no date.

Solberg, Mary. "El Salvador." *Migration Today* (1982), 10(2):8–12.

Sowell, Thomas, ed. *American Ethnic Groups.* Washington: Urban Institute, 1978.

Sowell, Thomas. *Ethnic America.* New York: Basic Books, 1981.

Sparadlin, T. Richard. "The Mexican Farm Labor Importation Program: Review and Reform." *George Washington Law Review* (October 1961), 30:84–122.

Staub, Shalom. *Yemenis in New York City: The Folklore of Ethnicity.* Philadelphia: Balch Institute Press, 1989.

Strand, Paul J. and Woodrow Jones, Jr. *Indochinese Refugees in America: Problems of Adaptation and Assimilation.* Durham: Duke University Press, 1985.

Starr, Paul. *The Transformation of American Medicine: The Rise of a Sovereign Profession and the Making of a Vast Industry,* New York: Basic Books, 1982.

Starr, Paul D. "Troubled Waters: Vietnamese Fisherfolk on America's Gulf Coast." *International Migration Review* (Spring/Summer 1980), 15:226–38.

Starr, Paul D. "Vietnamese Fisherfolk and How They Grew." *Migration Today* (1981), 9(4/5):11–16.

Stein, Barry N. "Occupational Adjustment of Refugees: The Vietnamese in the United States." *International Migration Review* (Spring 1979), 13:25–45.

Stein, Barry N. and Silvano Tomasi. *Refugees Today: International Migration Review* (Spring/Summer 1981), no. 15. Entire issue.

Stern, William. "H. R. 1580, the Immigration and Nationality Amendments of 1965: A Case Study." Ph.D. dissertation, New York University, 1974.

Stevens, Rosemary, Stephen S. Mick, and Louis Goodman. *The Aliens Doctors: Foreign Medical Graduates in American Hospitals.* New York: Wiley, 1978.

Stoddard, Ellwyn R. "A Conceptual Analysis of the 'Alien Invasion': Institutionalized Support of Illegal Mexican Aliens in the United States." *International Migration Review* (Summer 1976), 10:157–89.

Stoddard, Ellwyn R. *Mexican Americans.* New York: Random House, 1973.

Sullivan, Maggie. "The Economic Impact of Undocumented Immigrants: The Orange County Report." *Migration Today* (April 1978), 6:7–9.

Sung, Betty Lee. *The Story of the Chinese in America.* New York: Collier Books, 1971.

Sutter, Valerie O'Connor. *The Indochinese Refugee Dilemma.* Baton Rouge: Louisiana State University Press, 1990.

Sutton, Constance R. and Elsa M. Chaney, eds. *Caribbean Life in New York City: Sociocultural Dimensions.* New York: Center for Migration Studies, 1987.

Synott, Marcia G. *The Half Opened Door: Discrimination in Admissions at Harvard, Yale, and Princeton: 1900–1970.* Westport, Conn.: Greenwood Press, 1979.

Takaki, Ronald. *Strangers From a Different Shore: A History of Asian Americans.* Boston: Little, Brown, 1989.

Tenhula, John. "Realities and Responsibilities: Refugee Resettlement in the U.S." *Migration Today* (June 1979), 6:9–13.

Thernstrom, Stephan, ed. *The Harvard Encyclopedia of American Ethnic Groups.* Cambridge: Harvard University Press, 1982.

"Those Amazing Cuban Emigres." *Fortune* (October 1966), 74:144–49.

Teitelbaum, Michael S. "Right Versus Right: Immigration and Refugee Policy in the United States." *Foreign Affairs* (Fall 1980), 59:21–59.

"To Eliminate Racial Discrimination in Immigration." Washington: Center for Migration Studies, 1965.

Tobier, Emanuel. "The Changing Face of Chinatown." *New York Affairs* (Spring 1979), 5:66–76.

Tollefson, James. *Alien Winds: The Reeducation of American Indochinese Refugees.* New York: Praeger, 1989.

Tucker, Robert W., Charles B. Keely, and Linda Wrigley, eds. *Immigration and U.S. Foreign Policy* Boulder, Colo.: Westview Press, 1990.

Ugalde, Antonio, Frank D. Bean, and Gilbert Cardenas. "International Migration from the Dominican Republic: Findings from a National Survey." *International Migration Review* (Summer 1979), 13:235–54.

Van Den Haag, Ernest. "More Immigration?" *National Review* (September 21, 1965), 17:821–22.

Wain, Barry. "The Indochina Refugee Crisis." *Foreign Affairs* (Fall 1979), 58:160–80.

Wain, Barry. *The Refused: The Agony of the Indochina Refugee.* New York: Simon and Schuster, 1981.

Waldinger, Roger D. *Through the Eye of the Needle: Immigrants and Enterprise in New York's Garment Trades.* New York: New York University Press, 1986.

Walsh, Bryan. "Cubans in Miami." *America* (February 26, 1966), 114:286–88.

Walter, Francis. "The Truth About the Immigration Act." *Reader's Digest* (May 1953), 62:126–32.

Walzer, Michael. "The Moral Problem of Refugees." *The New Republic* (February 10, 1979), 180:15–17.

Wang, John. "Behind the Boom: Power and Economics and Chinatown." *New York Affairs* (Spring 1979), 5:77–81.

Warren, Robert. "Recent Immigration and Current Data Collection." *Monthly Labor Review* (October 1977), 100:36–41.

Warren, Robert and Jennifer M. Peck. "Foreign-Born Emigration from the United States." *Demography* (February 1980), 17:71–81.

Wattenberg, Ben J. "The Case for More Immigrants." *U.S. News and World Report* (February 13, 1989), 106:29–31.

Weyr, Thomas. *Hispanic U.S.A.: Breaking the Melting Pot.* New York: Harper and Row, 1988.

"What Puts the Whiz in the Whiz Kids?" *U.S. News and World Report* (March 14, 1988), 48–53.

White, Theodore H. *America in Search of Itself: The Making of the President, 1956–1980.* New York: Harper and Row, 1982.

Williams, Jerry. *And Yet They Come: Portugese Immigration from the Azores to the United States.* New York: Center for Migration Studies, 1982.

Wyman, David S. *Paper Walls: America and the Refugee Crisis, 1938–1941.* Amherst: University of Massachusetts Press, 1968.

Yans-McLaughlin, Virginia, ed. *Immigration Reconsidered: History, Sociology, and Politics.* New York: Oxford University Press, 1990.

Zolberg, Aristide R. "The Main Gate and the Back Door: The Politics of American Immigration Policy, 1950–1976." Paper for Council on Foreign Relations, 1978.

Zucker, Norman L. and Naomi Flink Zucker. *The Guarded Gate: The Reality of American Refugee Policy.* New York: Harcourt Brace Jovanovich, 1987.

Newspapers, News Weeklies, Organizations, and
Organizational Publications

American Council of Voluntary Agencies for Foreign Service (New York City), Archives.

American Jewish Committee (New York City), Archives.

American Public Welfare Association, *Refugee Reports,* 1980–1983.

The (Bergen) Record, 1965–1991.

Boston Globe, 1986–1990.

CBS-*Times* Poll.

Center for immigration Studies, *Backgrounder* and *Scope.*

Chicago Tribune, 1972–1983.

Christian Science Monitor, 1943–1991.

Congressional Quarterly, 1943–1991.

Congressional Quarterly Almanac.

Daily News, 1990.

Detroit News, 1976–1983.

Editorials on File.

Environmental Defense Fund, Miscellaneous publications.

Federation of Americans for Immigration Reform, *Immigration Reports* (1979–1991), *Information Exchange* and *Immigration Papers.*

Gallup Poll.

Harris Poll.

Herbert Lehman Papers, Columbia University.

Houston Post, 1976–1983.

Interpreter Releases, 1943–1983.

Irish Echo, 1980–1990.

Irish Immigration Reform Movement, *Newsletters,* 1990.

Irish Voice, 1989–1991.

Los Angeles Times, 1972–1991.

Miami Herald, 1986–1990.

National Catholic Welfare Conference (Center for Migration Studies, Staten Island, New York), Archives.

National Forum on Immigration and Refugee Policy, Miscellaneous publications.

National Lutheran Council, Immigration and Refugee Department (New York City), Archives.

New Orleans Times-Picayune, 1972–1983.

New York Times, 1943–1991.

San Francisco Chronicle, 1986–1989.

St. Louis Post Dispatch, 1976–1983.

Wall Street Journal, 1965–1991.

Washington Post, 1965–1991.

Zero Population Growth, Miscellaneous publications.

Government Documents

Civil Rights Digest (Fall 1976), no. 9. Entire issue on Asians.

Commission on Population Growth and the American Future. *Population and the American Future*. New York: New American Library, 1972.

Commission on Wartime Relocation and Internment of Civilians.

   Personal Justice Denied. Washington: GPO, 1983.

   Summary and Conclusions. Washington: GPO, 1983.

Comptroller General of the United States.

   Employer Sanctions. Washington: GPO, 1990.

   Illegal Aliens: Estimating Their Impact on the United States. Washington: GPO, 1980.

   Illegal Aliens: Influence of Illegal Workers on Wages and Working Conditions of Legal Workers. Washington: GPO, 1988.

   Immigration and Marriage Fraud: Controls in Most Countries Surveyed Stronger Than in U.S. Washington: GPO, 1986.

   Immigration Reform: Major Changes Likely Under S. 358. Washington: GPO, 1989.

   Immigration—Need to Reassess U.S. Policy. Washington: GPO, 1976.

   The Indochinese Exodus: A Humanitarian Dilemma. Washington: GPO, 1979.

   More Needs to Be Done to Reduce the Number and Adverse Impact of Illegal Aliens in the United States. Washington: GPO, 1973.

   The Need to Reduce Public Expenditures for Newly Arrived Immigrants and Correct Inequality in Current Immigration Law. Washington: GPO, 1975.

Number of Undocumented Aliens Residing in the United States Unknown. Washington: GPO, 1981.

Prospects Dim for Effectively Enforcing Immigration Laws. Washington: GPO, 1980.

Reissuing Tamper-Resistant Cards Will Not Eliminate Misuse of Social Security Numbers. Washington: GPO, 1980.

Smugglers, Illicit Documents, and Schemes Are Undermining U.S. Controls Over Immigration. Washington: GPO, 1976.

Congressional Record, 1943–1990.

Immigration and Naturalization Service.

Annual Reports, 1943–1987.

Statistical Yearbooks, 1978–1989.

Unpublished data, 1981–1983.

National Commission for Employment Policy. *Hispanics and Jobs: Barriers to Progress.* Washington: GPO, 1982.

National Commission for Manpower Policy. Special Report No. 10. *Manpower and Immigration Policies in the United States.* Washington: GPO, 1978.

National Council for Employment Policy. *Illegal Aliens: Assessment of the Issues.* Washington: GPO, 1976.

National Science Foundation.

Immigrant Scientists and Engineers in the United States: A Study of Characteristics. Washington: GPO, 1973.

Scientists and Engineers from Abroad, 1976–1978. Washington: GPO, 1981.

New York, City of. Dept. of City Planning. *Manhattan Bridge Area Study: Chinatown.* New York: New York City, 1979.

President's Commission on Immigration and Naturalization. *Whom Shall We Welcome?* Washington: GPO, 1953.

President's Commission on Migratory Labor in American Agriculture. *Final Report.* Washington: GPO, 1951.

President's Comprehensive Report on Immigration. *Report.* Washington: GPO, 1989.

Select Commission on Immigration and Refugee Policy.

Appendices. Washington: GPO, 1981.

Papers. Frederick, Md.: University Publications of America, 1982.

U.S. Immigration Policy and the National Interest. Washington: GPO, 1981.

Select Commission on Western Hemisphere Immigration. *Final Report.* Washington: GPO, 1968.

Smithsonian Institution. Research Institute on Immigration and Ethnic Studies.

Caribbean Immigration to the United States. Washington: GPO, 1976.

Exploratory Fieldwork on Latino Migrants and Indonesian Refugees. Washington: GPO, 1976.

Quantitative Data and Immigration Research. Washington: GPO, 1979.

State of Illinois. Survey of Indochinese Refugees: *Introduction, Summary and Recommendations.* Chicago: Illinois Department of Public Aid, 1980.

U.S. Civil Rights Commission.

Civil Rights Issues on Asian and Pacific Americans: Myths and Realities. Hearings and Papers. Washington: GPO, 1979.

Improving Unemployment Data: The Department of Labor's Continuing Obligation. Washington: GPO, 1978.

The Tarnished Golden Door: Civil Rights Issues in Immigration. Washington: GPO, 1980.

U.S. Civil Rights Commission. California Advisory Committee.

A Dream Unfulfilled: Korean and Filipino Health Professionals in California. Washington: GPO, 1975.

A Study of Federal Immigration Practices in Southern California. Washington: GPO, 1980.

Asian Americans and Pacific Peoples: A Case of Mistaken Identity. Washington: GPO, 1975.

U.S. Civil Rights Commission. Hawaiian Advisory Committee. *Immigration Issues in Hawaii.* Washington: GPO, 1979.

U.S. Civil Rights Commission. New York State Advisory Committee. *Asian Americans: An Agenda for Action.* Washington: GPO, 1980.

Documented and Undocumented Persons in New York City. Washington: GPO, 1982.

The Forgotten Minority: Asian Americans in New York City. Washington: GPO, 1977.

U.S. Civil Rights Commission. Texas Advisory Committee. *Without Papers: The Undocumented in Texas.* Washington: GPO, 1980.

U.S. Commission on Displaced Persons. *Memo to American: The DP Story.* Washington: GPO, 1952.

U.S. Congress, House. Committee on Education and Labor. *Refugee Education Assistance Act of 1980.* H. Rept. 96-1218, 96th Cong., 2d sess. Washington: GPO, 1980.

U. S. Congress, House. Committee on Government Operations. *Scientific Brain Drain from the Developing Countries.* Report, 90th Cong., 2d sess. Washington: GPO, 1968

U.S. Congress, House. Committee on Immigration and Naturalization.
To Deny Admission to the United States of Certain Aliens and Reduce Immigration Quotas. Hearings, 79th Cong., 2d sess. Washington: GPO, 1946.
Exclusion of Immigration from the Philippine Islands. Hearings, 71st Cong., 2d sess. Washington: GPO, 1930.
To Grant a Quota to Eastern Hemisphere Indians and to Make Them Racially Eligible for Naturalization. Hearings, 79th Cong., 1st sess. Washington: GPO, 1945.
Naturalization of Filipinos. Hearings, 78th Cong., 2d sess. Washington: GPO, 1944.
Repealing the Chinese Exclusion Laws. H. Rept. 732, 78th Cong., 1st sess. Washington: GPO, 1943.
Repeal of the Chinese Exclusion Acts. Hearings, 78th Cong., 1st sess. Washington: GPO, 1943.
To Return to the Philippine Islands Unemployed Filipinos. Hearings, 72d Cong., 2d sess., Washington: GPO, 1933.
U.S. Congress, House. Committee on Interstate and Foreign Commerce. *Current Health Manpower Issues.* Committee Print. 96th Cong. 1st sess. Washington: GPO, 1979.
U.S. Congress, House. Committee on the Judiciary.
Adjustment of Status for Indochina Refugees. H. Rept. 95-547, 95th Cong., 1st sess. Washington: GPO, 1977.
Amending the Immigration and Nationality Act, and for Other Purposes. H. Rept. 93-108, 93d Cong., 1st sess. Washington: GPO, 1973.
Cuban Refugees—Status. H. Rept. 1978, 89th Cong., 2d sess. Washington: GPO, 1966.
Hearings Before the President's Commission on Immigration and Naturalization. 82d Cong., 2d sess. Washington: GPO, 1952.
Illegal Aliens and Alien Labor; A Bibliography and Compilation of Background Materials (June 1970–June 1977). Committee Print, 95th Cong., 1st sess. Washington: GPO, 1977.
Illegal Aliens: Analysis and Background. Committee Print, 95th Cong., 1st sess. Washington: GPO, 1977.
Immigration—Alien Spouses. H. Rept. 478, 80th Cong., 1st sess. Washington: GPO, 1947.
Immigration and Reform and Control Act of 1982. H. Rept. 97-890, 97th Cong., 2d sess. Washington: GPO, 1982.
Providing the Privilege of Becoming a Naturalized Citizen of the United States. H. Rept. 65, 81st Cong., 1st sess. Washington: GPO, 1948.

Refugee Relief Act of 1953: Final Report. Committee Print, 83d Cong., 1st sess. Washington: GPO, 1958.

U.S. Congress, House. Committee on Science and Technology, *Demographic Trends and the Scientific and Engineering Work Force*. Background Rept. No. 9, 99th Cong., 2d sess.

U.S. Congress, House. *Immigration Act of 1990*. Conference Rept. 101-955, 101st Cong., 2d sess. Washington: GPO, 1990.

U.S. Congress, House. Select Committee on Population.
Final Report, 95th Cong., 2d sess. Washington: GPO, 1978.
Immigration to the United States. Hearings, 95th Cong., 2d sess. Washington: GPO, 1978.

U.S. Congress, House. Special Subcommittee of the Committee on the Judiciary to Review Immigration, Refugee, and Nationality Problems. *Report*. 93d Cong., 1st sess. Washington: GPO, 1973.

U.S. Congress, House. Subcommittee on Census and Population of the Committee on Post Office and Civil Service. *Hispanic Immigration and the Select Commission on Immigration's Final Report*. Hearings, 97th Cong., 1st sess. Washington: GPO, 1981.

U.S. Congress, House. Subcommittee of the Committee on Appropriations, Depts. of State, Justice, Commerce, and the Judiciary and Related Agencies. *Appropriations*. Hearings, 95th Cong., 2d sess. Washington: GPO, 1978.

U.S. Congress, House. Subcommittee on Compensation and Employment of the Committee on the Post Office and Civil Service. *Reductions in Force and Budget Cuts*. Hearings, 97th Cong., 1st sess. Washington: GPO, 1981.

U.S. Congress, House. Subcommittee on Equipment, Supplies, and Manpower of the Committee on Agriculture.
Extension of the Mexican Farm Labor Program. Hearings, 86th Cong., 2d sess. Washington: GPO, 1960.
Mexican Farm Labor Program. Hearings, 84th Cong., 1st sess. Washington: GPO, 1955.

U.S. Congress, House. Subcommittee on Europe and the Middle East of the Committee on Foreign Affairs and the Subcommittee on Immigration, Refugees, and International Law of the Committee on the Judiciary. *Processing of Soviet Refugees*. Jr. Hearings, 101st Cong., 1st sess. Washington: GPO, 1989.

U.S. Congress, House. Subcommittee on Immigration and Naturalization of the Committee on the Judiciary.
Permitting Admission of 400,000 Displaced Persons into the United States. Hearings, 80th Cong., 1st sess. Washington: GPO, 1947.

Providing for Equality Under Naturalization and Immigration Laws.
Hearings, 80th Cong., 2d sess. Washington: GPO, 1948.

U.S. Congress, House. Subcommittee on Immigration, Citizenship, and International Law of the Committee on the Judiciary.

Admission of Refugees into the United States. Hearings, Parts I–II, 95th Cong., 1st sess. Washington: GPO, 1977 and 1978.

Extension of the Indochina Refugee and Assistance Programs. Hearings, 95th Cong., 1st sess. Washington: GPO, 1977.

Haitian Emigration. Report on Claims for Asylum and Requests for Administration Relief under the Immigration and Naturalization Act. 94th Cong., 2d sess. Washington: GPO, 1976.

Illegal Immigration and the U.S.—Mexican Border Control: Analysis and Recommendation. Committee Print, 95th Cong., 2d sess. Washington: GPO, 1978.

Indochina Refugees—Adjustment of Status. Hearings, 95th Cong., 1st sess. Washington: GPO, 1977.

Refugees from Indochina. Hearings, 94th Cong., 1st and 2d sess. Washington: GPO, 1975 and 1976.

Review of Immigration Problems. Hearings, 94th Cong., 1st sess. Washington: GPO, 1975 and 1976.

Waivers, Foreign Students, Immigration Benefits to Illegitimate Children. Hearings, 94th Cong., 1st and 2d sess. Washington: GPO, 1976.

Western Hemisphere Immigration. Hearings, 94th Cong., 1st and 2d sess. Washington: GPO, 1975 and 1976.

U.S. Congress, House. Subcommittee on Immigration, Refugees, and International Law of the Committee on the Judiciary.

Central American Asylum Seekers, Hearings, 101st Cong., 1st sess. Washington: GPO, 1989.

Central American Studies and Temporary Relief Act of 1987. Hearings, 100th Cong., 1st sess. Washington: GPO, 1987.

Family Unification and Employment Opportunity Act of 1990. H. Rept. 101-723, 101st Cong., 2d sess. Washington: GPO, 1990.

Immigration Act of 1989. Hearings (Part 1–3), 101st Cong., 1st and 2d sess. Washington: GPO, 1989.

Immigration and Refugee Issues in Southern California: An Investigative Trip. Committee Print, 97th Cong., 1st sess. Washington: GPO, 1981.

Immigration Nursing Relief Act of 1989. Hearing, 101st Cong., 1st sess. Washington: GPO, 1989.

The Indochinese Refugee Problem. Hearings, 96th Cong., 1st sess. Washington: GPO, 1979.

Legal Immigration. Hearing, 99th Cong., 2d sess. Washington: GPO, 1986.

Reform of Legal Immigration. Hearings, 100th Cong., 2d sess. Washington: GPO, 1988.

Refugee Act of 1980 Amendment. Hearings, 97th Cong., 1st sess. Washington: GPO, 1981.

Stay of Deportation for Undocumented Salvadorans and Nicaraguans. Hearing, 100th Cong., 1st sess. Washington: GPO, 1987.

Temporary Safe Haven Act of 1987. Hearings, 100th Cong., 1st sess. Washington: GPO, 1987.

Temporary Suspension of the Deportation of Certain Salvadorans and Nicaraguans. Hearing, 99th Cong., 2d sess. Washington: GPO, 1986.

U.S. Congress, House. Subcommittee on Inter-American Affairs of the Committee on International Relations.

Undocumented Workers: Implications for U.S. Policy in the Western Hemisphere. Hearings, 95th Cong., 2d sess. Washington: GPO, 1978.

United States-Mexican Relations: An Update. Hearings, 97th Cong., 1st sess. Washington: GPO, 1981.

U.S. Congress, House. Subcommittee on International Operations of the Committee on Foreign Affairs. *The Refugee Act of 1979.* Hearings, 96th Cong., 1st sess. Washington: GPO, 1979.

U.S. Congress, House. Subcommittee No. 1 of the Committee on the Judiciary.

Adjustment of Status for Cuban Refugees. Hearings, 89th Cong., 2d sess. Washington: GPO, 1966.

Amending the Displaced Persons Act of 1948. Hearings, 81st Cong., 1st sess. Washington: GPO, 1949.

Illegal Aliens. Hearings, 92d Cong., 1st sess. Washington: GPO, 1971.

Illegal Aliens: A Review of Hearings Conducted during the 92d Congress. 93d Cong., 1st sess. Washington: GPO, 1973.

Immigration. Hearings, 88th Cong., 2d sess. Washington: GPO, 1964.

Immigration. Hearings, 89th Cong., 1st sess. Washington: GPO, 1965.

Immigration. Hearings, 90th Cong., 2d sess. Washington: GPO, 1968.

Immigration. Hearings, 91st Cong., 2d sess. Washington: GPO, 1970.

Migration and Refugee Assistance. Hearings, 87th Cong., 1st sess. Washington: GPO, 1961.

Western Hemisphere Immigration. Hearings, 93d Cong., 1st sess. Washington: GPO, 1973.

U.S. Congress, Joint Economic Committee.
Economic and Demographic Consequences of Immigration. Print, 99th Cong., 2d sess. Washington: GPO, 1986.
Indochina Refugees: The Impact on First Asylum Countries and Implications for American Policy. Rept., 96th Cong., 2d sess. Washington: GPO, 1980.

U.S. Congress, Senate. Committee on Agriculture and Forestry.
Farm Labor Program. Hearings, 82d Cong., 1st sess. Washington: GPO, 1951.
Importation of Foreign Agricultural Workers. Hearings, 89th Cong., 1st sess. Washington: GPO, 1965.

U.S. Congress, Senate. Committee on Immigration. *Restriction of Western Hemisphere Immigration.* Hearings, 70th Cong., 1st sess. Washington: GPO, 1928.

U.S. Congress, Senate. Committee on the Judiciary.
Amending the Displaced Persons Act of 1948. S. Rept. 1237, 81st Cong., 2d sess. Washington: GPO, 1950.
Amending the Immigration and Nationality Act and for Other Purposes. S. Rept. 748, 89th Cong., 1st sess. Washington: GPO, 1965.
Caribbean Refugee Crisis: Cubans and Haitians. Hearings, 96th Cong., 2d sess. Washington: GPO, 1980.
Dept. of Justice Authorization and Oversight, 1981. Hearings, 97th Cong., 2d sess. Washington: GPO, 1980.
Displaced Persons in Europe. S. Rept. 950, 80th Cong., 2d sess. Washington: GPO, 1948.
History of the Immigration and Naturalization Service. Report for use of the Select Commission on Immigration and Refugee Policy, 96th Cong., 2d sess. Washington: GPO, 1980.
Immigration and Nationality Act: Amendments. S. Rept. 748, 89th Cong., 1st sess. Washington: GPO, 1965.
Immigration and Nationality Efficiency Act of 1979. Hearings, 96th Cong., 1st sess. Washington: GPO, 1979.
Immigration and Naturalization Systems of the United States. S. Rept. 1515, 81st Cong., 2d sess. Washington: GPO, 1950.
Records and Correspondence Relating to Immigration and Nationality Act. HR. 2850, 89th Cong. National Archives.
The Refugee Act of 1979. Hearings, 96th Cong., 1st sess. Washington: GPO, 1979.
The Refugee Act of 1980. S. Rept. 96-256, 96th Cong., 2d sess. Washington: GPO, 1980.

Review of U.S. Refugee Resettlement Programs and Policies. Committee Print, 96th Cong., 2d sess. Washington: GPO, 1980.

Revision of Immigration and Nationality Laws. Report, 82d Cong., 2d sess. Washington: GPO, 1952.

S. 2252: Alien Adjustment and Employment Act of 1977. Hearings, 95th Cong., 2d sess. Washington: GPO, 1978.

The Seizure of Vehicles Used to Illegally Transport Persons into the United States. Hearings, 95th Cong., 2d sess. Washington: GPO, 1978.

Selected Readings on U.S. Immigration Policy and Law. Committee Print, 96th Cong., 2d sess. Washington: GPO, 1980.

Temporary Workers Program: Backgrounds and Issues. Report for the Select Commission on Immigration and Refugee Policy, 96th Cong., 2d sess. Washington: GPO, 1980.

U.S. Immigration Law and Policy: 1952–1979. Committee Print, 96th Cong., 1st sess. Washington: GPO, 1979.

World Refugee Crisis: The International Community's Response. Committee Print, 96th Cong., 1st sess. Washington: GPO, 1979.

U.S. Congress, Senate. Committee on Labor and Human Resources. *Farmworker Collective Bargaining, 1979.* Hearings, 96th Cong., 1st sess. Washington: GPO, 1979.

U.S. Congress, Senate. Permanent Subcommittee on Investigations of the Committee on Government Affairs. *Federal Identification Cards.* Report, 98th Cong., 1st sess. Washington: GPO, 1983.

U.S. Congress, Senate. *Repealing the Chinese Exclusion Laws and to Establish Quotas.* S. Rept. 535, 78th Cong., 1st sess. Washington: GPO, 1943.

U.S. Congress, Senate. Select Committee on Small Business. *The Effects of Proposed Legislation Prohibiting the Employment of Illegal Aliens on Small Businesses.* Hearings, 94th Cong., 2d sess. Washington: GPO, 1977.

U.S. Congress, Senate. Subcommittee of the Committee on the Judiciary. *Emergency Migration of Escapees, Expellees, and Refugees.* Hearings, 83d Cong., 1st sess. Washington: GPO, 1953.

U.S. Congress, Senate. Subcommittee on Immigration and Naturalization of the Committee on the Judiciary.
Immigration. Hearings, 89th Cong., 1st sess. Washington: GPO, 1965.
Immigration 1976. Hearings, 94th Cong., 2d sess. Washington: GPO, 1976.

U.S. Congress, Senate. Subcommittee on Immigration and Refugee Affairs of the Committee on the Judiciary.
Immigration Marriage Fraud. Hearing, 99th Cong., 1st sess. Washington: GPO, 1986.

Legal Immigration to the United States: A Demographic Analysis of the Fifth Preference Visa Admissions. Staff Report. 100th Cong., 1st sess. Washington: GPO, 1987.

Asylum and Migration Issues: the Case of South Texas. Staff Report, 101st Cong., 1st sess. Washington: GPO, 1989.

Immigration Reform. Hearing, 101st Cong., 1st sess. Washington: GPO, 1990.

The Knowing Employment of Illegal Immigrants. Hearings, 97th Cong., 1st sess. Washington: GPO, 1981.

Legalization of Illegal Immigrants. Hearings, 97th Cong., 2d sess. Washington: GPO, 1981.

Systems to Verify Authorization to Work in the U.S. Hearings, 97th Cong., 1st sess. Washington: GPO, 1981.

The Preference System. Hearings, 97th Cong., 1st sess. Washington: GPO, 1981.

U.S. Congress, Senate. Subcommittee on Migratory Labor of the Committee on Labor and Public Welfare. *Migrant and Seasonal Farmworkers Powerlessness.* Hearings, 91st Cong., 1st and 2d sess. Washington: GPO, 1969 and 1970.

U.S. Congress, Senate. Subcommittee to Investigate Problems Connected with Refugees and Escapees of the Committee on the Judiciary.

Cuban Refugee Problems. Hearings, 89th Cong., 2d sess. Washington: GPO, 1966.

Humanitarian Problems in Lebanon. Hearings, 94th Cong., 2d sess. Washington: GPO, 1976.

Indochina Evacuation and Refugee Problems. Parts I–V. Hearings, 94th Cong., 1st sess. Washington: GPO, 1975.

Indochina Evacuation and Refugee Problems. Committee Print, 94th Cong., 1st sess. Washington: GPO, 1975.

Refugee and Humanitarian Problems in Chile. Hearings, Part III, 94th Cong., 1st sess. Washington: GPO, 1975.

U.S. Congress. Subcommittee on Economic Resources, Competitiveness, and Security Economics of the Joint Economic Committee. *Economic and Demographic Consequences of Immigration.* Hearings, 99th Cong., 2d sess. Washington: GPO, 1987.

U.S. Congress. Subcommittee on Immigration and Refugee Policy of the Senate Committee on the Judiciary and Subcommittee on Immigration, Refugees, and International Law of the House Committee on the Judiciary.

Final Report on the Select Commission on Immigration and Refugee Policy. Joint Hearings, 97th Cong., 1st sess. Washington: GPO, 1981.

Immigration Reform and Control Act of 1982. Joint Hearings, 97th Cong., 2d sess. Washington: GPO, 1982.

U.S. Congress. Subcommittee of the Committee on the Judiciary. House and Senate. *Revision of Immigration, Naturalization, and Nationality Laws*. Joint Hearings. 82d Cong., 1st sess. Washington: GPO, 1951.

U.S. Dept. of Commerce. Bureau of the Census.

Current Population Reports. P-23, No. 116. *Ancestry and Language in the United States*. Washington: GPO, 1979.

Current Population Reports. P-20, No. 347. *Population Characteristics: Persons of Spanish Origin in the United States (March 1979): Advance Report*. Washington: GPO, 1979.

Current Population Reports. P-20, No. 361. *Population Characteristics: Persons of Spanish Origin in the United States (March 1980): Advance Report*. Washington: GPO, 1981.

Preliminary Review of Existing Studies of the Number of Illegal Residents in the United States. Washington: GPO, 1980.

Supplementary Reports. *Ancestry of the Population by State: 1980*. Washington: GPO, 1983.

U.S. Dept. of Education. Office of Educational Research and Improvement. *Conference on the Educational and Occupational Needs of Asian-Pacific Women*. Washington: GPO, 1980.

U.S. Dept. of Health, Education, and Welfare. Social Security Administration, Office of Refugee Affairs. *Indochinese Refugee Assistance Programs*. Rept. to Congress, December 1979. Washington: GPO, 1979.

U.S. Dept. of Health, Education, and Welfare. *Summary and Recommendations of Conference on Pacific and Asian American Families*. Washington: GPO, 1978.

U.S. Dept. of Health and Human Services. Office of Refugee Resettlement. *Report to Congress: Refugee Resettlement Programs*. Washington: GPO, 1981.

U.S. Depts. of Justice, Labor, and State. Interagency Task Force on Immigration Policy. *Staff Report*. Washington: GPO, 1979.

U.S. Dept. of Labor. Bureau of International Labor Affairs. *The Effects of Immigration on the U.S. Economy and Labor Market*. Washington: GPO, 1989.

U.S. Dept. of Labor. Employment and Training Administration.

Chinese Population in Lower Manhattan, 1978. Washington: GPO, 1978.

Seven Years Later: The Experience of the 1970 Cohort of Immigrants in the United States. Washington: GPO, 1979.

U.S. Dept. of Labor. Manpower Administration. *Immigrants and the Ameri-*

can Labor Market. National Technical Information Service, Dept. of Commerce, 1973.

U.S. Dept. of Labor. Office of Information. Employment Standards Administration. *News Release.* February 15, 1980.

U.S. Dept. of State. *Bulletins.* 1943–1983.

U.S. Domestic Council. Committee on Illegal Aliens. *Preliminary Report.* Washington: GPO, 1976.

Weekly Compilation of Presidential Documents.

Index